D0936203

VISUAL
DICTIONARY

VISUAL

DICTIONARY

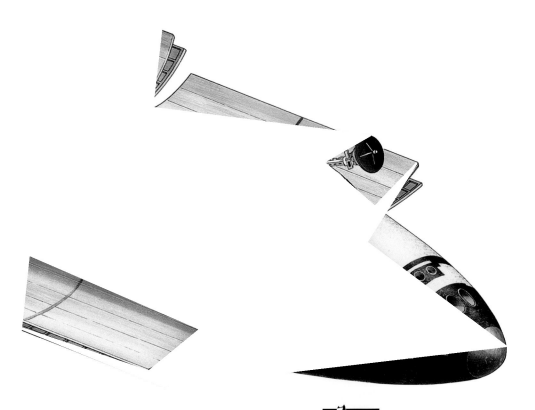

FOG CITY PRESS

Published by Fog City Press
814 Montgomery Street
San Francisco, CA 94133 USA

Copyright © 2003 Weldon Owen Pty Ltd

All rights reserved. Unauthorized reproduction,
in any manner, is prohibited.
A catalog record for this book is available from
the Library of Congress, Washington, D.C.

First printed 2003
Reprinted 2004

ISBN 1 877019 11 9

Color reproduction by Colourscan Co Pte Ltd
Printed by Tien Wah Press (PTE) Limited
Printed in Singapore

A Weldon Owen Production

WELDON OWEN PUBLISHING
Publisher: Sheena Coupe
Creative Director: Sue Burk
Project Editors: Sarah Anderson, Paul McNally
Project Designers: Suzanne Tawansi, Heather Menzies

Fog City Press
Chief Executive Officer: John Owen
President: Terry Newell
Publisher: Lynn Humphries
Managing Editors: Janine Flew, Angela Handley
Design Manager: Helen Perks
Editorial Coordinator: Jennifer Losco
Production Manager: Caroline Webber
Production Coordinator: James Blackman
Sales Manager: Emily Jahn
Vice President International Sales: Stuart Laurence

Contents

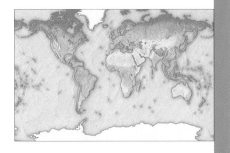

Solar System

BIRTH OF THE SOLAR SYSTEM

Dust and gas collapse to form a dense core surrounded by a broad disk called the solar nebula.

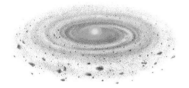

The nebula's densest part attracts dust and gas. It grows larger and hotter, becoming the proto-Sun.

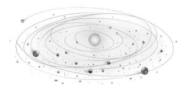

Particles of rock and ice stick together to become planetesimals—the building blocks of planets.

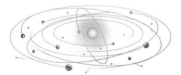

The planetesimals clump together to form larger bodies called proto-planets.

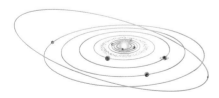

The Sun becomes a star and its radiation blows away leftover gas, leaving behind nine planets.

Pluto

Neptune

Path of orbit

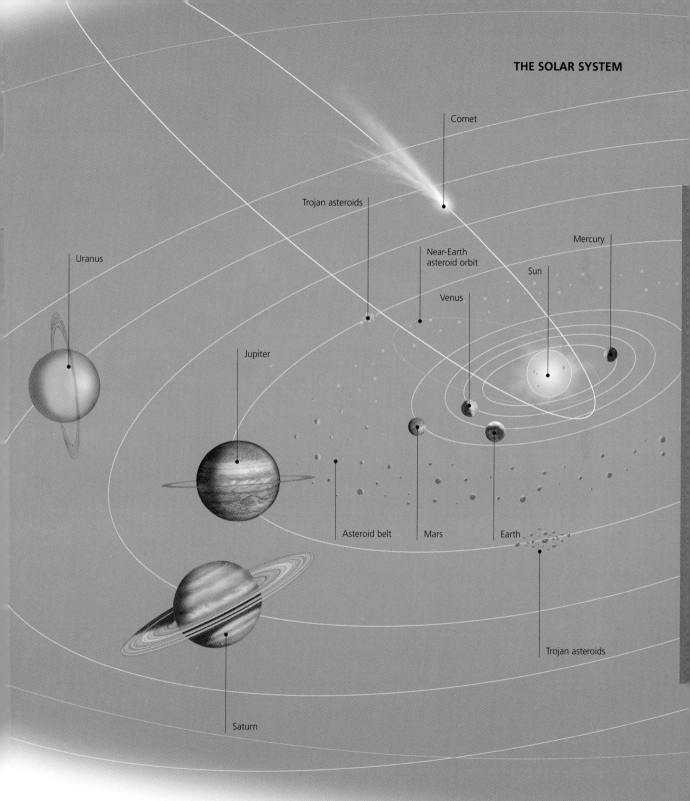

Comet

Trojan asteroids

Near-Earth
asteroid orbit

Mercury

Sun

Venus

Uranus

Jupiter

Asteroid belt

Mars

Earth

Trojan asteroids

Saturn

Mercury

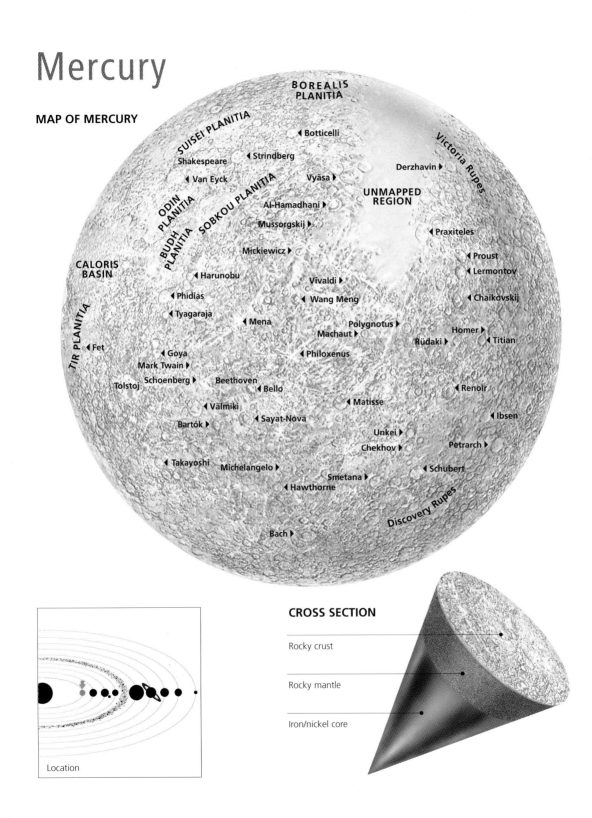

MAP OF MERCURY

BOREALIS
PLANITIA

SUISEI PLANITIA

◄ Botticelli

Shakespeare   ◄ Strindberg

◄ Van Eyck   Vyāsa ▶

Derzhavin ▶

Victoria Rupes

ODIN
PLANITIA

SOBKOU PLANITIA

Al-Hamadhani ▶

UNMAPPED
REGION

BUDH
PLANITIA

Mussorgskij ▶

Mickiewicz ▶

◄ Praxiteles

◄ Proust

CALORIS
BASIN

◄ Harunobu

Vivaldi ▶

◄ Lermontov

◄ Phidias

◄ Wang Meng

◄ Chaikovskij

◄ Tyagaraja

◄ Mena

Polygnotus ▶

Homer ▶

TIR PLANITIA

Machaut ▶

Rüdaki ▶   ◄ Titian

◄ Fet

◄ Goya

◄ Philoxenus

Mark Twain ▶

Schoenberg ▶   Beethoven

◄ Renoir

Tolstoj

◄ Bello

◄ Matisse

◄ Ibsen

◄ Vālmiki

◄ Sayat-Nova

Bartók ▶

Unkei ▶

Chekhov ▶   Petrarch ▶

◄ Takayoshi   Michelangelo ▶

◄ Schubert

Smetana ▶

◄ Hawthorne

Discovery Rupes

Bach ▶

Location

CROSS SECTION

Rocky crust

Rocky mantle

Iron/nickel core

MERCURY'S ORBIT

Mercury has a year of 88 Earth days, while a full solar day from noon to noon lasts 176 Earth days.

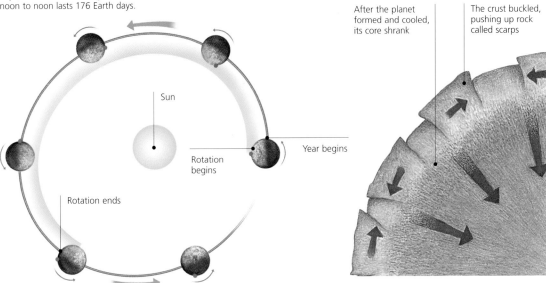

Sun

Year begins

Rotation begins

Rotation ends

MERCURY'S SURFACE

After the planet formed and cooled, its core shrank

The crust buckled, pushing up rock called scarps

CALORIS BASIN

The Caloris Basin formed when a huge object slammed into Mercury's surface

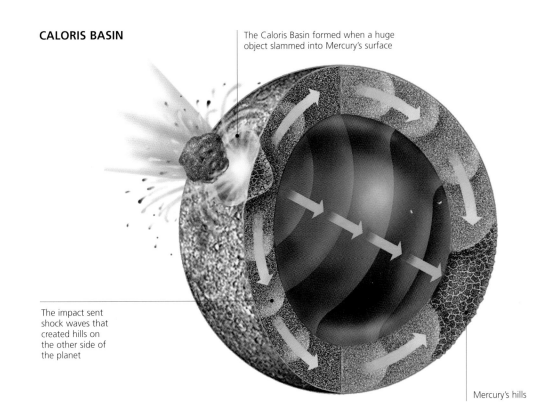

The impact sent shock waves that created hills on the other side of the planet

Mercury's hills

Venus

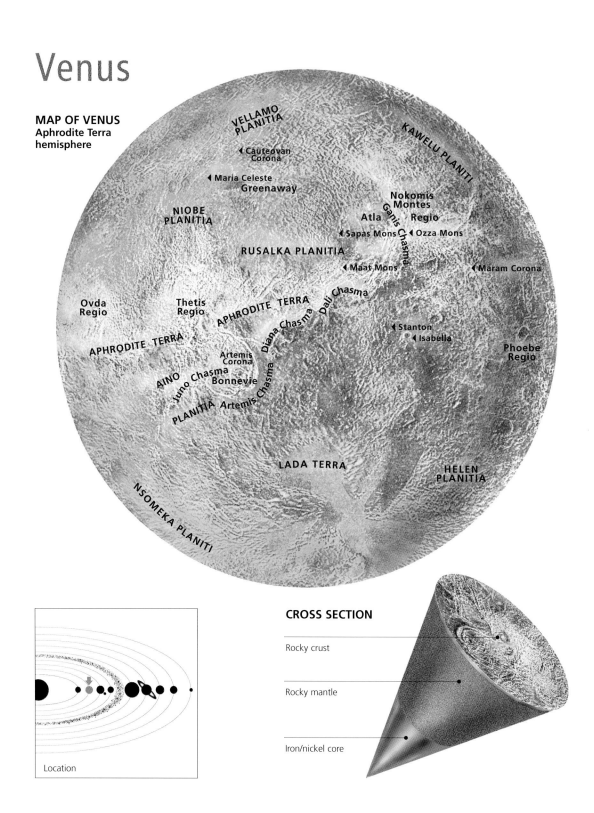

MAP OF VENUS
Aphrodite Terra
hemisphere

VELLAMO
PLANITIA

KAWELU PLANITI

◄ Cauteovan
Corona

◄ Maria Celeste
Greenaway

Nokomis
Montes
Atla Ganis Chasma Regio
◄ Sapas Mons ◄ Ozza Mons

NIOBE
PLANITIA

RUSALKA PLANITIA

◄ Maat Mons ◄ Maram Corona

Ovda
Regio

Thetis
Regio

APHRODITE TERRA

Diana Chasma

Dali Chasma

◄ Stanton
◄ Isabella

Phoebe
Regio

APHRODITE TERRA

Artemis
Corona

AINO

Juno Chasma

Bonnevie

PLANITIA Artemis Chasma

LADA TERRA

HELEN
PLANITIA

NSOMEKA PLANITI

CROSS SECTION

Rocky crust

Rocky mantle

Iron/nickel core

Location

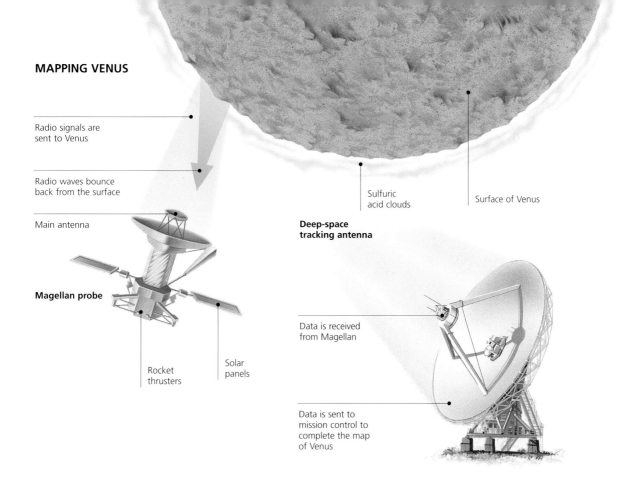

MAPPING VENUS

Radio signals are
sent to Venus

Radio waves bounce
back from the surface

Main antenna

Magellan probe

Rocket
thrusters

Solar
panels

Sulfuric
acid clouds

Surface of Venus

**Deep-space
tracking antenna**

Data is received
from Magellan

Data is sent to
mission control to
complete the map
of Venus

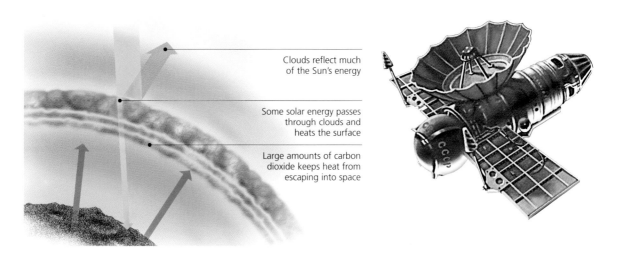

GREENHOUSE EFFECT
Venus suffers from a severe greenhouse effect.

Clouds reflect much
of the Sun's energy

Some solar energy passes
through clouds and
heats the surface

Large amounts of carbon
dioxide keeps heat from
escaping into space

VENERA
Venus spacecraft

Earth

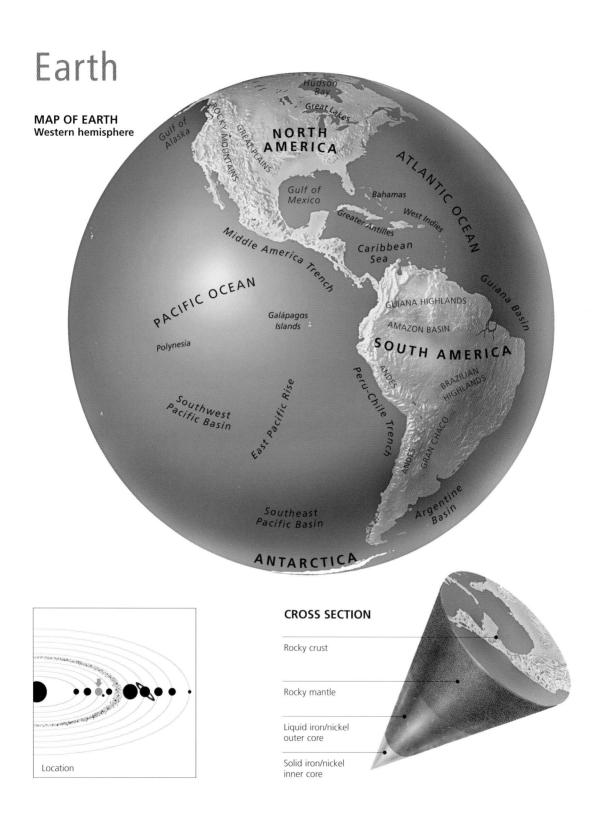

MAP OF EARTH
Western hemisphere

Hudson
Bay

Great Lakes

NORTH
AMERICA

Gulf of
Alaska

ROCKY MOUNTAINS

GREAT PLAINS

ATLANTIC OCEAN

Gulf of
Mexico

Bahamas

Greater Antilles

West Indies

Caribbean
Sea

Middle America Trench

PACIFIC OCEAN

Galápagos
Islands

GUIANA HIGHLANDS

Guiana Basin

AMAZON BASIN

SOUTH AMERICA

Polynesia

Southwest
Pacific Basin

East Pacific Rise

Peru-Chile Trench

ANDES

BRAZILIAN
HIGHLANDS

ANDES

GRAN CHACO

Southeast
Pacific Basin

Argentine
Basin

ANTARCTICA

Location

CROSS SECTION

Rocky crust

Rocky mantle

Liquid iron/nickel
outer core

Solid iron/nickel
inner core

MAP OF EARTH
Eastern hemisphere

EUROPE
ASIA
Siberia
Caspian Sea
TIAN SHAN MOUNTAINS
GOBI DESERT
Plateau of Tibet
Hindu Kush
HIMALAYAS
ARABIAN PENINSULA
Ganges Basin
DECCAN PLATEAU
Yangtze Basin
Sea of Japan (East Sea)
Honshu
East China Sea
Sahara Desert
Arabian Sea
Bay of Bengal
Mekong Basin
South China Sea
PACIFIC OCEAN
Philippine Islands
AFRICA
Sri Lanka
Lake Victoria
GREAT RIFT VALLEY
Sumatra
Borneo
New Guinea
Java
Java Trench
INDIAN OCEAN
Madagascar
Great Sandy Desert
AUSTRALIA
GREAT DIVIDING RANGE
Great Australian Bight
ANTARCTICA

MARTIAN ROCKS ON EARTH

An asteroid smashes into Mars and blasts pieces of the planet into space.

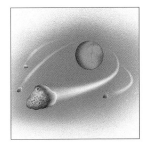

These Martian rocks go into orbit around the Sun for millions of years.

Some of the rocks collide with Earth and fall to the ground as meteorites.

Mars

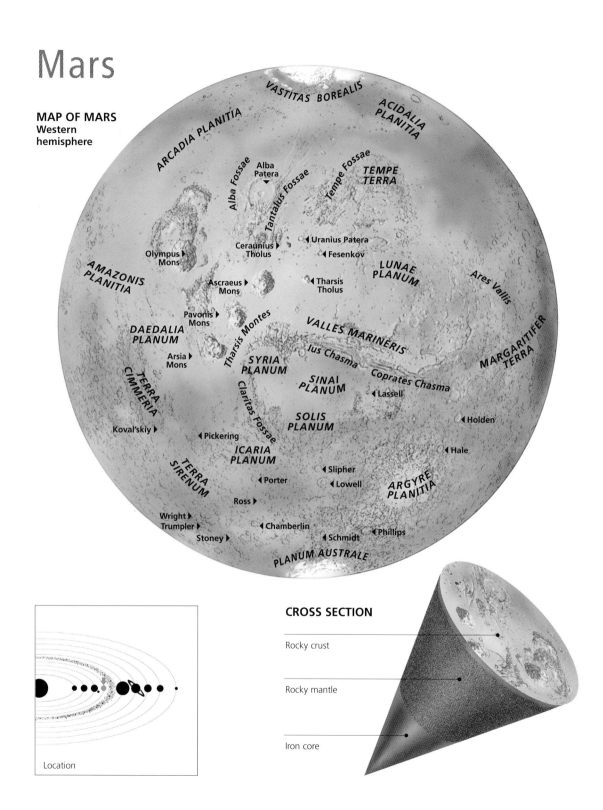

The Solar System

SPACE

MAP OF MARS
Western
hemisphere

VASTITAS BOREALIS

ACIDALIA PLANITIA

ARCADIA PLANITIA

Alba Fossae

Alba Patera ▼

Tantalus Fossae

Tempe Fossae

TEMPE TERRA

Ceraunius ▶ Tholus

◀ Uranius Patera

◀ Fesenkov

Olympus ▶ Mons

AMAZONIS PLANITIA

Ascraeus ▶ Mons

◀ Tharsis Tholus

LUNAE PLANUM

Ares Vallis

Pavonis ▶ Mons

DAEDALIA PLANUM

Tharsis Montes

VALLES MARINERIS

MARGARITIFER TERRA

Arsia ▶ Mons

SYRIA PLANUM

Ius Chasma

Coprates Chasma

SINAI PLANUM

Claritas Fossae

◀ Lassell

TERRA CIMMERIA

◀ Holden

SOLIS PLANUM

Koval'skiy ▶

◀ Pickering

◀ Hale

ICARIA PLANUM

TERRA SIRENUM

◀ Slipher

◀ Porter

◀ Lowell

ARGYRE PLANITIA

Ross ▶

Wright ▶
Trumpler ▶

◀ Chamberlin

◀ Schmidt

◀ Phillips

Stoney ▶

PLANUM AUSTRALE

CROSS SECTION

Rocky crust

Rocky mantle

Iron core

Location

PATHFINDER MISSION TO MARS

SOJOURNER ROVER

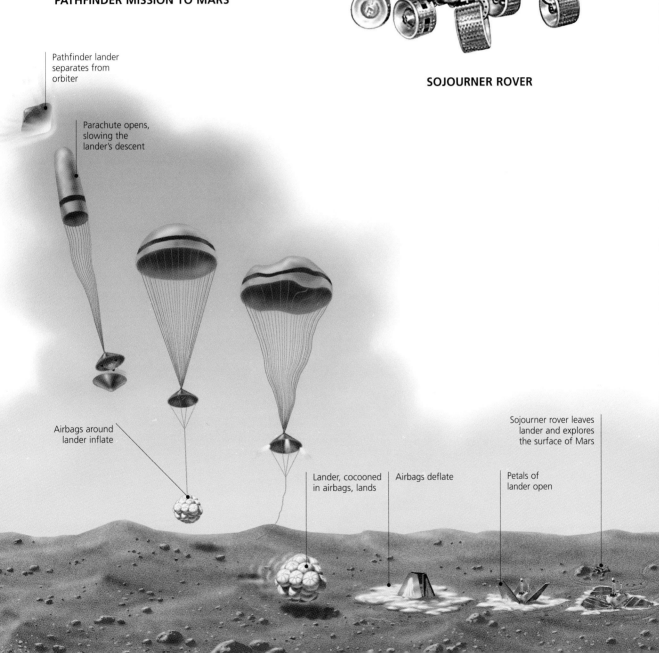

Pathfinder lander separates from orbiter

Parachute opens, slowing the lander's descent

Airbags around lander inflate

Lander, cocooned in airbags, lands

Airbags deflate

Petals of lander open

Sojourner rover leaves lander and explores the surface of Mars

Jupiter

GALILEO ORBITER

In 1995, the Galileo orbiter shot an entry probe into Jupiter's atmosphere.

GALILEO PROBE

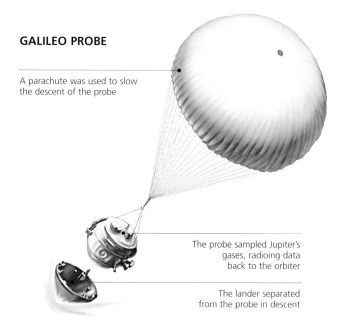

A parachute was used to slow the descent of the probe

The probe sampled Jupiter's gases, radioing data back to the orbiter

The lander separated from the probe in descent

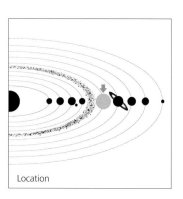

Location

CROSS SECTION

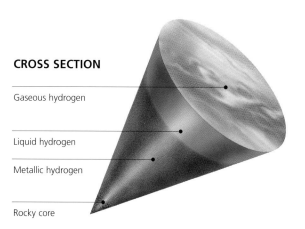

Gaseous hydrogen

Liquid hydrogen

Metallic hydrogen

Rocky core

North pole

North polar region

North temperate belt

North tropical zone

North equatorial belt

Equatorial zone

South equatorial belt

Great Red Spot

South tropical zone

South temperate zone

South polar region

South pole

Saturn

CREATING SATURN'S RINGS

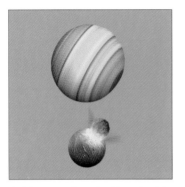

1. A large comet or asteroid smashes into an icy moon orbiting Saturn.

2. The impact shatters the moon into a cloud of icy particles. These orbit Saturn.

3. Constant collisions among the icy particles grind them into smaller pieces.

4. Over years, these particles spread out to form a broad ring around the planet.

B ring

Cassini division

A ring

Encke division

F ring

Location

CROSS SECTION

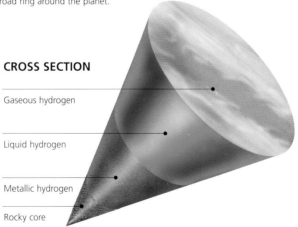

Gaseous hydrogen

Liquid hydrogen

Metallic hydrogen

Rocky core

MAP OF SATURN

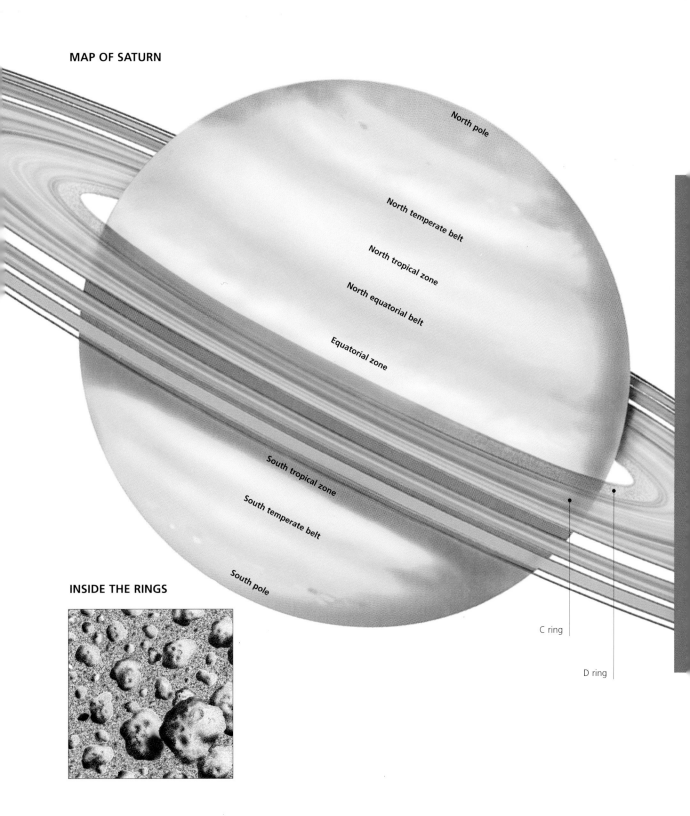

North pole

North temperate belt

North tropical zone

North equatorial belt

Equatorial zone

South tropical zone

South temperate belt

South pole

C ring

D ring

INSIDE THE RINGS

Uranus

SEASONS OF URANUS

Uranus's orbit takes 84 Earth years, so each pole receives a long period of constant sunlight followed by a long period of darkness.

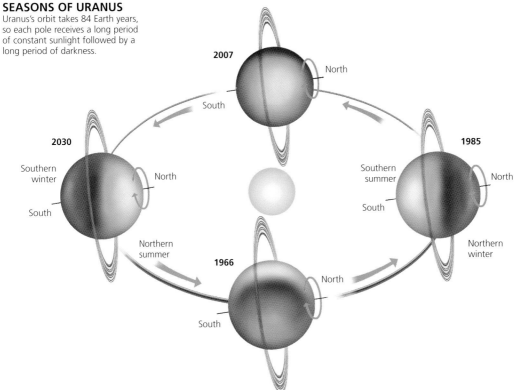

2007
North
South

2030
Southern winter
North
South
Northern summer

1966
North
South

1985
Southern summer
North
South
Northern winter

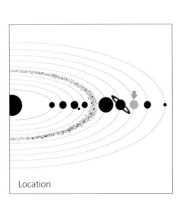

Location

CROSS SECTION

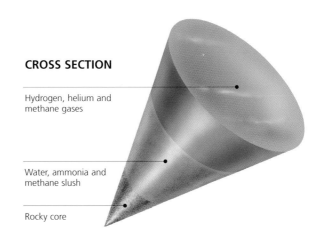

Hydrogen, helium and methane gases

Water, ammonia and methane slush

Rocky core

The Solar System

SPACE

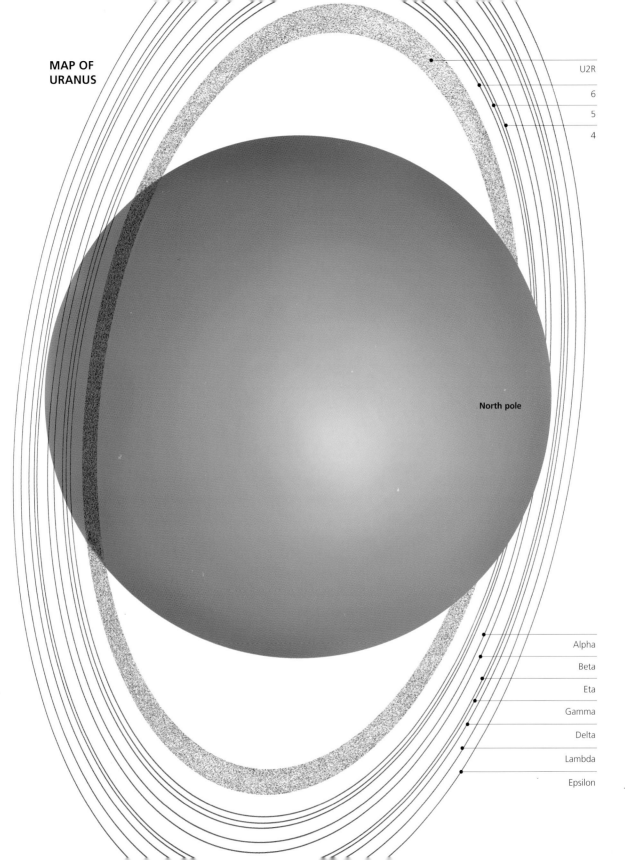

MAP OF URANUS

U2R

6

5

4

North pole

Alpha

Beta

Eta

Gamma

Delta

Lambda

Epsilon

Neptune

VOYAGER 2

Voyager 2 flew past Neptune
in 1986, relaying data to Earth.

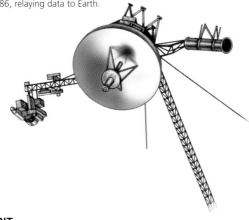

ORBIT

Neptune's orbit takes 165 Earth years.
Since it was first seen in 1846, it has still
not made a full orbit around the Sun.

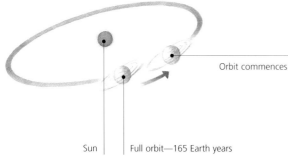

Orbit commences

Sun | Full orbit—165 Earth years

Location

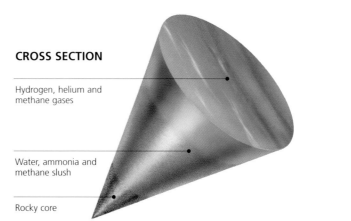

CROSS SECTION

Hydrogen, helium and
methane gases

Water, ammonia and
methane slush

Rocky core

North pole

South pole

Leverrier   Lassell   Arago   Adams   Galle

Pluto

MAP OF PLUTO

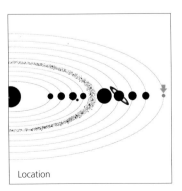

Location

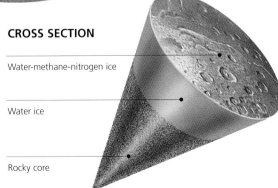

CROSS SECTION

Water-methane-nitrogen ice

Water ice

Rocky core

PLUTO'S DAY AND MONTH

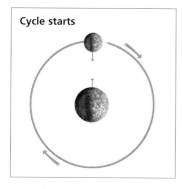

Cycle starts

Due to the exact length of Pluto's rotation and its moon's orbit, Pluto's day and month are identical.

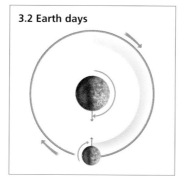

3.2 Earth days

Pluto and its moon Charon keep the same faces turned toward each other.

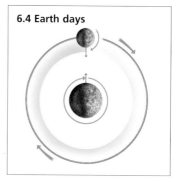

6.4 Earth days

Pluto has completed its rotation and Charon has completed its orbit.

KUIPER BELT

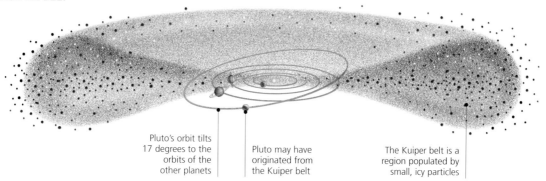

Pluto's orbit tilts 17 degrees to the orbits of the other planets

Pluto may have originated from the Kuiper belt

The Kuiper belt is a region populated by small, icy particles

SIZE COMPARISON

Pluto

Earth's moon

Jupiter's moon—Ganymede

Size Comparison of Planets

RELATIVE SIZES

Jupiter

Mercury

Venus

Earth

Mars

The Solar System

SPACE

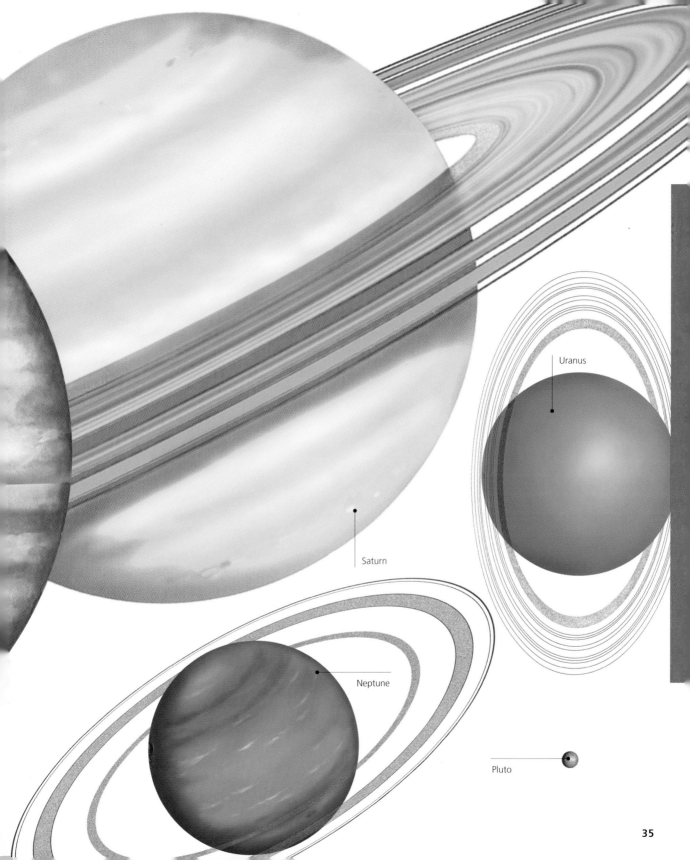

Uranus

Saturn

Neptune

Pluto

Asteroids and Meteoroids

TYPES OF METEORITES

Iron meteorite

Stony meteorite

Stony-iron meteorite

ASTEROID BELT

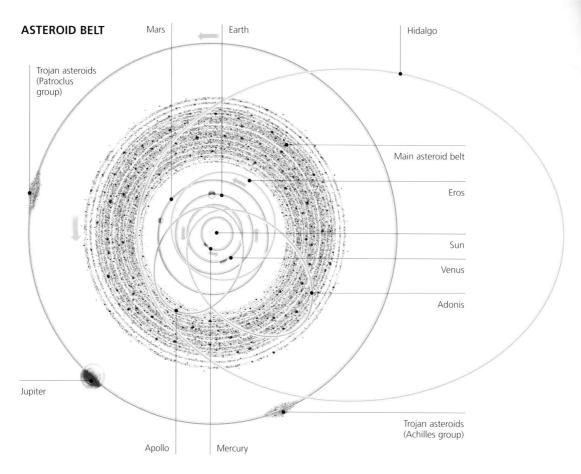

Mars

Earth

Hidalgo

Trojan asteroids
(Patroclus
group)

Main asteroid belt

Eros

Sun

Venus

Adonis

Jupiter

Trojan asteroids
(Achilles group)

Apollo

Mercury

METEOR SHOWER
Although no large meteorite impact
has occurred in human history, scientists
believe it is just a matter of time.

Comets

COMET ORBITS

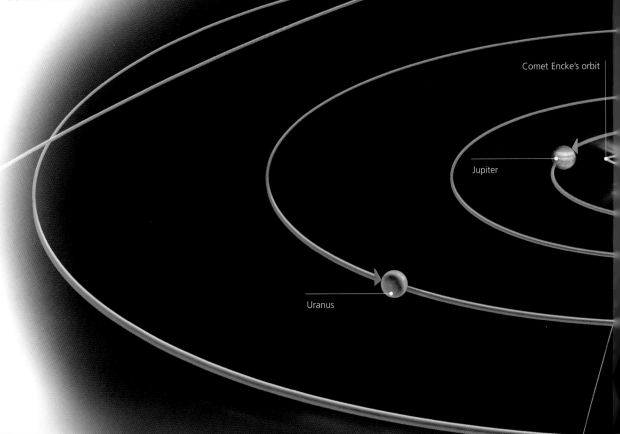

Comet Encke's orbit

Jupiter

Uranus

COMET CROSS SECTION

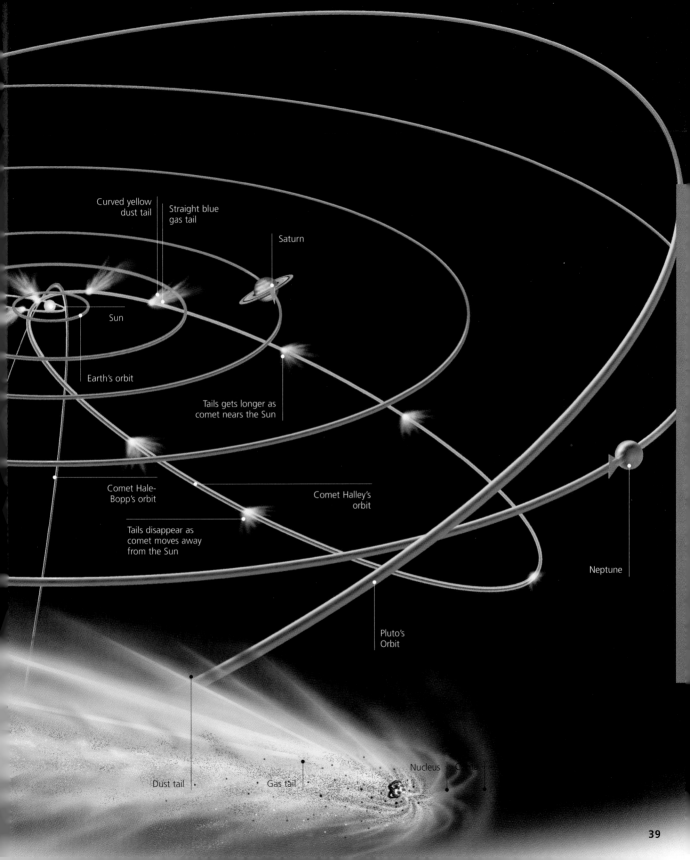

Curved yellow
dust tail

Straight blue
gas tail

Saturn

Sun

Earth's orbit

Tails gets longer as
comet nears the Sun

Comet Hale-
Bopp's orbit

Comet Halley's
orbit

Tails disappear as
comet moves away
from the Sun

Neptune

Pluto's
Orbit

Dust tail

Gas tail

Nucleus

Earth's Moon

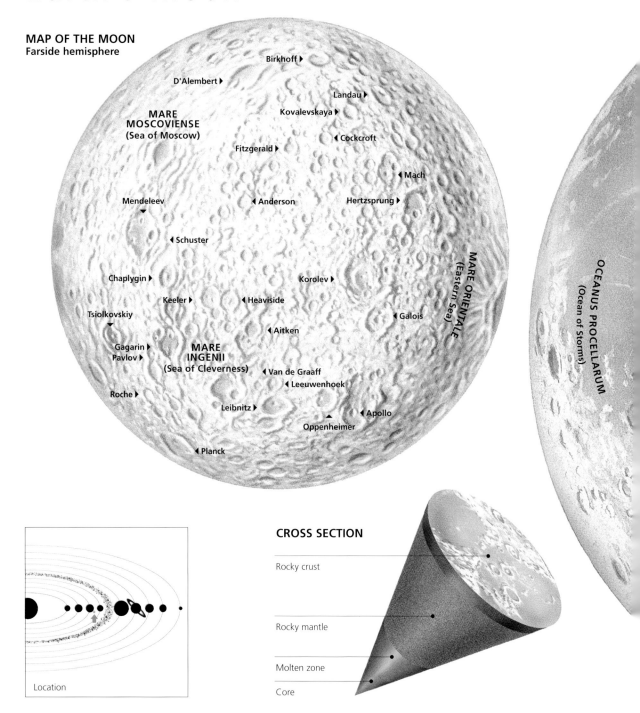

MAP OF THE MOON
Farside hemisphere

Birkhoff ▶

D'Alembert ▶

Landau ▶

Kovalevskaya ▶

**MARE
MOSCOVIENSE**
(Sea of Moscow)

◀ Cockcroft

Fitzgerald ▶

◀ Mach

Mendeleev ▼

◀ Anderson

Hertzsprung ▶

◀ Schuster

Chaplygin ▶

Korolev ▶

Keeler ▶

◀ Heaviside

Tsiolkovskiy ▼

◀ Galois

◀ Aitken

Gagarin ▶
Pavlov ▶

**MARE
INGENII**
(Sea of Cleverness)

◀ Van de Graaff

◀ Leeuwenhoek

Roche ▶

Leibnitz ▶

◀ Apollo

Oppenheimer ▲

◀ Planck

MARE ORIENTALE
(Eastern Sea)

OCEANUS PROCELLARUM
(Ocean of Storms)

Location

CROSS SECTION

Rocky crust

Rocky mantle

Molten zone

Core

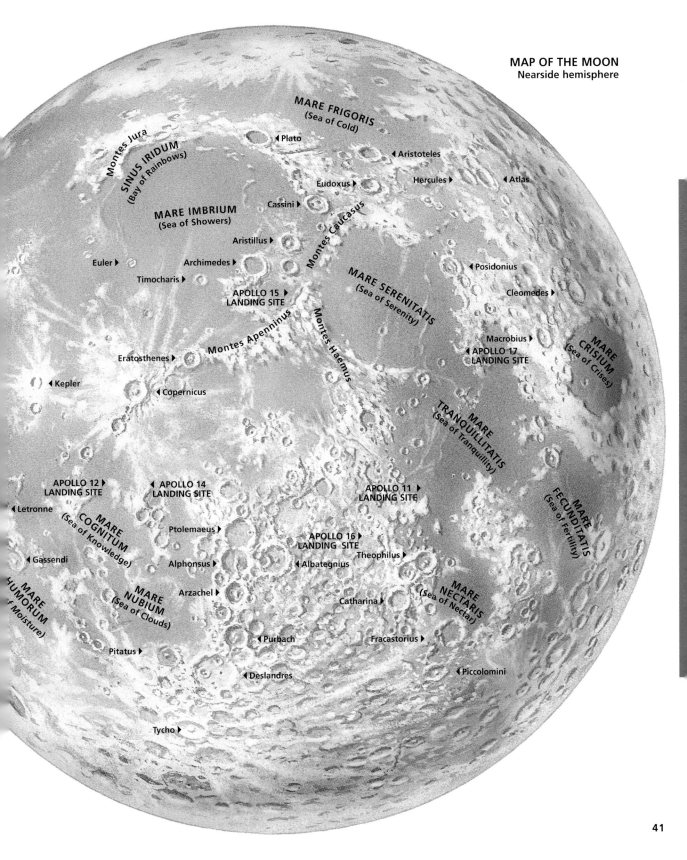

MARE FRIGORIS
(Sea of Cold)

Montes Jura

SINUS IRIDUM
(Bay of Rainbows)

◄ Plato

◄ Aristoteles

Eudoxus ►

Hercules ►

◄ Atlas

Cassini ►

MARE IMBRIUM
(Sea of Showers)

Montes Caucasus

Aristillus ►

Euler ►

Archimedes ►

◄ Posidonius

Timocharis ►

MARE SERENITATIS
(Sea of Serenity)

Cleomedes ►

APOLLO 15 ►
LANDING SITE

Montes Apenninus

Macrobius ►

◄ APOLLO 17
LANDING SITE

MARE
CRISIUM
(Sea of Crises)

Eratosthenes ►

Montes Haemus

◄ Kepler

◄ Copernicus

MARE
TRANQUILLITATIS
(Sea of Tranquillity)

APOLLO 12 ►
LANDING SITE

◄ APOLLO 14
LANDING SITE

APOLLO 11 ►
LANDING SITE

MARE
FECUNDITATIS
(Sea of Fertility)

◄ Letronne

MARE
COGNITUM
(Sea of Knowledge)

Ptolemaeus ►

APOLLO 16 ►
LANDING SITE

◄ Gassendi

Theophilus ►

Alphonsus ►

◄ Albategnius

MARE
HUMORUM
(Sea of Moisture)

MARE
NUBIUM
(Sea of Clouds)

Arzachel ►

MARE
NECTARIS
(Sea of Nectar)

Catharina ►

◄ Purbach

Fracastorius ►

Pitatus ►

◄ Deslandres

◄ Piccolomini

Tycho ►

41

Earth's Moon

THE MOON'S FORMATION

Earth was struck by a large object.

The debris circled around Earth.

Eventually the debris clumped together.

LUNAR PROSPECTOR
This craft studied the Moon's composition, relaying data back to Earth.

LUNA 16
This Soviet Union craft was the first to collect Moon rocks automatically.

LUNOKHOD 1
In 1970, this was the the first roving remote-controlled robot on the Moon.

Luna 16 was the first robotic probe to land on the Moon and return a sample to Earth

MISSION TO THE MOON
From 1968 to 1972, 27 astronauts visited the Moon in the Apollo spacecraft.

During the 1971 Apollo 14 mission, Alan Shepard played golf on the Moon

Lunar module

Due to the Moon's low gravity, the ball was hit a great distance

Solar and Lunar Eclipses

PHASES OF THE MOON

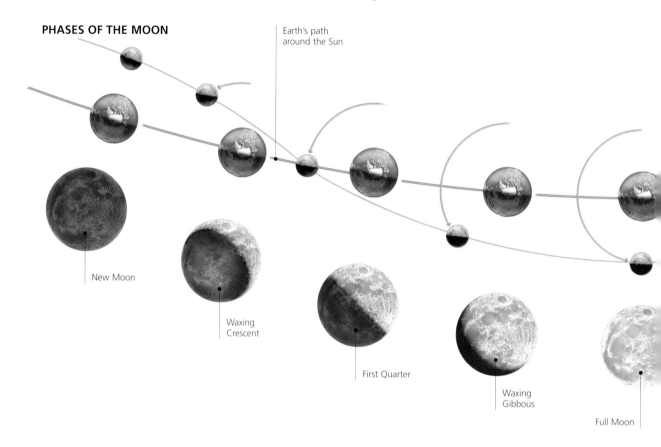

Earth's path
around the Sun

New Moon

Waxing
Crescent

First Quarter

Waxing
Gibbous

Full Moon

LUNAR ECLIPSE

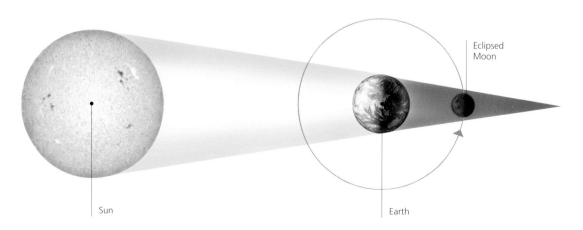

Sun

Earth

Eclipsed
Moon

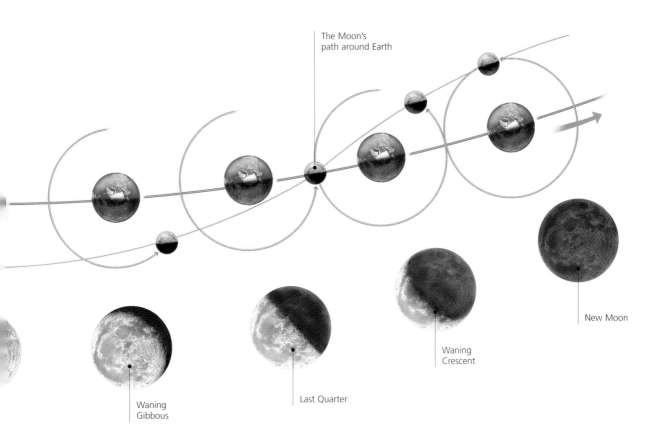

The Moon's path around Earth

New Moon

Waning
Crescent

Waning
Gibbous

Last Quarter

SOLAR ECLIPSE

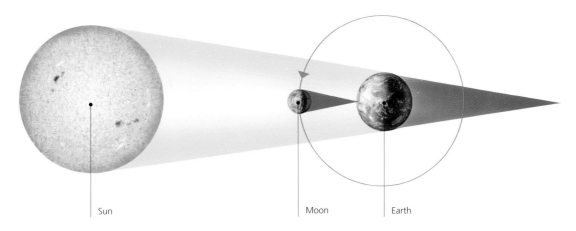

Sun

Moon

Earth

Moons

SATURN'S MAJOR MOONS

Iapetus

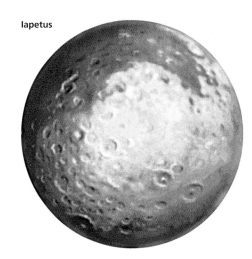

Mimas

Enceladus

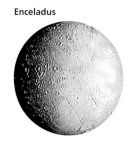

Titan

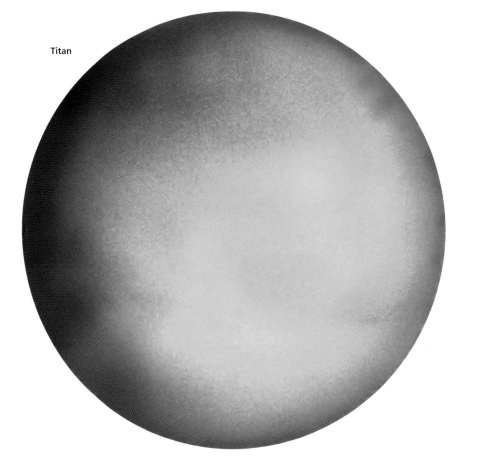

URANUS'S MAJOR MOONS

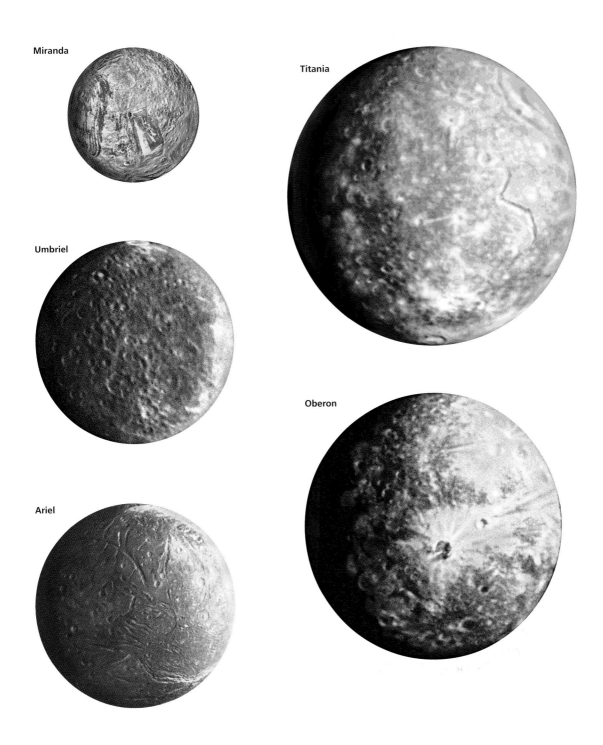

Miranda

Titania

Umbriel

Oberon

Ariel

Moons

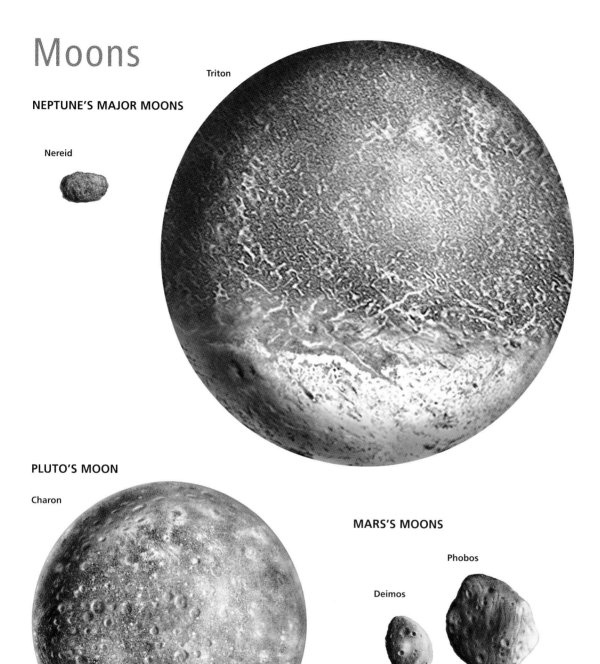

Triton

NEPTUNE'S MAJOR MOONS

Nereid

PLUTO'S MOON

Charon

MARS'S MOONS

Phobos

Deimos

JUPITER'S MAJOR MOONS

Ganymede

Europa

Io

Callisto

The Sun

MAP OF THE SUN

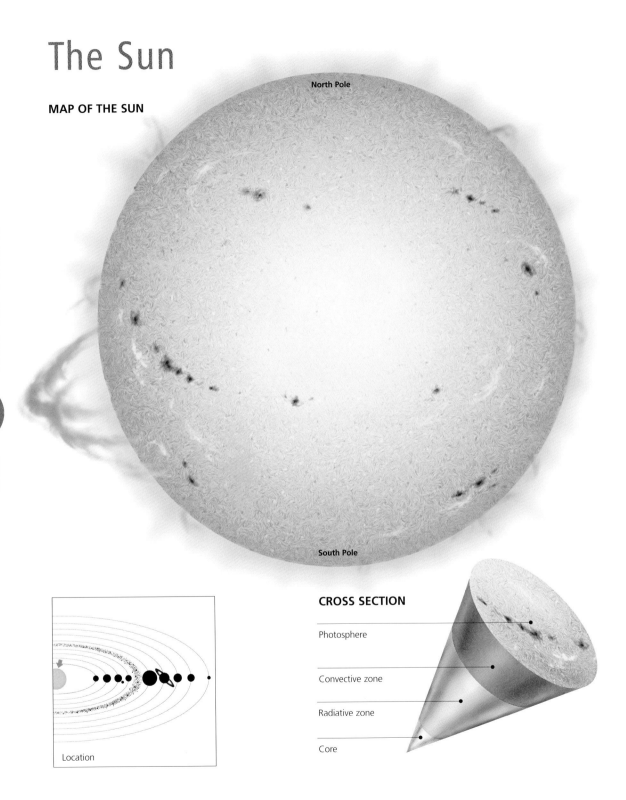

North Pole

South Pole

Location

CROSS SECTION

Photosphere

Convective zone

Radiative zone

Core

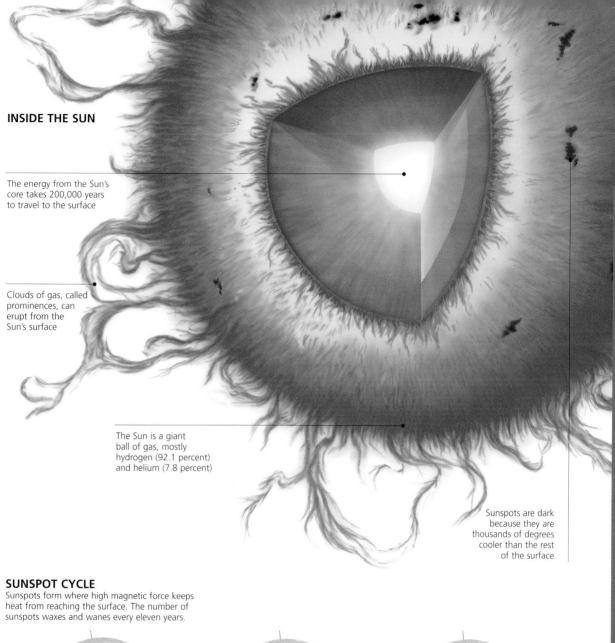

INSIDE THE SUN

The energy from the Sun's core takes 200,000 years to travel to the surface

Clouds of gas, called prominences, can erupt from the Sun's surface

The Sun is a giant ball of gas, mostly hydrogen (92.1 percent) and helium (7.8 percent)

Sunspots are dark because they are thousands of degrees cooler than the rest of the surface

SUNSPOT CYCLE

Sunspots form where high magnetic force keeps heat from reaching the surface. The number of sunspots waxes and wanes every eleven years.

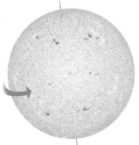

Year 1—sunspot minimum

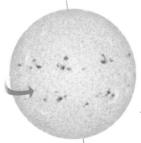

Year 5—sunspot maximum

Year 9—approaching minimum

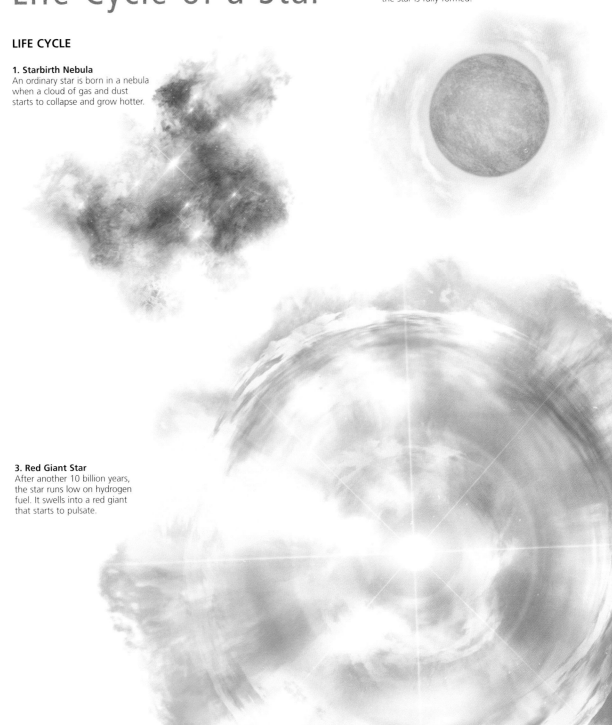

Life Cycle of a Star

LIFE CYCLE

1. Starbirth Nebula
An ordinary star is born in a nebula when a cloud of gas and dust starts to collapse and grow hotter.

2. Main Sequence Star
About 40 million years later, the star is fully formed.

3. Red Giant Star
After another 10 billion years, the star runs low on hydrogen fuel. It swells into a red giant that starts to pulsate.

4. Planetary Nebula
Three billion years later, the
pulsations grow stronger and the
bloated star sheds it outer layers.

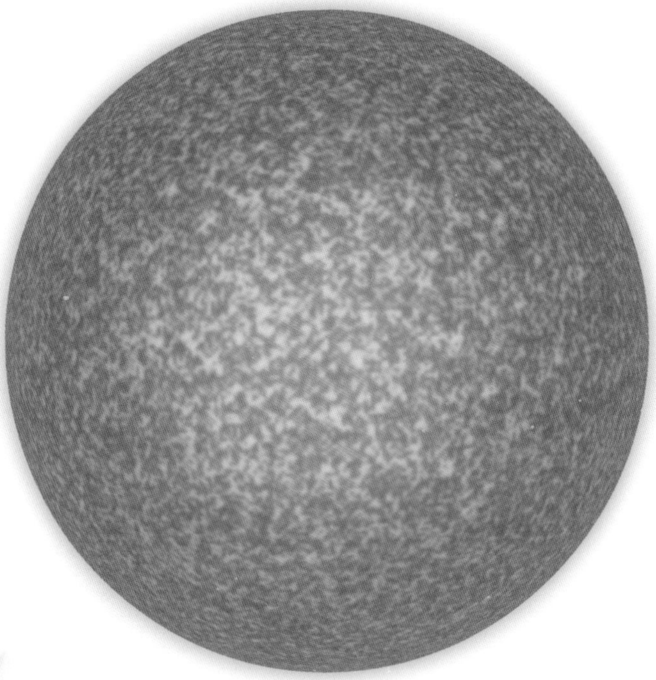

STAR SIZE COMPARISON

Red supergiant

Red giant

5. White Dwarf Star
In less than 50,000 years, the
planetary nebula disperses into
space. It leaves behind a white
dwarf, the star's white-hot core.

Sun

White dwarf

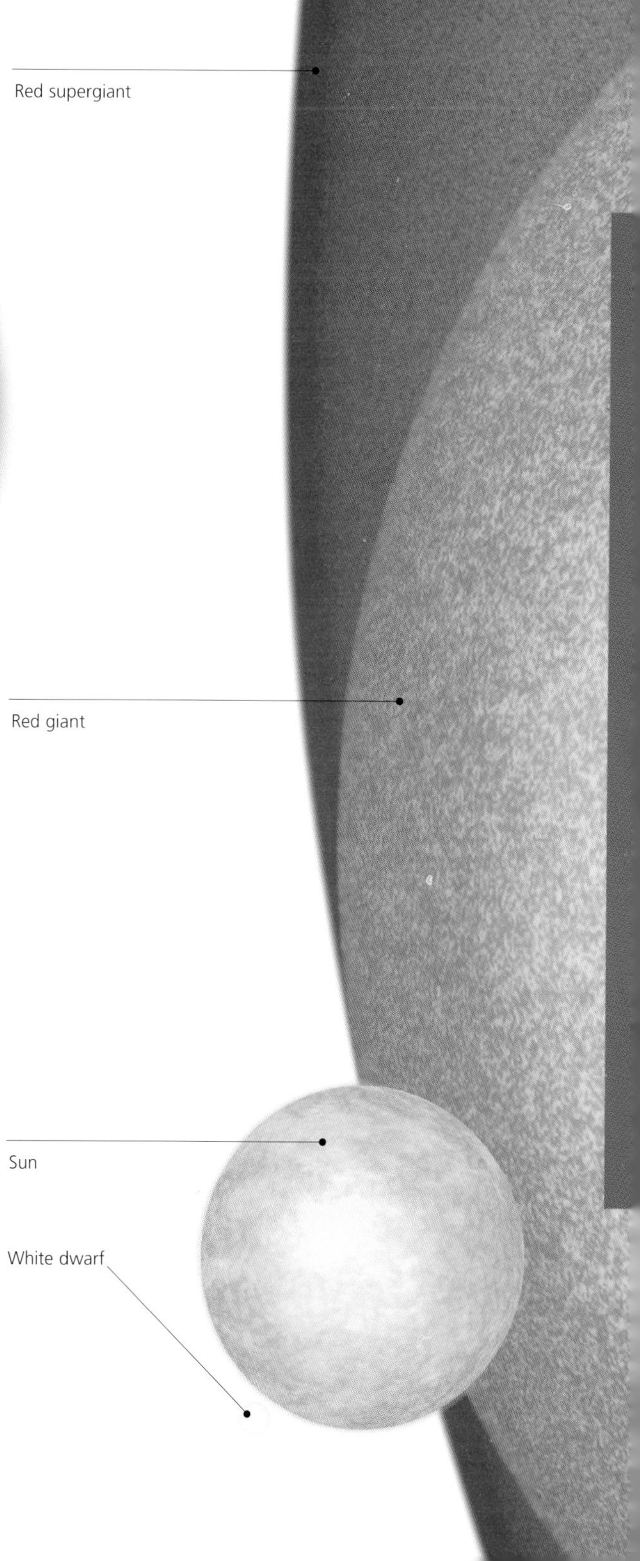

Stars and Supernovas

MASSIVE-STAR SUPERNOVA
This type of supernova signals the explosive death of a massive star.

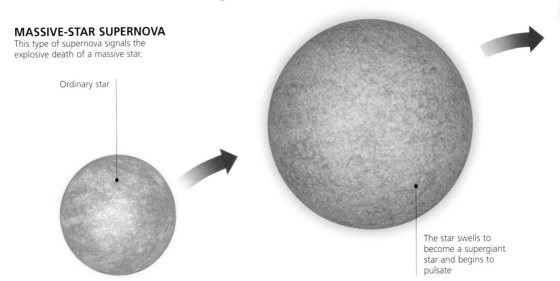

Ordinary star

The star swells to become a supergiant star and begins to pulsate

PULSARS
A neutron star is only a few miles across but it spins rapidly. If Earth lies in the beam of its energy, we see a repeating signal of light.

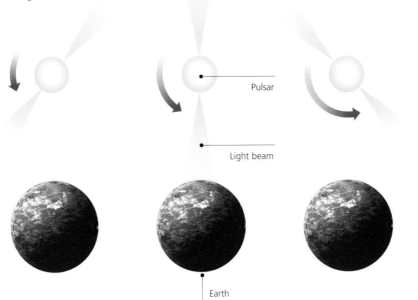

Pulsar

Light beam

Earth

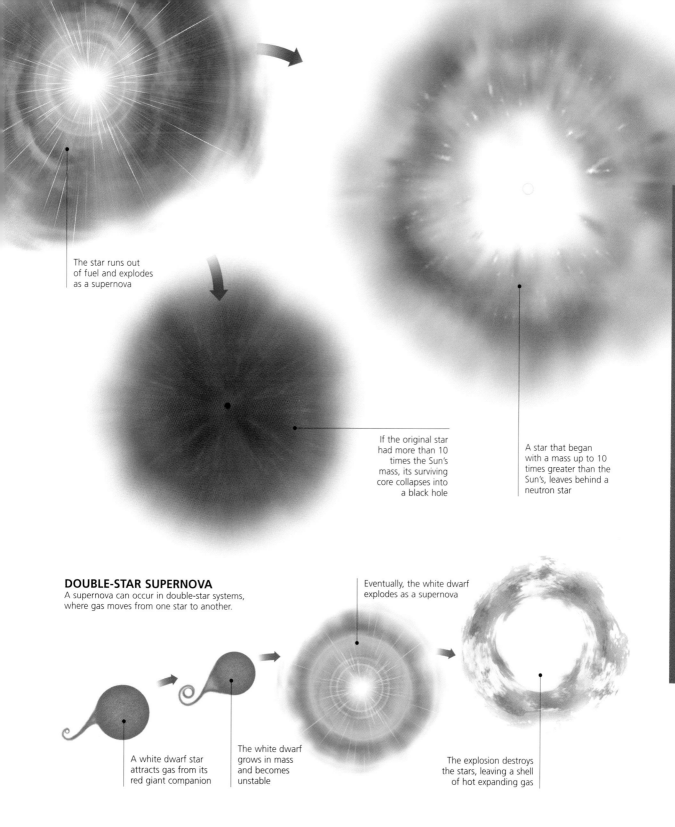

The star runs out
of fuel and explodes
as a supernova

If the original star
had more than 10
times the Sun's
mass, its surviving
core collapses into
a black hole

A star that began
with a mass up to 10
times greater than the
Sun's, leaves behind a
neutron star

DOUBLE-STAR SUPERNOVA
A supernova can occur in double-star systems,
where gas moves from one star to another.

Eventually, the white dwarf
explodes as a supernova

A white dwarf star
attracts gas from its
red giant companion

The white dwarf
grows in mass
and becomes
unstable

The explosion destroys
the stars, leaving a shell
of hot expanding gas

Clusters

MILKY WAY CLUSTERS

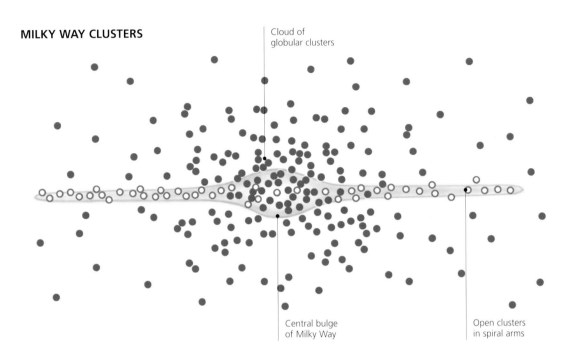

Cloud of globular clusters

Central bulge of Milky Way

Open clusters in spiral arms

GLOBULAR CLUSTERS

Young

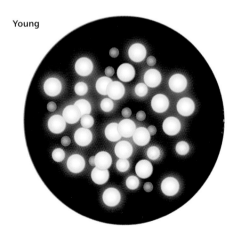

A young cluster has many white-hot stars, plus yellow stars like the Sun and dim red dwarfs.

Old

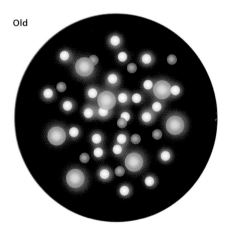

Stars in the original population have evolved, becoming red giants and white dwarfs.

OPEN CLUSTERS OVER TIME

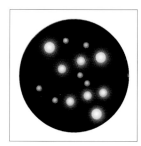

Members of the open cluster drift apart as the galaxy's gravity pulls.

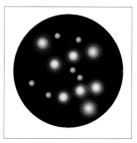

The cluster members evolve, with massive stars becoming red giants.

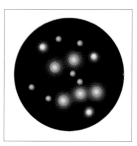

As the cluster becomes fainter, the red giants become white dwarfs.

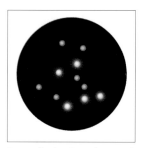

Eventually, the cluster becomes hard to tell apart from the rest of the galaxy.

THE PLEIADES

The Pleiades is an open cluster in the constellation of Taurus. It lies 375 light-years away from Earth

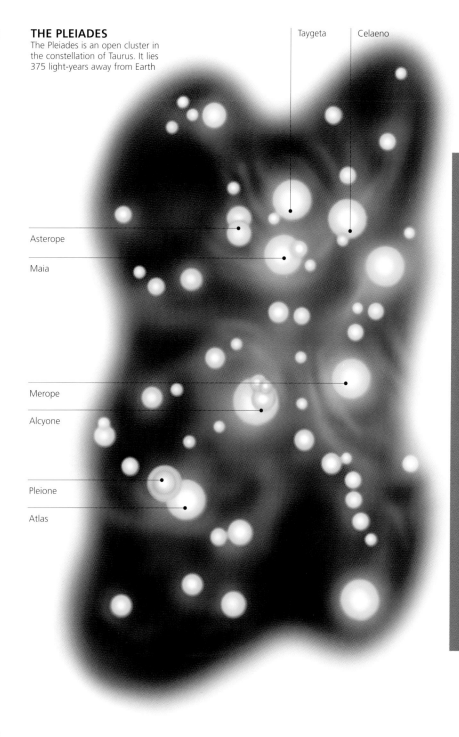

Taygeta

Celaeno

Asterope

Maia

Merope

Alcyone

Pleione

Atlas

The Milky Way

SIDE VIEW

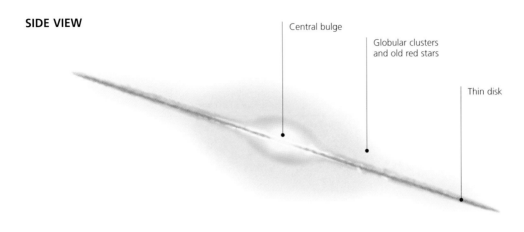

Central bulge

Globular clusters
and old red stars

Thin disk

GALACTIC NEIGHBORS

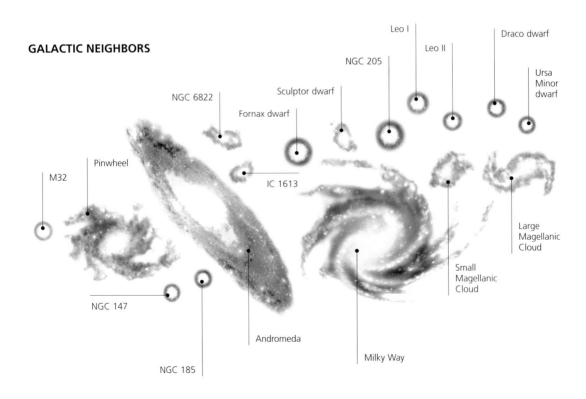

Leo I

Leo II

Draco dwarf

NGC 205

Ursa
Minor
dwarf

NGC 6822

Sculptor dwarf

Fornax dwarf

M32

Pinwheel

IC 1613

Large
Magellanic
Cloud

NGC 147

Small
Magellanic
Cloud

Andromeda

Milky Way

NGC 185

CROSS SECTION

Sun

Central bulge

Cygnus arm

Orion arm

Crux-
Centaurus
arm

Sagittarius
arm

Halo of
globular
clusters

Galaxies and Black Holes

MULTIPLE IMAGES

A black hole is so powerful that it can bend light—creating the optical illusion of a double galaxy.

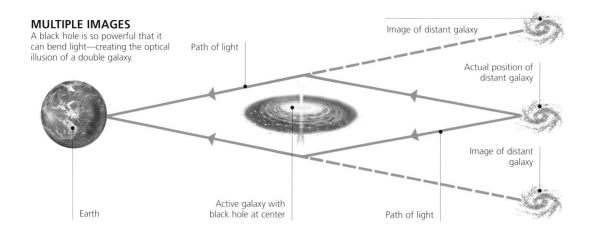

Path of light

Image of distant galaxy

Actual position of distant galaxy

Image of distant galaxy

Earth

Active galaxy with black hole at center

Path of light

GALACTIC BLACK HOLE

Active galaxies produce a huge amount of energy in a very small space

Black hole

As gas falls into the black hole, it becomes extremely hot and emits lots of energy

GALAXY CLASSIFICATION

Edwin Hubble developed this scheme for classifying galaxies by shape.

Hubble thought ellipticals evolved to become spirals or barred spirals

Spirals

Elliptical

Barred spirals

Today's astronomers think most spirals and barred spirals are born that way

TYPES OF GALAXIES

Elliptical galaxy

Irregular galaxy

Spiral galaxy

Barred spiral galaxy

Using a Star Map

STAR MOVEMENT

The path of star movement depends on latitude.

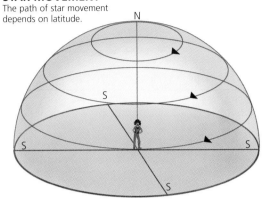

North Pole—90°N

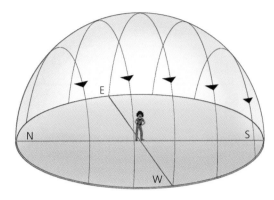

Equator—0°

FINDING THE POLES

Northern Hemisphere

First locate the Big Dipper using the correct map for your location and season. Then draw an imaginary line from the end of the Dipper's bowl to Polaris.

Southern Hemisphere

First locate Crux using the correct map for your location and season. Then draw imaginary lines between the other bright stars marked below, to find the pole.

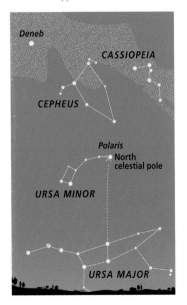

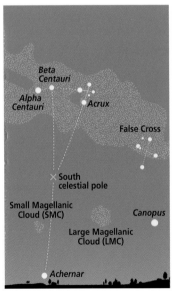

KEY TO MAP SYMBOLS

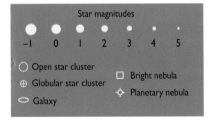

Sky maps show star brightness using dots sized according to their magnitude. Fainter stars have higher magnitude numbers, while the brightest stars have negative magnitudes.

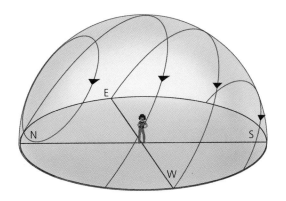

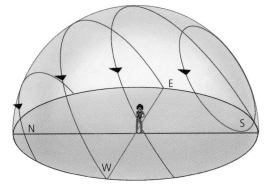

Northern middle latitudes—40°N

Southern middle latitudes—40°S

A GUIDE TO STAR MAPS

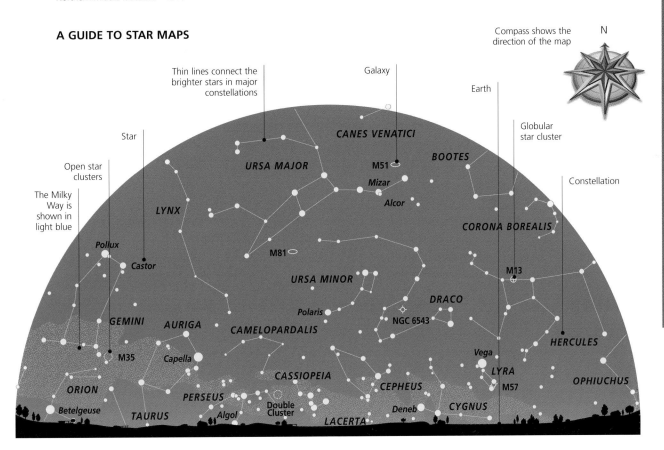

Thin lines connect the brighter stars in major constellations

Galaxy

Compass shows the direction of the map

N

Star

Earth

Open star clusters

Globular star cluster

Constellation

The Milky Way is shown in light blue

CANES VENATICI

URSA MAJOR

M51

BOOTES

Mizar

Alcor

LYNX

CORONA BOREALIS

Pollux

M81

Castor

URSA MINOR

M13

GEMINI

Polaris

DRACO

NGC 6543

HERCULES

AURIGA

CAMELOPARDALIS

Vega

M35

Capella

LYRA

OPHIUCHUS

CASSIOPEIA

M57

ORION

CEPHEUS

Betelgeuse

PERSEUS

CYGNUS

Deneb

TAURUS

Algol

Double Cluster

LACERTA

Winter Stars of the Northern Skies

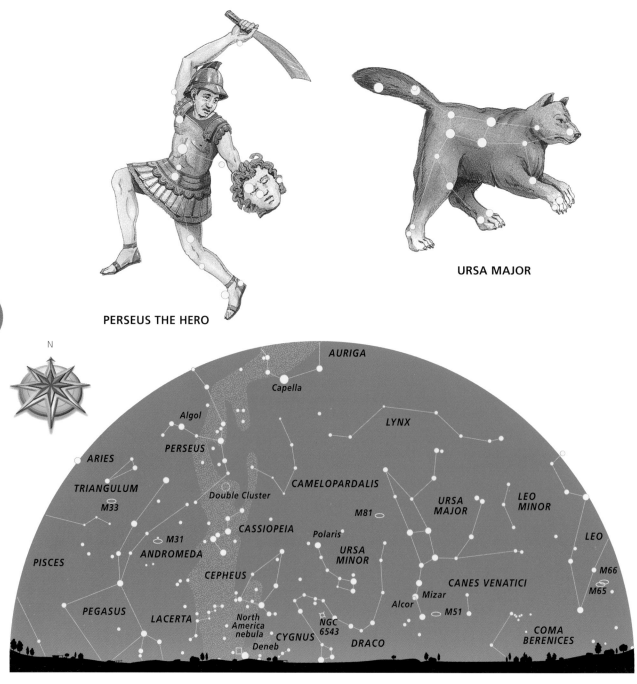

PERSEUS THE HERO

URSA MAJOR

N

AURIGA

Capella

Algol

LYNX

PERSEUS

ARIES

CAMELOPARDALIS

TRIANGULUM

LEO
MINOR

URSA
MAJOR

M33

Double Cluster

M81

LEO

CASSIOPEIA

Polaris

M31

ANDROMEDA

URSA
MINOR

M66

PISCES

CEPHEUS

CANES VENATICI

M65

Mizar

PEGASUS

Alcor

M51

LACERTA

North
America
nebula

NGC
6543

COMA
BERENICES

CYGNUS

DRACO

Deneb

ORION THE HUNTER

CANIS MAJOR

TAURUS THE BULL

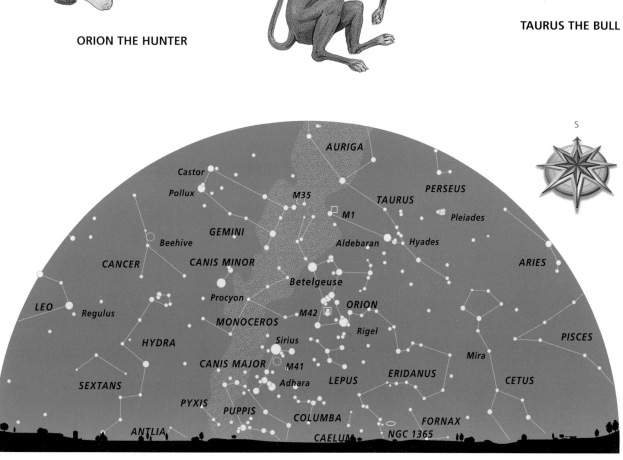

S

Spring Stars of the Northern Skies

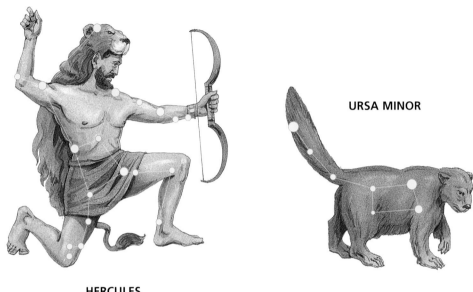

HERCULES

URSA MINOR

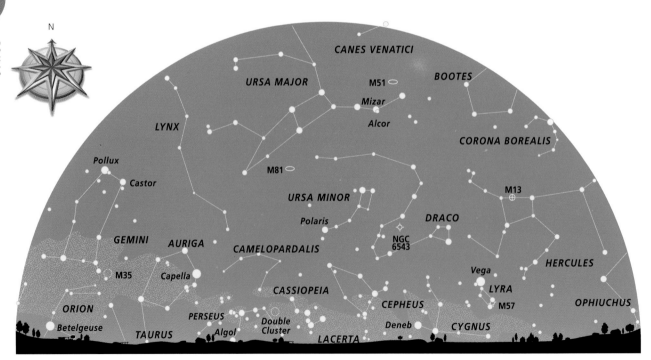

N

CANES VENATICI

URSA MAJOR

M51

BOOTES

Mizar

Alcor

LYNX

CORONA BOREALIS

Pollux

M81

M13

Castor

URSA MINOR

Polaris

DRACO

GEMINI

AURIGA

CAMELOPARDALIS

NGC
6543

HERCULES

Vega

M35

Capella

CASSIOPEIA

LYRA

M57

OPHIUCHUS

ORION

CEPHEUS

Betelgeuse

Deneb

CYGNUS

TAURUS

PERSEUS

Algol

Double
Cluster

LACERTA

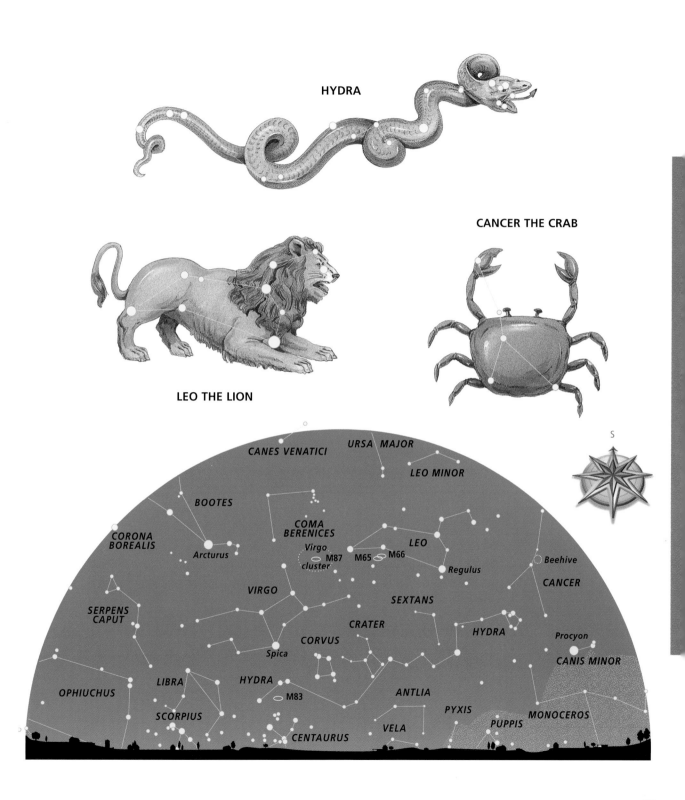

HYDRA

CANCER THE CRAB

LEO THE LION

CANES VENATICI
URSA MAJOR
LEO MINOR
BOOTES
COMA BERENICES
LEO
CORONA BOREALIS
Virgo
M87
M65 M66
Beehive
Arcturus
Virgo cluster
Regulus
CANCER
VIRGO
SEXTANS
SERPENS CAPUT
CRATER
HYDRA
Procyon
CORVUS
CANIS MINOR
Spica
OPHIUCHUS
LIBRA
HYDRA
ANTLIA
PYXIS
MONOCEROS
SCORPIUS
M83
PUPPIS
CENTAURUS
VELA

S

Summer Stars of the Northern Skies

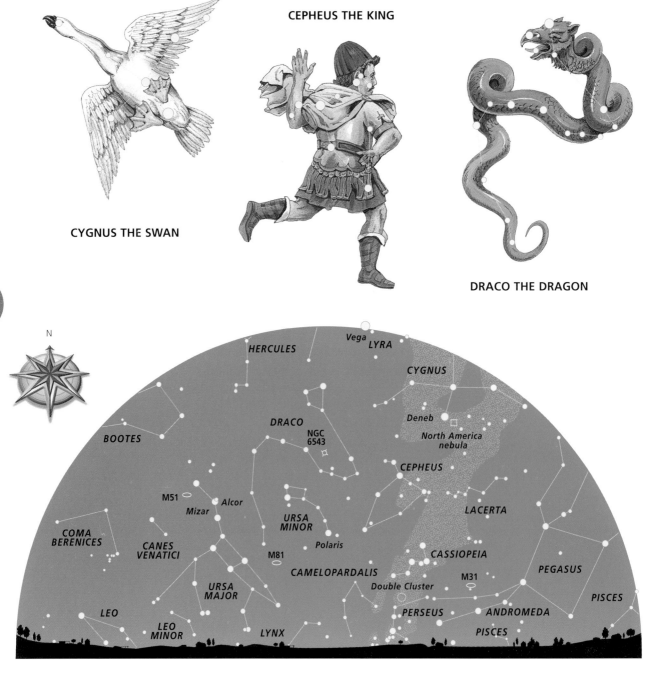

CEPHEUS THE KING

CYGNUS THE SWAN

DRACO THE DRAGON

N

HERCULES

Vega LYRA

CYGNUS

DRACO

Deneb

NGC 6543

North America nebula

BOOTES

CEPHEUS

LACERTA

M51

Alcor

Mizar

URSA MINOR

COMA BERENICES

CANES VENATICI

Polaris

M81

CASSIOPEIA

PEGASUS

CAMELOPARDALIS

Double Cluster

M31

URSA MAJOR

PISCES

LEO

PERSEUS

ANDROMEDA

LEO MINOR

LYNX

PISCES

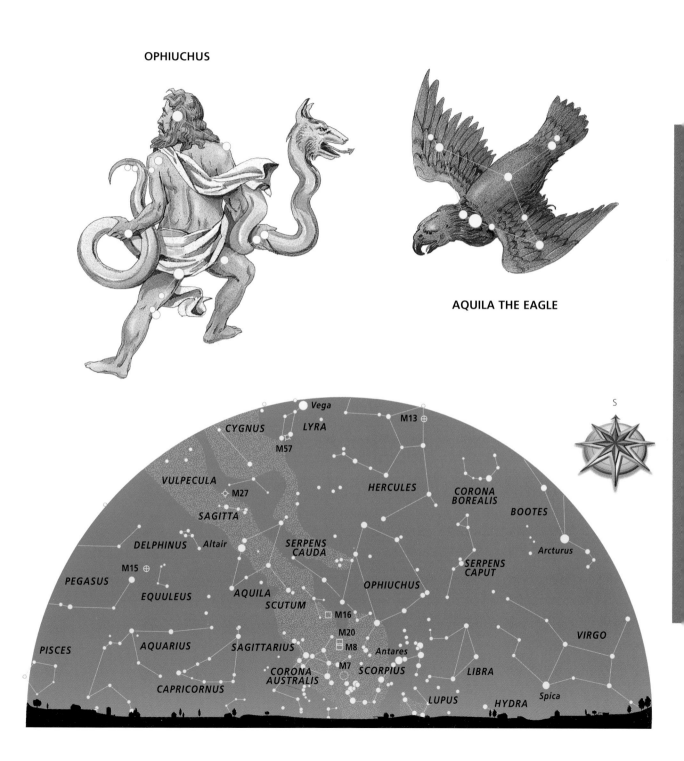

OPHIUCHUS

AQUILA THE EAGLE

CYGNUS
Vega
LYRA
M13
M57
HERCULES
CORONA
BOREALIS
VULPECULA
BOOTES
M27
SAGITTA
SERPENS
CAUDA
Arcturus
DELPHINUS
Altair
SERPENS
CAPUT
PEGASUS
M15
OPHIUCHUS
EQUULEUS
AQUILA
SCUTUM
VIRGO
M16
M20
PISCES
M8
AQUARIUS
SAGITTARIUS
Antares
LIBRA
Spica
CORONA
AUSTRALIS
M7
SCORPIUS
CAPRICORNUS
LUPUS
HYDRA

S

Autumn Stars of the Northern Skies

Constellations

SPACE

LYRA THE LYRE

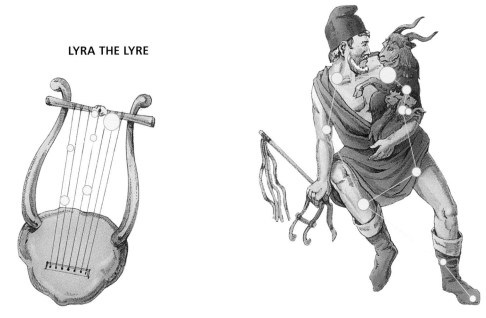

AURIGA THE CHARIOTEER

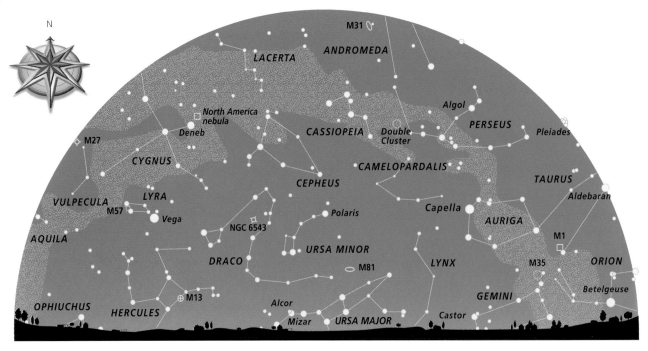

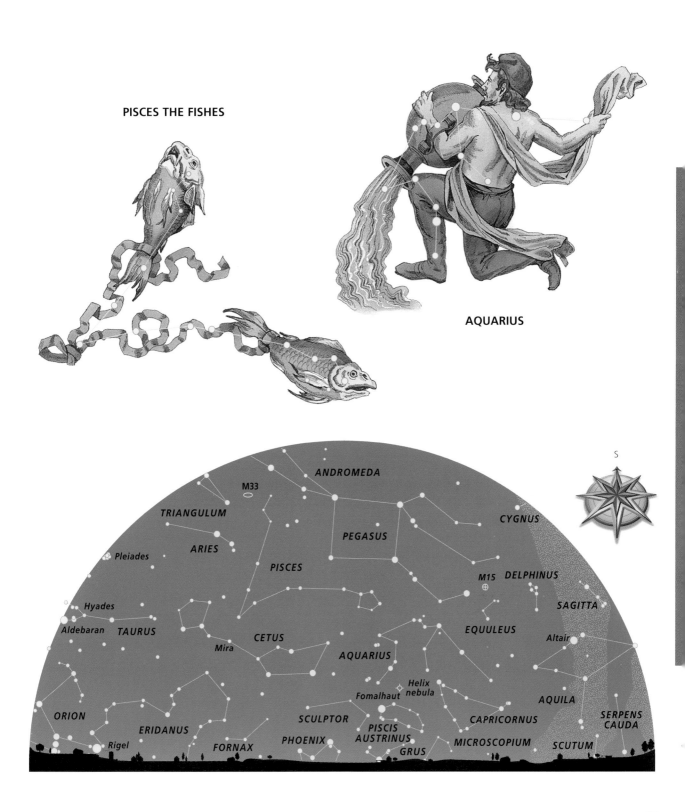

PISCES THE FISHES

AQUARIUS

ANDROMEDA

M33

TRIANGULUM

CYGNUS

ARIES

PEGASUS

Pleiades

PISCES

M15

DELPHINUS

Hyades

SAGITTA

Aldebaran

TAURUS

EQUULEUS

Altair

Mira

CETUS

AQUARIUS

Helix
nebula

Fomalhaut

AQUILA

ORION

Rigel

ERIDANUS

FORNAX

PHOENIX

SCULPTOR

PISCIS
AUSTRINUS

GRUS

CAPRICORNUS

MICROSCOPIUM

SERPENS
CAUDA

SCUTUM

S

Winter Stars of the Southern Skies

SERPENS THE SERPENT

SAGITTARIUS THE ARCHER

LIBRA THE SCALES

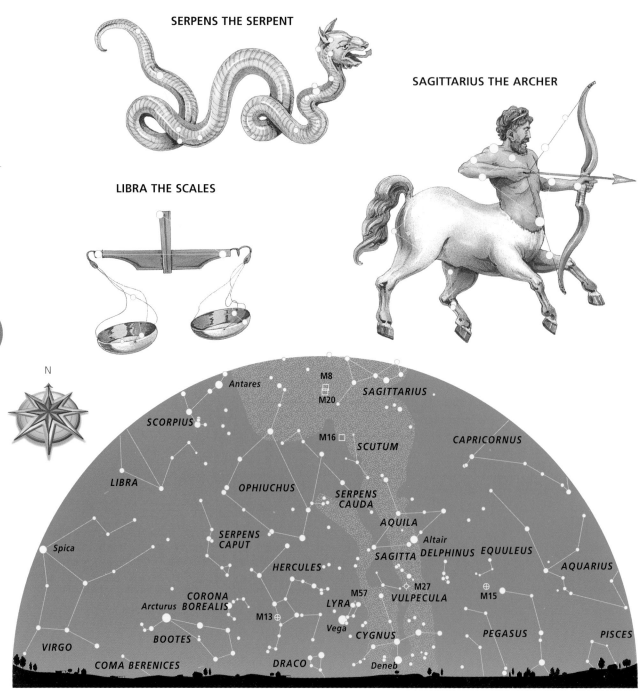

N

Antares
M8
M20
SAGITTARIUS

SCORPIUS
M16
SCUTUM
CAPRICORNUS

LIBRA
OPHIUCHUS
SERPENS CAUDA
AQUILA

Spica
SERPENS CAPUT
Altair
SAGITTA DELPHINUS EQUULEUS
AQUARIUS

HERCULES
M27 VULPECULA
M15

CORONA
M57
M13
LYRA
PEGASUS
PISCES

Arcturus BOREALIS
Vega
CYGNUS

VIRGO
BOOTES
DRACO
Deneb

COMA BERENICES

LUPUS THE WOLF

CORONA AUSTRALIS

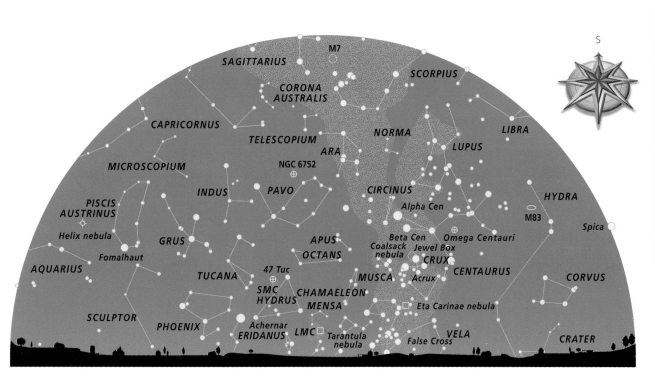

S

SAGITTARIUS   M7   SCORPIUS

CORONA
AUSTRALIS

CAPRICORNUS   NORMA   LIBRA

TELESCOPIUM   LUPUS

ARA   NGC 6752   CIRCINUS   HYDRA

MICROSCOPIUM   Alpha Cen   M83

INDUS   PAVO   Spica

PISCIS
AUSTRINUS   Beta Cen   Omega Centauri

Helix nebula   APUS   Coalsack   Jewel Box
nebula
GRUS   OCTANS   CRUX   CENTAURUS   CORVUS
Fomalhaut
MUSCA   Acrux
AQUARIUS   TUCANA   47 Tuc

SMC   CHAMAELEON   Eta Carinae nebula
SCULPTOR   HYDRUS   MENSA
PHOENIX   Achernar   LMC   Tarantula   VELA   CRATER
ERIDANUS   nebula   False Cross

73

Spring Stars of the Southern Skies

CETUS

PEGASUS

N

Fomalhaut
PISCIS AUSTRINUS
SCULPTOR
Helix nebula
CAPRICORNUS
AQUARIUS
CETUS
ERIDANUS
Mira
EQUULEUS
PISCES
AQUILA
DELPHINUS
M15
PEGASUS
ARIES
TAURUS
Altair
ANDROMEDA
M33
Pleiades
SCUTUM
SAGITTA
M31
TRIANGULUM
Hyades
Aldebaran
ORION
SERPENS
CAUDA
M27
VULPECULA
CYGNUS
LACERTA
CASSIOPEIA
PERSEUS
Algol
Deneb

GRUS THE CRANE

TUCANA THE TOUCAN

SCULPTOR
Fomalhaut
PISCIS
AUSTRINUS
PHOENIX
FORNAX
GRUS
ERIDANUS
MICROSCOPIUM
CAPRICORNUS
NGC 1365
Achernar
HOROLOGIUM
TUCANA
INDUS
47 Tuc
RETICULUM
SMC
HYDRUS
PAVO
CORONA
AUSTRALIS
CAELUM
NGC 6752
DORADO
TELESCOPIUM
LEPUS
Tarantula
MENSA
OCTANS
SAGITTARIUS
nebula
PICTOR
APUS
SCUTUM
LMC
CHAMAELEON
Rigel
M8
M16
COLUMBA
Canopus
VOLANS
M7
M42
MUSCA
M20
SERPENS
ORION
CANIS MAJOR
PUPPIS
CARINA
CIRCINUS
ARA
SCORPIUS
OPHIUCHUS
CAUDA
Adhara
VELA
NORMA
CRUX

S

75

Summer Stars of the Southern Skies

GEMINI THE TWINS

MONOCEROS THE UNICORN

N

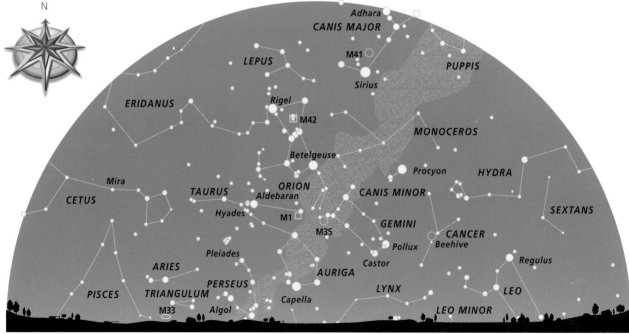

CANIS MAJOR
Adhara

LEPUS

M41

PUPPIS

Sirius

ERIDANUS

Rigel

M42

MONOCEROS

Betelgeuse

Procyon

HYDRA

Mira

ORION

CANIS MINOR

TAURUS

Aldebaran

CETUS

Hyades

M1

GEMINI

SEXTANS

M35

CANCER

Beehive

Pleiades

Pollux

Castor

Regulus

ARIES

AURIGA

LYNX

LEO

PISCES

PERSEUS

Capella

TRIANGULUM

M33

Algol

LEO MINOR

COLUMBA THE DOVE

ERIDANUS THE RIVER

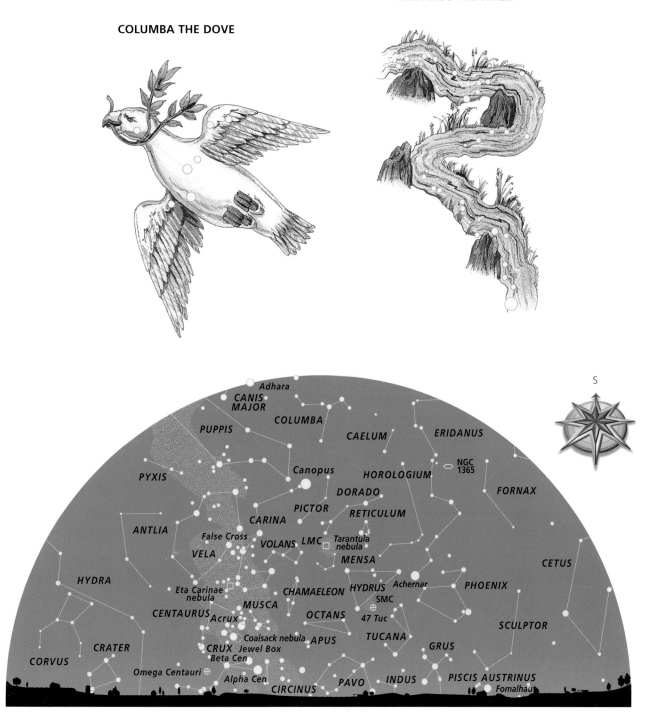

Adhara
CANIS
MAJOR
COLUMBA
CAELUM
ERIDANUS
PUPPIS
NGC
1365
HOROLOGIUM
PYXIS
Canopus
FORNAX
DORADO
PICTOR
RETICULUM
CARINA
ANTLIA
False Cross
VOLANS
LMC
Tarantula
nebula
VELA
MENSA
CETUS
HYDRA
Eta Carinae
nebula
CHAMAELEON
HYDRUS
Achernar
PHOENIX
SMC
MUSCA
CENTAURUS
OCTANS
47 Tuc
Acrux
SCULPTOR
Coalsack nebula
APUS
TUCANA
CRATER
CRUX
Jewel Box
GRUS
Beta Cen
CORVUS
Omega Centauri
PISCIS AUSTRINUS
Alpha Cen
PAVO
INDUS
Fomalhaut
CIRCINUS

S

77

Autumn Stars of the Southern Skies

VIRGO THE MAIDEN

BOOTES THE HERDSMAN

N

HYDRA
M83

CORVUS

CRATER

Spica

SEXTANS

LIBRA

HYDRA

VIRGO

Virgo
M66 M87 cluster
M65
Regulus

MONOCEROS

Procyon

LEO

Arcturus

Beehive

LEO MINOR

COMA
BERENICES

BOOTES

SERPENS
CAPUT

OPHIUCHUS

CANIS MINOR

CANCER

CORONA
BOREALIS

CANES VENATICI

Pollux

LYNX

M51

GEMINI

Castor

URSA MAJOR

Mizar

Alcor

HERCULES

Constellations

SPACE

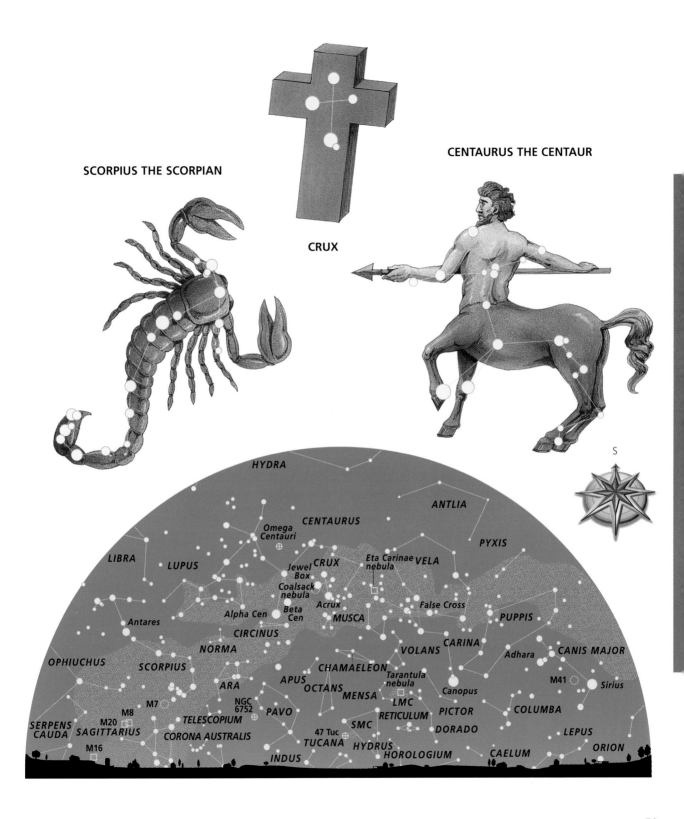

SCORPIUS THE SCORPIAN

CRUX

CENTAURUS THE CENTAUR

S

HYDRA

ANTLIA

CENTAURUS

Omega
Centauri

PYXIS

LIBRA

LUPUS

Jewel
Box

CRUX

Eta Carinae
nebula

VELA

Coalsack
nebula

Acrux

False Cross

PUPPIS

Antares

Alpha Cen

Beta
Cen

MUSCA

CIRCINUS

CARINA

NORMA

VOLANS

Adhara

CANIS MAJOR

OPHIUCHUS

SCORPIUS

CHAMAELEON

M41

Sirius

ARA

APUS

OCTANS

Tarantula
nebula

Canopus

M7

NGC
6752

MENSA

LMC

PICTOR

COLUMBA

SERPENS
CAUDA

M8

M20

TELESCOPIUM

PAVO

RETICULUM

DORADO

LEPUS

SAGITTARIUS

CORONA AUSTRALIS

47 Tuc

SMC

M16

TUCANA

HYDRUS

HOROLOGIUM

CAELUM

ORION

INDUS

Our Place in Space

EARTH IN THE UNIVERSE

Solar System
The Solar System is a tiny
speck in the millions of
stars in the galaxy.

Spiral Arm of Milky Way
The Sun and Solar System
lie near the edge of one of
the Milky Way's spiral arms.

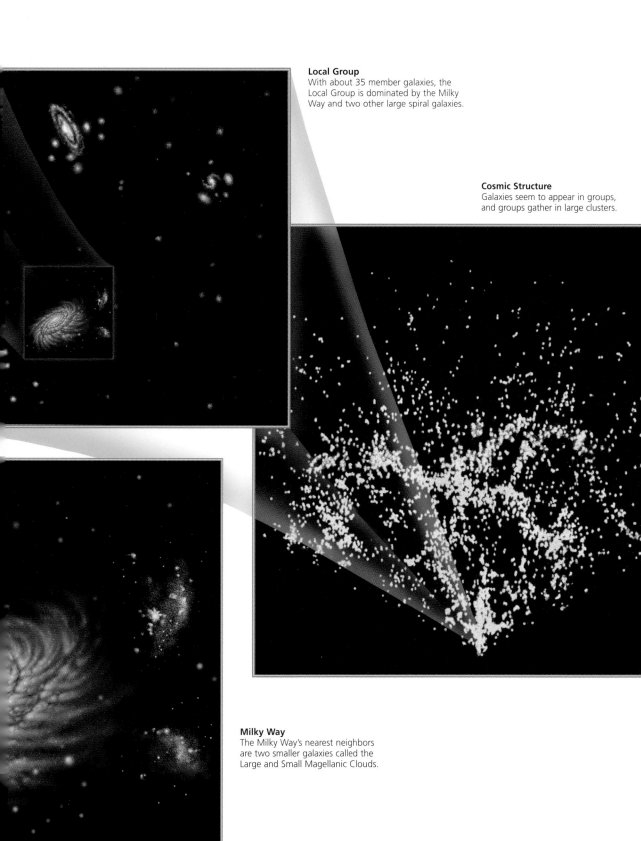

Local Group
With about 35 member galaxies, the Local Group is dominated by the Milky Way and two other large spiral galaxies.

Cosmic Structure
Galaxies seem to appear in groups, and groups gather in large clusters.

Milky Way
The Milky Way's nearest neighbors are two smaller galaxies called the Large and Small Magellanic Clouds.

81

Astronomy from Earth

TYPES OF TELESCOPES

Refractor

Reflector

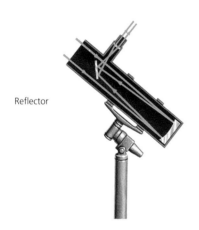

KECK TELESCOPES

Keck II dome

Each Keck telescope stands eight stories tall and weighs 300 tons (270 tonnes)

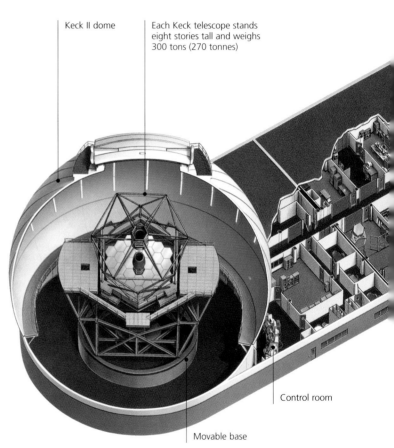

Control room

Movable base

ASTRONOMY MILESTONES

Galileo's refractor, 1609

Isaac Newton's reflector, 1671

William Herschel's reflector, 1781

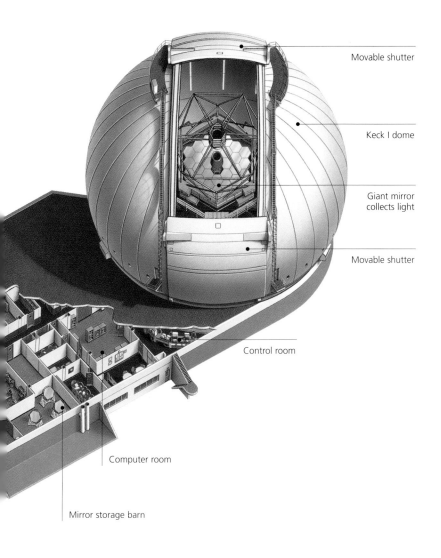

Movable shutter

Keck I dome

Giant mirror collects light

Movable shutter

Control room

Computer room

Mirror storage barn

A telescope's main lens gathers incoming light, while the eyepiece magnifies the image.

Kellner—3 lens elements

Plössl—4 lens elements

Nagler—8 lens elements

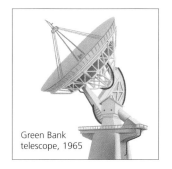

Green Bank telescope, 1965

Anglo-Australian telescope, 1974

ROSAT X-ray telescope, 1990

83

Astronomy from Space

ISO SATELLITE OBSERVATORY

SITF SATELLITE

CHANDRA X-RAY OBSERVATORY

ROSAT SPACE TELESCOPE

COROT TELESCOPE

KEPLER SPACE TELESCOPE

INTERNATIONAL SPACE STATION

IRAS SPACE TELESCOPE

COBE SATELLITE

HUBBLE SPACE TELESCOPE

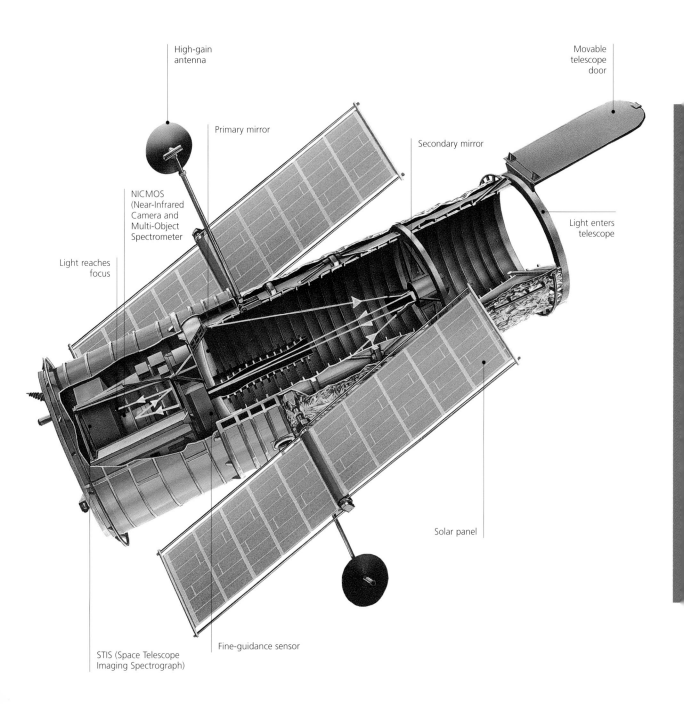

High-gain antenna

Movable telescope door

Primary mirror

Secondary mirror

NICMOS
(Near-Infrared
Camera and
Multi-Object
Spectrometer)

Light enters
telescope

Light reaches
focus

Solar panel

STIS (Space Telescope
Imaging Spectrograph)

Fine-guidance sensor

Robot Probes

Magellan Probe

EXPLORING VENUS

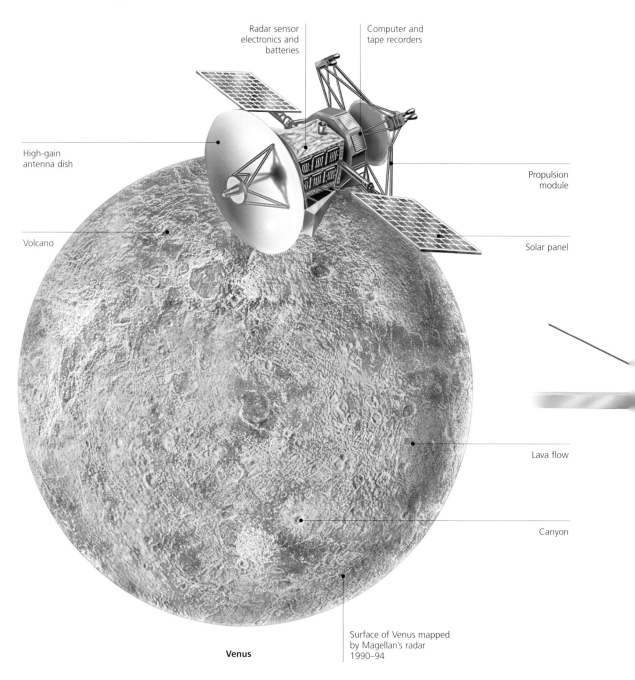

Radar sensor
electronics and
batteries

Computer and
tape recorders

High-gain
antenna dish

Propulsion
module

Volcano

Solar panel

Lava flow

Canyon

Surface of Venus mapped
by Magellan's radar
1990–94

Venus

COMPTON GAMMA-RAY OBSERVATORY

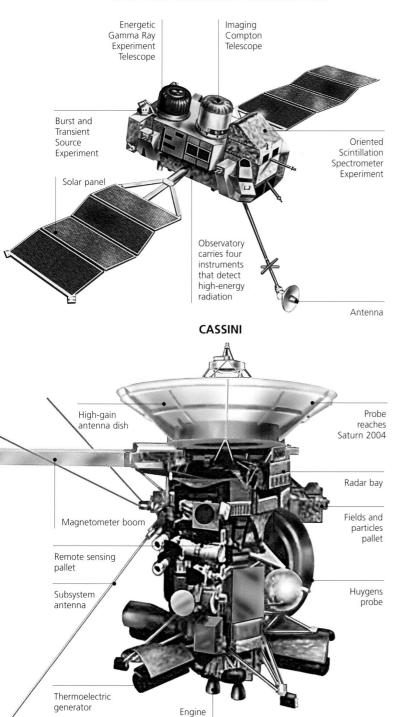

Energetic Gamma Ray Experiment Telescope

Imaging Compton Telescope

Burst and Transient Source Experiment

Oriented Scintillation Spectrometer Experiment

Solar panel

Observatory carries four instruments that detect high-energy radiation

Antenna

CASSINI

High-gain antenna dish

Probe reaches Saturn 2004

Radar bay

Magnetometer boom

Fields and particles pallet

Remote sensing pallet

Subsystem antenna

Huygens probe

Thermoelectric generator

Engine

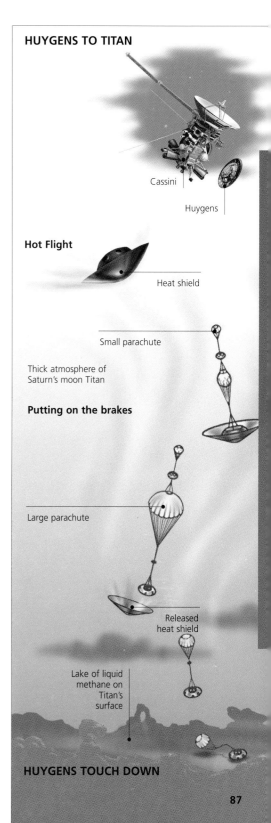

HUYGENS TO TITAN

Cassini

Huygens

Hot Flight

Heat shield

Small parachute

Thick atmosphere of Saturn's moon Titan

Putting on the brakes

Large parachute

Released heat shield

Lake of liquid methane on Titan's surface

HUYGENS TOUCH DOWN

Spacecraft

GIOTTO PROBE

PLUTO—KUIPER EXPRESS

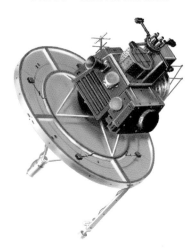

SPOT SATELLITE

MARINER 10 MERCURY PROBE

MARS SPACECRAFT

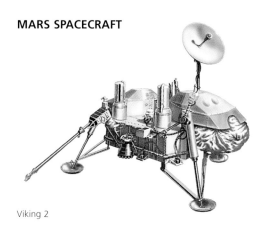

Viking 2

Mars Polar Lander

ASTEROID SPACECRAFT

Muses-C

NEAR (Near-Earth Asteroid Rendezvous) Spacecraft

SUN SPACECRAFT

SOHO (Solar and Heliospheric Observatory)

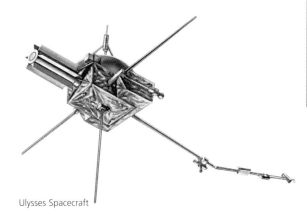

Ulysses Spacecraft

Space Travel

JOURNEY TO THE MOON

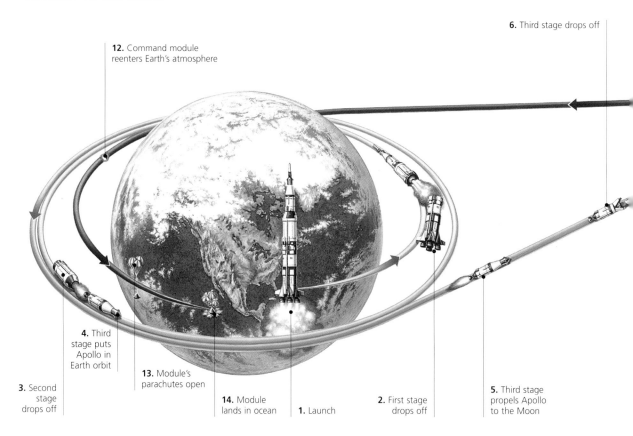

6. Third stage drops off

12. Command module reenters Earth's atmosphere

4. Third stage puts Apollo in Earth orbit

3. Second stage drops off

13. Module's parachutes open

14. Module lands in ocean

1. Launch

2. First stage drops off

5. Third stage propels Apollo to the Moon

MISSIONS TO SPACE

Vostok, 1961

Gemini, 1965

Soyuz, 1967

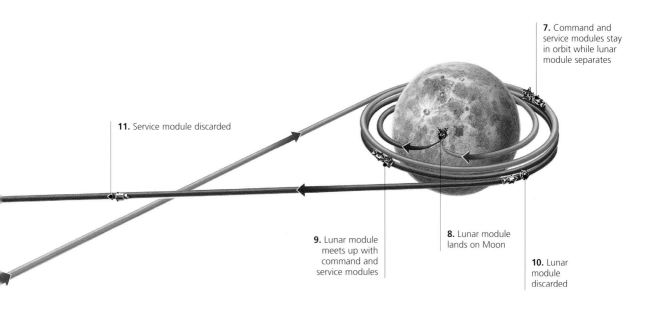

7. Command and service modules stay in orbit while lunar module separates

11. Service module discarded

9. Lunar module meets up with command and service modules

8. Lunar module lands on Moon

10. Lunar module discarded

FLYING THE SPACE SHUTTLE

Liftoff

SRB separation

Tank falls away

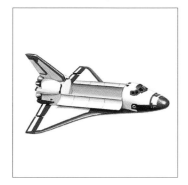

In orbit

Reentry

Touchdown

THE SHIFTING EARTH

ROCKS AND MINERALS

VOLCANOES AND EARTHQUAKES

The Earth's Structure

CROSS SECTION OF EARTH

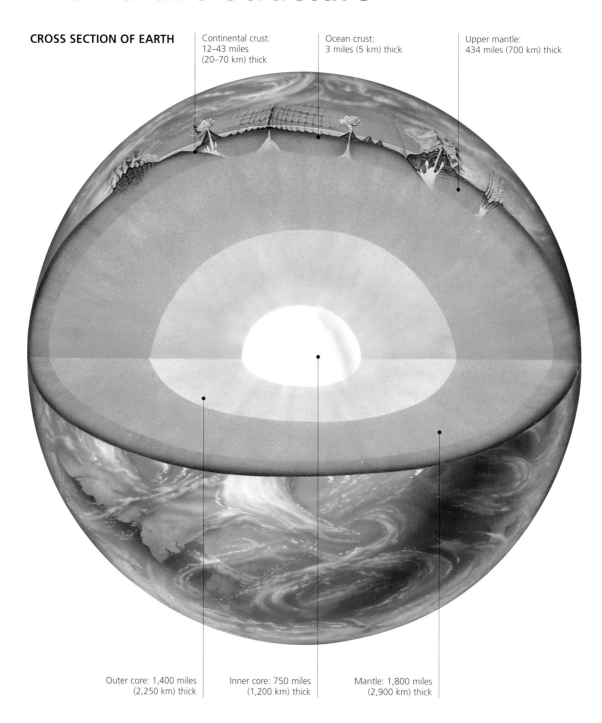

Continental crust:
12–43 miles
(20–70 km) thick

Ocean crust:
3 miles (5 km) thick

Upper mantle:
434 miles (700 km) thick

Outer core: 1,400 miles
(2,250 km) thick

Inner core: 750 miles
(1,200 km) thick

Mantle: 1,800 miles
(2,900 km) thick

CROSS SECTION OF THE GRAND CANYON

By studying fossils and rocks in the walls of the Grand Canyon, geologists can paint a picture of the canyon's history—which dates back more than two billion years.

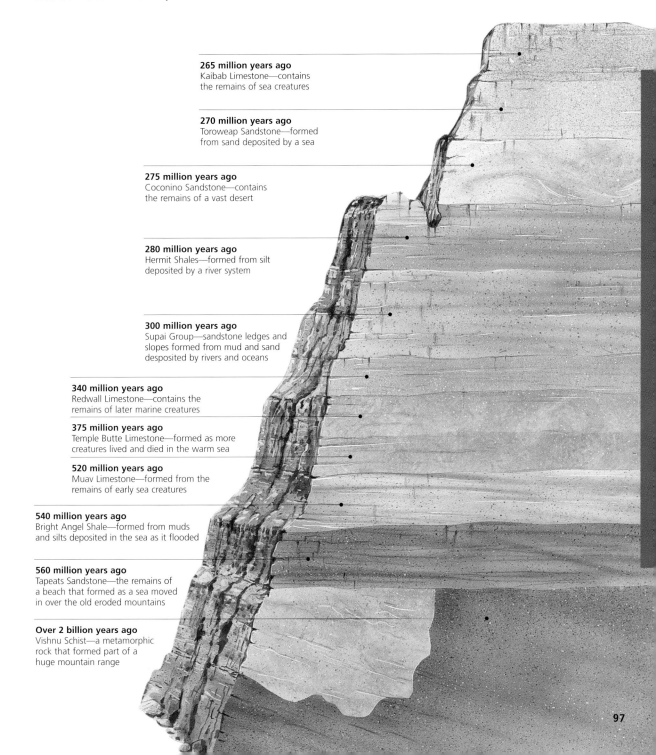

265 million years ago
Kaibab Limestone—contains the remains of sea creatures

270 million years ago
Toroweap Sandstone—formed from sand deposited by a sea

275 million years ago
Coconino Sandstone—contains the remains of a vast desert

280 million years ago
Hermit Shales—formed from silt deposited by a river system

300 million years ago
Supai Group—sandstone ledges and slopes formed from mud and sand desposited by rivers and oceans

340 million years ago
Redwall Limestone—contains the remains of later marine creatures

375 million years ago
Temple Butte Limestone—formed as more creatures lived and died in the warm sea

520 million years ago
Muav Limestone—formed from the remains of early sea creatures

540 million years ago
Bright Angel Shale—formed from muds and silts deposited in the sea as it flooded

560 million years ago
Tapeats Sandstone—the remains of a beach that formed as a sea moved in over the old eroded mountains

Over 2 billion years ago
Vishnu Schist—a metamorphic rock that formed part of a huge mountain range

Continental Drift

SHIFTING PLATES

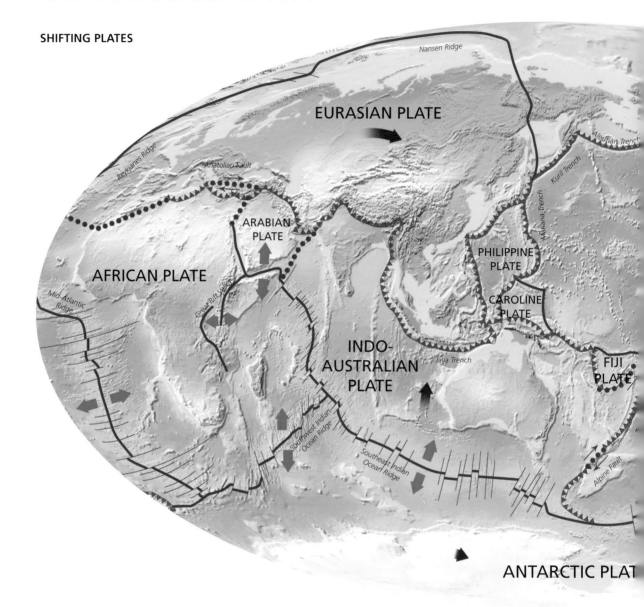

EURASIAN PLATE

Nansen Ridge

Reykjanes Ridge

Anatolian Fault

Aleutian Trench

Kuril Trench

Mariana Trench

ARABIAN PLATE

PHILIPPINE PLATE

AFRICAN PLATE

CAROLINE PLATE

Mid-Atlantic Ridge

Great Rift Valley

INDO-AUSTRALIAN PLATE

Java Trench

FIJI PLATE

Southwest Indian Ocean Ridge

Southeast Indian Ocean Ridge

Alpine Fault

ANTARCTIC PLATE

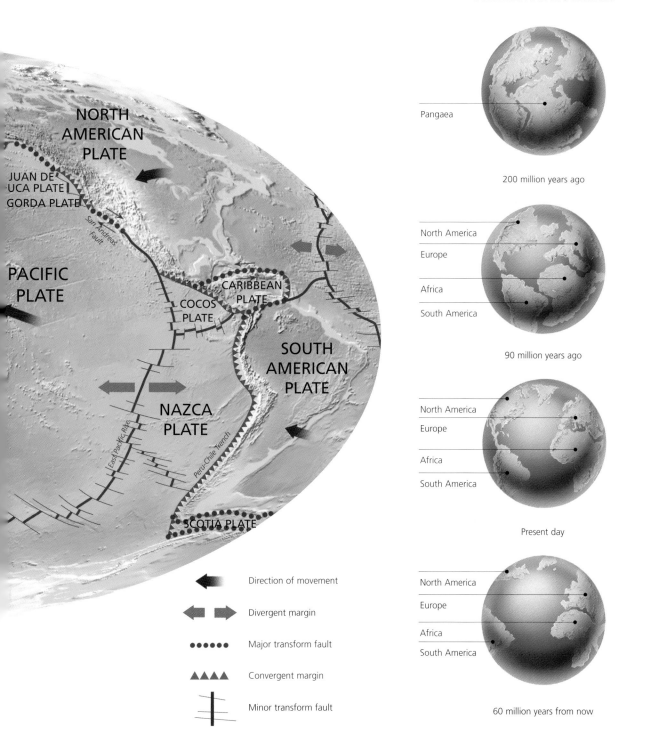

NORTH AMERICAN PLATE

JUAN DE FUCA PLATE
GORDA PLATE

San Andreas Fault

PACIFIC PLATE

COCOS PLATE

CARIBBEAN PLATE

SOUTH AMERICAN PLATE

NAZCA PLATE

East Pacific Rise

Peru-Chile Trench

SCOTIA PLATE

Direction of movement

Divergent margin

Major transform fault

Convergent margin

Minor transform fault

CONTINENTAL MOVEMENT

Pangaea

200 million years ago

North America
Europe
Africa
South America

90 million years ago

North America
Europe
Africa
South America

Present day

North America
Europe
Africa
South America

60 million years from now

Shifting Surface

SURFACE WEAR AND TEAR

Moving glaciers are formed by massive snowfalls and gouge wide, U-shaped valleys

Rivers carve mesas and canyons and wash away the surrounding rocks

Water can eat through some types of rock, forming elaborate cave systems

Ocean waves pound shorelines, cutting caves and creating stacks

In deserts, windblown sand wears away the rocks and forms shifting dunes

NATURAL SCULPTURE

Numbung Pinnacles, Australia

Devil's Tower, USA

Granite Tor, England

SPREADING SEA FLOOR

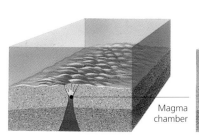

Magma chamber

1. As two plates with ocean crust move apart, a crack or rift forms.

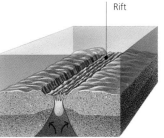

Rift

2. Magma from the mantle rises to fill the rift between the two plates.

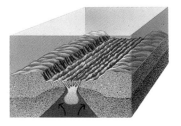

3. Magma cools and hardens and adds to the edges of the plates.

SPREADING CANYON

1. Sedimentary rocks are exposed when the sea level falls. Rivers cut deep into rocks, forming narrow pathways in the land.

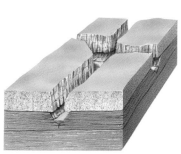

2. As the rivers cut deeper, they form steep-sided valleys. Reaching softer layers, the rivers start to dig under the hard rock.

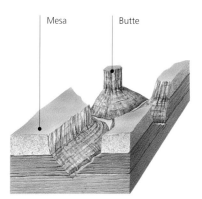

Mesa

Butte

3. The undercutting causes the upper layers to collapse and the valley widens. This creates mesas and buttes in the landscape.

Fault Lines

FAMOUS FAULT LINES

Himalayas

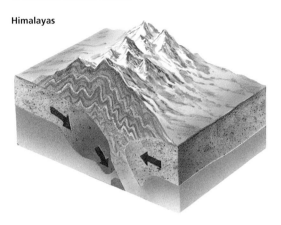

Formed at a convergent zone where two continental plates collided and squeezed together.

San Andreas

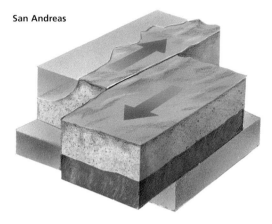

This fault line marks the transform boundary between the Pacific and North American plates.

TYPES OF FAULT LINES AND RIDGES

Reverse faults create mountains as one plate pushes against the other, the crust cracks and tilts

When two plates with ocean crust collide, magma breaks through, forming volcanoes

Magma rises through the gap and cools and hardens to form a mid-ocean ridge

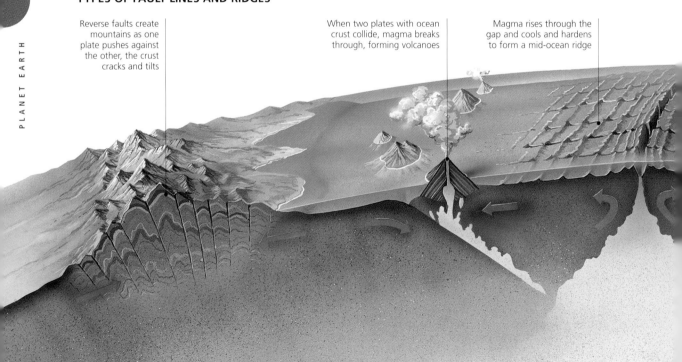

East African rift valley

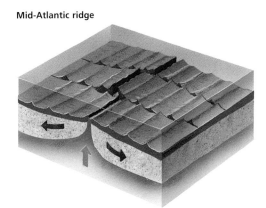

This rift valley represents a continental divergent zone, where Africa will split and a new ocean will form.

Mid-Atlantic ridge

This ridge is a mid-ocean divergent zone, where oceanic crust is formed continually.

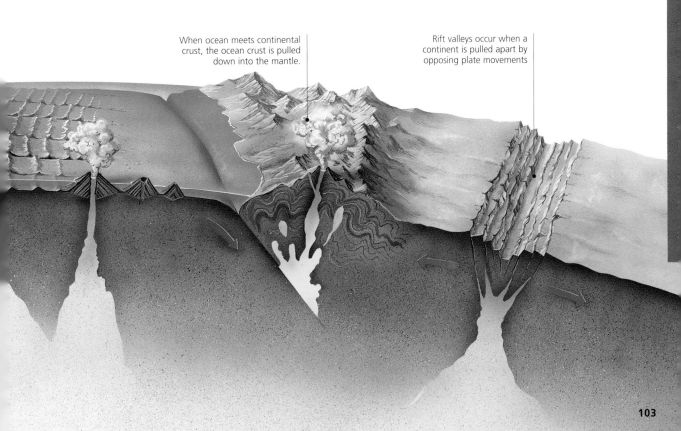

When ocean meets continental crust, the ocean crust is pulled down into the mantle.

Rift valleys occur when a continent is pulled apart by opposing plate movements

Types of Rocks

ROCK CYCLE

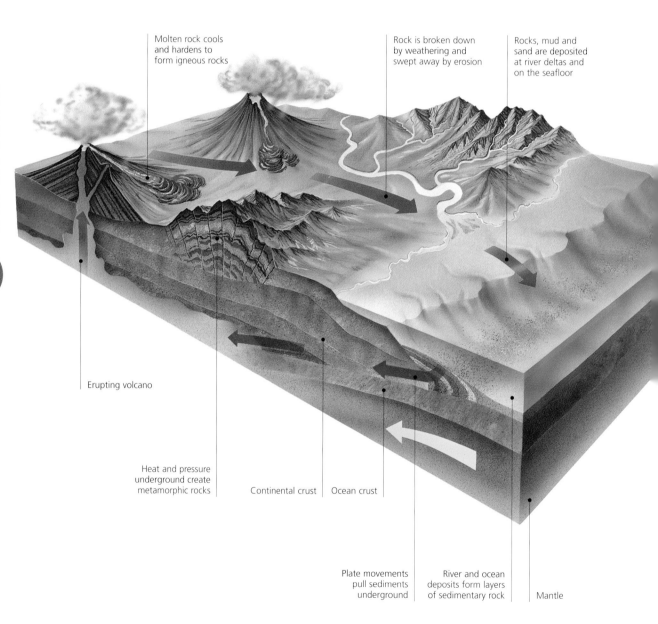

Molten rock cools
and hardens to
form igneous rocks

Rock is broken down
by weathering and
swept away by erosion

Rocks, mud and
sand are deposited
at river deltas and
on the seafloor

Erupting volcano

Heat and pressure
underground create
metamorphic rocks

Continental crust

Ocean crust

Plate movements
pull sediments
underground

River and ocean
deposits form layers
of sedimentary rock

Mantle

TYPES OF ROCKS

Igneous

Andesite

Gabbro

Obsidian

Sedimentary

Chert

Conglomerate

Sandstone

Metamorphic

Banded gneiss

Quartzite

Folded schist

Unusual

Pyrite sand dollar

Pumice

Dumbbell micrometeorite

Types of Minerals

ROCK AND MINERAL ENVIRONMENT

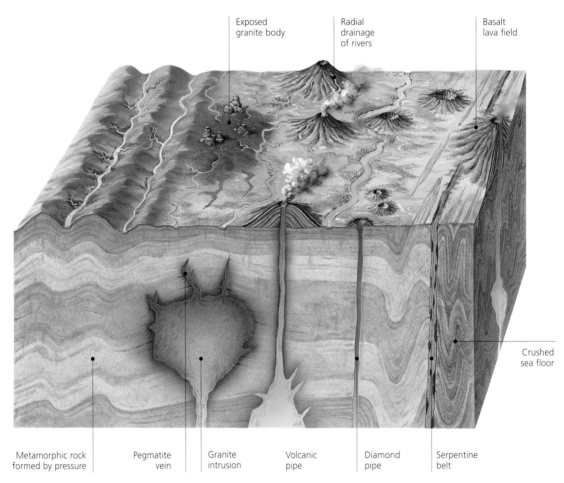

Exposed granite body

Radial drainage of rivers

Basalt lava field

Crushed sea floor

Metamorphic rock formed by pressure

Pegmatite vein

Granite intrusion

Volcanic pipe

Diamond pipe

Serpentine belt

MOHS SCALE OF HARDNESS
1 = softest, 10 = hardest

1. Talc

2. Gypsum

3. Calcite

4. Fluorite

5. Apatite

TYPES OF MINERAL STRUCTURE

Minerals are solid substances that occur naturally in Earth's crust.
They may take on a variety of forms.

Dendritic (treelike)

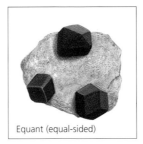

Equant (equal-sided)

Massive (rocklike)

TYPES OF ORE

Minerals that are useful and can be mined economically are called ores.
These minerals have been valued for thousands of years.

Bauxite—aluminum ore

Bornite—copper ore

Galena—lead ore

6. Orthoclase

7. Quartz

8. Topaz

9. Corundum

10. Diamond

Hotspot Volcanoes

THE HOTSPOT CYCLE

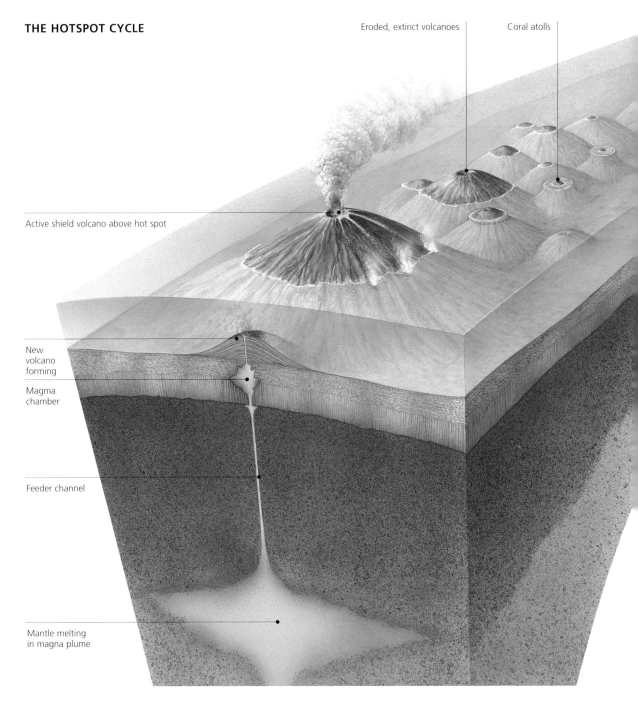

Eroded, extinct volcanoes

Coral atolls

Active shield volcano above hot spot

New volcano forming

Magma chamber

Feeder channel

Mantle melting in magma plume

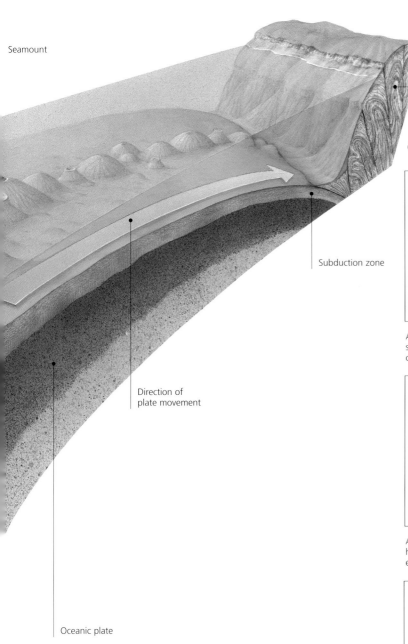

Seamount

Continental plate

Subduction zone

Direction of
plate movement

Oceanic plate

CHAIN FORMATION

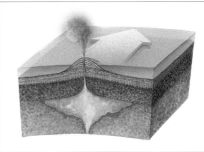

A single volcano forms above a hotspot, growing in size as the lava builds up. As the plate moves, it carries the volcano away from the hotspot.

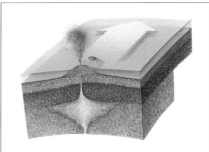

After millions of years, the volcano separates from the hotspot, its lava supply is cut off and it becomes extinct. A new volcano then forms above the hotspot.

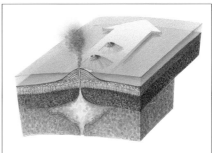

The chain of volcanoes continues to grow in the direction of the plate movement. If the hotspot fades, the chain of volcanoes stops growing.

Volcano Eruptions and Flows

TYPES OF ERUPTION

Hawaiian

Strombolian

Plinian

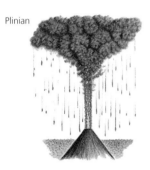

Vulcanian

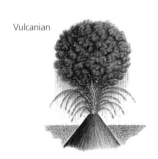

Peléean

TYPES OF PYROCLASTIC FLOW

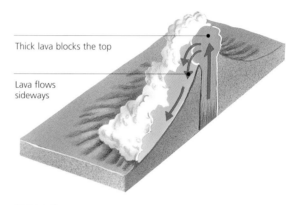

Thick lava blocks the top

Lava flows
sideways

Dome collapse

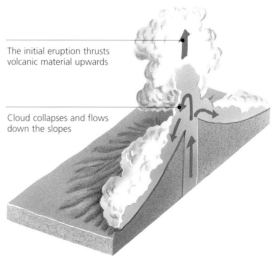

The initial eruption thrusts
volcanic material upwards

Cloud collapses and flows
down the slopes

Collapsing vertical eruption

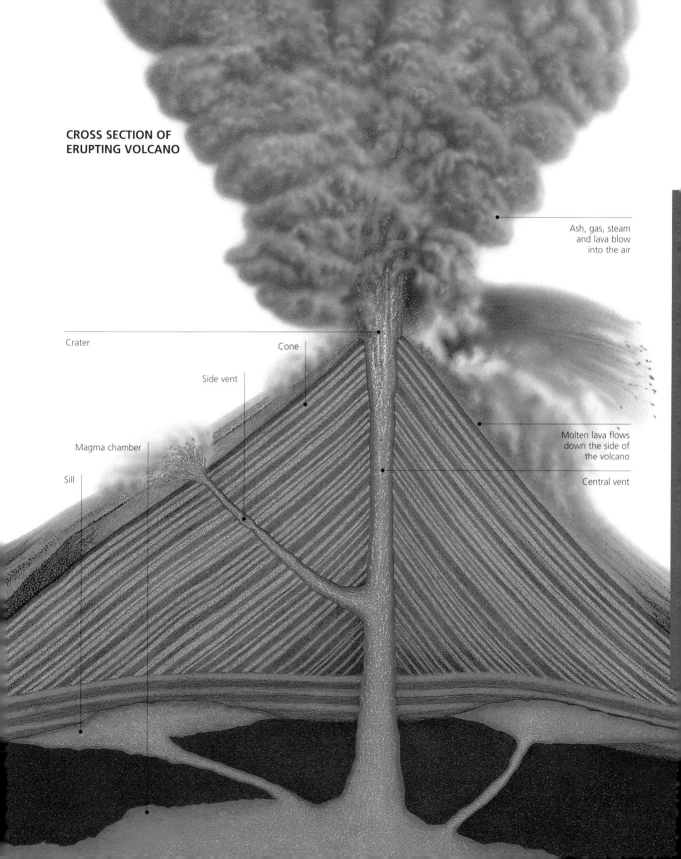

**CROSS SECTION OF
ERUPTING VOLCANO**

Ash, gas, steam
and lava blow
into the air

Crater

Cone

Side vent

Magma chamber

Sill

Molten lava flows
down the side of
the volcano

Central vent

Famous Volcanoes

WORLDWIDE VOLCANOES

COTOPAXI
Ecuador

MOUNT ST. HELENS
Washington, USA

TORRES DEL PAINE
Chile

MAYON
The Philippines

STROMBOLI
Italy

MOUNT FUJI
Japan

MOUNT ETNA
Italy

MOUNT AUGUSTINE
Alaska, USA

VILLARRICA
Chile

MOUNT RAINIER
Washington, USA

SANTORINI
Greece

MOUNT GARIBALDI
British Columbia, Canada

Earthquakes

MAJOR EARTHQUAKES

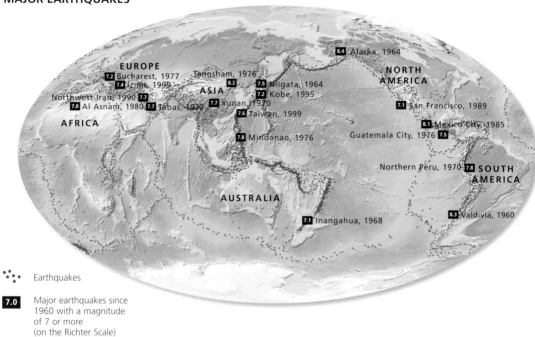

EUROPE
7.2 Bucharest, 1977
7.4 Izmit, 1999
Tangsham, 1976
ASIA
8.2
7.5 Niigata, 1964
7.2 Kobe, 1995
8.4 Alaska, 1964
NORTH AMERICA
Northwest Iran, 1990 **7.7**
7.0 Al Asnam, 1980 **7.7** Tabas, 1972
7.7 Yunan, 1970
7.1 San Francisco, 1989
AFRICA
7.6 Taiwan, 1999
8.1 Mexico City, 1985
7.8 Mindanao, 1976
Guatemala City, 1976 **7.5**
Northern Peru, 1970 **7.8** **SOUTH AMERICA**
AUSTRALIA
7.1 Inangahua, 1968
8.3 Valdivia, 1960

⋱ Earthquakes

7.0 Major earthquakes since 1960 with a magnitude of 7 or more (on the Richter Scale)

TYPES OF EARTHQUAKE WAVES

P-waves, or primary waves, are the first to arrive during an earthquake. They compress (push together) and dilate (pull apart) the rocks in the ground.

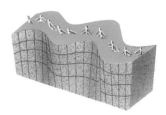

P- and S-waves are followed by surface waves, which only affect the Earth's surface. One type, Love waves, makes the surface move from side to side like a snake.

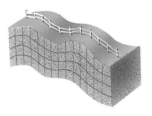

S-waves, or secondary waves, move more slowly than P-waves. They move rock layers up and down and from side to side.

Rayleigh waves are the second type of surface waves and cause the ground to rise and fall.

AFTER AN EARTHQUAKE
Earthquakes strike suddenly and
swiftly—often with devastating effect.

Tsunamis

EFFECTS OF AN EARTHQUAKE

Earthquakes that occur near the coast can trigger tsunamis—waves that spread across the ocean at great speed and rapidly grow in size as they near shore.

WAVE FORMATION

Unlike a surface wave, a tsunami is a whole column of water that reaches from the sea floor up.

Sometime after an earthquake, harbors can be drained dry as water is dragged out to the ocean to join the developing tsunami.

The power of the returning wave batters and floods the coast, causing enormous damage and loss of life. Tsunamis occur most often in the Pacific.

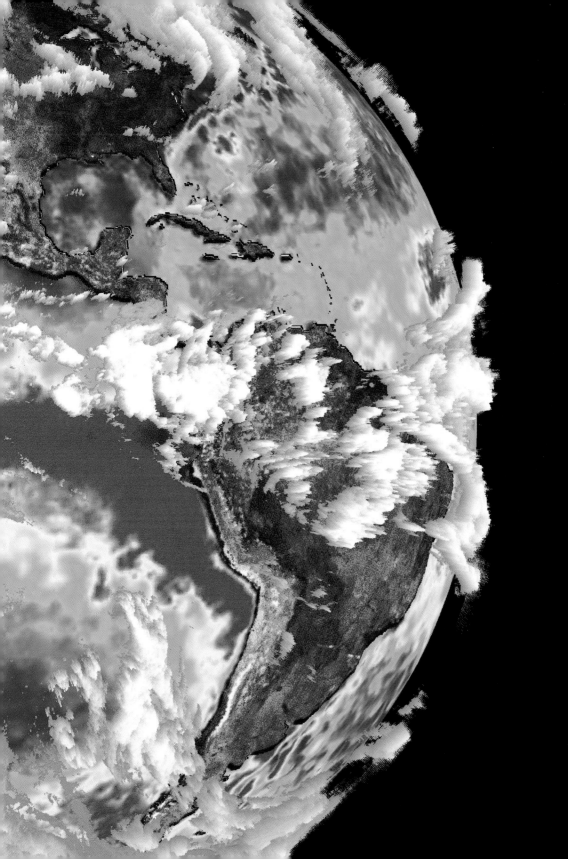

WEATHER

SEASONS AND CLIMATE

EARTH'S OCEANS

Earth's Atmosphere

OZONE LAYER

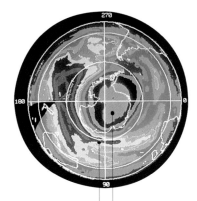

Thermosphere
Above 50 miles (80 km)

Mesosphere
30–50 miles (50–80 km)

Stratosphere
6–30 miles (10–50 km)

Troposphere
0–6 miles (0–10 km)

The ozone layer shields Earth from ultraviolet light

The light blue at the center of this picture shows a hole in the ozone layer situated over Antarctica

POLLUTION
The level of greenhouse gases in the atmosphere is increasing because of industrial pollution, deforestation, farming methods and the burning of fossil fuels.

Cows have a major effect on the atmosphere because they produce methane gas when they digest grass

More fossil fuels are being used each year. They provide power for transport and industry

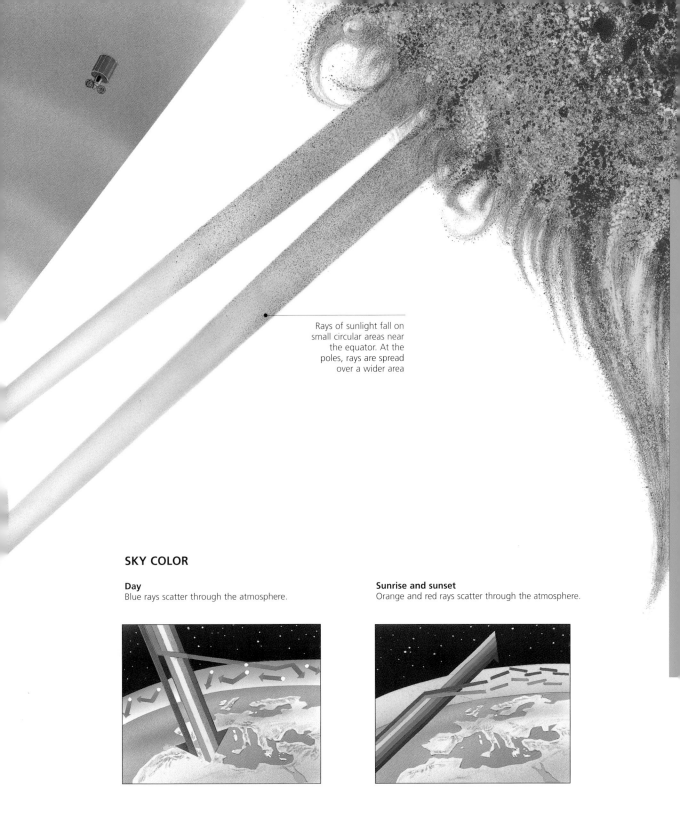

Rays of sunlight fall on small circular areas near the equator. At the poles, rays are spread over a wider area

SKY COLOR

Day
Blue rays scatter through the atmosphere.

Sunrise and sunset
Orange and red rays scatter through the atmosphere.

Water and Fog

MOVEMENT OF FOG

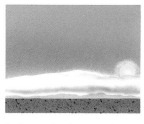

As the sun rises, it warms the edges of a bank of fog.

The fog bank gradually shrinks and rises as the sun rises higher.

By mid-morning, a thin deck of fog may remain suspended.

WATER CYCLE

Clouds build up over land

Water evaporates and forms clouds

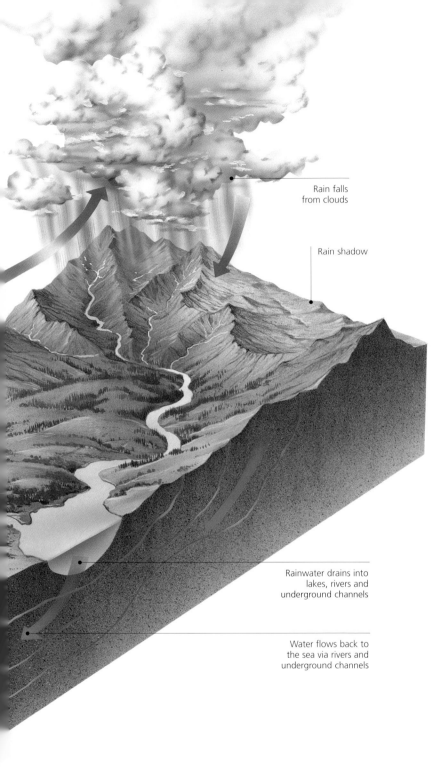

Rain falls
from clouds

Rain shadow

Rainwater drains into
lakes, rivers and
underground channels

Water flows back to
the sea via rivers and
underground channels

TYPES OF FOG

Advection

Fog forms when warm, humid air
moves over a cold surface.

Radiation

When land cools rapidly, the air
above is chilled, creating fog.

Stratus

Fog clears from the bottom up when
the ground warms quickly.

Clouds

CLOUD COLOR

Sunlight

Water droplets in cloud scatter the colors of sunlight evenly, so the cloud appears white

HOW CLOUDS LIFT

Convection
Ground heat causes air mass to rise.

Frontal formation
Warm air rises when it meets cooler air.

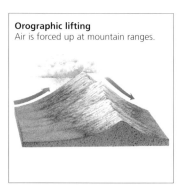

Orographic lifting
Air is forced up at mountain ranges.

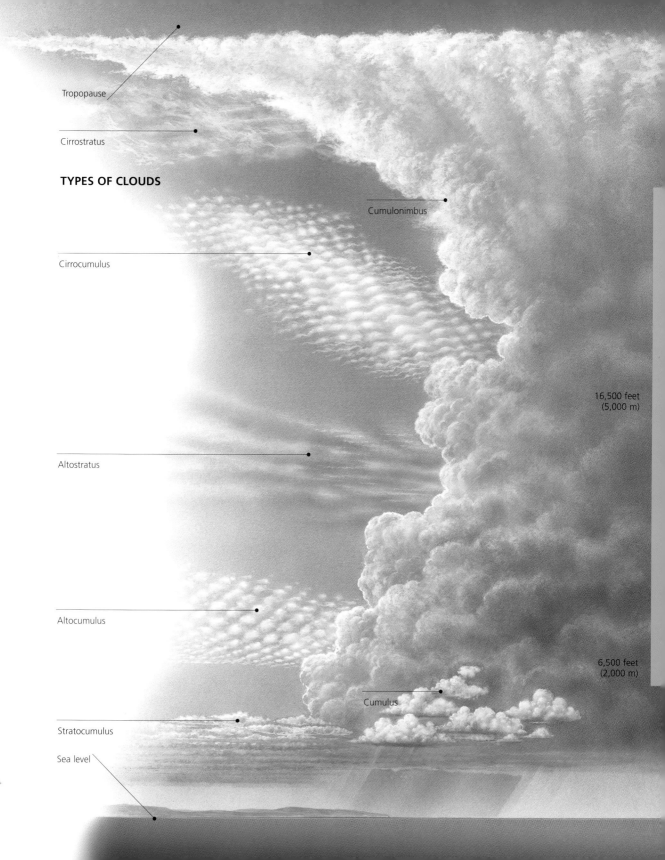

TYPES OF CLOUDS

Tropopause

Cirrostratus

Cumulonimbus

Cirrocumulus

16,500 feet
(5,000 m)

Altostratus

Altocumulus

6,500 feet
(2,000 m)

Cumulus

Stratocumulus

Sea level

Precipitation

AVALANCHE

Avalanches can occur when a new fall of snow builds up on top of old snow.

Snow slides with increasing speed when it can no longer support its own weight.

Rescuers often use sniffer dogs to locate survivors buried under the snow.

TYPES OF PRECIPITATION

Snow
Snow forms if the freezing level is below a height of 1,000 feet (300 m) above the ground, and the ice crystals do not have time to melt before they reach the ground.

SNOWFLAKES
Snowflakes are loose clusters of ice crystals usually with a flat, six-sided (hexagonal) shape. The exact shape of a snowflake depends on the temperature of the air—no two snowflakes are the same.

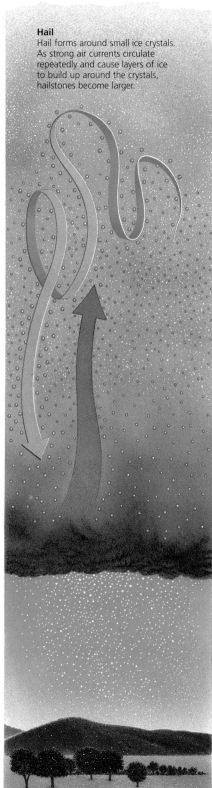

Hail
Hail forms around small ice crystals. As strong air currents circulate repeatedly and cause layers of ice to build up around the crystals, hailstones become larger.

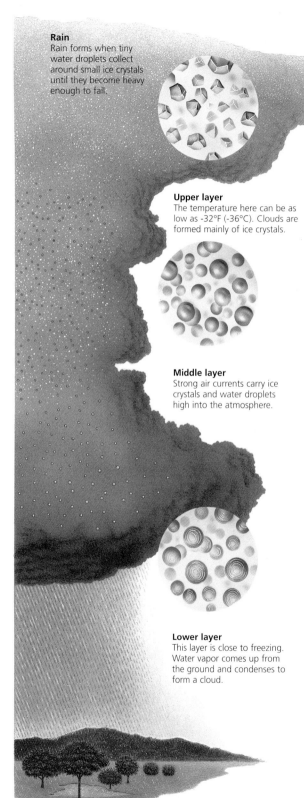

Rain
Rain forms when tiny water droplets collect around small ice crystals until they become heavy enough to fall.

Upper layer
The temperature here can be as low as -32°F (-36°C). Clouds are formed mainly of ice crystals.

Middle layer
Strong air currents carry ice crystals and water droplets high into the atmosphere.

Lower layer
This layer is close to freezing. Water vapor comes up from the ground and condenses to form a cloud.

Storms

HURRICANE
Hurricanes start life as small thunderstorms over warm water.

Eye of the storm

As the hurricane rotates, it continues to draw in moist air from the ocean, gaining energy all the time

Warm water heats the air and creates a rising current of moist air

Cool air is pulled in to replace the rising current

Huge banks of cumulonimbus clouds build up

THE STORM CYCLE

Building up
Rising air currents carry water vapor upward into cooler air. Moisture condenses and cumulus cloud forms.

At its peak
Cumulonimbus grows to the tropopause and spreads to form an anvil. The air sinks, creating heavy downdrafts.

On the wane
The downdrafts begin to outnumber the updrafts. The storm's supply of warm air is cut off and the cloud slowly disintegrates.

TYPES OF LIGHTNING

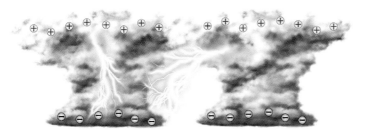

Cloud-to-cloud lightning
Lightning may jump within one cloud or
between opposite charges in adjacent clouds.

Cloud-to-ground lightning
If there is a positive charge on the ground,
lightning may strike from the base of a cloud.

Cloud-to-air lightning
Electricity may move from the cloud to the
surrounding, oppositely charged air.

HURRICANE LIFECYCLE

Day 1—a storm cluster forms

Day 2—storm starts to spin

Day 3—spiral shape develops

Day 6—eye emerges

Day 12—begins to fade

Mapping the Weather

Clear sky

Rain

Cloudy

Partly cloudy

Light wind

Moderate wind

H

High pressure

L

Low pressure

SYNOPTIC CHART

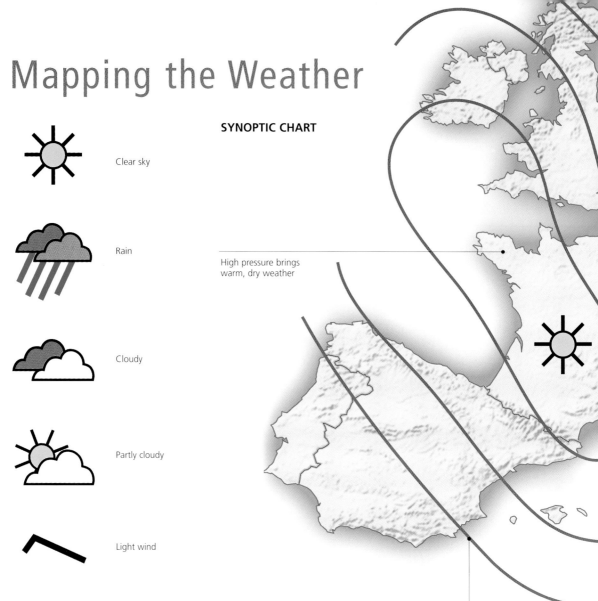

High pressure brings warm, dry weather

MAP SYMBOLS
Synoptic charts contain a wealth of information including air pressure, wind speed and direction, cloud cover, temperature and humidity.

Isobars link points with the same air pressure and are measured in hectapascals

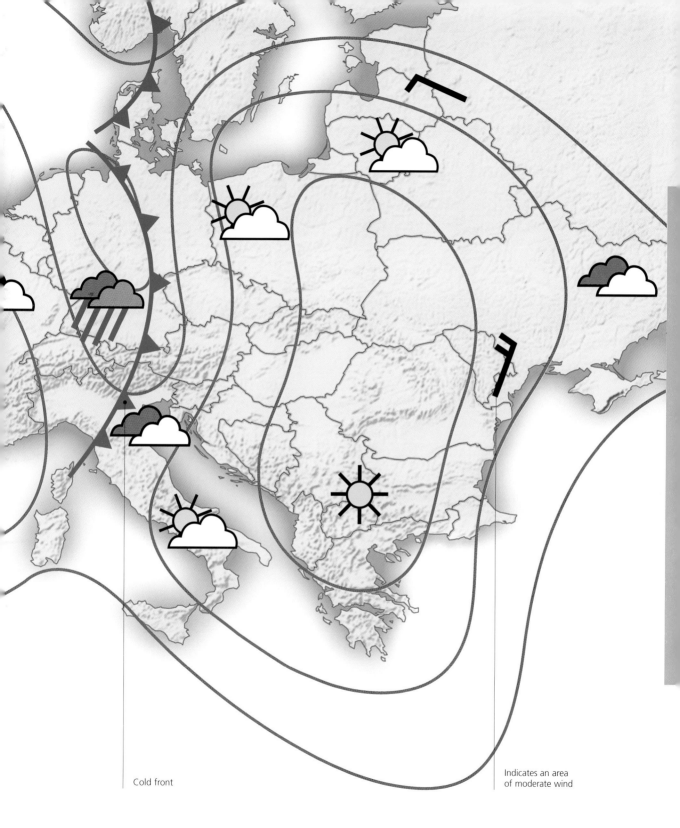

Cold front

Indicates an area
of moderate wind

Frontal Systems

LOW-PRESSURE SYSTEM

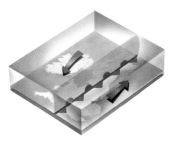

1. Low-pressure systems form when a cold air mass and a warm air mass meet.

2. Gradually, the warm air rises over the cold air. This creates an area of low pressure that the cold front moves into.

3. Rising air creates precipitation and clouds, and the fronts begin to rotate.

PRESSURE MOVEMENT

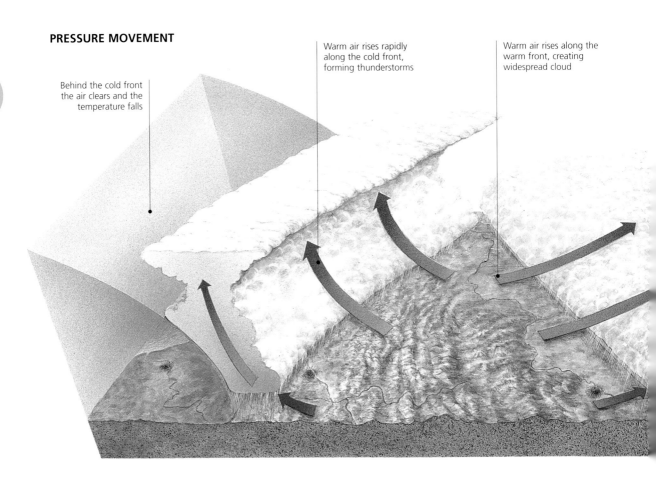

Behind the cold front the air clears and the temperature falls

Warm air rises rapidly along the cold front, forming thunderstorms

Warm air rises along the warm front, creating widespread cloud

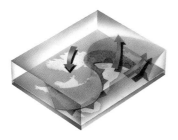 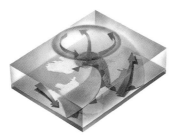 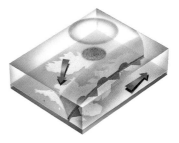

4. The faster-moving cold front starts to catch up with the warm front. Pressure decreases under the rising air, which intensifies precipitation.

5. When the cold front catches up with the warm front, an occluded front forms. This creates windy, unsettled weather.

6. The fully formed occluded front cuts off the supply of warm air, and winds and precipitation subside.

Spreading cloud produces light rain and snow

The leading edge of the warm front forms a band of high cloud

Prevailing westerly winds push the system further

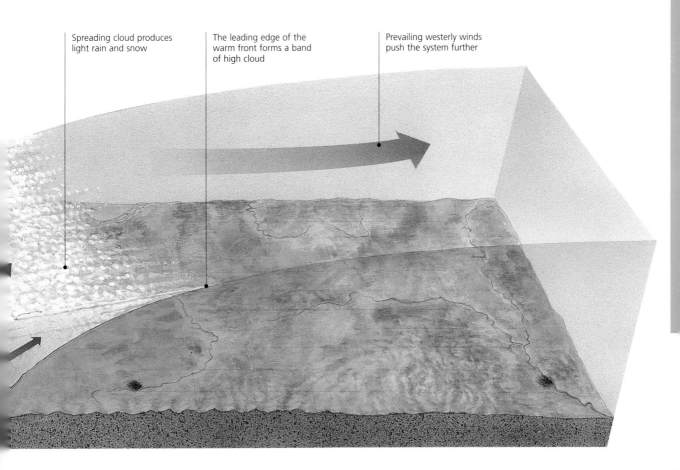

The Seasons

CLIMATE

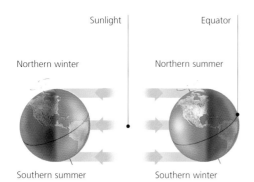

Sunlight   Equator

Northern winter   Northern summer

Southern summer   Southern winter

At the equator, the Sun's rays hit Earth almost directly all year long. This is the hottest zone on Earth. As you move farther away from the equator, the rays hit at more of an angle and the climate is cooler.

DAY AND NIGHT

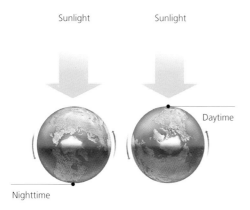

Sunlight   Sunlight

Daytime

Nighttime

At any moment, parts of the world are experiencing sunrise and sunset, noon and midnight.

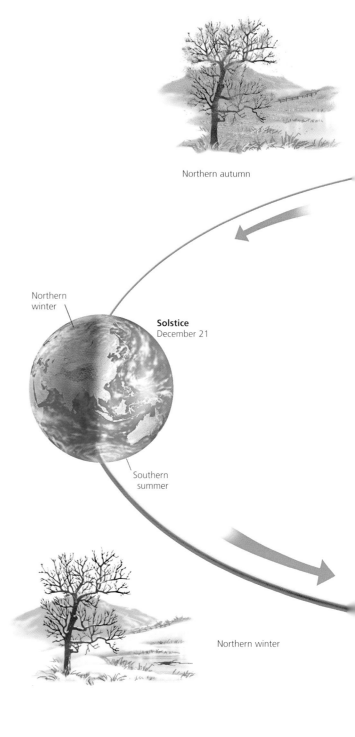

Northern autumn

Northern winter

Solstice
December 21

Southern summer

Northern winter

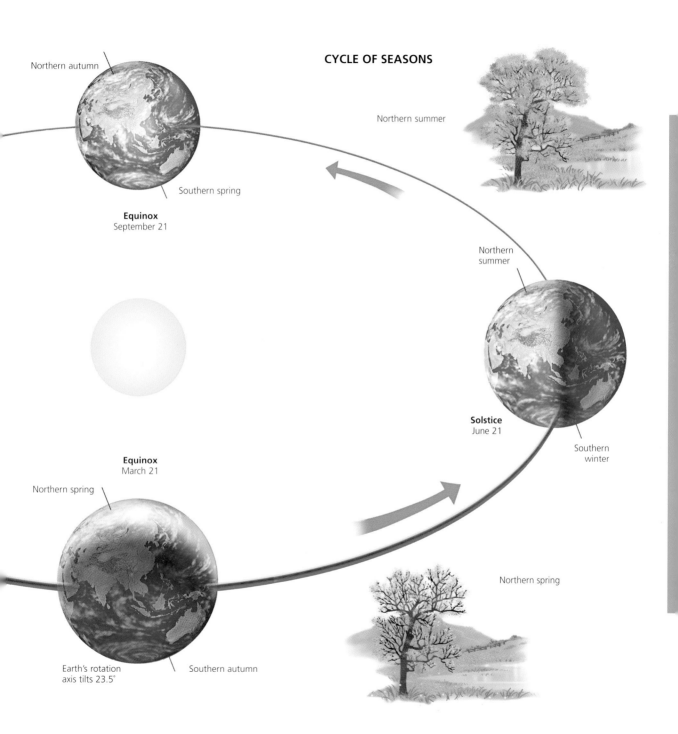

CYCLE OF SEASONS

Northern autumn

Southern spring

Equinox
September 21

Northern summer

Northern
summer

Solstice
June 21

Southern
winter

Equinox
March 21

Northern spring

Southern autumn

Earth's rotation
axis tilts 23.5°

Northern spring

Winds and Monsoons

GLOBAL AIR FLOW

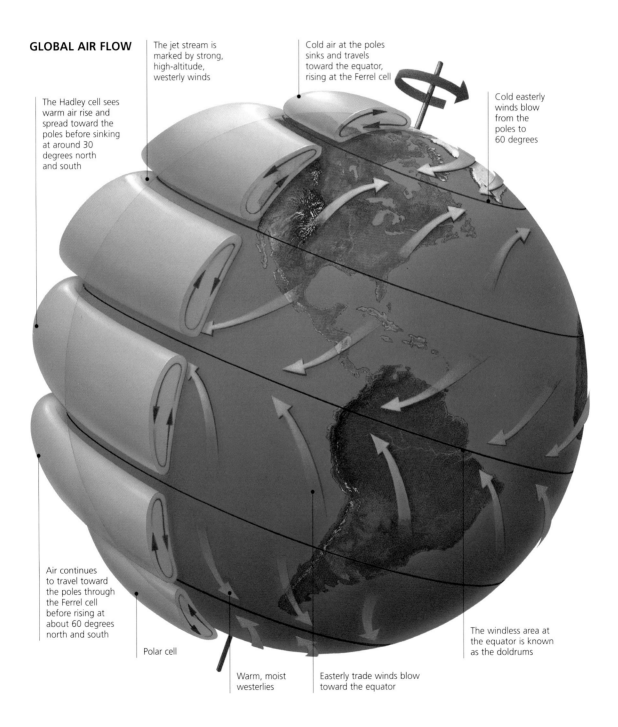

The jet stream is marked by strong, high-altitude, westerly winds

Cold air at the poles sinks and travels toward the equator, rising at the Ferrel cell

The Hadley cell sees warm air rise and spread toward the poles before sinking at around 30 degrees north and south

Cold easterly winds blow from the poles to 60 degrees

Air continues to travel toward the poles through the Ferrel cell before rising at about 60 degrees north and south

Polar cell

Warm, moist westerlies

Easterly trade winds blow toward the equator

The windless area at the equator is known as the doldrums

MOUNTAIN WIND

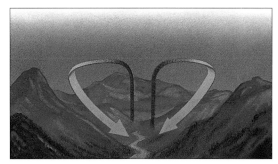

Warm air rises from mountain slopes. This cools and falls, creating a cool wind as it fills the space left by the rising warm air.

At night, warm mountain air cools and flows down the mountain slopes into the valley, creating a cool wind.

RAIN SHADOW

Most mountains experience dry wind which blows down the sheltered side. Moisture is deposited on the windward side.

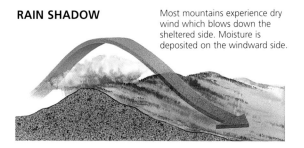

CORIOLIS EFFECT

As a result of the Earth's shape, air in the northern hemisphere moves clockwise and down around high pressure and anticlockwise and up around low pressure. The opposite occurs in the southern hemisphere.

DRY SEASON

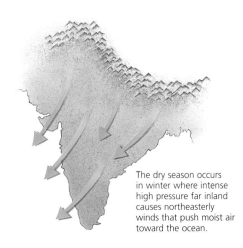

The dry season occurs in winter where intense high pressure far inland causes northeasterly winds that push moist air toward the ocean.

WET SEASON

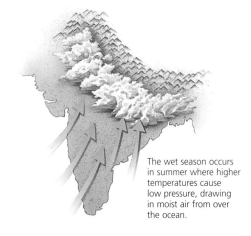

The wet season occurs in summer where higher temperatures cause low pressure, drawing in moist air from over the ocean.

Climate

WORLD CLIMATES

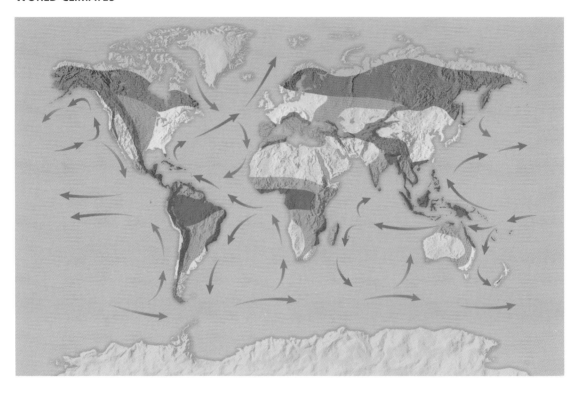

Cold temperate	Desert and semi-desert	Wet temperate	Mountain
Subtropical	Dry temperate	Tropical	Polar

Cool currents

Warm currents

LANDSCAPES

Desert

Forest

Arctic

MOUNTAIN ZONE

Nepal lies in the Himalayas. There is little flat land for villages, so houses are scattered. The warm, sunny, south-facing slopes are used for farming. The north-facing slopes are usually forested. As the steep slopes are difficult to farm, they have been gradually terraced to provide many small, level fields for farming. The higher pastures extend up to the permanent snow line.

EXTREME CLIMATES

High altitude

Desert

Arctic

Waves, Tides and Currents

OCEAN TIDES

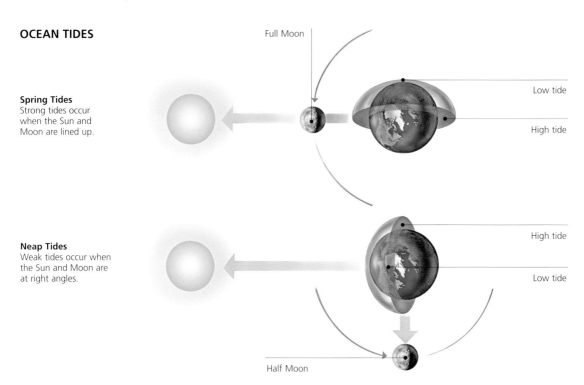

Spring Tides
Strong tides occur when the Sun and Moon are lined up.

Full Moon

Low tide

High tide

Neap Tides
Weak tides occur when the Sun and Moon are at right angles.

High tide

Low tide

Half Moon

OCEAN CURRENTS

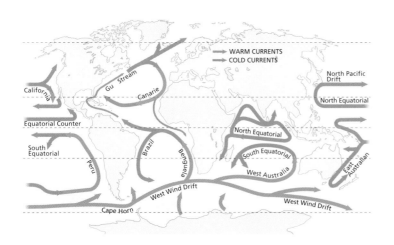

WARM CURRENTS
COLD CURRENTS

California

Gu Stream

Canarie

North Pacific Drift

North Equatorial

Equatorial Counter

South Equatorial

Peru

Brazil

Benguela

North Equatorial

South Equatorial

West Australia

East Australian

West Wind Drift

West Wind Drift

Cape Horn

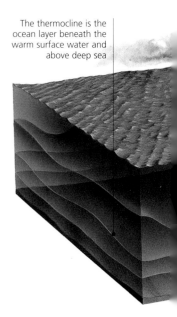

The thermocline is the ocean layer beneath the warm surface water and above deep sea

THE BEAUFORT SCALE

This scale uses the numbers
1 to 12 to indicate the strength
of wind at sea.

Force 2

Force 8

Force 12

WAVE FORMATION

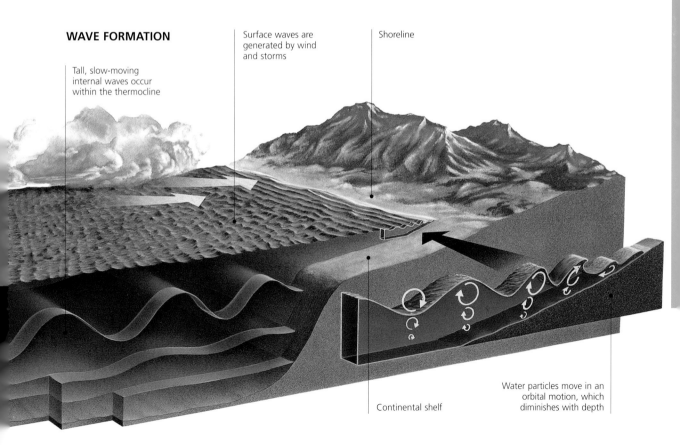

Tall, slow-moving
internal waves occur
within the thermocline

Surface waves are
generated by wind
and storms

Shoreline

Water particles move in an
orbital motion, which
diminishes with depth

Continental shelf

The Sea Floor

FOSSIL FUEL

Microscopic sea creatures die and fall to the ocean floor. Over millions of years, layers of mud and silt slowly cover the sea creatures and turn into sedimentary rocks.

The rock layers continue to pile up on top of the dead sea creatures. As the pressure from the rocks increases, the sea creatures slowly turn into oil and gas.

The oil and gas rise through the rock layers. They pass through porous rocks, such as sandstone, but are blocked by impermeable (nonporous) rocks, such as shale.

Under the right conditions, the oil and gas collect in a reservoir under the impermeable rocks, with the gas on top of the oil. Reservoirs are drilled to remove the fuels.

UNDERWATER LANDSCAPE

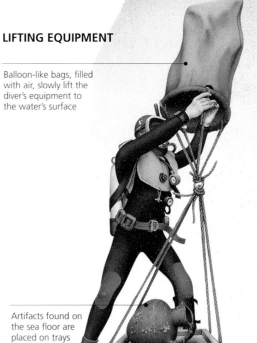

The continental shelf is a shallow extension of a continent, which is covered by water. This part of the ocean is rich in marine life. Oil exploration also takes place here

The continental slope is the gently sloping, submerged land near the coast that also forms the side of an ocean basin

LIFTING EQUIPMENT

Balloon-like bags, filled with air, slowly lift the diver's equipment to the water's surface

Artifacts found on the sea floor are placed on trays

Abyssal plains spread out flatly from the oceanic ridge to the edges of continents

Seamounts are underwater volcanoes. Those rising above the surface form islands

Guyots are flat-topped seamounts

Mapping the sea floor

An oceanic ridge rises when a new sea floor wells up from inside the Earth

A long, narrow valley, known as an oceanic trench, usually forms next to islands or beside coastal mountain ranges

The Shore

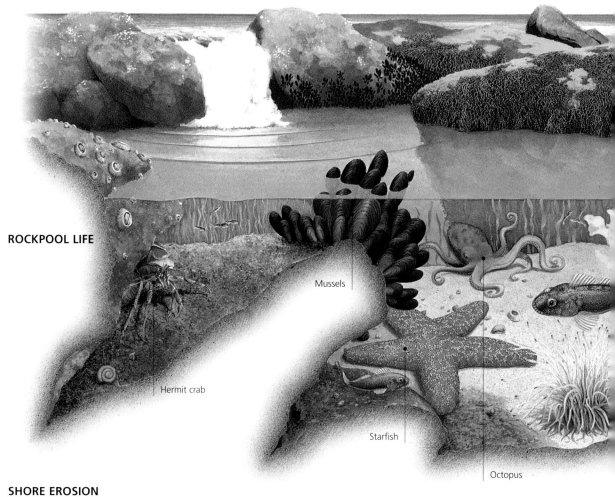

ROCKPOOL LIFE

Mussels

Hermit crab

Starfish

Octopus

SHORE EROSION

Headland

Sea arch

Sea stack

HOW THE SHORE FILTERS WATER

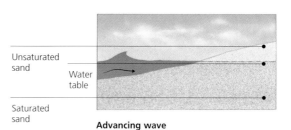

Unsaturated sand

Water table

Saturated sand

Advancing wave

Some water percolates through sand

High wave

Water filters back

Surface swash slides back to next oncoming breaker

Receding wave

Seaweed

SHORELINE

Sea cliffs

Sea stack

Blowholes form when the sea tunnels through a headland

Sand dunes form when wind blows loose, fine sand into large mounds

River mouth

Sediments deposited by rivers and waves may trap water, forming a coastal lagoon

PREHISTORIC LIFE

149

THE AGES OF PREHISTORY

TYPES OF DINOSAURS

AFTER THE DINOSAURS

Triassic Period

245–208 MILLION YEARS AGO

TRIASSIC ECOLOGY

Gingko tree

Coelophysis

Cycads

DINOSAUR FOOD

Dragonfly

Haramiya

Tree fern

Wielandiella

TRIASSIC WORLD

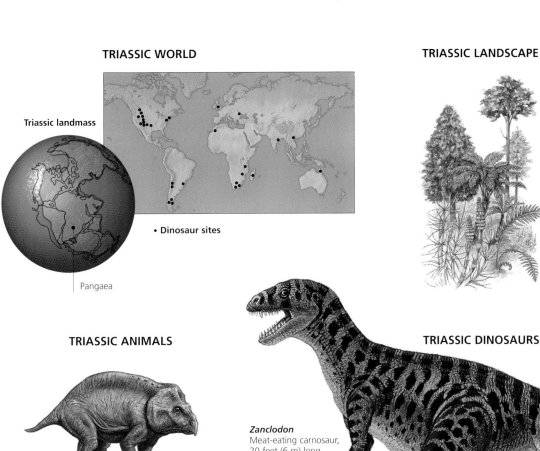

Triassic landmass

Pangaea

• Dinosaur sites

TRIASSIC LANDSCAPE

TRIASSIC ANIMALS

Synapsid
Kannemeyeria

Flying reptile
Eudimorphodon

TRIASSIC DINOSAURS

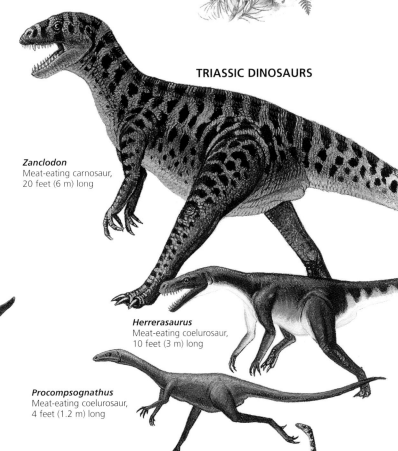

Zanclodon
Meat-eating carnosaur,
20 feet (6 m) long

Herrerasaurus
Meat-eating coelurosaur,
10 feet (3 m) long

Procompsognathus
Meat-eating coelurosaur,
4 feet (1.2 m) long

Saltopus
Meat-eating carnosaur,
2 feet (0.6 m) long

Jurassic Period

208–145 MILLION YEARS AGO

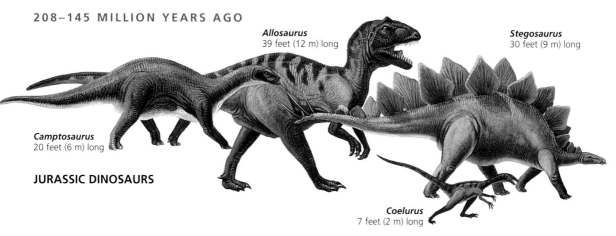

Allosaurus
39 feet (12 m) long

Stegosaurus
30 feet (9 m) long

Camptosaurus
20 feet (6 m) long

JURASSIC DINOSAURS

Coelurus
7 feet (2 m) long

JURASSIC WORLD

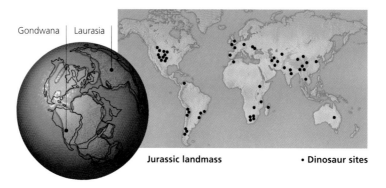

Gondwana   Laurasia

Jurassic landmass   • Dinosaur sites

JURASSIC PLANTS

Jurassic landscape

Cycad

Horsetail

154

DINOSAUR FOOD

Ginkgo

Cockroach

Turtle (*Pleisochelys*)

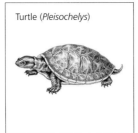

Dragonfly

JURASSIC ECOLOGY

Tree ferns

Diplodocus

Cycads

Ground
cover ferns

Cretaceous Period

145–65 MILLION YEARS AGO

CRETACEOUS ANIMALS

Early lizard
Polyglyphanodon

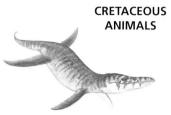

Marine reptile
Kronosaurus

Snake
Pachyrhachis

CRETACEOUS WORLD

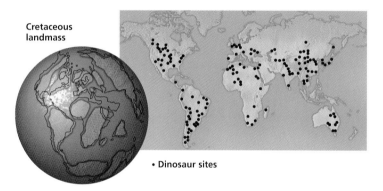

Cretaceous landmass

• **Dinosaur sites**

Ancient mammal
Crusafontia

CRETACEOUS DINOSAURS

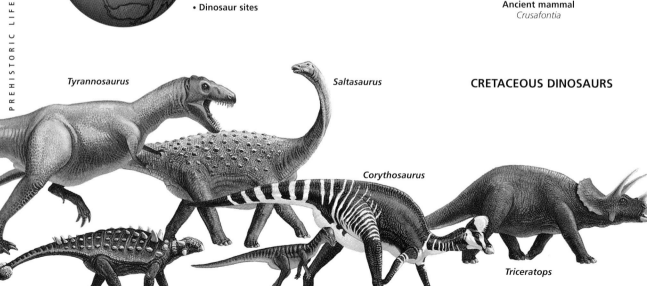

Tyrannosaurus

Saltasaurus

Corythosaurus

Triceratops

Euoplocephalus

Pachycephalosaurus

Conifer forest

Prenocephale

Magnolias

Protoceratops

Velociraptor

Dinosaur Anatomy

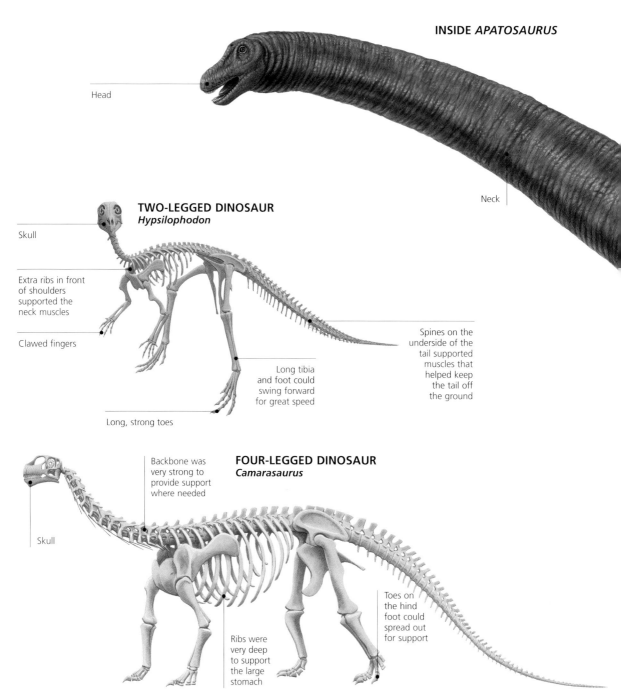

INSIDE *APATOSAURUS*

Head

Neck

TWO-LEGGED DINOSAUR
Hypsilophodon

Skull

Extra ribs in front
of shoulders
supported the
neck muscles

Clawed fingers

Long tibia
and foot could
swing forward
for great speed

Spines on the
underside of the
tail supported
muscles that
helped keep
the tail off
the ground

Long, strong toes

FOUR-LEGGED DINOSAUR
Camarasaurus

Backbone was
very strong to
provide support
where needed

Skull

Ribs were
very deep
to support
the large
stomach

Toes on
the hind
foot could
spread out
for support

JAWS

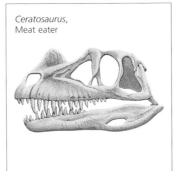

Ceratosaurus,
Meat eater

Ouranosaurus,
Plant eater

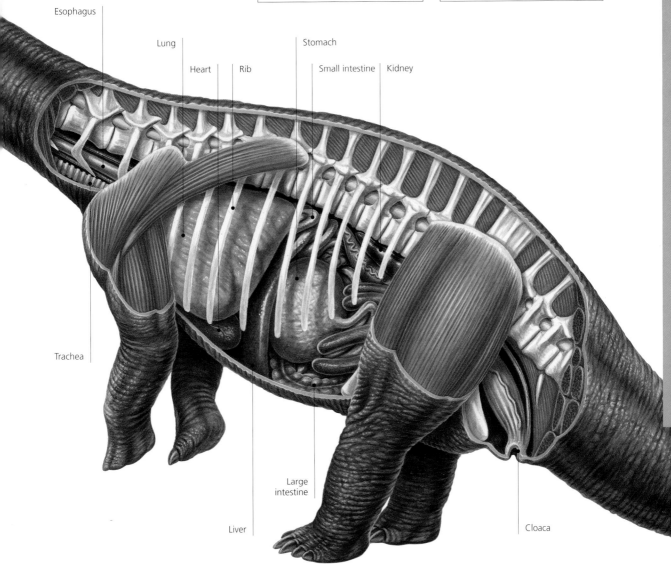

Esophagus

Lung

Stomach

Heart

Rib

Small intestine

Kidney

Trachea

Large
intestine

Liver

Cloaca

Dinosaur Hips

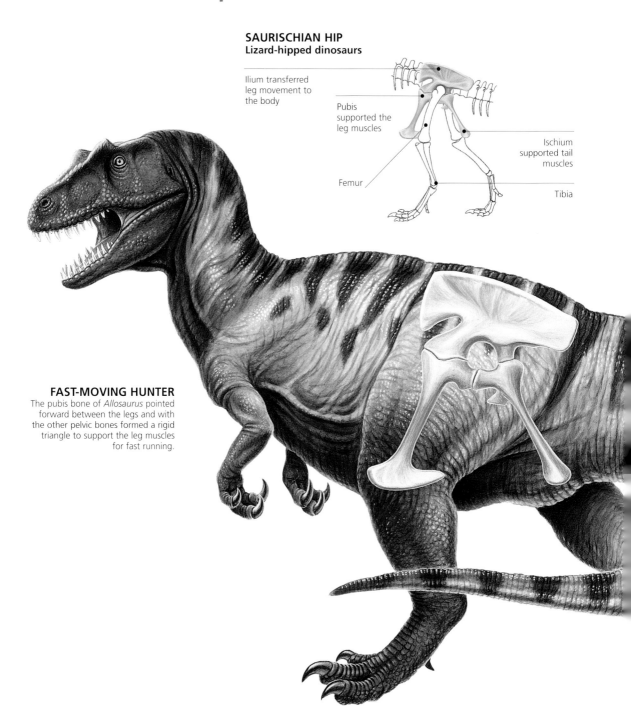

SAURISCHIAN HIP
Lizard-hipped dinosaurs

Ilium transferred
leg movement to
the body

Pubis
supported the
leg muscles

Ischium
supported tail
muscles

Femur

Tibia

FAST-MOVING HUNTER
The pubis bone of *Allosaurus* pointed
forward between the legs and with
the other pelvic bones formed a rigid
triangle to support the leg muscles
for fast running.

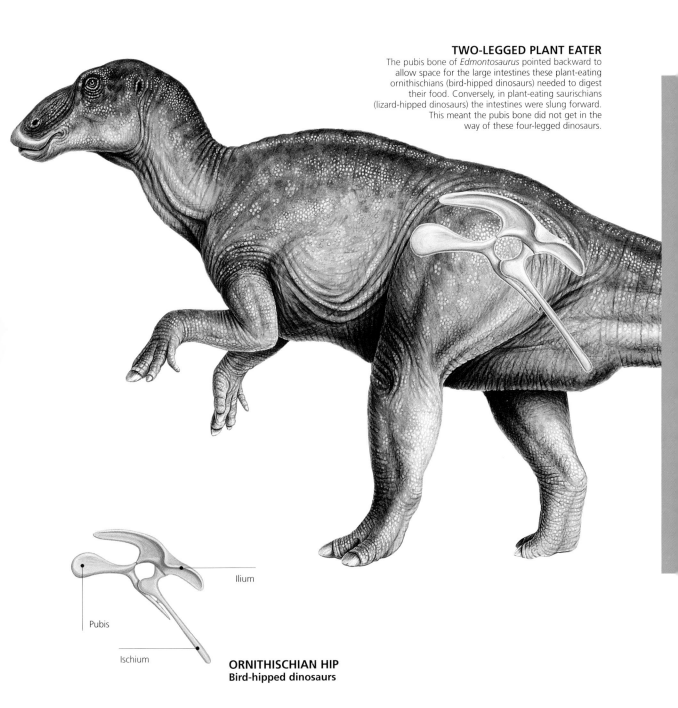

TWO-LEGGED PLANT EATER

The pubis bone of *Edmontosaurus* pointed backward to allow space for the large intestines these plant-eating ornithischians (bird-hipped dinosaurs) needed to digest their food. Conversely, in plant-eating saurischians (lizard-hipped dinosaurs) the intestines were slung forward. This meant the pubis bone did not get in the way of these four-legged dinosaurs.

Ilium

Pubis

Ischium

ORNITHISCHIAN HIP
Bird-hipped dinosaurs

Meat Eaters

SKULL TYPES

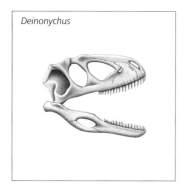

Deinonychus

Allosaurus

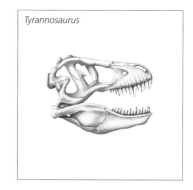

Tyrannosaurus

BYRONOSAURUS

DEINONYCHUS

HAND VARIETIES

Velociraptor

Allosaurus

Deinocheirus

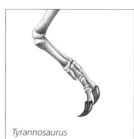

Tyrannosaurus

OVIRAPTOR

SCIPIONYX

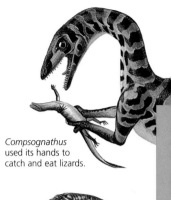

Compsognathus used its hands to catch and eat lizards.

Baryonyx used the huge hook on its hand to spear its prey.

MAJUNGATHOLUS

IRRITATOR

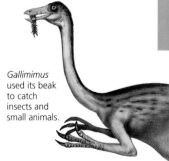

Albertosaurus used its powerful jaws to tear off pieces of meat.

Gallimimus used its beak to catch insects and small animals.

163

Plant Eaters

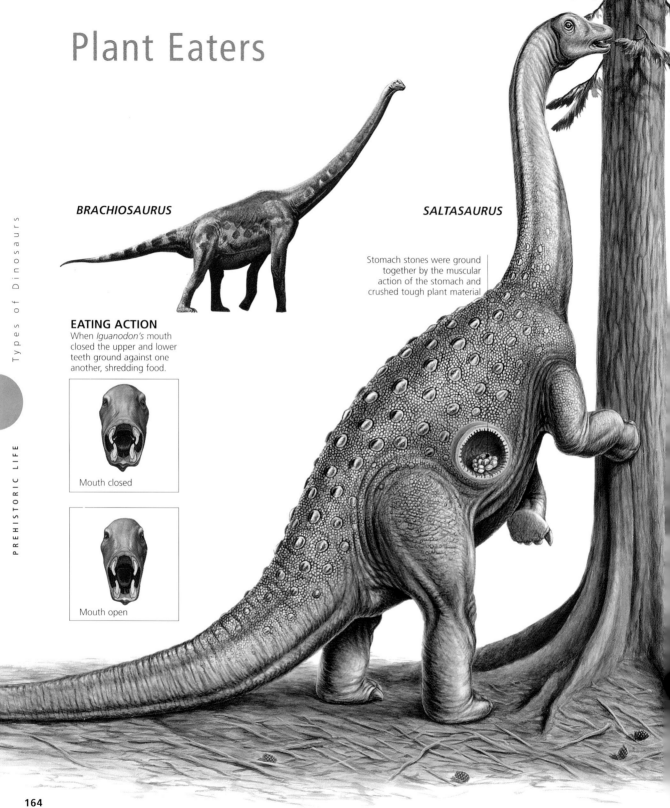

BRACHIOSAURUS

SALTASAURUS

Stomach stones were ground together by the muscular action of the stomach and crushed tough plant material

EATING ACTION

When *Iguanodon's* mouth closed the upper and lower teeth ground against one another, shredding food.

Mouth closed

Mouth open

KINDS OF FOOD

Pine cone

Flowering magnolia plant

OTHNIELIA
This dinosaur used its five-fingered hands to push aside and hold down a fern while eating.

Ginkgo

Tree fern

TEETH VARIATIONS

Brachiosaurus stripped leaves from tall trees.

Heterodontosaurus had cutting teeth in front, fanglike teeth in the middle and chopping teeth in the back of its mouth.

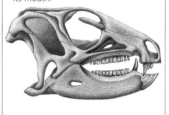

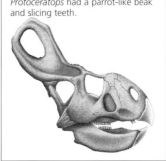

Protoceratops had a parrot-like beak and slicing teeth.

Lambeosaurus had a horny beak and grinding teeth.

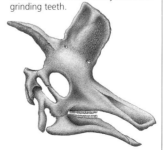

Long-necked Dinosaurs

BAROSAURUS SKELETON

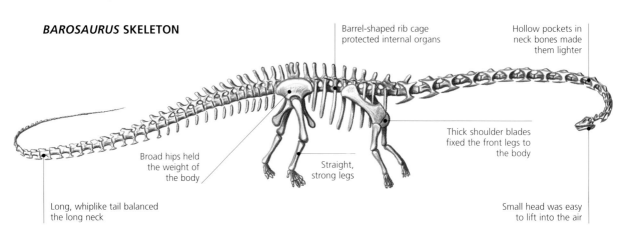

Barrel-shaped rib cage
protected internal organs

Hollow pockets in
neck bones made
them lighter

Thick shoulder blades
fixed the front legs to
the body

Broad hips held
the weight of
the body

Straight,
strong legs

Long, whiplike tail balanced
the long neck

Small head was easy
to lift into the air

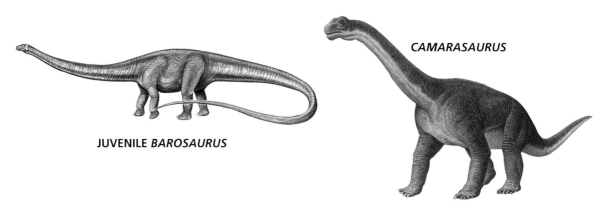

CAMARASAURUS

JUVENILE *BAROSAURUS*

SAUROPOD FEATURES

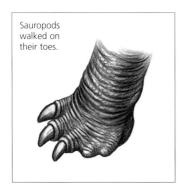

Sauropods
walked on
their toes.

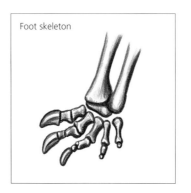

Foot skeleton

Long tails
balanced
long necks.

LONGEST NECK

Mamenchisaurus had the longest neck of any animal—36 feet (11 m).

COMPACT BODY

Barosaurus had a relatively compact body that supported a long neck and tail.

MAMENCHISAURUS

SALTASAURUS

APATOSAURUS

167

Armored Dinosaurs

HEAD PROTECTION

Centrosaurus had a heavy, short neck shield.

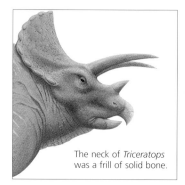

The neck of *Triceratops* was a frill of solid bone.

Chasmosaurus had a light head shield.

KENTROSAURUS

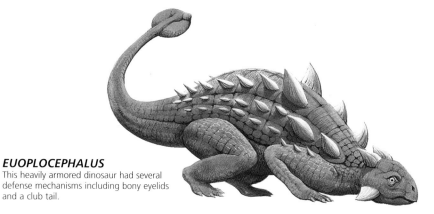

EUOPLOCEPHALUS
This heavily armored dinosaur had several defense mechanisms including bony eyelids and a club tail.

STEGOSAURUS

SCUTELLOSAURUS

POLACANTHUS

SAUROPELTA

CHASMOSAURUS

EDMONTONIA

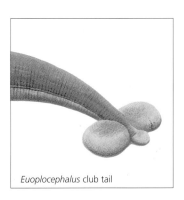

DEFENSIVE FEATURES

Triceratops horn

Euoplocephalus bony eyelids

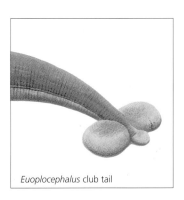

Euoplocephalus club tail

Duckbilled Dinosaurs

PARASAUROLOPHUS HEADS

Adult male

Adult female

Juvenile

DUCKBILLED COMMUNICATION

A male *Parasaurolophus* could bellow by forcing air from its mouth up into its hollow crest

Hollow crest

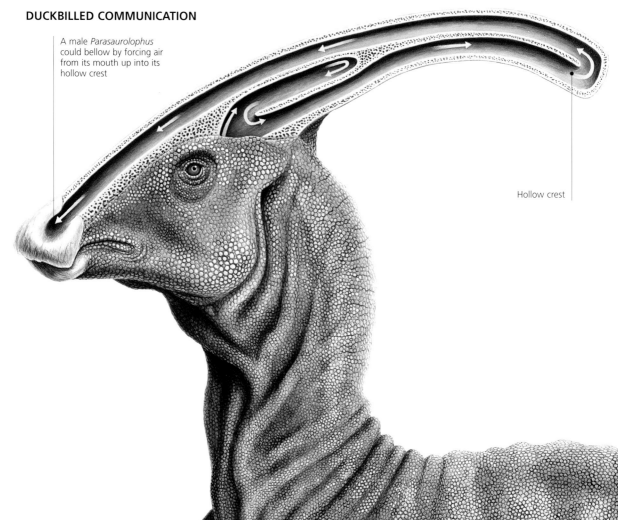

Homalocephale

Kritosaurus

Shantungosaurus

HEAD VARIETIES

HEAD FEATURES

Edmontosaurus had a flat head and an inflatable sac of skin on the front of its face, which enabled it to make sounds.

DILOPHOSAURUS

SAUROLOPHUS

Stegoceras had a dome of solid bone on its head.

Saurolophus had head spike and possibly an inflatable nose sac.

EDMONTOSAURUS

CORYTHOSAURUS

Lambeosaurus had a hollow crest on its head.

Disappearance of the Dinosaurs

EXTINCTION THEORIES

Cold climate change

Hot climate change

Volcanic eruptions

Baryonyx

Crocodile

DISTANT RELATIVES

Baryonyx had a head very similar to a crocodile. Their jaws look alike because they probably did the same job— catch fish.

DINOSAUR EXTINCTION

Dinosaurs suddenly vanished 65 million years ago. Scientists have several theories about what caused this. Some believe there were major weather changes or a volcanic disaster. The main theory is that a huge meteorite hit Earth causing environmental chaos.

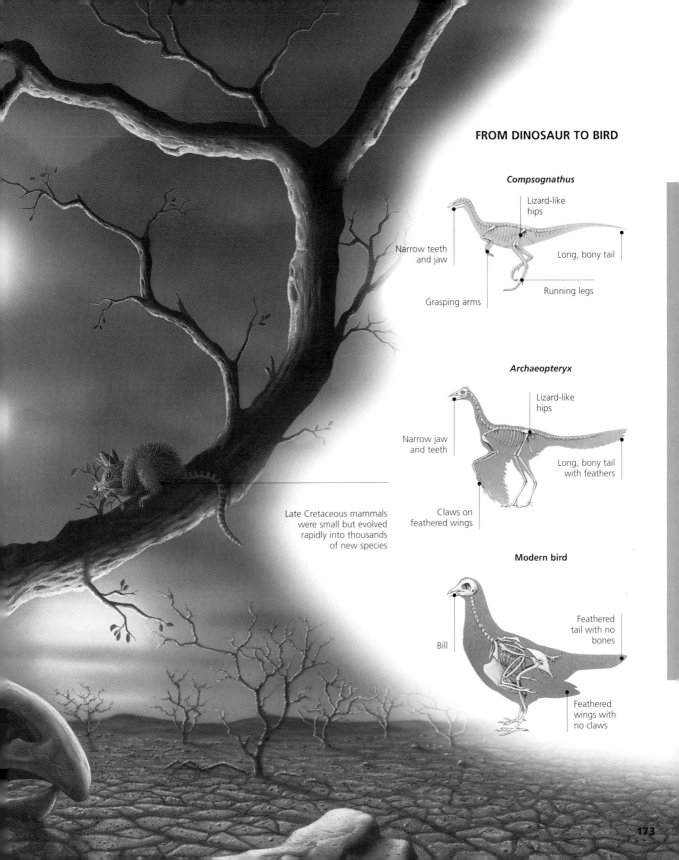

FROM DINOSAUR TO BIRD

Compsognathus

Lizard-like hips

Narrow teeth and jaw

Long, bony tail

Grasping arms

Running legs

Archaeopteryx

Lizard-like hips

Narrow jaw and teeth

Long, bony tail with feathers

Claws on feathered wings

Late Cretaceous mammals were small but evolved rapidly into thousands of new species

Modern bird

Feathered tail with no bones

Bill

Feathered wings with no claws

Fossils and Other Clues

KINDS OF FOSSILS

Conifer pine

Cycad

Gingko

Limulus

RECONSTRUCTING *BARYONYX*

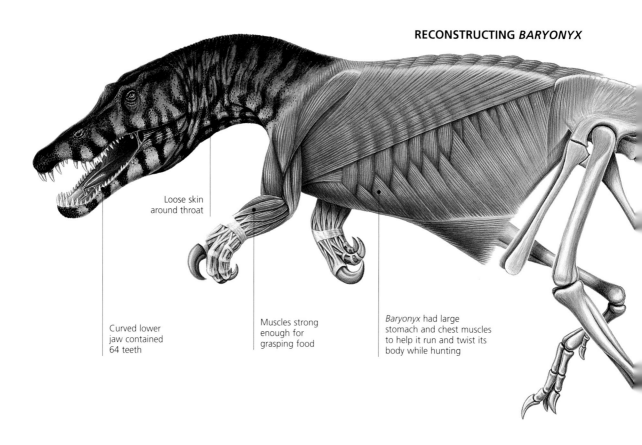

Loose skin
around throat

Curved lower
jaw contained
64 teeth

Muscles strong
enough for
grasping food

Baryonyx had large
stomach and chest muscles
to help it run and twist its
body while hunting

HOW A FOSSIL FORMS

1. Beneath the surface of a lake, a dead dinosaur is safe from scavengers. Its flesh rots but the skeleton remains intact.

2. Layers of sand cover the bones.

3. Bones are gradually replaced by minerals that are harder than the rocks around them.

4. Millions of years later movements in Earth's crust return the fossilized skeleton to the surface.

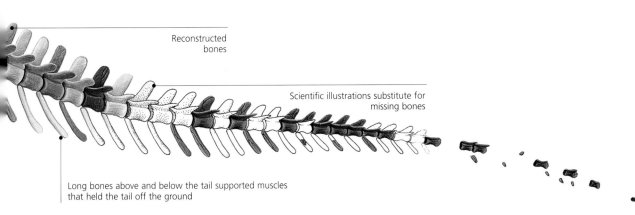

Reconstructed bones

Scientific illustrations substitute for missing bones

Long bones above and below the tail supported muscles that held the tail off the ground

FOSSILIZED FOOTPRINTS

Small theropod tracks

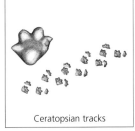

Ceratopsian tracks

Large theropod tracks

Sauropod tracks

PLANT CHARACTERISTICS

FERNS AND TREES

FLOWERS AND FOOD PLANTS

PLANT HABITATS

Plant Parts

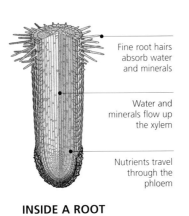

Fine root hairs absorb water and minerals

Water and minerals flow up the xylem

Nutrients travel through the phloem

INSIDE A ROOT

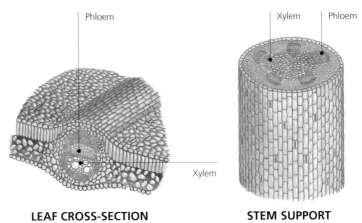

Phloem

Xylem

LEAF CROSS-SECTION

Xylem   Phloem

STEM SUPPORT

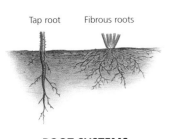

Tap root   Fibrous roots

ROOT SYSTEMS

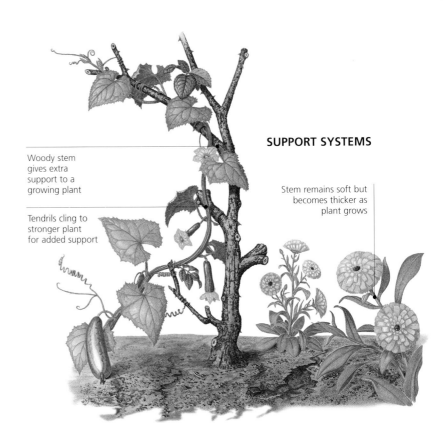

Woody stem gives extra support to a growing plant

Tendrils cling to stronger plant for added support

SUPPORT SYSTEMS

Stem remains soft but becomes thicker as plant grows

AERIAL ROOTS

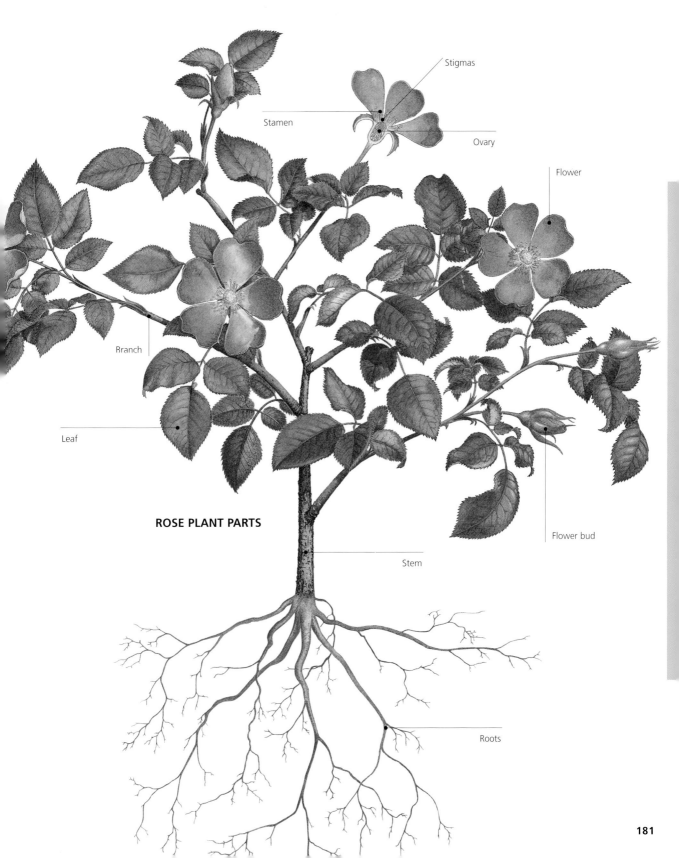

Stigmas

Stamen

Ovary

Flower

Branch

Leaf

ROSE PLANT PARTS

Flower bud

Stem

Roots

181

Plant Processes

SAVING WATER

Plants lose water through their leaves. Some trees shed their leaves in the cold or dry season to save water.

LEAF VARIATIONS

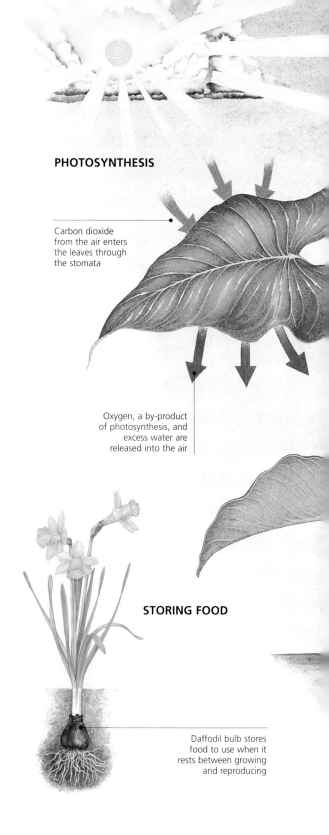

PHOTOSYNTHESIS

Carbon dioxide from the air enters the leaves through the stomata

Oxygen, a by-product of photosynthesis, and excess water are released into the air

STORING FOOD

Daffodil bulb stores food to use when it rests between growing and reproducing

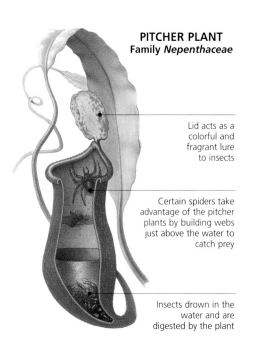

PITCHER PLANT
Family *Nepenthaceae*

Lid acts as a colorful and fragrant lure to insects

Certain spiders take advantage of the pitcher plants by building webs just above the water to catch prey

Insects drown in the water and are digested by the plant

The flower needs energy from the plant's sugars to grow

Phloem cells transport the sugars from leaves to other parts of the plant

Green chlorophyll in the leaf cells absorbs sunlight

Rainwater lands on the soil where the roots collect it

Xylem cells transport water and mineral salts from the roots to the leaves

Phosphates, nitrates and other mineral salts are absorbed by the roots

183

Ferns and Mosses

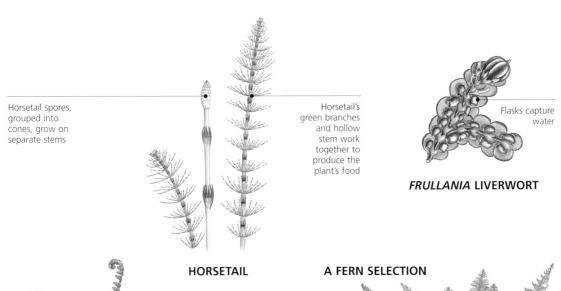

Horsetail spores, grouped into cones, grow on separate stems

Horsetail's green branches and hollow stem work together to produce the plant's food

HORSETAIL

Flasks capture water

***FRULLANIA* LIVERWORT**

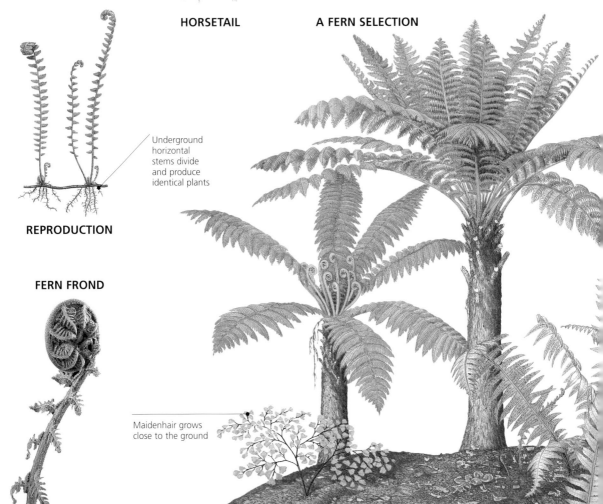

Underground horizontal stems divide and produce identical plants

REPRODUCTION

FERN FROND

A FERN SELECTION

Maidenhair grows close to the ground

Elkhorn ferns can grow on trees without harming them

When the spore case opens, spores scatter to the wind.

FERN LIFECYCLE
Ferns have a unique lifecycle. The first generation produces asexual spores. The seond generation produces sex cells (or gametes) and these grow into the third generation of spore producers.

Spores have no sex and form in spore cases (sporangia) on the underside of the fern's fronds.

The spore grows into a tiny plant called a gametophyte, which has male and female sex cells.

The male cell needs at least a film of water to swim to and join a female cell before the new spore-producing fern can grow.

Tree ferns can grow as tall as palm trees

Rasp fern reproduces rapidly from its horiztonal stems

Tree Types

MORETON BAY FIG
Ficus macrophylla

COMMON BEECH
Fagus sylvatica

COASTAL SHE-OAK
Casuarina equisetifolia

ENGLISH OAK
Quercus robur

AMERICAN ELM
Ulmus americana

BATSWING CORAL-TREE
Erythrina vespertilio

MONTEREY PINE
Pinus radiata

SILVER BIRCH
Betula pendula

SUGAR MAPLE
Acer saccharum

LAWSON CYPRESS
Chamaecyparis lawsoniana

BALSAM FIR
Abies balsamea

SENEGAL DATE PALM
Pheonix reclinata

SOUTHERN BLUE GUM
Eucalyptus bicostata

ATLAS CEDAR
Cedrus atlantica

187

Conifers

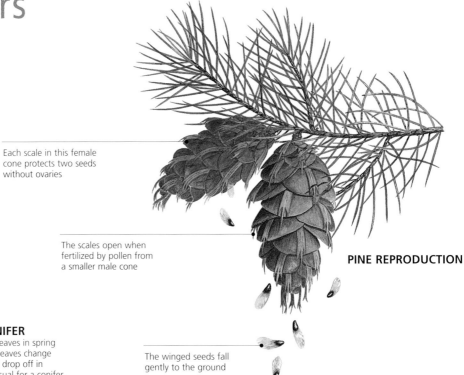

Each scale in this female cone protects two seeds without ovaries

The scales open when fertilized by pollen from a smaller male cone

PINE REPRODUCTION

The winged seeds fall gently to the ground

UNUSUAL CONIFER

Larches have green leaves in spring and summer. These leaves change color in autumn and drop off in winter, which is unusual for a conifer.

INSIDE A TREE TRUNK

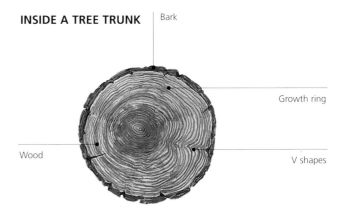

Bark

Growth ring

Wood

V shapes

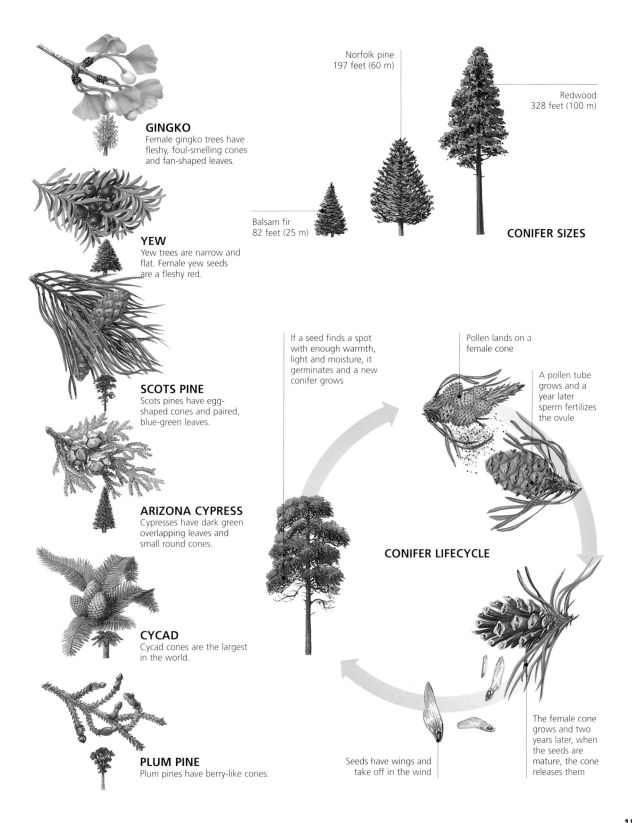

GINGKO
Female gingko trees have fleshy, foul-smelling cones and fan-shaped leaves.

YEW
Yew trees are narrow and flat. Female yew seeds are a fleshy red.

SCOTS PINE
Scots pines have egg-shaped cones and paired, blue-green leaves.

ARIZONA CYPRESS
Cypresses have dark green overlapping leaves and small round cones.

CYCAD
Cycad cones are the largest in the world.

PLUM PINE
Plum pines have berry-like cones.

Norfolk pine
197 feet (60 m)

Redwood
328 feet (100 m)

Balsam fir
82 feet (25 m)

CONIFER SIZES

If a seed finds a spot with enough warmth, light and moisture, it germinates and a new conifer grows

Pollen lands on a female cone

A pollen tube grows and a year later sperm fertilizes the ovule

CONIFER LIFECYCLE

The female cone grows and two years later, when the seeds are mature, the cone releases them

Seeds have wings and take off in the wind

Flowering Plants

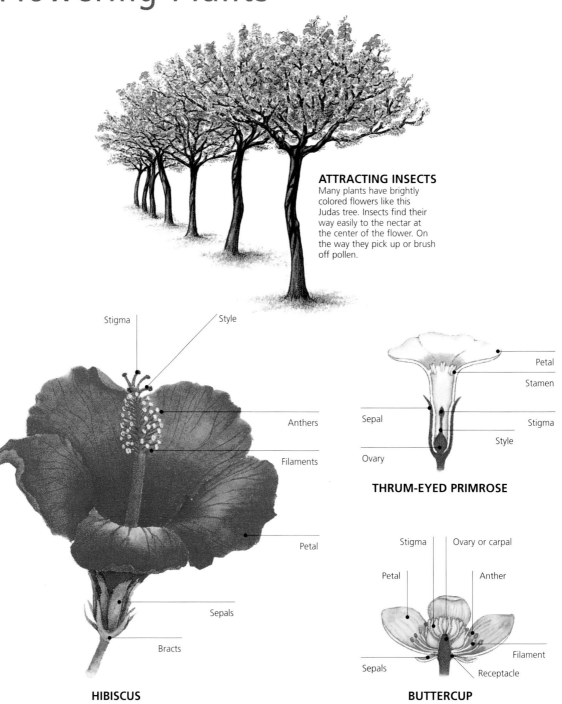

ATTRACTING INSECTS
Many plants have brightly
colored flowers like this
Judas tree. Insects find their
way easily to the nectar at
the center of the flower. On
the way they pick up or brush
off pollen.

Stigma

Style

Anthers

Filaments

Petal

Sepals

Bracts

HIBISCUS

Petal

Stamen

Sepal

Stigma

Style

Ovary

THRUM-EYED PRIMROSE

Stigma

Ovary or carpal

Petal

Anther

Filament

Sepals

Receptacle

BUTTERCUP

EUCALYPTUS FLOWERS

Eucalpypts are evergreen, flowering trees. They are the dominant trees in Australia.

BULB REPRODUCTION

Daffodil bulbs split and grow new bulbs on the side of the parent bulb.

PUMPKIN REPRODUCTION

The male and female pumpkin flowers grow on the same vine. A male can pollinate its sister female flower—this is called self-pollination. To avoid this, the male and female flowers mature at different times.

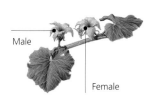

Male

Female

Male pumpkin flower

Female pumpkin flower

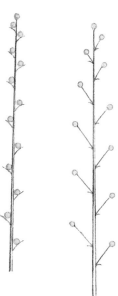

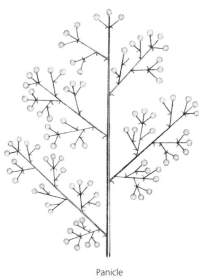

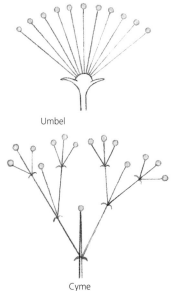

Umbel

Panicle

Spike

Raceme

KINDS OF INFLORESCENCE

Cyme

Flowering Plant Cycles

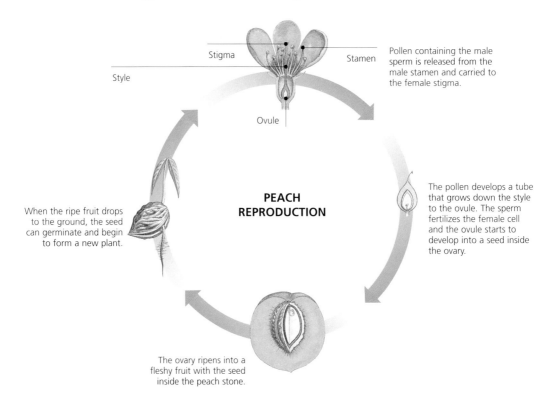

Stigma

Stamen

Style

Ovule

PEACH REPRODUCTION

Pollen containing the male sperm is released from the male stamen and carried to the female stigma.

The pollen develops a tube that grows down the style to the ovule. The sperm fertilizes the female cell and the ovule starts to develop into a seed inside the ovary.

The ovary ripens into a fleshy fruit with the seed inside the peach stone.

When the ripe fruit drops to the ground, the seed can germinate and begin to form a new plant.

FOUR SEASONS
The London plane tree has four very different stages in its yearly cycle.

Spring
Yellow male and red female flowers hang in separate clusters on the same tree. Once fertilized, the female flower begins to grow fruit.

Summer
The clusters of tightly packed green fruits grow larger and protect the seeds inside.

Autumn
As the leaves change color, the hairy fruits also change to a brown color. They are dispersed with the wind.

Winter
The leaves and their stalks drop off the branches. The sticky buds on the end of bare twigs protect the young leaves, which emerge in the spring.

A TREE'S YEAR

Summer

Autumn

Spring

Winter

193

Types of Flowering Plants

ROSE
Family *Rosaceae*

POPPY
Family *Papaveraceae*

STURT'S DESERT PEA
Swainsona formosa

LILAC
Family *Oleaceae*

SUNFLOWER
Family *Compositae*

MADONNA LILY
Family *Liliaceae*

IMPERIAL CRIMSON LILY
Family *Liliaceae*

DAYLILY
Family *Liliaceae*

FOXGLOVE
Family *Scorphulariaceae*

MARIGOLD
Family *Compositae*

EDELWEISS
Leontopodium alpinum

Food and Medicinal Plants

CHIVE
Allium schoenoprasum

ANISE
Pimpinella anisum

BASIL
Ocimum basilicum

MEADOWSWEET
Filipendula ulmaria

ECHINACEA
Echinacea purpurea

FRUIT AND VEGETABLES

 A strawberry is a fruit with many ovaries, each with one seed.

 An orange is the fruit of an evergreen tree.

 A carrot is an orange-colored tap root.

 A potato is the thick part of an underground stem called a tuber.

 A tomato is a fruit originally from the Americas.

 An onion is an underground bulb.

 A pumpkin is a fruit grown on a vine.

 Ginger is an underground stem.

 Lettuce is a plant with crisp, green leaves usually eaten raw.

Asparagus is a green stem with reduced leaves, or bracts.

CABBAGE FAMILY

Savoy cabbage

Cauliflower

Broccoli

Brussel sprouts

Kohlrabi

Wild cabbage

GARLIC CLOVE

NUT VARIATIONS

197

Forests and Rainforests

ROOT SYSTEMS

Temperate forest
In forests that grow on rich soils the roots of trees penetrate deep down and take nutrients as needed

Rainforest
The roots of trees growing in poor soils remain near the soil surface where they take nutrients before they are lost at deeper levels

Root tips attach themselves to fallen leaves

LIFE IN A TANK BROMELIAD

The leaves of a tank bromeliad form a watertight bowl that accumulates rainwater. Bromeliads are non-parasitic epiphytic plants. They gain their nutrients from the animal matter that filters to the bottom of the pool.

Velvet worms have been discovered in bromeliads, far above their usual home on the forest floor

A female poison arrow frog deposits tadpoles into the water-filled bromeliad

A mouse opossum eats a damsel fly larva from the bromeliad pool

The bromeliad pool is a perfect breeding ground for mosquitos

An alligator lizard drinks from the pool

Beetle larvae prey on tadpoles

A variety of land snails forage and hide between the leaves

Predatory and scavenging ants patrol the area for anything they can find

Rainforest Life

RAINFOREST CANOPY
High above the ground the leaves of the tall trees almost meet to form a roof or canopy. Tropical rainforests are home to a wider range of plants and animals than any other habitat.

STRANGLER FIG
This epiphyte grows from a bird-borne seed high in a host tree. It grows roots into the soil and forms a woody "corset" around the trunk. Because the host tree cannot grow outward, it rots and dies. The strangler fig then stands alone.

ANT HOUSE
Ants live inside the cavities of this epiphytic ant plant.

ENERGY FLOW
Dead plant and animal matter are raw materials for the rainforest nutrient cycle. These cells must be broken down by fungi and bacteria before nutrients can be released into the soil.

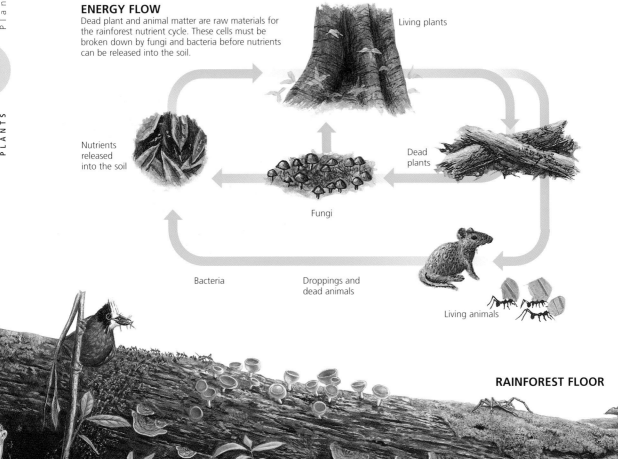

Living plants

Nutrients released into the soil

Dead plants

Fungi

Bacteria

Droppings and dead animals

Living animals

RAINFOREST FLOOR

Bird Characteristics

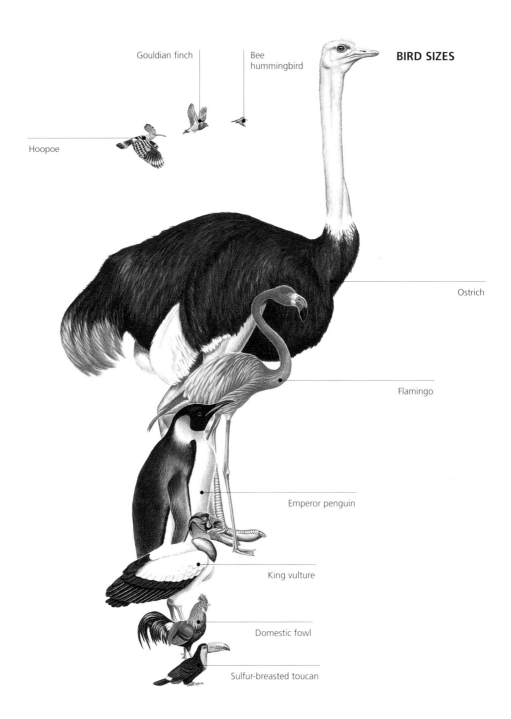

Gouldian finch

Bee hummingbird

BIRD SIZES

Hoopoe

Ostrich

Flamingo

Emperor penguin

King vulture

Domestic fowl

Sulfur-breasted toucan

BILL VARIETIES

African spoonbill

Pileated woodpecker

Palm cockatoo

Far eastern curlew

Bald eagle

Ring-necked pheasant

Ring-necked pheasant skeleton

Wire-tailed manakin

Wire-tailed manakin skeleton

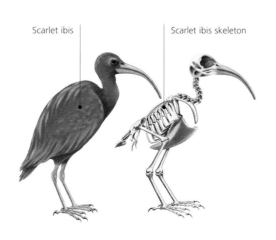

Scarlet ibis

Scarlet ibis skeleton

FEET VARIETIES

Black-capped lorikeet

Mallard

Northern jacana

Rhea

Bird Anatomy

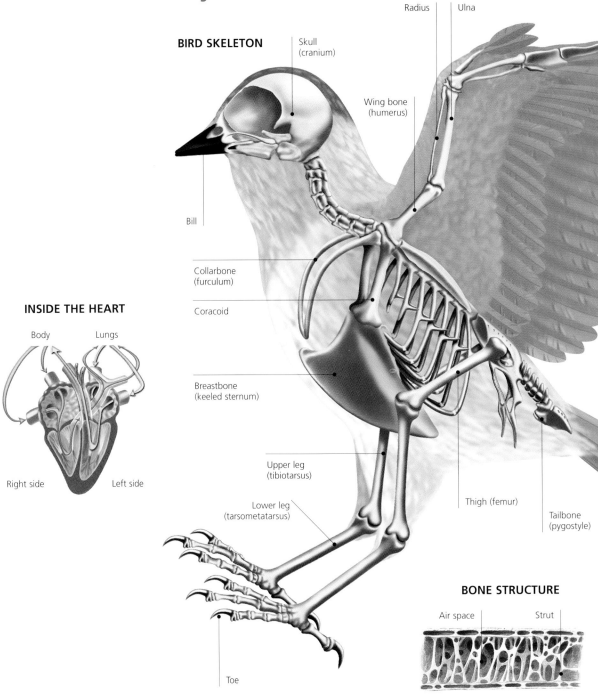

BIRD SKELETON

Skull
(cranium)

Radius

Ulna

Wing bone
(humerus)

Bill

Collarbone
(furculum)

Coracoid

Breastbone
(keeled sternum)

Upper leg
(tibiotarsus)

Thigh (femur)

Tailbone
(pygostyle)

Lower leg
(tarsometatarsus)

Toe

INSIDE THE HEART

Body

Lungs

Right side

Left side

BONE STRUCTURE

Air space

Strut

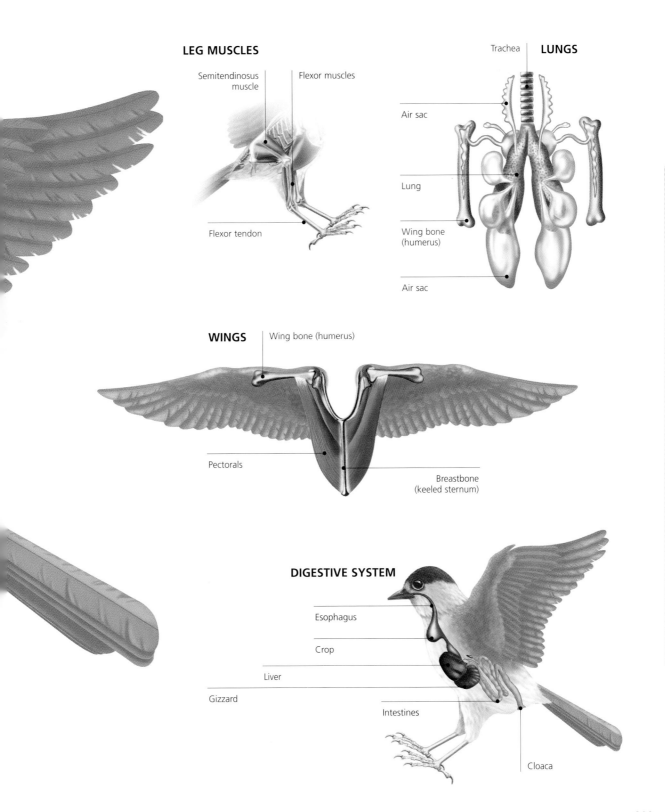

LEG MUSCLES

Semitendinosus
muscle

Flexor muscles

Flexor tendon

Trachea | **LUNGS**

Air sac

Lung

Wing bone
(humerus)

Air sac

WINGS | Wing bone (humerus)

Pectorals

Breastbone
(keeled sternum)

DIGESTIVE SYSTEM

Esophagus

Crop

Liver

Gizzard

Intestines

Cloaca

Feathers and Flight

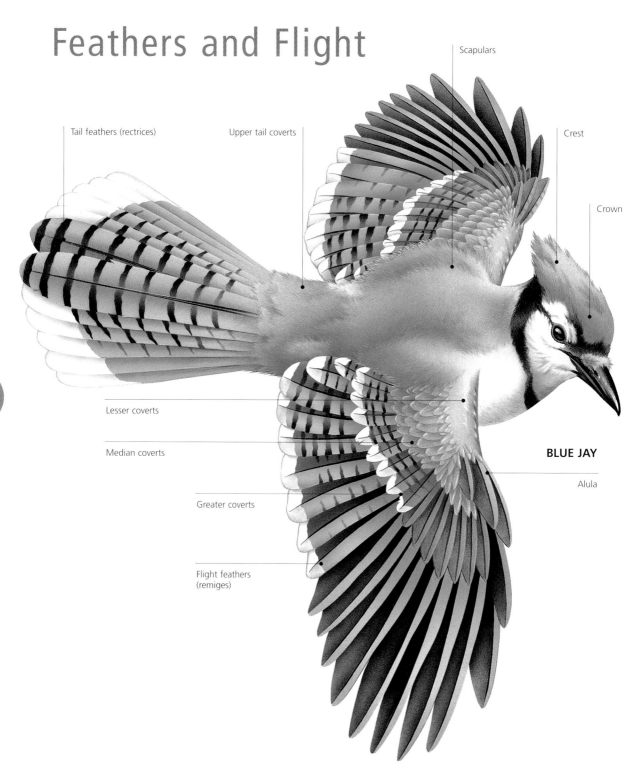

Scapulars

Tail feathers (rectrices)

Upper tail coverts

Crest

Crown

Lesser coverts

Median coverts

BLUE JAY

Alula

Greater coverts

Flight feathers
(remiges)

AMERICAN CROW FLIGHT

SCARLET MINIVET FLIGHT

PEACOCK PLUMAGE

FLIGHT OR CONTOUR FEATHER

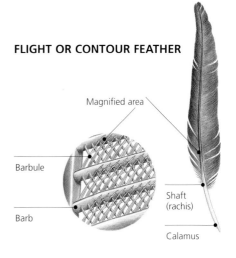

Magnified area

Barbule

Barb

Shaft
(rachis)

Calamus

SEMI PLUME OR DOWN FEATHER

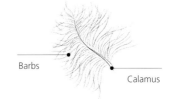

Barbs

Calamus

FEATHER GROWTH

Worn feather

New feather
pushes out
old feather

New feather

Feather
unfurls from
the shaft

Waterbirds

MUTE SWAN
Cygnus olor

GEESE FLYING IN "V" FORMATION

KING EIDER
Somateria spectabilis

WOOD DUCK
Aix sponsa

RED-BREASTED GOOSE
Branta ruficollis

PURPLE GALLINULE
Porphyrio martinica

WALDRAPP
Geronticus eremita

PAINTED STORK
Mycteria leucocephala

PURPLE HERON
Ardea purpurea

NORTHERN SCREAMER
Chauna chavaria

CROWNED CRANE
Balearica pavonina

Seabirds and Shorebirds

BROWN PELICAN
Pelecanus occidentalis

LESSER GOLDEN PLOVER
Pluvialis dominica

BANDED LAPWING
Vanellus tricolor

Birds

ANIMALS

BLUE-FOOTED BOOBY
Sula nebouxii

GREAT AUK
Pinguinus impennis

ATLANTIC PUFFIN
Fratercula arctica

BLACK SKIMMER
Rhynchops niger

Penguins

Feathers and blubber provide insulation.

Tough toenails grip the ice.

EMPEROR PENGUIN ANATOMY

EMPEROR PENGUIN
Aptenodytes forsteri

CHINSTRAP PENGUIN
Pygoscelis antarctica

YELLOW-EYED PENGUIN
Megadyptes antipodes

KING PENGUIN
Aptenodytes patagonicus

ROCKHOPPER PENGUIN
Eudyptes chrysocome

FIORDLAND PENGUIN
Eudyptes pachyrhynchus

MAGELLANIC PENGUIN
Spheniscus magellanicus

FAIRY PENGUIN
Eudyptula minor

217

Flightless Birds

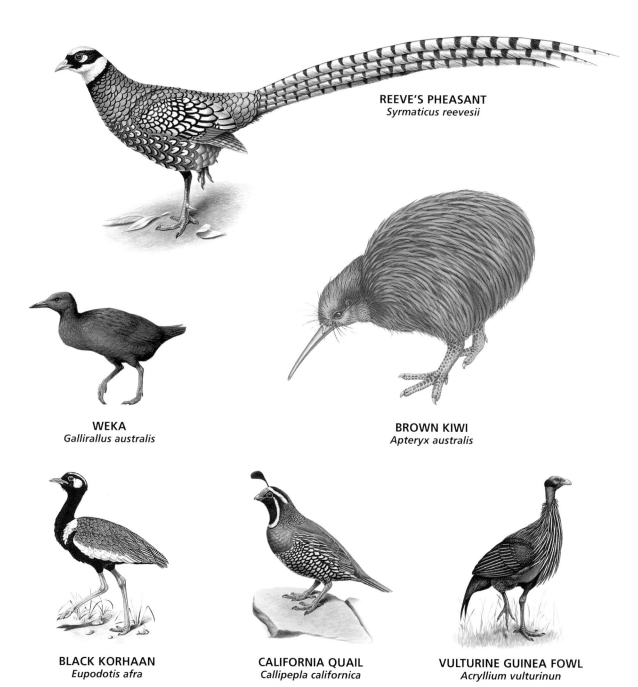

REEVE'S PHEASANT
Syrmaticus reevesii

WEKA
Gallirallus australis

BROWN KIWI
Apteryx australis

BLACK KORHAAN
Eupodotis afra

CALIFORNIA QUAIL
Callipepla californica

VULTURINE GUINEA FOWL
Acryllium vulturinun

KAKAPO
Strigops habroptilus

TAKAHE
Porphyrio mantelli

EMU
Dromaius novaehollandiae

Raptor Characteristics

RAPTOR TALONS

Osprey

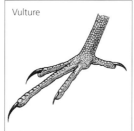

Vulture

Harpy eagle

Sparrowhawk

Birds

ANIMALS

RAPTOR ANATOMY

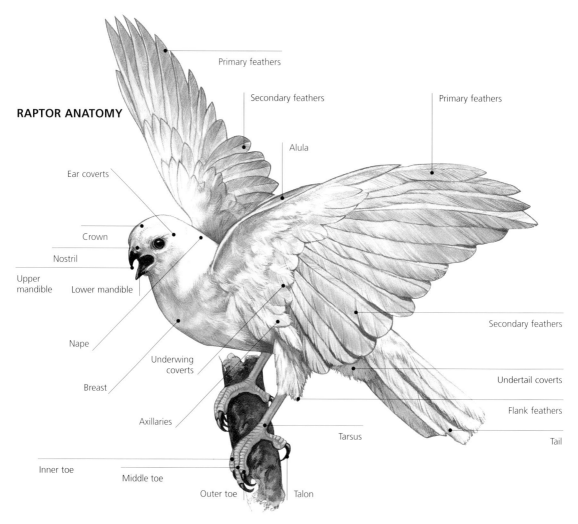

Primary feathers

Secondary feathers

Primary feathers

Alula

Ear coverts

Crown

Nostril

Upper mandible

Lower mandible

Secondary feathers

Nape

Underwing coverts

Undertail coverts

Breast

Flank feathers

Axillaries

Tarsus

Tail

Inner toe

Middle toe

Outer toe

Talon

SNAIL KITE
Rostrhamus sociabilis

BLACK-SHOULDERED KITE
Elanus caeruleus

PEARL KITE
Gampsonyx swainsonii

BRAHMINY KITE
Haliastur indus

BEARDED VULTURE
Gypaetus barbatus

RAPTOR WINGSPANS

Andean condor
9 ½ feet (2.9 m)

Bearded vulture
8 feet (2.5 m)

Secretarybird
6 ¾ feet (2.1 m)

**White-bellied
sea eagle**
6 ½ feet (2.0 m)

**Rough-legged
buzzard**
4 ½ feet (1.5 m)

Peregrine falcon
3 ¼ feet (1.0 m)

Lesser kestrel
2 ¾ feet (0.7 m)

Little sparrowhawk
1 ¼ feet (0.4 m)

Raptors

BATELEUR
Terathopius ecaudatus

CRESTED CARACARA
Polyborus plancus

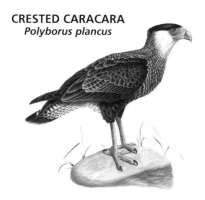

BLACK KITE
Milvus migrans

AMERICAN KESTREL
Falco sparverius

BARN OWL AND SKULL
Tyto alba

Asymmetrical ears
enhance the owl's
"stereo" hearing

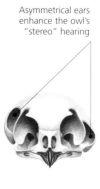

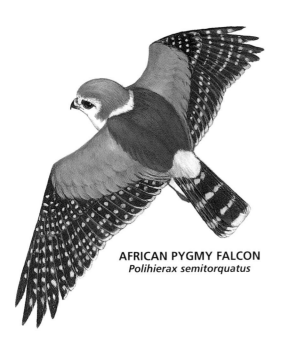

AFRICAN PYGMY FALCON
Polihierax semitorquatus

WHITE-EYED KESTREL
Falco rupicoloides

EURASIAN GRIFFON
Gyps fulvus

PALMNUT VULTURE
Gypohierax angolensis

223

Hawks and Eagles

Birds

ANIMALS

BONELLI'S EAGLE
Hieraaetus fasciatus

ORNATE HAWK EAGLE
Spizaetus ornatus

CRESTED SERPENT EAGLE
Spilornis cheela

GREAT PHILIPPINE EAGLE
Pithecophaga jefferyi

WHITE-BELLIED SEA EAGLE
Haliaeetus leucogaster

ROUGH-LEGGED HAWK
Buteo lagopus

SLATE-COLORED HAWK
Leucopternis schistacea

Pigeons and Parrots

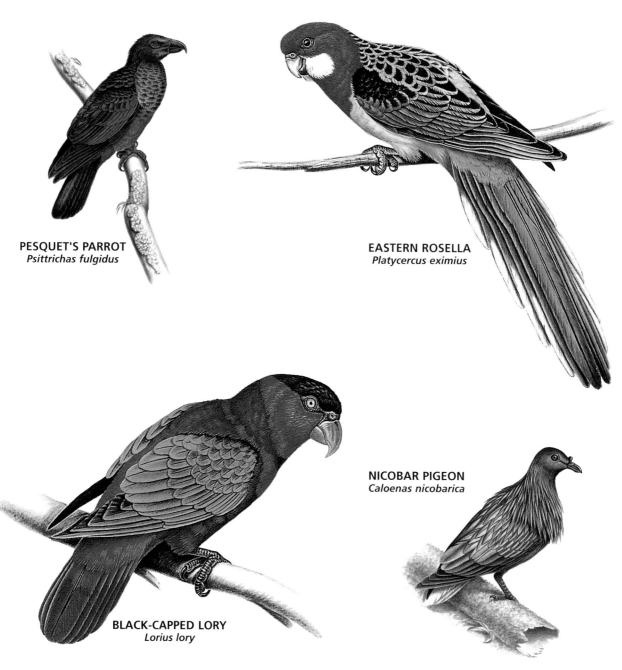

PESQUET'S PARROT
Psittrichas fulgidus

EASTERN ROSELLA
Platycercus eximius

BLACK-CAPPED LORY
Lorius lory

NICOBAR PIGEON
Caloenas nicobarica

ANIMALS

SUPERB FRUIT DOVE
Ptilinopus superbus

HAWK-HEADED PARROT
Deroptyus accipitrinus

PIN-TAILED SANDGROUSE
Pterocles alchata

Hummingbirds

BLACK-CHINNED HUMMINGBIRD
Archilochus alexandri

ANNA'S HUMMINGBIRD
Clypte anna

RUBY-THROATED HUMMINGBIRD
Archilochus colubris

Hummingbirds have long tongues that are brush-tipped to aid in nectar feeding

This male's ruby-red throat makes him unmistakeable

EXTRACTING NECTAR
This male ruby-throated hummingbird (*Archilochus colubris*) hovers in front of a flower and inserts its bill to extract the nectar. Hummingbirds also eat insects, which form a large part of their diet.

HUMMINGBIRD FLIGHT

Flying forward
Hummingbirds flap their wings up and down to move forward.

Hovering
Hummingbirds move their wings in a rapid figure-of-eight motion to hover in place.

Flying backward
Hummingbirds flap their wings above and behind their heads to move backward.

BROAD-BILLED HUMMINGBIRD
Cynanthus latirostris

CALLIOPE HUMMINGBIRD
Stellula calliope

RUFOUS HUMMINGBIRD
Selasphorus rufus

Kingfishers and their Allies

ANIMALS

Birds

SPANGLED KOOKABURRA
Dacelo tyro

DIVING FOR FISH
This belted kingfisher
(*Ceryle alcyon*) plunges head-
first into water to catch fish.

YELLOW-BILLED
HORNBILL
Tockus flavirostris

RAINBOW BEE-EATER
Merops ornatus

WHITE-THROATED
KINGFISHER
Halcyon smyrnensis

BLUE-CROWNED
MOTMOT
Momotus momota

MALACHITE
KINGFISHER
Alcedo cristata

LILAC-BREASTED ROLLER
Coracias caudata

231

Woodpeckers and Barbets

Birds

ANIMALS

**RUFOUS-TAILED
JACAMAR**
Galbula ruficauda

**RED-AND-YELLOW
BARBET**
*Trachyphonus
erythrocephalus*

HAIRY WOODPECKER
Picoides villosus

ACORN WOODPECKER
Melanerpes formicivorus

DOWNY WOODPECKER
Picoides pubescens

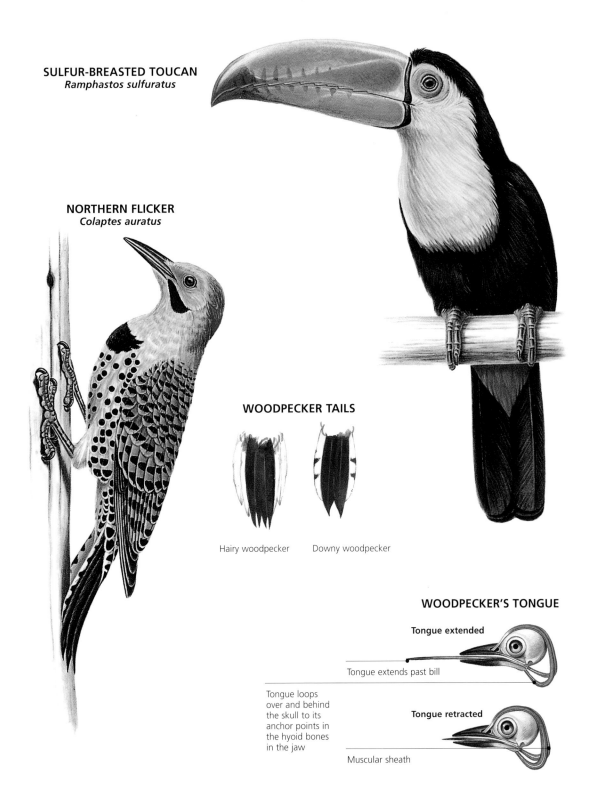

SULFUR-BREASTED TOUCAN
Ramphastos sulfuratus

NORTHERN FLICKER
Colaptes auratus

WOODPECKER TAILS

Hairy woodpecker

Downy woodpecker

WOODPECKER'S TONGUE

Tongue extended

Tongue extends past bill

Tongue loops over and behind the skull to its anchor points in the hyoid bones in the jaw

Tongue retracted

Muscular sheath

Land Birds

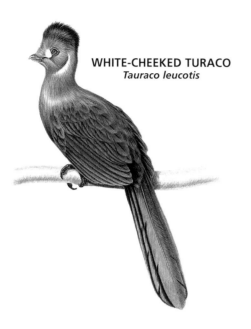

WHITE-CHEEKED TURACO
Tauraco leucotis

CHANNEL-BILLED CUCKOO
Scythrops novaehollandia

GREAT KISKADEE
Pitangus sulphuratus

GREATER ROADRUNNER
Geococcyx californianus

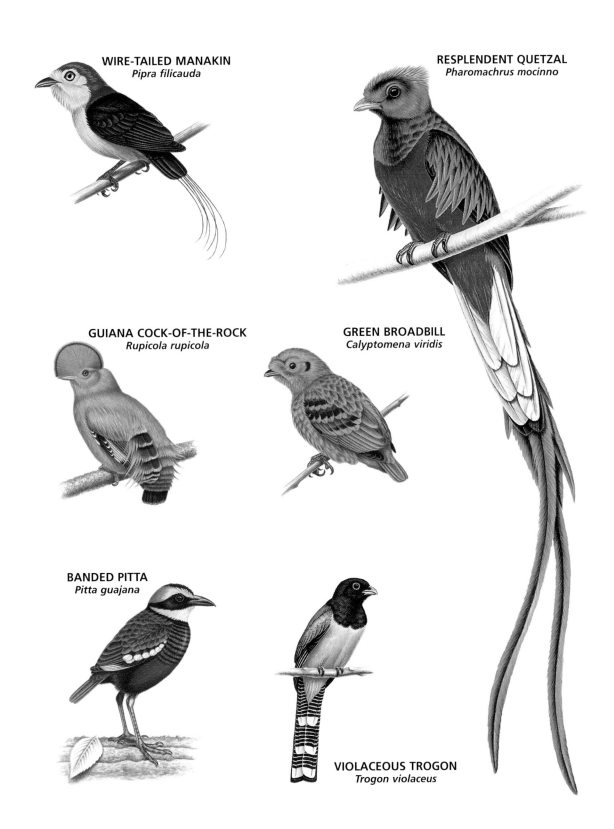

WIRE-TAILED MANAKIN
Pipra filicauda

RESPLENDENT QUETZAL
Pharomachrus mocinno

GUIANA COCK-OF-THE-ROCK
Rupicola rupicola

GREEN BROADBILL
Calyptomena viridis

BANDED PITTA
Pitta guajana

VIOLACEOUS TROGON
Trogon violaceus

235

Songbirds

Birds

ANIMALS

BARRED CUCKOOSHRIKE
Coracina lineata

**GOLDEN-FRONTED
LEAFBIRD**
Chloropsis aurifrons

RED-BILLED LEIOTHRIX
Leiothrix lutea

GOLDEN-CROWNED KINGLET
Regulus satrapa

RUFOUS-BELLIED NILTAVA
Niltava sundara

SHRIKE-TIT
Falcunculus frontatus

SPECTACLED MONARCH
Monarcha trivirgatus

REGAL SUNBIRD
Nectarinia regia

RUFOUS-BACKED SHRIKE
Lanius schach

WHITE'S THRUSH
Zoothera dauma

WHITE-RUMPED SHAMA
Copsychus malabaricus

ORANGE CHAT
Epthianura aurifrons

SPLENDID FAIRY-WREN
Malurus splendens

RED-CAPPED ROBIN
Petroica goodenovii

SPOTTED PARDALOTE
Pardalotus punctatus

EASTERN SPINEBILL
Acanthorhynchus tenuirostris

REGENT HONEYEATER
Xanthomyza phrygia

PAINTED BUNTING
Passerina ciris

RED-LEGGED HONEYCREEPER
Cyanerpes cyaneus

SUPERB TANAGER
Tangara fastuosa

237

Finches and Starlings

EURASIAN GOLDFINCH
Carduelis carduelis

CHAFFINCH
Fringilla coelebs

JAVA SPARROW
Padda oryzivora

GOULDIAN FINCH
Chloebia gouldiae

RED BISHOP
Euplectes orix

MELBA FINCH
Pytilia melba

Birds

ANIMALS

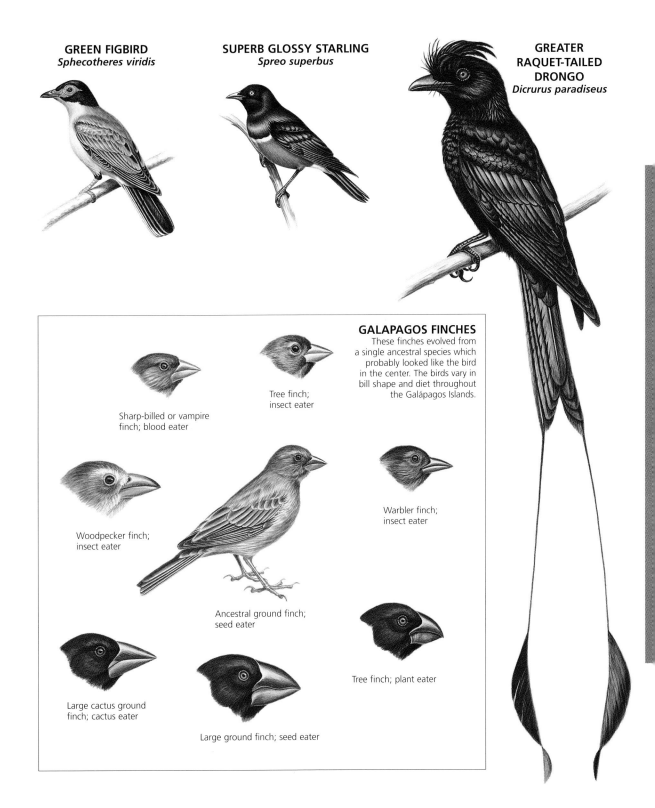

GREEN FIGBIRD
Sphecotheres viridis

SUPERB GLOSSY STARLING
Spreo superbus

GREATER RAQUET-TAILED DRONGO
Dicrurus paradiseus

GALAPAGOS FINCHES
These finches evolved from a single ancestral species which probably looked like the bird in the center. The birds vary in bill shape and diet throughout the Galápagos Islands.

Sharp-billed or vampire finch; blood eater

Tree finch; insect eater

Woodpecker finch; insect eater

Warbler finch; insect eater

Ancestral ground finch; seed eater

Large cactus ground finch; cactus eater

Large ground finch; seed eater

Tree finch; plant eater

Monotremes and Marsupials

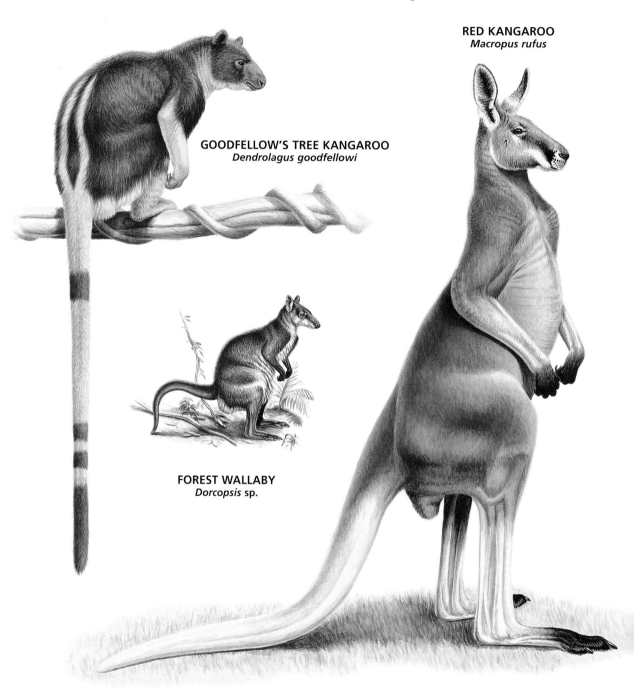

GOODFELLOW'S TREE KANGAROO
Dendrolagus goodfellowi

RED KANGAROO
Macropus rufus

FOREST WALLABY
Dorcopsis sp.

Mammals

ANIMALS

PLATYPUS ANATOMY

Watertight closed eyes

Open eyes

Webbed feet fold back to reveal claws.

Poisonous spur and venom gland

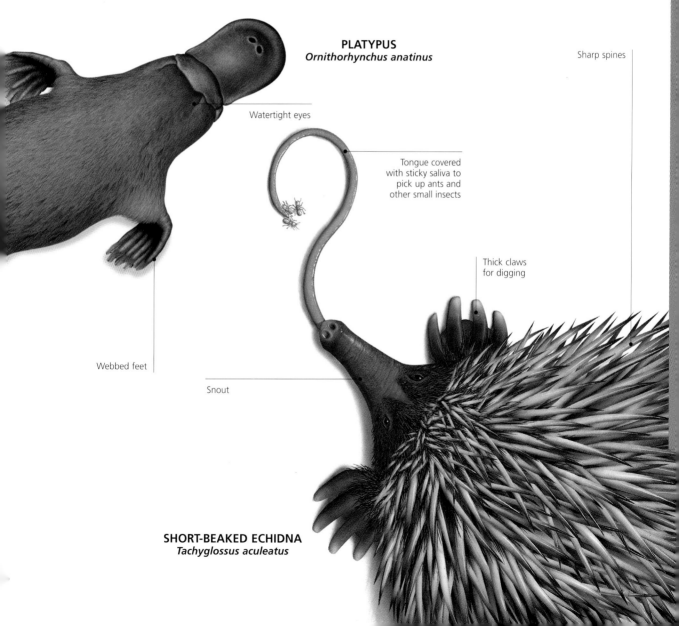

PLATYPUS
Ornithorhynchus anatinus

Sharp spines

Watertight eyes

Tongue covered with sticky saliva to pick up ants and other small insects

Thick claws for digging

Webbed feet

Snout

SHORT-BEAKED ECHIDNA
Tachyglossus aculeatus

Marsupials

BILBY
Macrotis lagotis

KOALA
Phascolarctos cinereus

SQUIRREL GLIDER
Petaurus norfolcensis

MUSKY RAT-KANGAROO
Hypsiprymnodon moschatus

NUMBAT
Myrmecobius fasciatus

COMMON SPOTTED CUSCUS
Spilocuscus maculatus

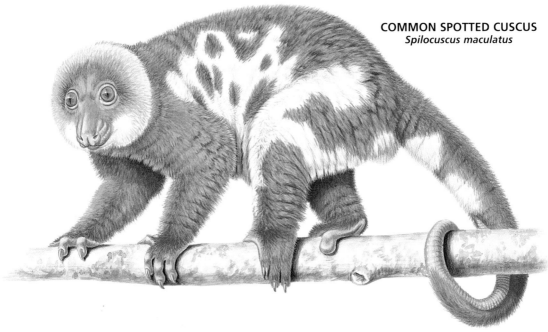

WOOLLY OPOSSUM
Caluromys sp.

SPOTTED-TAILED QUOLL
Dasyurus maculatus

WATER OPOSSUM
Chironectes minimus

STRIPED POSSUM
Dactylopsila trivirgata

243

Insect-eating Mammals

GREATER MOONRAT
Echinosorex gymnura

PYRENEAN DESMAN
Galemys pyranaicus

PANGOLIN
Manis sp.

Mammals

ANIMALS

NOSE VARIETIES

Algerian hedgehog

European mole

African aardvark

Pyreanean desman

THREE-BANDED ARMADILLO
Tolypeutes tricinctus

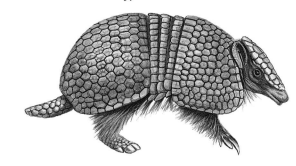

To defend itself from predators the three-banded armadillo rolls into a tight ball using its thick bony plating like armor

TAMANDUA
Tamandua sp.

Bats

Mammals

ANIMALS

LONG-EARED BAT
Family Vespertilionidae

ORANGE HORSESHOE BAT
Rhinonicteris aurantius

TENT-BUILDING BAT
Uroderma bilobatum

SWORD-NOSED BAT
Lonchorhina sp.

GAMBIAN EPAULETTED FRUIT BAT
Epomorphorus gambianus

LESSER BARE-BACKED FRUIT BAT
Dobsonia minor

COMMON VAMPIRE BAT
Desmodus rotundus

**AFRICAN YELLOW-WINGED
FALSE VAMPIRE BAT**
Lavia frons

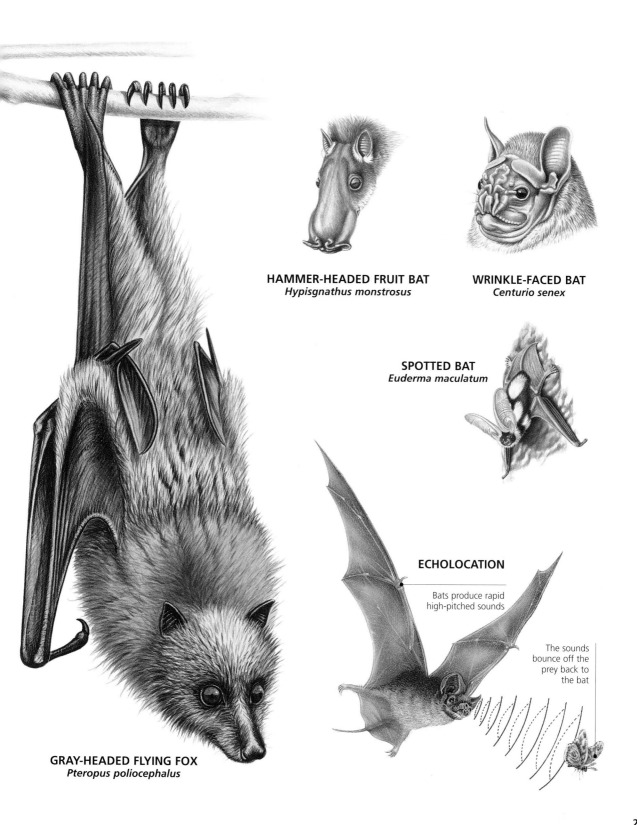

HAMMER-HEADED FRUIT BAT
Hypisgnathus monstrosus

WRINKLE-FACED BAT
Centurio senex

SPOTTED BAT
Euderma maculatum

ECHOLOCATION

Bats produce rapid
high-pitched sounds

The sounds
bounce off the
prey back to
the bat

GRAY-HEADED FLYING FOX
Pteropus poliocephalus

Primates

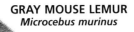

GRAY MOUSE LEMUR
Microcebus murinus

PRIMATE FEET AND HANDS

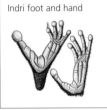

Indri foot and hand

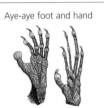

Aye-aye foot and hand

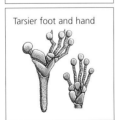

Tarsier foot and hand

Gorilla foot and hand

LAR GIBBON
Hylobates lar

RED RUFFED LEMUR
Varecia variegata rubra

GOLDEN POTTO
Arctocebus aureus

BRACHIATION
The orang-utan (*Pongo pygmaeus*) moves through the trees primarily via brachiation—swinging hand over hand from branch to branch.

Mobile shoulder joints

Long arms

Curved hands

PHILIPPINES TARSIER
Tarsius syrichta

INDRI
Indri indri

AYE-AYE
Daubentonia madagascariensis

Old World Monkeys

Old World monkeys
Monkeys from Africa and Asia have prominent noses with narrow nostrils that face forward.

CELEBES MACAQUE
Macaca nigra

BLACK AND WHITE COLOBUS
Colobus guereza

DUSKY LEAF MONKEY
Trachypithecus obscurus

MANDRILL
Mandrillus sphinx

DIANA GUENON
Cercopithecus diana

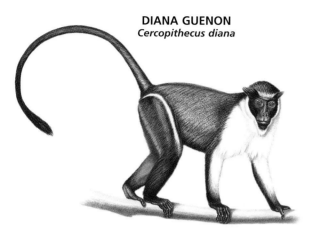

GELADA
Theropithecus gelada

PROBOSCIS MONKEY
Nasalis larvatus

GOLDEN SNUB-NOSED MONKEY
Rhinopithecus roxellana

251

New World Monkeys

New World monkeys
Monkeys from Central and South America have flattened noses with nostrils that face sideways.

NIGHT MONKEY
Aotus trivirgatus

BLACK HOWLER MONKEY
Alouatta caraya

RED UAKARI
Cacajao calvus

RED HOWLER MONKEY
Aloutta seniculus

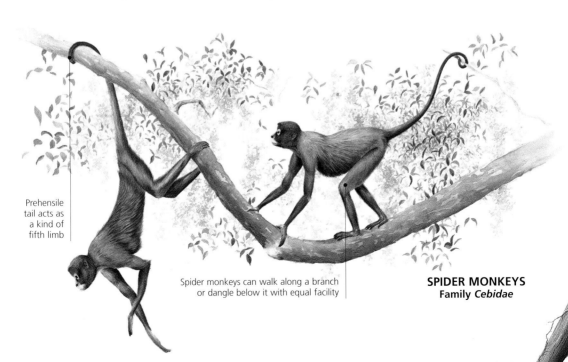

Prehensile tail acts as a kind of fifth limb

Spider monkeys can walk along a branch or dangle below it with equal facility

SPIDER MONKEYS
Family *Cebidae*

South American spider monkeys are herbivores, or plant eaters

SOUTH AMERICAN SPIDER MONKEYS
Aletes sp.

Baby spider monkeys use their tails to grip on to their mothers

Dogs

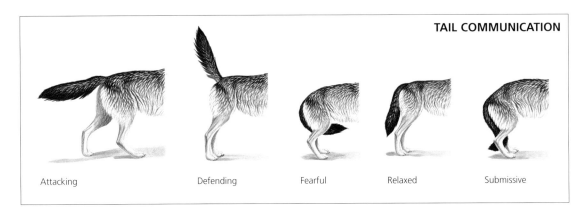

TAIL COMMUNICATION

Attacking   Defending   Fearful   Relaxed   Submissive

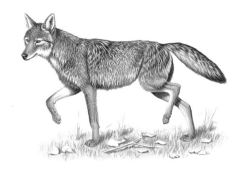

RED WOLF
Canis rufus

RACOON DOG
Nyctereutes procyonoides

MANED WOLF
Chrysocyon brachyurus

COYOTE
Canis latrans

BUSH DOG
Speothos ·ᵥₐnaticus

BAT-EARED FOX
Octocyon megalotis

AFRICAN HUNTING DOG
Lycaon pictus

GRAY FOX
Urocyon cinereoargenteus

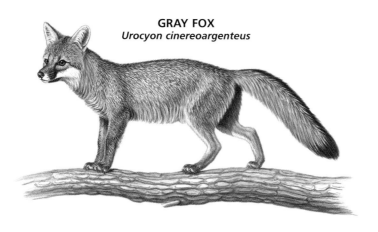

COYOTE FACIAL EXPRESSIONS

Attacking

Defending

Submissive

Playful

Friendly

Cat Characteristics

CAT SKELETON

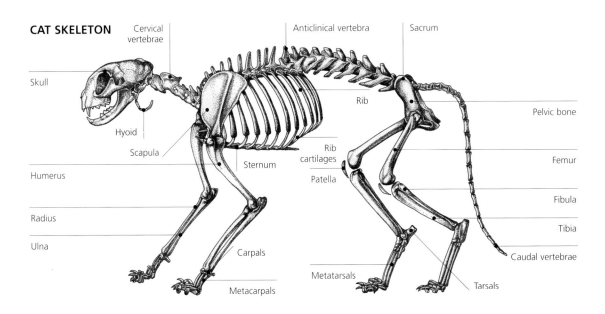

- Cervical vertebrae
- Skull
- Hyoid
- Scapula
- Humerus
- Radius
- Ulna
- Sternum
- Carpals
- Metacarpals
- Anticlinical vertebra
- Rib
- Rib cartilages
- Patella
- Metatarsals
- Sacrum
- Pelvic bone
- Femur
- Fibula
- Tibia
- Caudal vertebrae
- Tarsals

FACIAL EXPRESSIONS

Attacking

Defending

CAT CLAWS

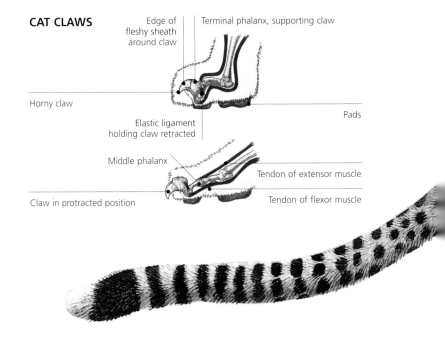

- Edge of fleshy sheath around claw
- Terminal phalanx, supporting claw
- Horny claw
- Pads
- Elastic ligament holding claw retracted
- Middle phalanx
- Tendon of extensor muscle
- Tendon of flexor muscle
- Claw in protracted position

LEOPARD
Panthera pardus

SNOW LEOPARD
Panthera uncia

PUMA
Felis concolor

FASTEST ANIMAL

Cheetahs are the fastest land animal. They reach speeds of 70 miles (110 km) per hour. The cheetah's long tail acts as a rudder.

CHEETAH
Acinonyx jubatus

Great Cats

BOBCAT
Lynx rufus

NORTH AMERICAN LYNX
Lynx canadensis

CARACAL
Lynx caracal

EURASIAN LYNX
Lynx lynx

JAGUAR
Panthera onca

SPANISH LYNX
Lynx pardinus

TIGER
Panthera tigris

LION
Panthera leo

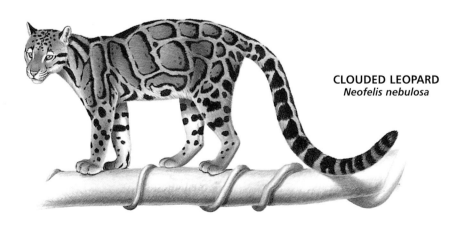

CLOUDED LEOPARD
Neofelis nebulosa

259

Small Cats

FISHING CAT
Felis viverrina

SERVAL
Felis serval

ASIAN GOLDEN CAT
Felis temminckii

MARGAY
Felis wiedii

ONCILLA
Felis tigrina

LEOPARD CAT
Felis bengalensis

PALLAS' CAT
Felis manul

WILD CAT
Felis silvestris

JUNGLE CAT
Felis chaus

AFRICAN GOLDEN CAT
Felis aurata

KODKOD
Felis guigna

OCELOT
Felis pardalis

ANDEAN MOUNTAIN CAT
Felis jacobita

GEOFFROY'S CAT
Felis geoffroyi

BLACK-FOOTED CAT
Felis nigripes

CHINESE DESERT CAT
Felis bieti

SAND CAT
Felis margarita

Bears

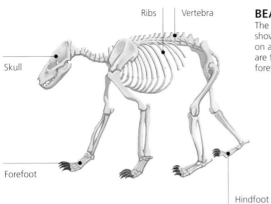

Ribs | Vertebra

Skull

Forefoot

Hindfoot

BEAR POSTURE
The skeleton of this brown bear shows its posture when standing on all four feet. The bear's hindfeet are flat to the ground and the forefeet are partly flat to ground.

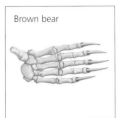

Brown bear

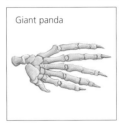

Giant panda

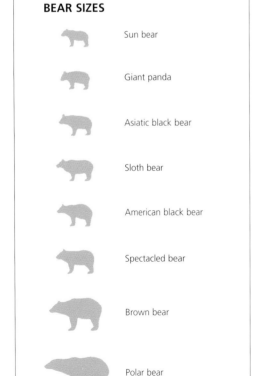

BEAR SIZES

Sun bear

Giant panda

Asiatic black bear

Sloth bear

American black bear

Spectacled bear

Brown bear

Polar bear

BROWN BEAR
Ursus arctos

Mammals

ANIMALS

BEAR FEET

Forefoot

Forefoot

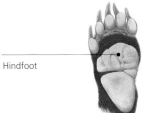

Hindfoot

Hindfoot

American black bear
(Ursus americanus)

Giant panda
(Ailuropoda melanoleuca)

ASIATIC BLACK BEAR
Ursus thibetanus

SUN BEAR
Ursus malayanus

SLOTH BEAR
Ursus ursinus

Bears

TREE CLIMBERS
American black bears are
excellent tree climbers and
often sleep in tree-tops.

GIANT PANDA
Ailuropoda melanoleuca

SPECTACLED BEAR
Tremarctos ornatus

Cinnamon color

Black color

AMERICAN BLACK BEAR
Ursus americanus

RED PANDA
Ailurus fulgens

POLAR BEAR
Ursus maritimus

Whales, Dolphins and Porpoises

WHALE TAILS

Humpback whale

Blue whale

Southern right whale

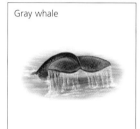
Gray whale

DOLPHIN ANATOMY

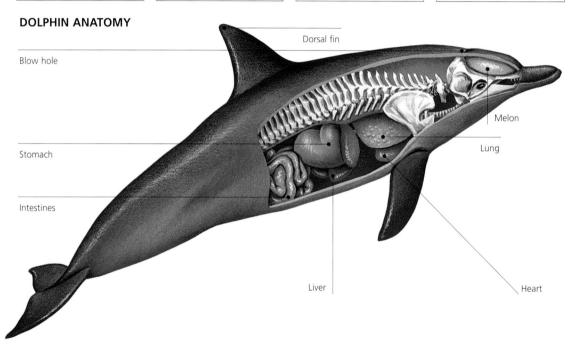

Dorsal fin

Blow hole

Melon

Lung

Stomach

Intestines

Liver

Heart

Mammals

ANIMALS

HEAD TYPES

Minke whale

Right whale

Sperm whale

Bottlenose dolphin

BALEEN WHALE
Pygmy right whale (*Caperea marginata*)

TOOTHED WHALE
Atlantic white-sided dolphin (*Lagenorhynchus acutus*)

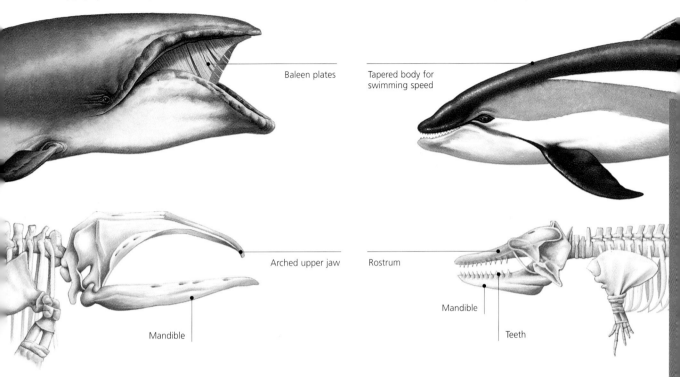

Baleen plates

Tapered body for swimming speed

Arched upper jaw

Rostrum

Mandible

Mandible

Teeth

DIFFERENCES BETWEEN BALEEN AND TOOTHED WHALES

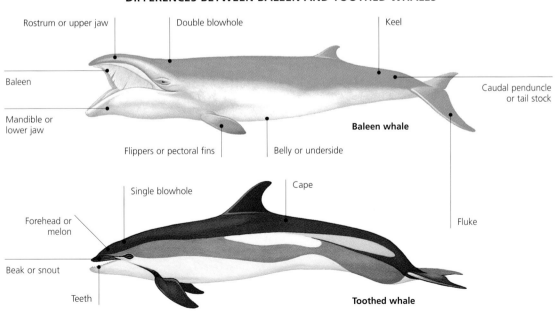

Rostrum or upper jaw

Double blowhole

Keel

Baleen

Mandible or lower jaw

Caudal penduncle or tail stock

Baleen whale

Flippers or pectoral fins

Belly or underside

Single blowhole

Cape

Forehead or melon

Fluke

Beak or snout

Teeth

Toothed whale

Whales, Dolphins and Porpoises

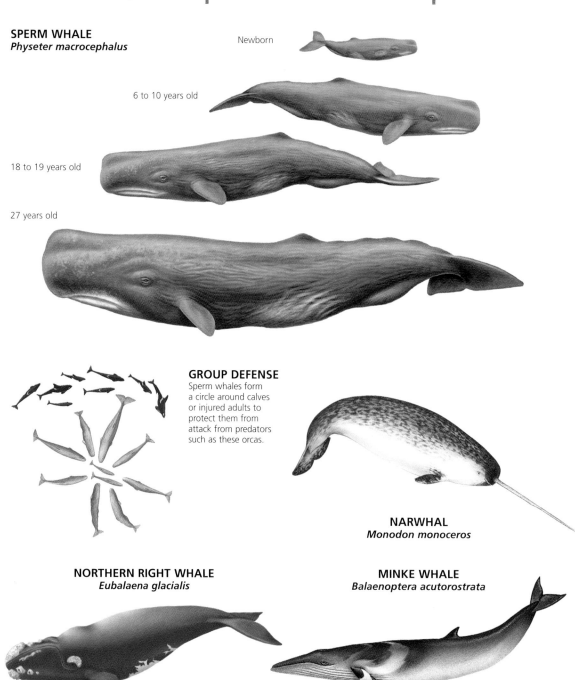

SPERM WHALE
Physeter macrocephalus

Newborn

6 to 10 years old

18 to 19 years old

27 years old

Mammals

ANIMALS

GROUP DEFENSE
Sperm whales form a circle around calves or injured adults to protect them from attack from predators such as these orcas.

NARWHAL
Monodon monoceros

NORTHERN RIGHT WHALE
Eubalaena glacialis

MINKE WHALE
Balaenoptera acutorostrata

DIVE SEQUENCES

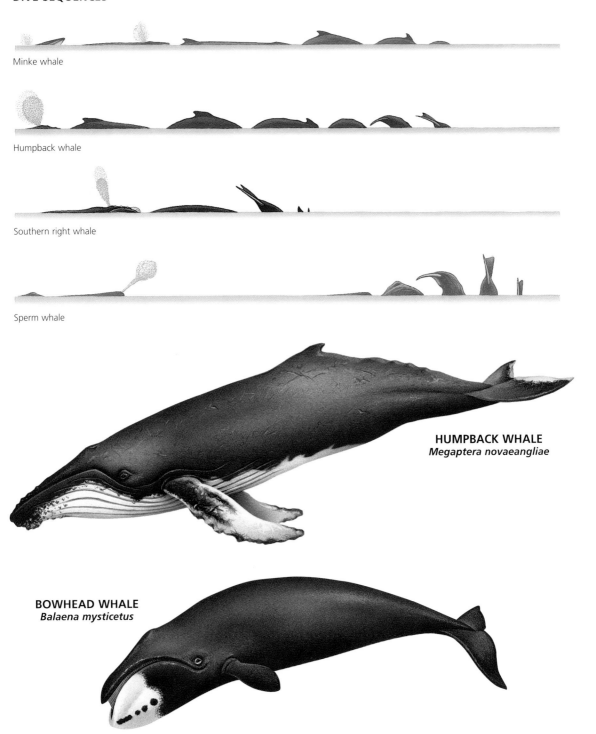

Minke whale

Humpback whale

Southern right whale

Sperm whale

HUMPBACK WHALE
Megaptera novaeangliae

BOWHEAD WHALE
Balaena mysticetus

Whales, Dolphins and Porpoises

ENDANGERED SPECIES

Vaquita
Phocoena sinus

Indus River dolphin
Platanista minor

Baiji
Lipotes vexillifer

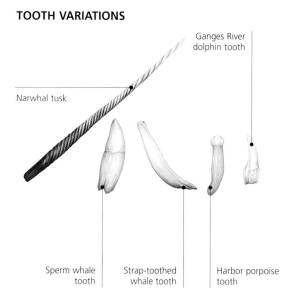

FINLESS PORPOISE
Neophocaena phocaenoides

HARBOR PORPOISE
Phocoena phocoena

TOOTH VARIATIONS

Ganges River
dolphin tooth

Narwhal tusk

Sperm whale
tooth

Strap-toothed
whale tooth

Harbor porpoise
tooth

SOUND PRODUCTION

Melon

Low density oil

High density oil

Blow hole

Nasal air sacs
and passages

Muscles that
alter melon
shape

"lips"—
sound source

DALL'S PORPOISE
Phocoenoides dalli

ORCA
Orcinus orca

DOLPHIN PROPULSION

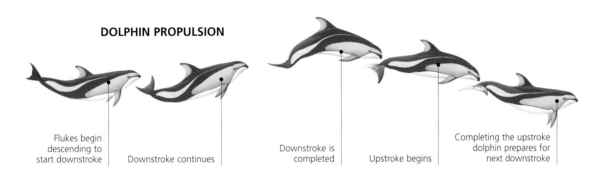

Flukes begin
descending to
start downstroke

Downstroke continues

Downstroke is
completed

Upstroke begins

Completing the upstroke
dolphin prepares for
next downstroke

PACIFIC WHITE-SIDED DOLPHIN
Lagenorhynchus obliquidens

Elephants

FOREST AFRICAN ELEPHANT
Loxodonta cyclotis

MAINLAND ASIAN ELEPHANT
Elephas maximus indicus

SUMATRAN ASIAN ELEPHANT
Elephas maximus sumatranus

SRI LANKAN ASIAN ELEPHANT
Elephas maximus maximus

AFRICAN AND ASIAN ELEPHANT DIFFERENCES

Large ears

Hips as high as shoulders

African elephant

Three toes

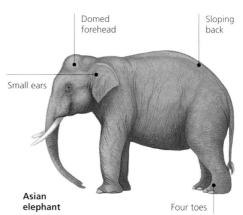

Domed forehead

Sloping back

Small ears

Asian elephant

Four toes

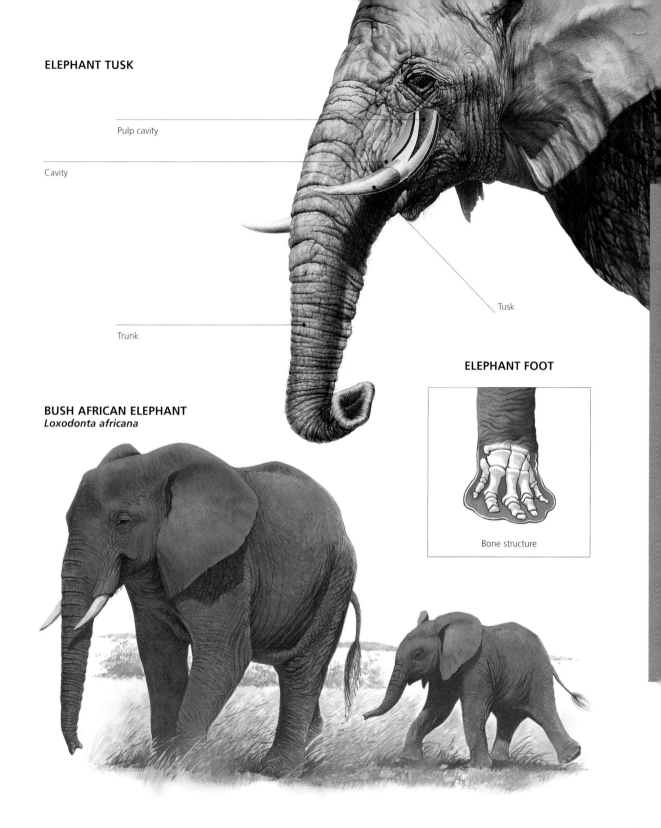

ELEPHANT TUSK

Pulp cavity

Cavity

Tusk

Trunk

ELEPHANT FOOT

Bone structure

BUSH AFRICAN ELEPHANT
Loxodonta africana

Hoofed Mammals

ZEBRA
Equus burchelli

WHITE RHINOCEROS
Ceratotherium simum

DROMEDARY CAMEL
Camelus dromedarius

Three toes

One toe or hoof

Two toes

BLACK RHINOCEROS
Diceros bicornis

GAUR
Bos gaurus

MOUNTAIN ANOA
Bubalus quarlesi

BARBARY SHEEP
Ammotragus lervia

BIGHORN SHEEP
Ovis canadensis

HIMALAYAN TAHR
Hemitragus jemlahicus

MUSK OX
Ovibos moschatus

WILD GOAT
Capra aegragus

Deer, Gazelles and Antelopes

Early spring

Late summer

Autumn

Winter

GROWING ANTLERS

BLUE WILDEBEEST
Connochaetes taurinus

WAPITI
Cervus elaphus

MOOSE
Alces alces

FOUR-HORNED ANTELOPE
Tetracerus quadricornus

GERENUK
Litocranius walleri

INDIAN ANTELOPE
Antilope cervicapra

Mammals

ANIMALS

276

BONTEBOK
Damaliscus dorcas

FALLOW DEER
Dama dama

THOMPSON'S GAZELLE
Gazella thompsonii

PUDU
Pudu puda

BANDED DUIKER
Cephalophus zebra

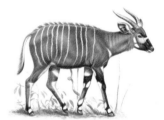

BONGO
Tragelaphus euryceros

SAIGA
Saiga tatarica

INDIAN MUNTJAC
Muntiacus muntjac

KLIPSPRINGER
Oreotragus oreotragus

REINDEER
Rangifer tarandus

GEMSBOK
Oryx gazella

GIANT SABLE ANTELOPE
Hippotragus niger variani

277

Rodents

GERBIL
Family *Muridae*

GIANT BLACK SQUIRREL
Ratufa bicolor

SOUTHERN FLYING SQUIRREL
Glaucomys volans

LEAST CHIPMUNK
Tamias minimus

COLUMBIAN GROUND SQUIRREL
Spermophilus columbianus

HOARY MARMOT
Marmota caligata

CAPYBARA
Hydrochaerus hydrochaeris

PATAGONIAN MARA
Dolichotis patagonum

CRESTED PORCUPINE
Hystrix cristata

GOLDEN AGOUTI
Dasyprocta leporina

PLAINS VISCACHA
Lagostomus maximus

EURASIAN RED SQUIRREL
Sciurus vulgaris

BLACK RAT
Rattus rattus

PREHENSILE-TAILED PORCUPINE
Coendou prehensilis

SPINY RAT
Proechimys sp.

279

Turtle and Tortoise Anatomy

TORTOISE SKELETON

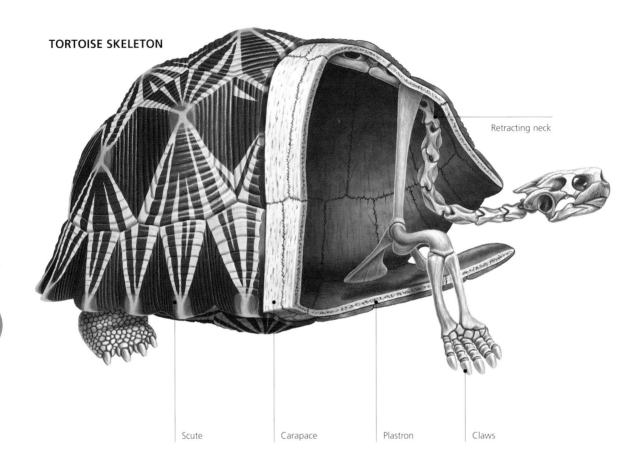

Retracting neck

Scute

Carapace

Plastron

Claws

LEG TYPES

Sea turtle

Land tortoise

Pond turtle

MUSK TURTLE
Sternotherus odoratus

Musk turtles produce
a strong, unpleasant
smell when picked up

ORNATE BOX TURTLE
Terrapene ornata

The box turtle pulls its
legs and head inside its
shell for protection

LOGGERHEAD SEA TURTLE
Caretta caretta

Sea turtles
"cry" to
remove salt
from their eyes

LAND TORTOISE SHELL
Domed shell, slow moving

SEMI-TERRESTRIAL TURTLE SHELL
Flattened shell for land and water

SEA TURTLE SHELL
Streamlined shell for swimming

POND TURTLE SHELL
Small flattened shell

Turtles and Tortoises

GREEN TURTLE
Chelonia mydas

SEA TURTLE
Family *Cheloniidae*

**EASTERN SPINY
SOFTSHELL TURTLE**
Apalone spinifera spinifera

TURTLE'S CARAPACE

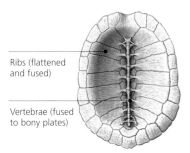

Ribs (flattened
and fused)

Vertebrae (fused
to bony plates)

View from below

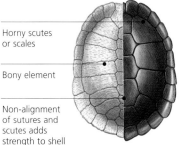

Horny scutes
or scales

Bony element

Non-alignment
of sutures and
scutes adds
strength to shell

View from above

TURTLE REPRODUCTION
Female green turtles (*Chelonia mydas*) leave the sea to lay their eggs on specific nesting beaches.

YELLOW-SPOTTED AMAZON
RIVER TURTLE
Podocnemis unifilis

TWIST-NECKED TURTLE
Platemys platycephala platycephala

PACIFIC HAWKSBILL TURTLE
Eretmochelys imbricata bissa

SOUTHERN LOGGERHEAD
MUSK TURTLE
Sternotherus minor minor

EASTERN BOX TURTLE
Terrapene carolina carolina

PANCAKE TORTOISE
Malacochersus tornieri

VIETNAMESE
BIG-HEADED TURTLE
Platysternon megacephalum shiui

PAINTED TURTLE
Chrysemys picta belli

DESERT TORTOISE
Gopherus agassizii

RADIATED TORTOISE
Asterochelys radiata

MALAYAN SNAIL-EATING TURTLE
Malayemys subtrijuga

SPINED TURTLE
Heosemys spinosa

Crocodiles and Alligators

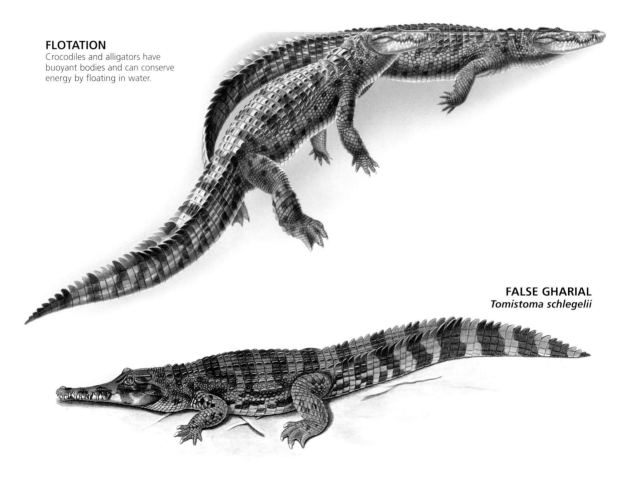

FLOTATION
Crocodiles and alligators have buoyant bodies and can conserve energy by floating in water.

FALSE GHARIAL
Tomistoma schlegelii

CUVIER'S DWARF CAIMAN
Paleosuchus palpebrosus

SNOUT VARIETIES

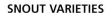

American crocodile, side view

American crocodile, top view

Gharial, side view

Gharial, top view

Black caiman, side view

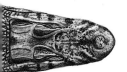

Black caiman, top view

AQUATIC ADAPTATIONS
Crocodiles and alligators can breathe while almost totally submerged as they have nostrils on the top of their snouts that remain above the water.

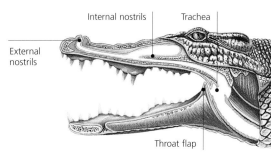

Internal nostrils   Trachea

External nostrils

Throat flap

GHARIAL ANATOMY

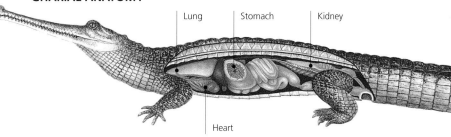

Lung   Stomach   Kidney

Heart

NILE CROCODILE
Crocodylus niloticus

Amphisbaenians and Tuataras

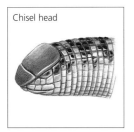

Chisel head

Shovel head

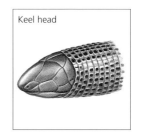

Keel head

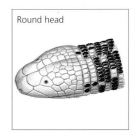

Round head

AMPHISBAENIAN HEAD TYPES

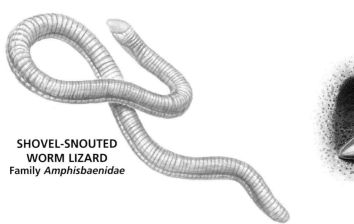

**SHOVEL-SNOUTED
WORM LIZARD**
Family *Amphisbaenidae*

KEEL-SNOUTED WORM LIZARD
Keel-snouted worm lizards occur in South
America and Africa.

SHOVEL-SNOUTED WORM LIZARD
This worm lizard grows up to 30 inches (75 cm)
long. It uses its hard head to push soil upwards
and compact it into the top of the tunnel.

Recessed mouth

Hard scale
on snout

Invisible eye

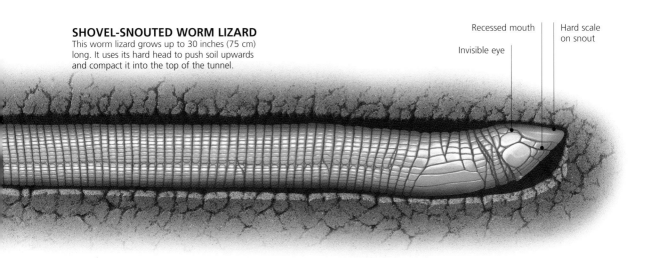

TUATARA
Sphenodon sp.
These ancient reptiles are found only in New Zealand.

NIGHT HUNTERS
Tuataras spend the day sleeping or basking in the sun at the entrance to their burrows. They hunt insects and other prey at night.

Female tuataras weigh about half as much as males and are about 6 inches (15 cm) shorter

GENDER DIFFERENCES

Male tuataras weigh up to 2.2 pounds (1 kg) and can grow up to 2 feet (60 cm) long

Male tuataras have larger spines on their necks and backs

287

Iguanas, Chameleons and Agamids

Reptiles

ANIMALS

CUBAN BROWN ANOLE
Anolis sagrei sagrei

BASILISK LIZARD
Basiliscus basiliscus

FIJIAN CRESTED IGUANA
Brachylophus vitiensis

COLLARED LIZARD
Croptaphytus collaris

BEARDED DRAGON LIZARD
Family *Agamidae*

MILITARY DRAGON
Ctenophorus isolepis gularis

MALAGASY CHAMELEON
Furcifer lateralis

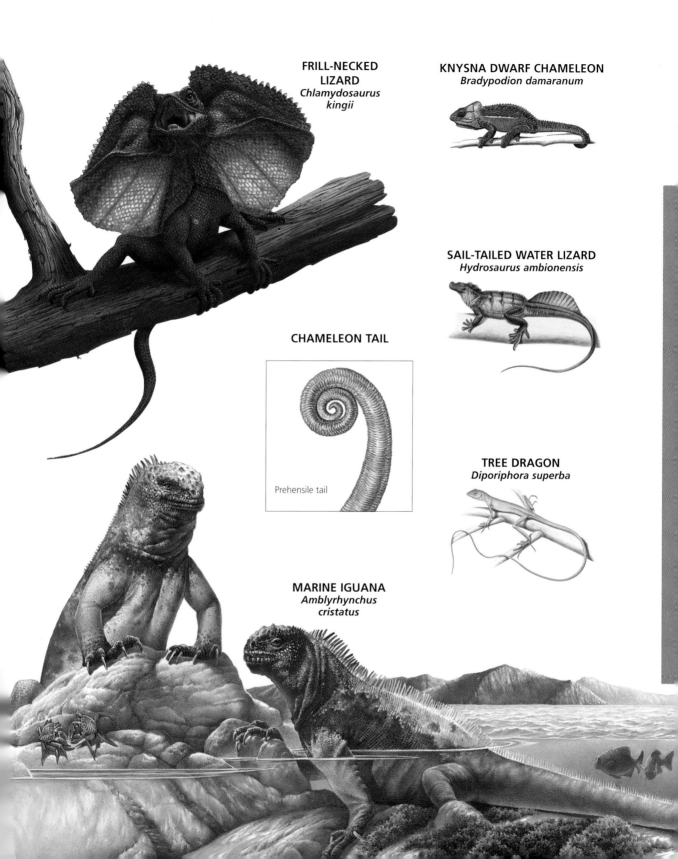

**FRILL-NECKED
LIZARD**
*Chlamydosaurus
kingii*

KNYSNA DWARF CHAMELEON
Bradypodion damaranum

SAIL-TAILED WATER LIZARD
Hydrosaurus ambionensis

CHAMELEON TAIL

Prehensile tail

TREE DRAGON
Diporiphora superba

MARINE IGUANA
*Amblyrhynchus
cristatus*

Geckos

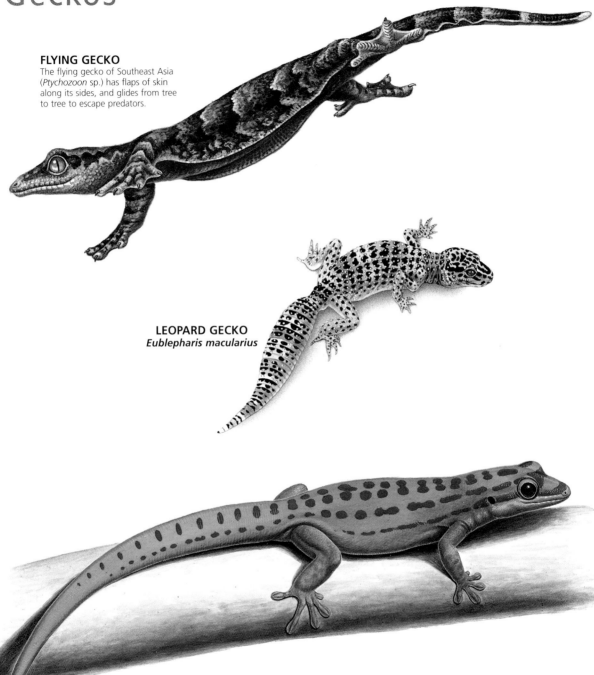

FLYING GECKO
The flying gecko of Southeast Asia
(*Ptychozoon* sp.) has flaps of skin
along its sides, and glides from tree
to tree to escape predators.

LEOPARD GECKO
Eublepharis macularius

BLUE-TAILED DAY GECKO
Phelsuma cepediana

SPOTTED VELVET GECKO
Oedura tryoni

Leaf-tailed
gecko tail

Desert gecko's
foot

RING-TAILED GECKO
Cyrtodactylus louisiadensis

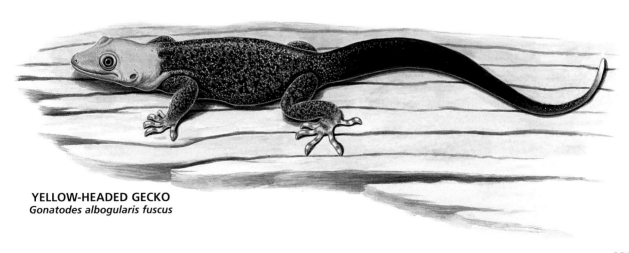

YELLOW-HEADED GECKO
Gonatodes albogularis fuscus

Lizards

FLAP-FOOTED LIZARD
Delma tincta

GOULD'S MONITOR LIZARD
Varanus gouldii

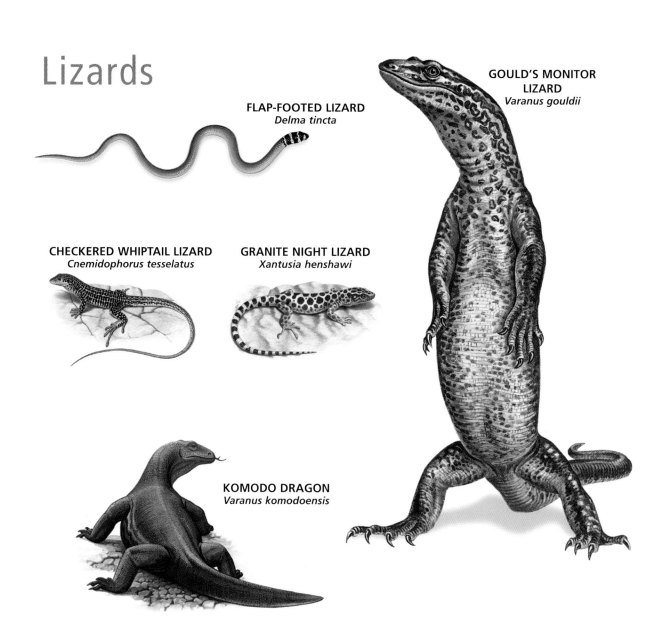

CHECKERED WHIPTAIL LIZARD
Cnemidophorus tesselatus

GRANITE NIGHT LIZARD
Xantusia henshawi

KOMODO DRAGON
Varanus komodoensis

ITALIAN WALL LIZARD
Podarcis sicula

DWARF FLAT LIZARD
Platysaurus guttatus

JUNGLE RUNNER
Ameiva ameiva

LIZARD TAILS

Skink tail

Shingleback
lizard tail

PERENTIE GOANNA
Varanus giganteus

RED-TAILED SKINK
Morethia ruficauda exquisita

LIZARD SENSES

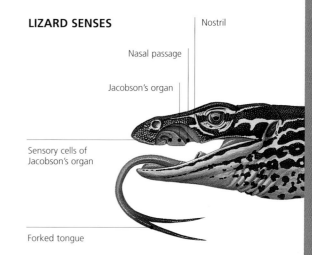

Nostril

Nasal passage

Jacobson's organ

Sensory cells of
Jacobson's organ

Forked tongue

PINK-TONGUED SKINK
Cyclodomorphus gerrardii

TONGUE TYPES

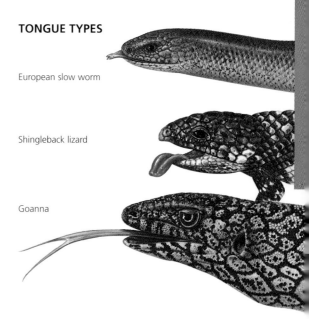

European slow worm

Shingleback lizard

Goanna

FIVE-LINED SKINK
Eumeces fasciatus

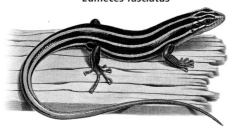

Snake Anatomy

Vine snake

SNAKE SKIN TYPES

Keeled scales

Granular scales

Smooth scales

SNAKE EYES

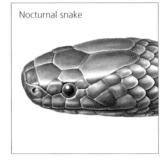

Nocturnal snake

FANG VARIETIES

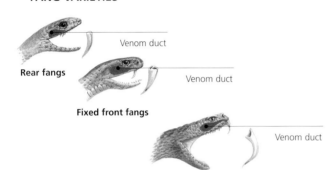

Rear fangs

Venom duct

Venom duct

Fixed front fangs

Venom duct

Swinging front fangs

Diurnal snake

RATTLESNAKE ANATOMY

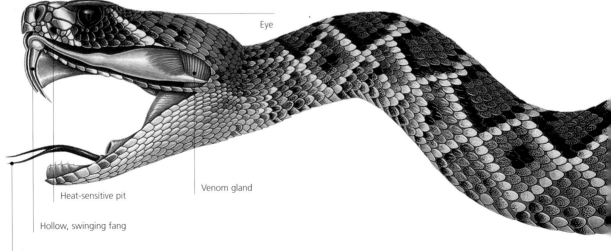

Eye

Heat-sensitive pit

Venom gland

Hollow, swinging fang

Forked tongue

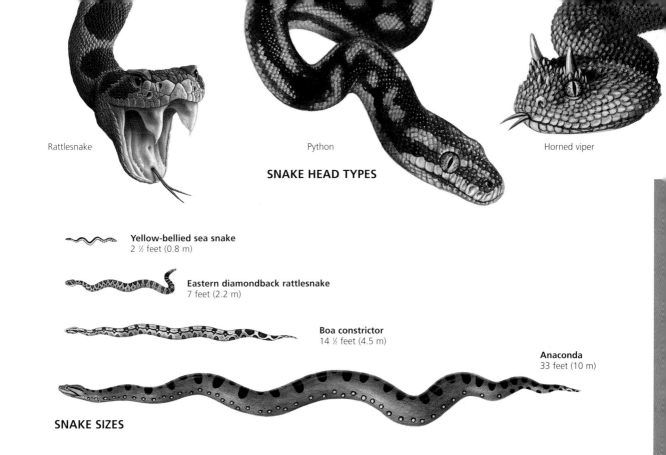

Rattlesnake

Python

Horned viper

SNAKE HEAD TYPES

Yellow-bellied sea snake
2 ½ feet (0.8 m)

Eastern diamondback rattlesnake
7 feet (2.2 m)

Boa constrictor
14 ½ feet (4.5 m)

Anaconda
33 feet (10 m)

SNAKE SIZES

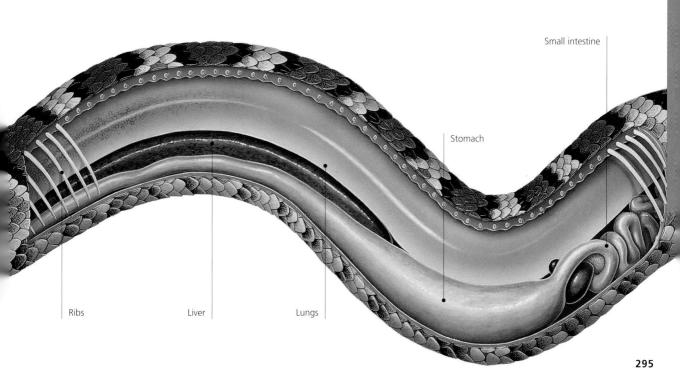

Small intestine

Stomach

Ribs

Liver

Lungs

Snakes

LANCE-HEADED RATTLESNAKE
Crotalus polystictus

RHINOCEROS VIPER
Bitis nasicornis

**SOUTH AMERICAN
CORAL PIPE SNAKE**
Anilius scytale

BLOOD PYTHON
Python curtus

BRAZILIAN RAINBOW BOA
Epicrates cenchria cenchria

KENYAN SAND BOA
Eryx colubrinus loveridgei

SPITTING COBRA
Spitting cobras (Family
Elapidae) spray venom at the
eyes of their attackers. They
can hit targets nearly 10 feet
(3 m) away.

URUTU
Bothrops alternatus

BLUNT-HEADED TREE SNAKE
Imantodes cenchoa

ARIZONA CORAL SNAKE
Micruroides euryxanthus

EASTERN RIBBON SNAKE
Thamnophis sauritus

CARPET PYTHON
Morelia spilota

YELLOW-LIPPED SEA KRAIT
Laticauda colubrina

BLOTCHED PIPE SNAKE
Cylindrophus maculatus

IMITATION COLORS

Some harmless snakes avoid predators
by copying the colors and patterns of
venomous snakes. The false coral
snake imitates the dangerous Mayan
coral snake.

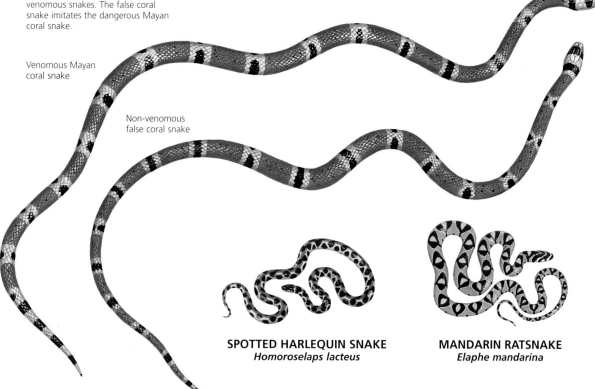

Venomous Mayan
coral snake

Non-venomous
false coral snake

SPOTTED HARLEQUIN SNAKE
Homoroselaps lacteus

MANDARIN RATSNAKE
Elaphe mandarina

Salamanders, Newts and Caecilians

CAECILIAN ANATOMY

The caecilian skull is powerfully built with a pointed snout and a recessed mouth, both of which are ideal for burrowing. Caecilians are the only vertebrates with an extra set of jaw-closing muscles.

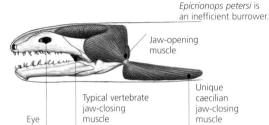

Epicrionops petersi is an inefficient burrower.

Jaw-opening muscle

Typical vertebrate jaw-closing muscle

Unique caecilian jaw-closing muscle

Eye

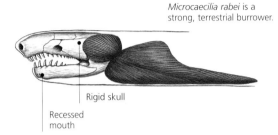

Microcaecilia rabei is a strong, terrestrial burrower.

Rigid skull

Recessed mouth

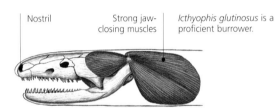

Nostril

Strong jaw-closing muscles

Icthyophis glutinosus is a proficient burrower.

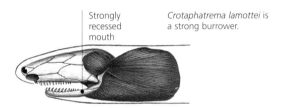

Strongly recessed mouth

Crotaphatrema lamottei is a strong burrower.

AQUATIC CAECILIAN
Typhlonectes natans

TERRESTRIAL CAECILIAN
Dermophis mexicanus

SOUTHEAST ASIAN CAECILIAN
Ichthyophis kohtaoensis

MARBLED NEWT
Triturus marmoratus

CONGO EEL
Amphiuma means

ALPINE NEWT
Triturus alpestris

TWO-LINED SALAMANDER
Eurycea bislineata cirrigera

RED SALAMANDER
Pseudotriton ruber

DWARF SIREN
Pseudobranchus striatus

MUDPUPPY
Necturus maculosus

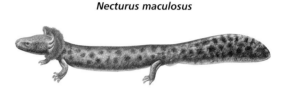

TIGER SALAMANDER
Ambystoma tigrinum mavortium

PACIFIC GIANT SALAMANDER
Dicamptodon ensatus

LIFECYCLE OF AN AMPHIBIOUS SALAMANDER

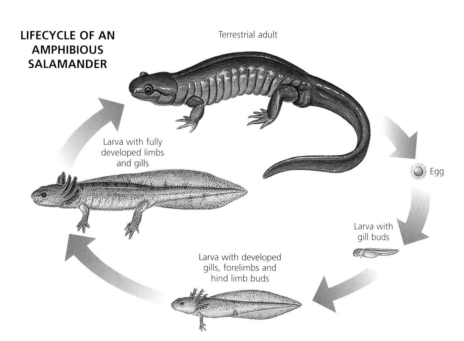

Terrestrial adult

Larva with fully developed limbs and gills

Egg

Larva with gill buds

Larva with developed gills, forelimbs and hind limb buds

Frogs and Toads

COUCH'S SPADEFOOT
Scaphiopus couchii

MEXICAN BURROWING TOAD
Rhinophrynus dorsalis

SOUTH AMERICAN BULLFROG
Leptodactylus pentadactylus

Amphibians

ANIMALS

LIFECYCLE OF A FROG

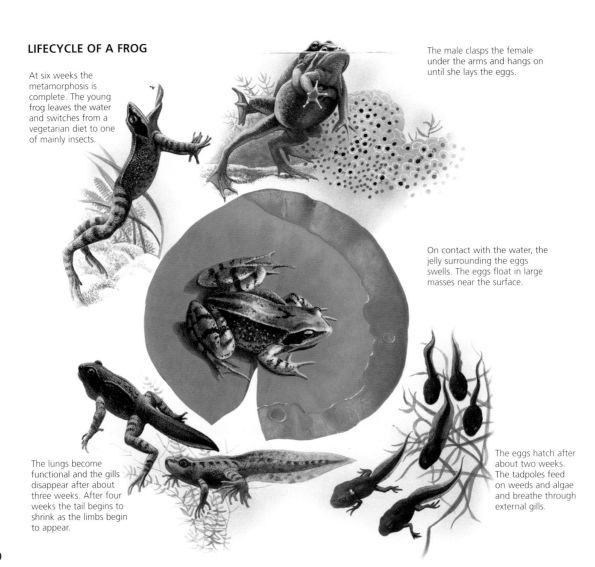

At six weeks the metamorphosis is complete. The young frog leaves the water and switches from a vegetarian diet to one of mainly insects.

The male clasps the female under the arms and hangs on until she lays the eggs.

On contact with the water, the jelly surrounding the eggs swells. The eggs float in large masses near the surface.

The lungs become functional and the gills disappear after about three weeks. After four weeks the tail begins to shrink as the limbs begin to appear.

The eggs hatch after about two weeks. The tadpoles feed on weeds and algae and breathe through external gills.

ORNATE HORNED TOAD
Ceratophrys ornata

TAILED FROG
Ascaphus truei

WESTERN BARKING FROG
Eleutherodactylus augusti cactorum

EUROPEAN PAINTED FROG
Discoglossus pictus

CAPE CLAWED FROG
Xenopus gilli

ASIAN HORNED TOAD
Megophyrus nasuta

Frogs and Toads

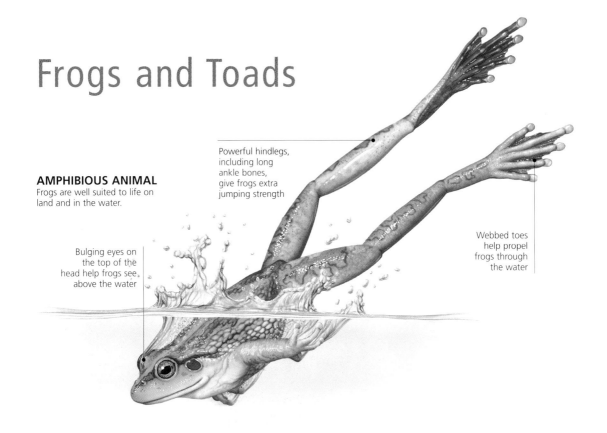

AMPHIBIOUS ANIMAL
Frogs are well suited to life on land and in the water.

Powerful hindlegs, including long ankle bones, give frogs extra jumping strength

Webbed toes help propel frogs through the water

Bulging eyes on the top of the head help frogs see above the water

SPOTTED GRASS FROG
Limnodynastes tasmaniensis

CRUCIFIX TOAD
Notaden bennettii

LEOPARD TOAD
Bufo pardalis

CORROBOREE FROG
Pseudophryne corroboree

BURROWING TREEFROG
Pternohyla fodiens

GREEN AND GOLDEN BELL FROG
Litoria aurea

FUNEREAL POISON FROG
Phyllobates lugubris

ORANGE AND BLACK POISON FROG
Dendrobates leucomelas

VARIABLE HARLEQUIN FROG
Atelopus varius

ASIATIC CLIMBING TOAD
Pedostibes hosii

STRAWBERRY POISON FROG
Dendrobates pumilio

RED-EYED TREEFROG
Agalychnis callidryas

Frogs and Toads

ORNATE BURROWING FROG
Hildebrandtia ornata

PICKEREL FROG
Rana palustris

SOLOMON ISLANDS TREEFROG
Platymantis guppyi

ASIAN PAINTED FROG
Kaloula pulchra

EASTERN NARROW-MOUTHED TOAD
Gastrophryne carolinensis

RED-BANDED CREVICE CREEPER
Phrynomerus bifasciatus

CAPE GHOST FROG
Heleophryne purcelli

PARADOX FROG
Pseudis paradoxa

DARWIN'S FROG
Rhinoderma darwinii

GOLD FROG
Brachycephalus ephippium

WALLACE'S FLYING FROG
Racophorus nigropalmatus

PAINTED REED FROG
Hyperolius marmoratus

SENEGAL RUNNING FROG
Kassina senegalensis

Shark Anatomy

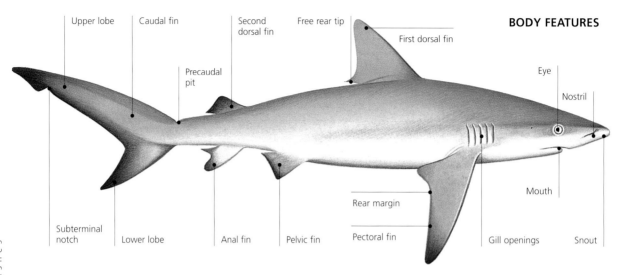

BODY FEATURES

Upper lobe

Caudal fin

Second dorsal fin

Free rear tip

First dorsal fin

Precaudal pit

Eye

Nostril

Subterminal notch

Lower lobe

Anal fin

Pelvic fin

Rear margin

Pectoral fin

Mouth

Gill openings

Snout

INTERNAL ANATOMY

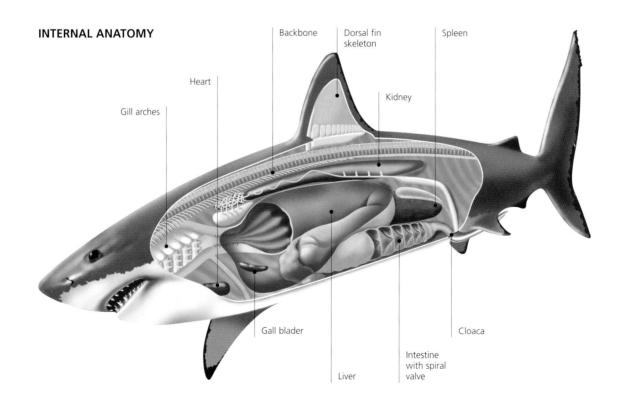

Backbone

Dorsal fin skeleton

Spleen

Heart

Kidney

Gill arches

Gall blader

Liver

Intestine with spiral valve

Cloaca

VARIETIES OF TAILS

Cookiecutter shark

Thresher shark

Porbeagle shark

Mako shark

Nurse shark

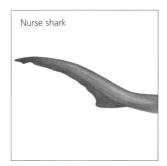

Tiger shark

SHARK SENSES

Vibration-sensitive nerve cells, arranged in a series called the lateral line, run along a shark's sides. They help the shark to "feel" objects some distance away.

Sharks can also feel contact on their skin

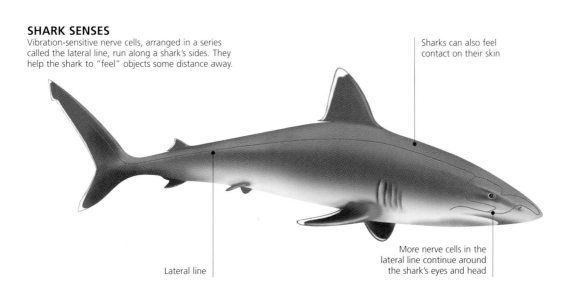

Lateral line

More nerve cells in the lateral line continue around the shark's eyes and head

Shark Variations

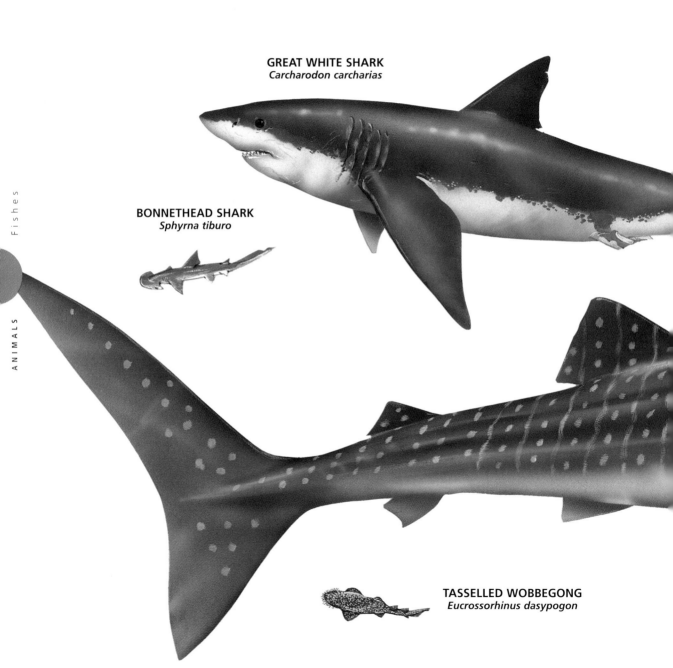

GREAT WHITE SHARK
Carcharodon carcharias

BONNETHEAD SHARK
Sphyrna tiburo

TASSELLED WOBBEGONG
Eucrossorhinus dasypogon

ANIMALS

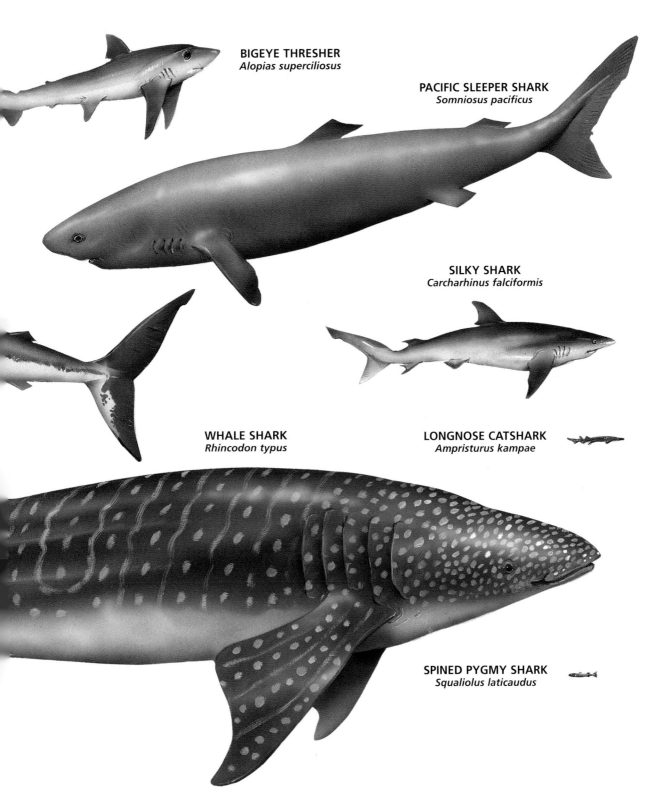

BIGEYE THRESHER
Alopias superciliosus

PACIFIC SLEEPER SHARK
Somniosus pacificus

SILKY SHARK
Carcharhinus falciformis

WHALE SHARK
Rhincodon typus

LONGNOSE CATSHARK
Ampristurus kampae

SPINED PYGMY SHARK
Squaliolus laticaudus

Rays and Chimaeras

RAY FEATURES

Upperside view

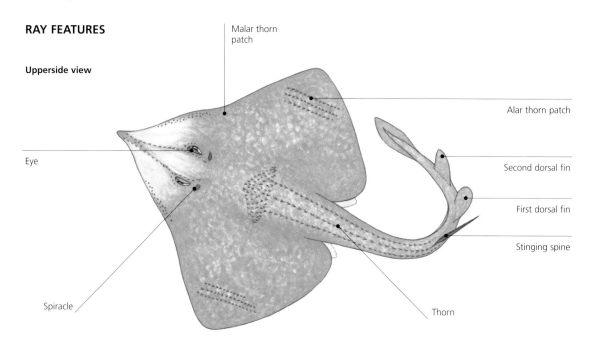

Malar thorn patch

Alar thorn patch

Eye

Second dorsal fin

First dorsal fin

Stinging spine

Spiracle

Thorn

Underside view

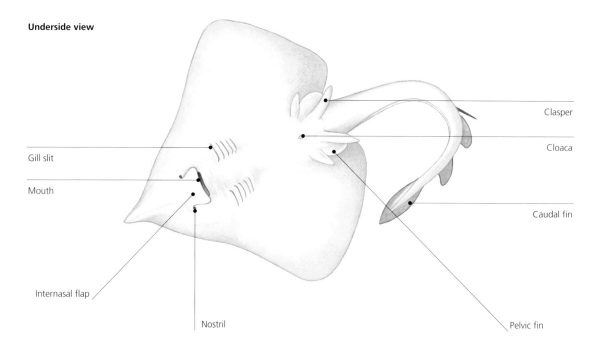

Clasper

Cloaca

Gill slit

Mouth

Caudal fin

Internasal flap

Nostril

Pelvic fin

Fishes

ANIMALS

PORT DAVEY SKATE
Raja sp.

LEG SKATE
Anacanthobatis sp.

BLUE SKATE
Notoraja sp.

GUITARFISH
Family *Rhinobatidae*

OCELLATED FRESHWATER STINGRAY
Potamotrygon motoro

BLUNT-NOSED CHIMAERA
Hydrolagus colliei

SIXGILL STINGRAY
Hexatrygon bickelli

BLIND ELECTRIC RAY
Typhlonarke aysoni

SKATE
Family *Rajidae*

ELEPHANTFISH
Family *Callorhynchidae*

SPOOKFISH
Family *Rhinochimaeridae*

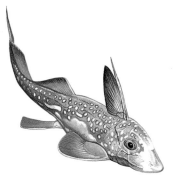

SHORTNOSE CHIMAERA
Family *Chimaeridae*

Bony Fishes

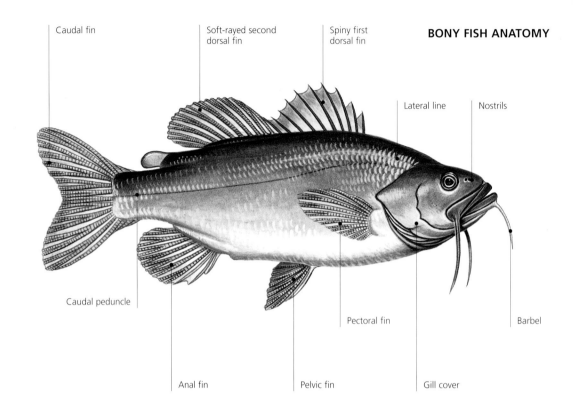

BONY FISH ANATOMY

Caudal fin

Soft-rayed second dorsal fin

Spiny first dorsal fin

Lateral line

Nostrils

Caudal peduncle

Anal fin

Pelvic fin

Gill cover

Pectoral fin

Barbel

BUTTERFLYFISH
Pantodon buchholzi

COELACANTH
Latimeria chalumnae

ELEPHANTNOSE
Gnathonemus petersi

SOUTH AMERICAN LUNGFISH
Lepidosiren paradoxa

STERLET
Acipenser ruthenus

SPOTTED GAR
Lepisosteus oculatus

RIBBON EEL
Rhinomuraena quaesita

SPOTTED AFRICAN LUNGFISH
Protopterus dolloi

BLACK-SPOTTED MORAY EEL
Gymnothorax favagineus

AUSTRALIAN LUNGFISH
Neoceratodus forsteri

CLOWN KNIFEFISH
Chitala chitala

Bony Fishes

STRIPED JULIE
Julidochromis regani

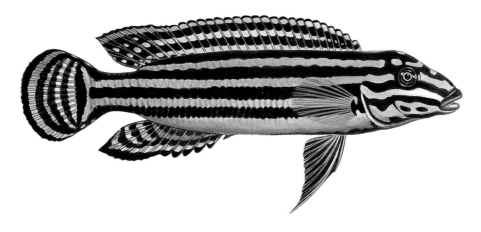

MEYER'S BUTTERFLYFISH
Chaetodon meyeri

MOORISH IDOL
Zanclus cornutus

PURPLEQUEEN
Pseudanthis tuka

LAKE MALAWI ZEBRA CICHLID
Pseudotropheus zebra

LICORICE GOURAMI
Paraosphromenus dreissneri

GIANT GROUPER
Epinephalus lanceolatus

SIXLINE SOAPFISH
Grammistes sexlineatus

VELVET CICHLID
Astronotus ocellatus

SOUTHEAST ASIAN PIKEHEAD
Luciocephalus pulcher

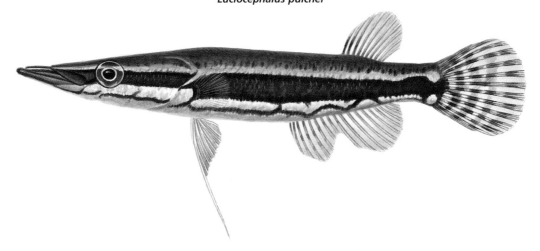

Freshwater Fishes

RED-BELLIED PIRANHA
Pygocentrus nattereri

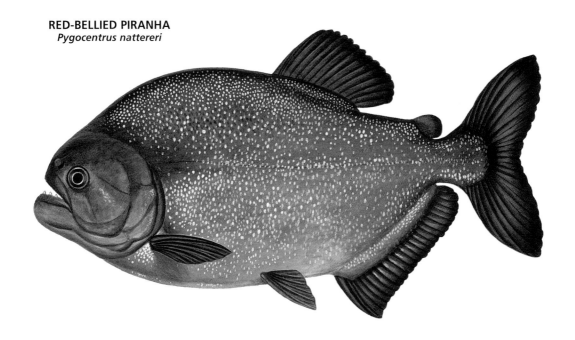

ELECTRIC CATFISH
Malapterurus electricus

ZEBRA DANIO
Brachydanio rerio

MARBLED HATCHETFISH
Carnegiella strigata

STRIPED HEADSTANTER
Anostomus anostomus

SADDLED HILLSTREAM LOACH
Homaloptera orthogoniata

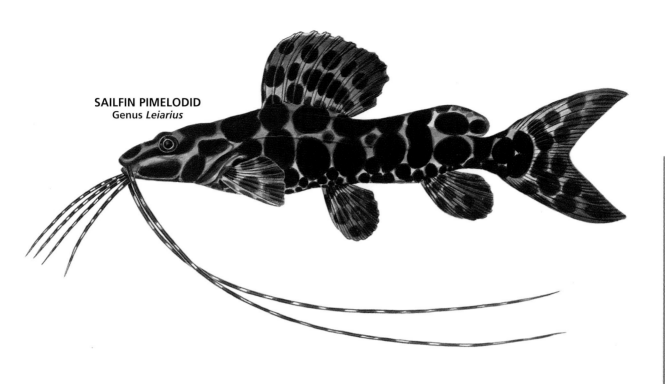

SAILFIN PIMELODID
Genus Leiarius

SLIMY LOACH
Acantophthalmus myersi

WHITE-SPOTTED SPINY EEL
Mastacembelus armatus

Freshwater Fishes

STEEL-BLUE KILLIFISH
Aphyosemion gardneri

CLOWN KILLIFISH
Aplocheilus annulatus

MALAYAN HALFBEAK
Dermogenys pusilla

PIRATE PERCH
Aphredoderus sayanus

AUSTRALIAN RAINBOWFISH
Melanotaenia boesemani

CUATRO OJOS
Anableps anableps

MADAGASCAR RAINBOWFISH
Bedotia geayi

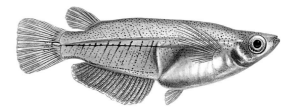

JAVANESE RICEFISH
Oryzias javaniaus

SWORDTAIL
Xiphophorus helleri

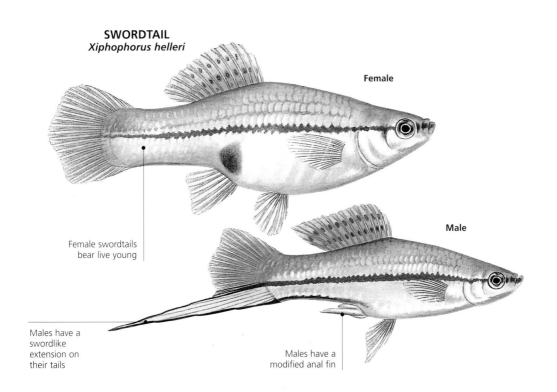

Female

Male

Female swordtails
bear live young

Males have a
swordlike
extension on
their tails

Males have a
modified anal fin

Ocean Fishes

VARIEGATED LIZARDFISH
Synodus variegatus

Fishes

ANIMALS

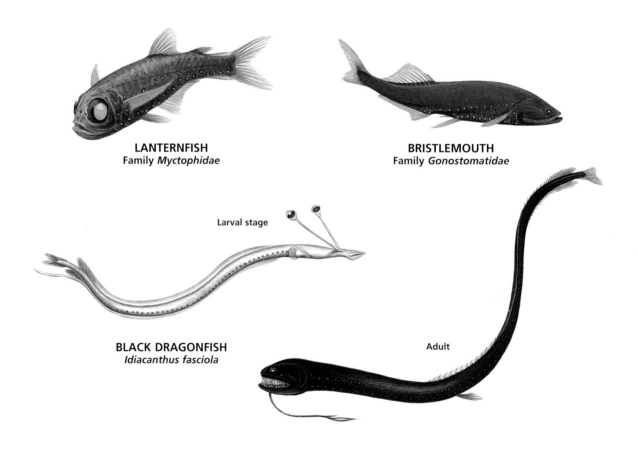

LANTERNFISH
Family *Myctophidae*

BRISTLEMOUTH
Family *Gonostomatidae*

Larval stage

Adult

BLACK DRAGONFISH
Idiacanthus fasciola

ARTHUR'S PARAGALAXIAS
Paragalaxias mesotes

ALASKA BLACKFISH
Dallia pectoralis

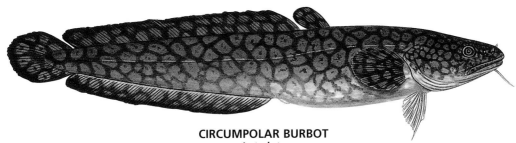

CIRCUMPOLAR BURBOT
Lota lota

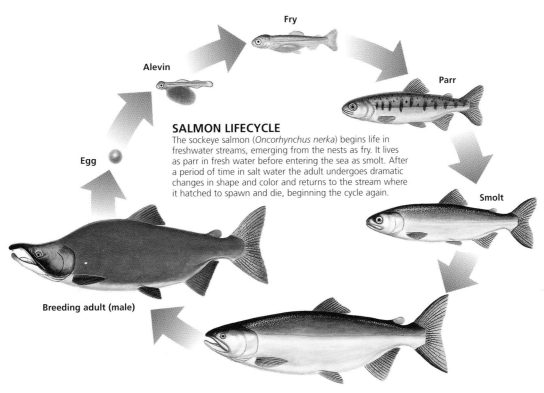

Fry

Alevin

Parr

Egg

SALMON LIFECYCLE

The sockeye salmon (*Oncorhynchus nerka*) begins life in freshwater streams, emerging from the nests as fry. It lives as parr in fresh water before entering the sea as smolt. After a period of time in salt water the adult undergoes dramatic changes in shape and color and returns to the stream where it hatched to spawn and die, beginning the cycle again.

Smolt

Breeding adult (male)

Sea-going adult

Ocean Fishes

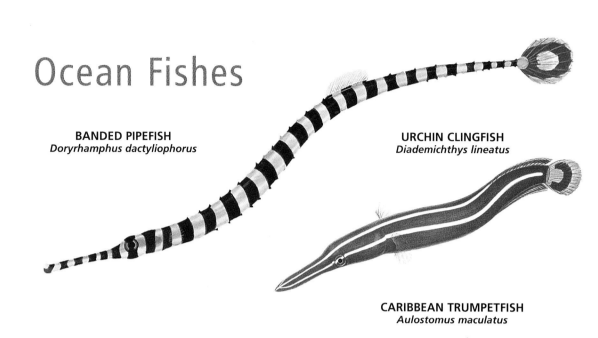

BANDED PIPEFISH
Doryrhamphus dactyliophorus

URCHIN CLINGFISH
Diademichthys lineatus

CARIBBEAN TRUMPETFISH
Aulostomus maculatus

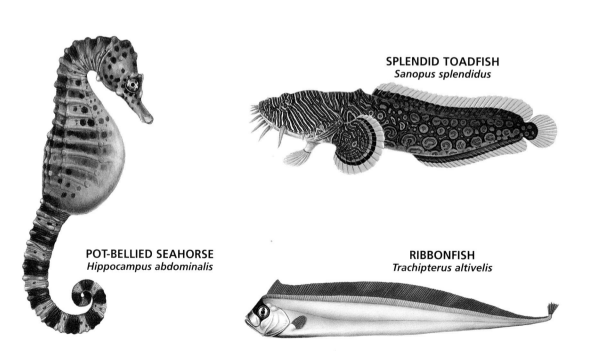

SPLENDID TOADFISH
Sanopus splendidus

POT-BELLIED SEAHORSE
Hippocampus abdominalis

RIBBONFISH
Trachipterus altivelis

OPAH
Lampris guttatus

AUSTRALIAN PINEAPPLEFISH
Cleidopus gloriamaris

SPOTTED OREO
Pseudocyttus maculatus

FLASHLIGHT FISH
Photoblepharon palpebratus

SOUTHERN ROUGHY
Trachichthys australis

TIGER ROCKFISH
Sebastes nigrocinctus

COCKATOO WASPFISH
Ablabys taenionotus

PAXTON'S WHIPNOSE ANGLER
Gigantactis paxtoni

LUMPSUCKER
Cyclopterus lumpus

MANDARIN FISH
Synchiropus splendidus

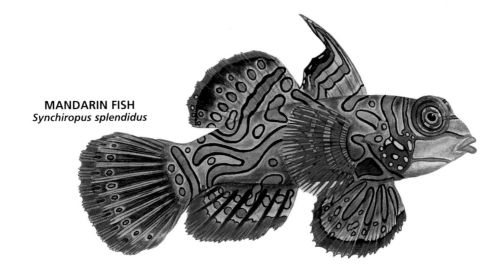

Ocean Fishes

Fishes

ANIMALS

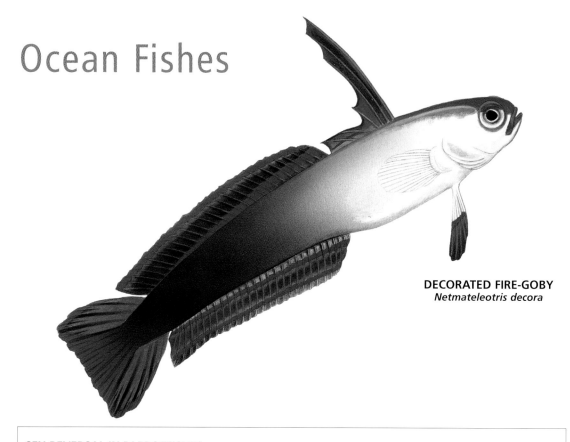

DECORATED FIRE-GOBY
Netmateleotris decora

SEX REVERSAL IN PARROTFISHES
In its lifetime the highfin parrotfish (*Scarus altipinnis*) travels through three color phases as well as gender change.

Juvenile—usually female, not sexually active

Initial phase—usually female

Terminal phase—always a mature male

SPINE-CHEEK ANEMONEFISH
Premnas biaculeatus

HARLEQUIN TUSKFISH
Choerodon fasciatus

DORIA'S BUMBLEBEE GOBY
Brachygobius doriae

BLACK-HEADED BLENNY
Lipophrys nigriceps

BLUEBANDED GOBY
Lythrypnus dalli

FIGURE-EIGHT PUFFER
Tetraodon biocellatus

IMITATION PUFFERFISH

As a defense mechanism the mimic filefish (*Paraluteres prionurus*) has evolved to look almost exactly like the highly toxic black-saddled puffer (*Canthigaster valentini*).

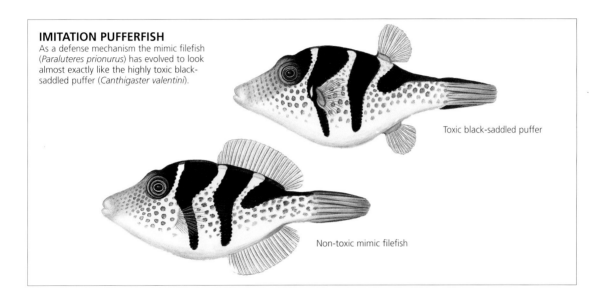

Toxic black-saddled puffer

Non-toxic mimic filefish

CLOWN TRIGGERFISH
Balistoides conspicillum

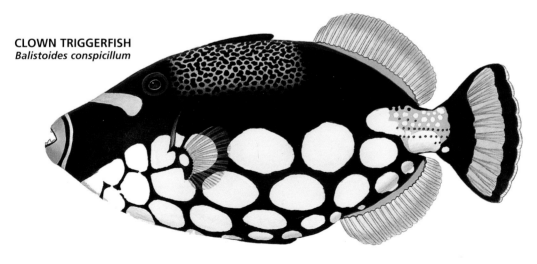

Insect Anatomy

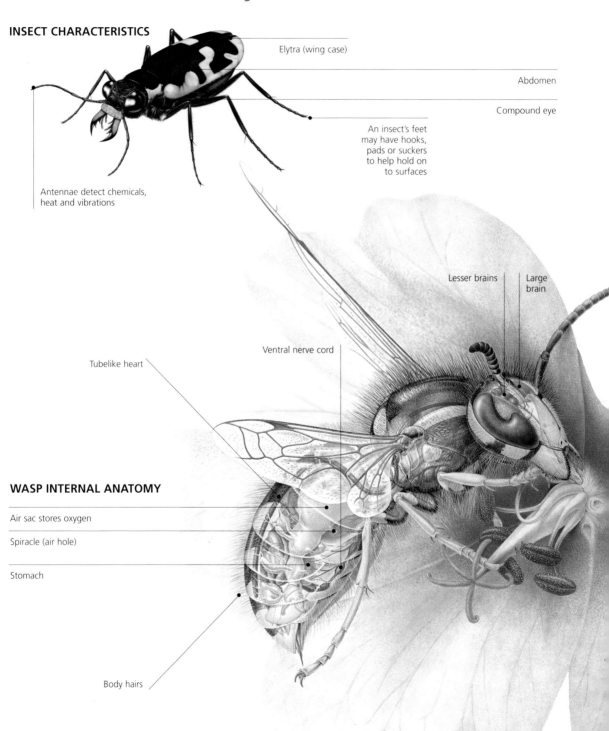

INSECT CHARACTERISTICS

Elytra (wing case)

Abdomen

Compound eye

An insect's feet may have hooks, pads or suckers to help hold on to surfaces

Antennae detect chemicals, heat and vibrations

Lesser brains

Large brain

Ventral nerve cord

Tubelike heart

WASP INTERNAL ANATOMY

Air sac stores oxygen

Spiracle (air hole)

Stomach

Body hairs

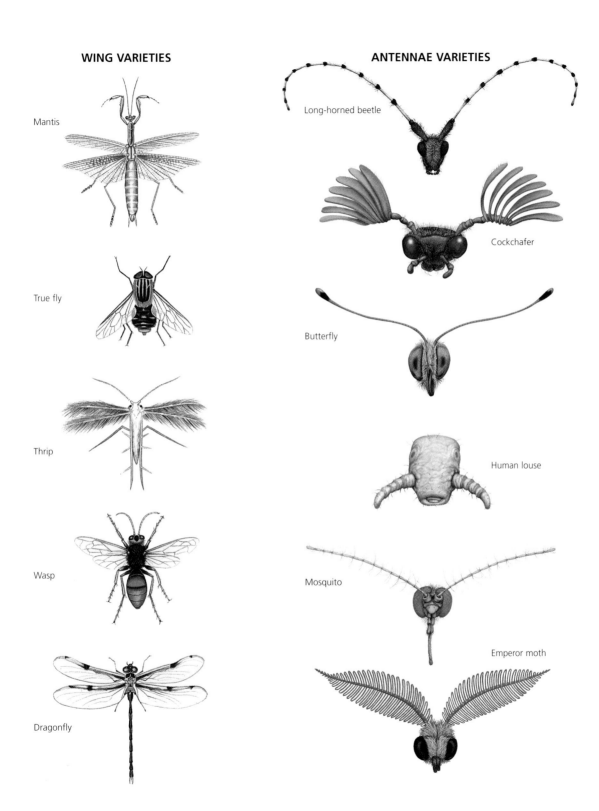

WING VARIETIES

Mantis

True fly

Thrip

Wasp

Dragonfly

ANTENNAE VARIETIES

Long-horned beetle

Cockchafer

Butterfly

Human louse

Mosquito

Emperor moth

Beetles and Bugs

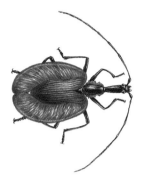

VIOLIN BEETLE
Family *Buprestidae*

WEEVIL
Family *Curculionidae*

GIRAFFE WEEVIL
Family *Brentidae*

FIVE-SPOTTED LADYBIRD
Family *Coccinellidae*

TEN-SPOTTED LADYBIRD
Family *Coccinellidae*

TORTOISE BEETLE
Family *Chrysomelidae*

STINK BUG
Family *Pentatomidae*

SOUTH AMERICAN LONGHORN BEETLE
Family *Cerambycidae*

LONG-HORNED BEETLE
Family *Cerambycidae*

LADYBIRD IN FLIGHT

BOX ELDER BUG
Family *Rhopalidae*

Adult   Nymph

BEE-EATING BEETLE
Family *Cleridae*

BLISTER BEETLE
Family *Meloidae*

HARLEQUIN BEETLE
Family *Cerambycidae*

ROVE BEETLE
Family *Staphylinidae*

CARDINAL BEETLE FLIGHT
Family *Pyrochroidae*

Takeoff

In flight

Butterflies and Moths

SWALLOWTAIL BUTTERFLY
Family *Papilionidae*

HELICONIID MIMIC BUTTERFLY
Family *Nymphalidae*

ORCHARD BUTTERFLY CATERPILLAR
Family *Papilionidae*

SILK MOTH CATERPILLAR
Family *Bombycidae*

HERCULES MOTH CATERPILLAR
Family *Saturniidae*

MALAY LACEWING BUTTERFLY
Cethosia hypsea hypsina

88 BUTTERFLY
Family *Nymphalidae*

PAINTED LADY BUTTERFLY
Family *Nymphalidae*

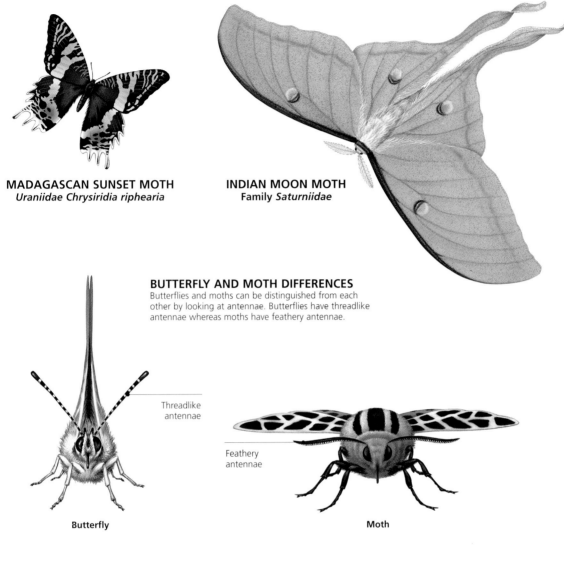

MADAGASCAN SUNSET MOTH
Uraniidae Chrysiridia riphearia

INDIAN MOON MOTH
Family *Saturniidae*

BUTTERFLY AND MOTH DIFFERENCES

Butterflies and moths can be distinguished from each other by looking at antennae. Butterflies have threadlike antennae whereas moths have feathery antennae.

Threadlike antennae

Feathery antennae

Butterfly

Moth

SHEEP MOTH
Family *Saturniidae*

YELLOW EMPEROR MOTH
Family *Saturniidae*

FIVE-SPOTTED BURNET MOTH
Family *Sphingidae*

Bees, Wasps and Ants

POLLINATION

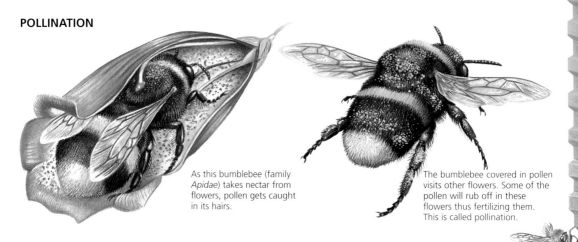

As this bumblebee (family *Apidae*) takes nectar from flowers, pollen gets caught in its hairs.

The bumblebee covered in pollen visits other flowers. Some of the pollen will rub off in these flowers thus fertilizing them. This is called pollination.

MUD DAUBER
Family *Sphecidae*

TORYMID WASP
Family *Torymidae*

BEE HIVE

Larva

HAIRY-LEGGED MINING BEE
Family *Andrenidae*

HORNET
Family *Vespidae*

Cell

Larva in a capped cell spins a cocoon and pupates for several weeks

A worker bee caps the cell of a mature larva with a wax seal

SPIDER WASP
Family *Pompilidae*

COW KILLER WASP
Family *Mutillidae*

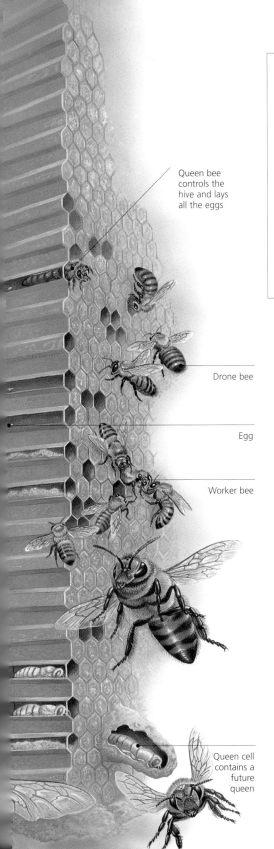

Queen bee controls the hive and lays all the eggs

Drone bee

Egg

Worker bee

Queen cell contains a future queen

BIG-HEADED ANT
Family *Formicidae*

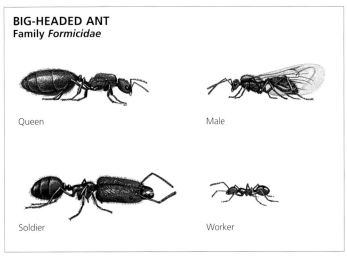

Queen

Male

Soldier

Worker

ANT
Family *Formicidae*

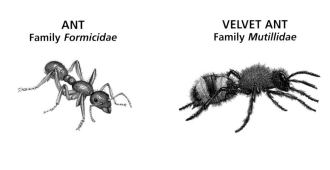

VELVET ANT
Family *Mutillidae*

BULLDOG ANT
Myrmecia sp.

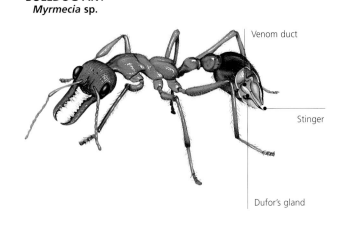

Venom duct

Stinger

Dufor's gland

Flies and Dragonflies

DEER FLY IN MOTION
Family *Tabanidae*

Front edge of
wings raised

Upstroke

MOSQUITO
Family *Culicidae*

Front edge
of wings
begins to dip

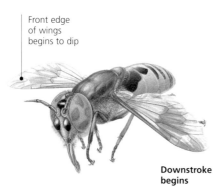

Downstroke
begins

GREEN BOTTLE FLY
Family *Calliphoridae*

Wings push air backward,
thrusting the fly forward

Downstroke
completed

HOVER FLY
Family *Syrphidae*

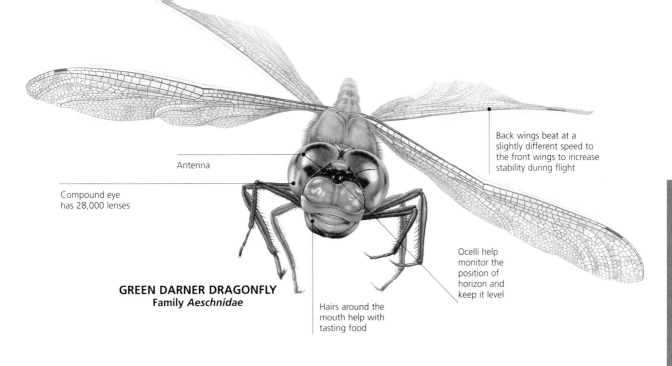

Antenna

Compound eye
has 28,000 lenses

Back wings beat at a
slightly different speed to
the front wings to increase
stability during flight

Ocelli help
monitor the
position of
horizon and
keep it level

Hairs around the
mouth help with
tasting food

GREEN DARNER DRAGONFLY
Family *Aeschnidae*

SOLDIER FLY
Family *Stratiomyidae*

HAIRY BEE FLY
Family *Bombyliidae*

MIDGE
Family *Chironomidae*

FLY FOOD

House flies eat most
organic matter.

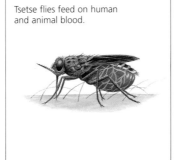

Tsetse flies feed on human
and animal blood.

Fruit flies feed on
rotting fruit.

Grasshoppers and Crickets

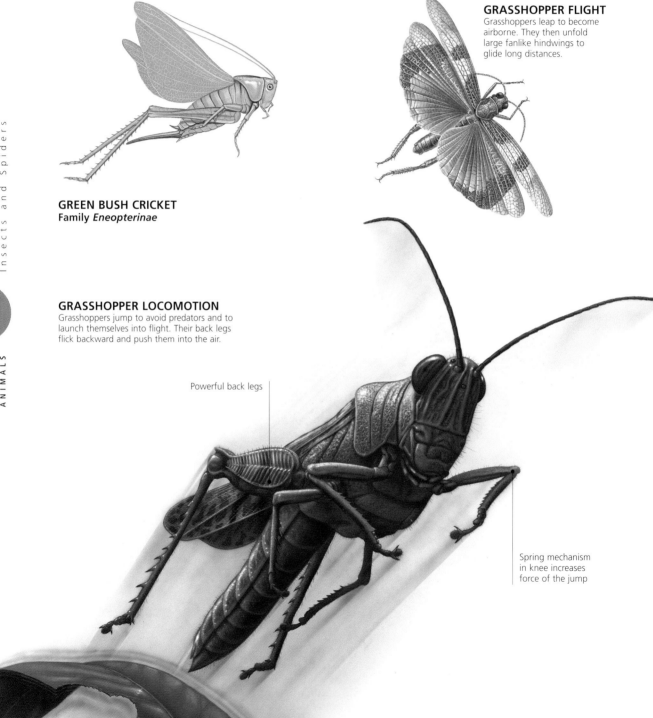

GREEN BUSH CRICKET
Family *Eneopterinae*

GRASSHOPPER FLIGHT
Grasshoppers leap to become airborne. They then unfold large fanlike hindwings to glide long distances.

GRASSHOPPER LOCOMOTION
Grasshoppers jump to avoid predators and to launch themselves into flight. Their back legs flick backward and push them into the air.

Powerful back legs

Spring mechanism in knee increases force of the jump

FIELD CRICKET
Family *Gryllidae*

JERUSALEM CRICKET
Family *Stenopelmatidae*

GRASSHOPPER SENSES
Grasshoppers and locusts have ears on their abdomen. They are particularly sensitive to calls from their own species.

DESERT LOCUST
Family *Acrididae*

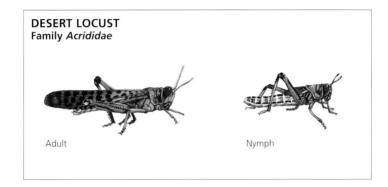

Adult

Nymph

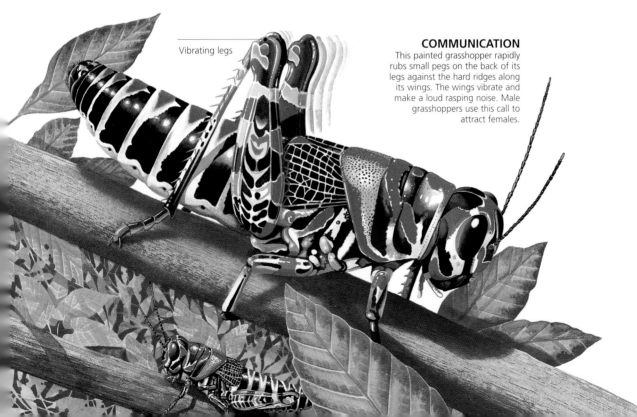

Vibrating legs

COMMUNICATION
This painted grasshopper rapidly rubs small pegs on the back of its legs against the hard ridges along its wings. The wings vibrate and make a loud rasping noise. Male grasshoppers use this call to attract females.

Spider Anatomy

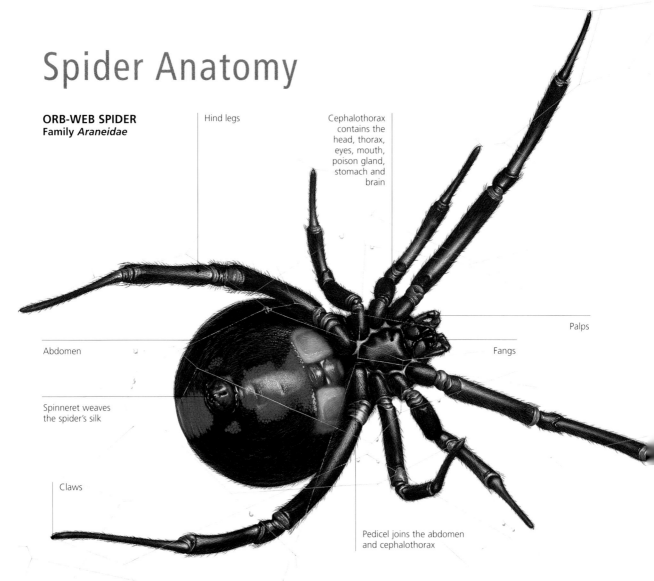

ORB-WEB SPIDER
Family *Araneidae*

Hind legs

Cephalothorax contains the head, thorax, eyes, mouth, poison gland, stomach and brain

Palps

Abdomen

Fangs

Spinneret weaves the spider's silk

Claws

Pedicel joins the abdomen and cephalothorax

SPIDER FANGS

Fangs hinge downward

Fangs hinge sideways

SPIDER EYES

Huntsman spider

Woodlouse-eating spider

Crab spider

Ogre-faced spider

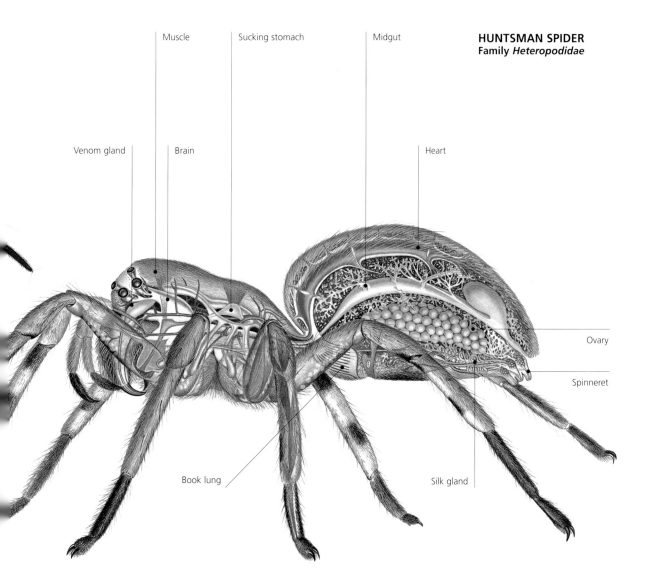

Muscle

Sucking stomach

Midgut

Venom gland

Brain

Heart

Ovary

Spinneret

Book lung

Silk gland

HUNTSMAN SPIDER
Family *Heteropodidae*

Spider Varieties

JUMPING SPIDER
Family *Salticidae*

WHITE LADY SPIDER
Family *Sparassidae*

TRAPDOOR SPIDER
Family *Ctenizidae*

HUNTSMAN SPIDER
Family *Heteropodidae*

TARANTULA
Family *Theraphosidae*

COMB-FOOTED SPIDER
Family *Theridiidae*

LYNX SPIDER
Family *Oxyopidae*

RED WIDOW SPIDER
Family *Theridiidae*

HUNTSMAN SPIDER LIFECYCLE

Eggs and egg sac

Spiderling

Juvenile

Adult

SPINY ORB WEAVER
Family *Araneidae*

LONG-JAWED ORB WEAVER
Family *Araneidae*

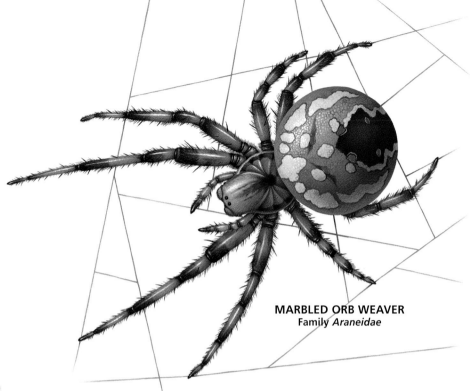

MARBLED ORB WEAVER
Family *Araneidae*

CLOSE RELATIVES

Northern black widow spider
Family *Theridiidae*

Redback spider
Family *Theridiidae*

MOUSE SPIDER
Missulena sp.

CRAB SPIDER
Family *Thomisidae*

Spider Behavior

SPIDER WEB VARIETIES

Orb web

Sheet web

Lace-sheet web

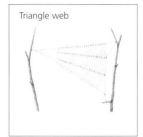

Triangle web

VENOMOUS SPIDERS

Insects and Spiders

ANIMALS

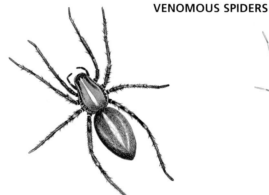

Brazilian wandering spider
Family *Ctenidae*

Violin spider
Family *Loxoscelidae*

Southern black widow spider
Family *Theridiidae*

Funnel-web spider
Family *Dipluridae*

SHEDDING SKIN

Old exoskeleton splits on edge of the cephalothorax.

Old skin on abdomen comes away.

Spider pulls legs clear.

New exoskeleton hardens.

SPIDER DISGUISES

Scorpion spiders (family *Araneidae*) hang in the air imitating a dead leaf to discourage predators.

This Brazilian ant-mimicking spider (family *Araneidae*) uses its disguise to get up close to ants and eat them.

As a defense mechanism this jumping spider from Borneo (family *Salticidae*) imitates the dangerous Asian multillid wasp.

JUMPING SPIDER COURTSHIP DISPLAY

ATTACKING SPIDER

The funnel-web spider (family *Dipluridae*) has large fangs and highly potent venom. The spider raises its head to attack and stabs its prey by moving its head down.

Venom

Head raised in attacking position

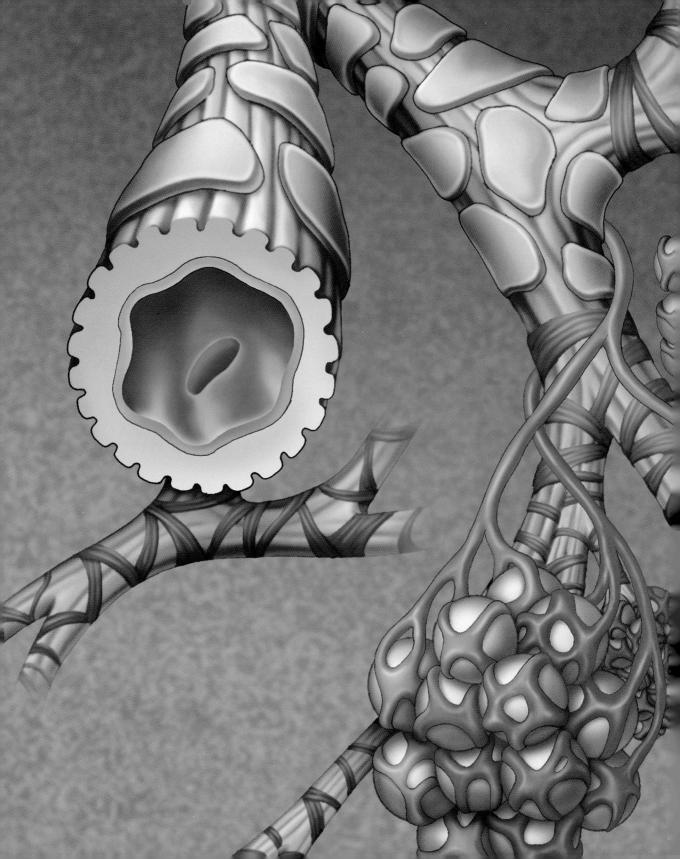

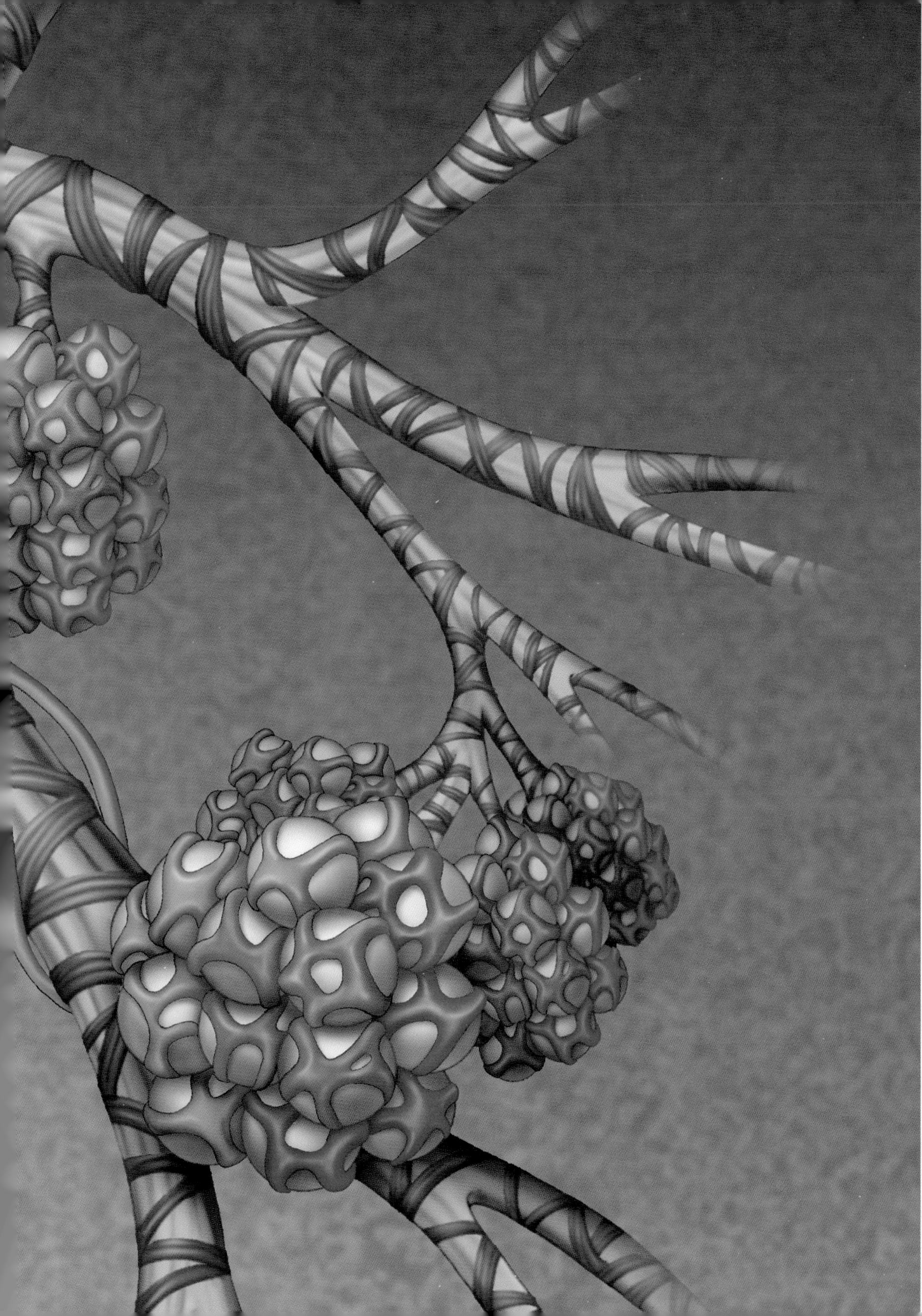

THE HUMAN BODY

THE VITAL SYSTEMS

BONES, MUSCLES AND SKIN

SENSES AND NERVES

Cells

INSIDE A CELL

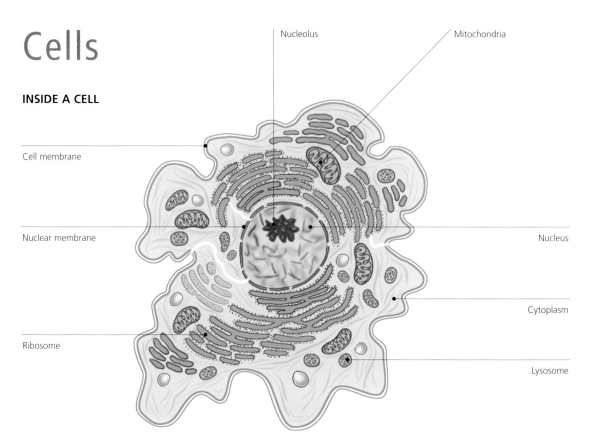

Nucleolus

Mitochondria

Cell membrane

Nuclear membrane

Nucleus

Cytoplasm

Ribosome

Lysosome

CELL CLONING

Cells form when a parent cell divides in two. This is called mitosis.

HELPFUL BACTERIA

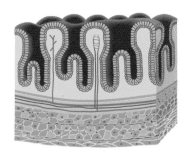

Some bacteria can destroy healthy tissue. Bacteria in the lining of the stomach, however, help the body use vitamins from food.

VIRUSES

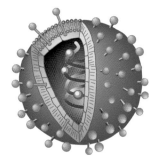

Viruses invade cells and trick them into making more viruses. This process changes the cells chemically. They are damaged or they die.

TYPES OF CELLS

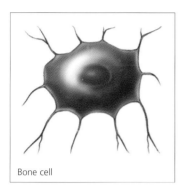

Bone cell

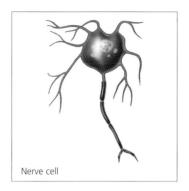

Nerve cell

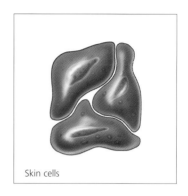

Skin cells

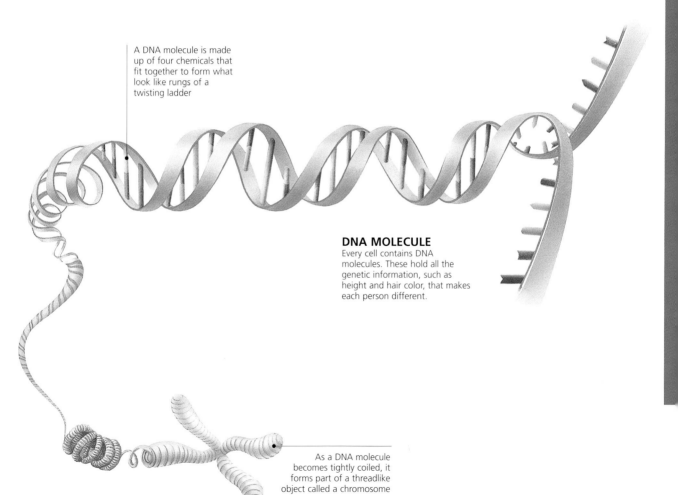

A DNA molecule is made up of four chemicals that fit together to form what look like rungs of a twisting ladder

DNA MOLECULE
Every cell contains DNA molecules. These hold all the genetic information, such as height and hair color, that makes each person different.

As a DNA molecule becomes tightly coiled, it forms part of a threadlike object called a chromosome

Blood

BLOOD CLOTTING

At a wound, platelets and sticky fibers trap red cells, white cells and germs. A clot is formed that seals the leak.

Cells at the wound's edge multiply to make new skin as healing begins. The clot hardens into a protective scab.

Capillaries under the skin reseal, and new cells grow together. Eventually the scab falls off and the wound is healed.

BLOOD TYPES

Type A   Type B   Type AB   Type O

ARTERY

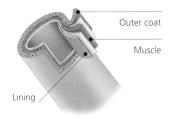

Outer coat

Muscle

Lining

VEIN

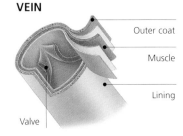

Outer coat

Muscle

Lining

Valve

CAPILLARY

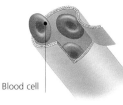

Blood cell

BLOOD CIRCULATION

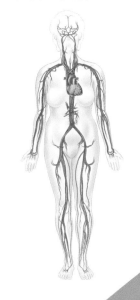

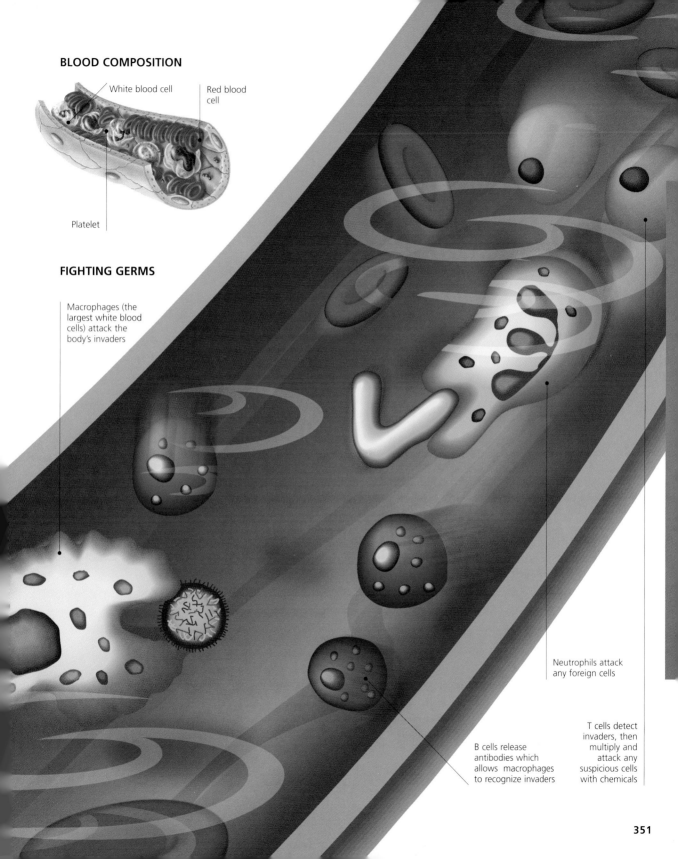

BLOOD COMPOSITION

White blood cell

Red blood cell

Platelet

FIGHTING GERMS

Macrophages (the largest white blood cells) attack the body's invaders

Neutrophils attack any foreign cells

T cells detect invaders, then multiply and attack any suspicious cells with chemicals

B cells release antibodies which allows macrophages to recognize invaders

The Heart

INSIDE THE HEART

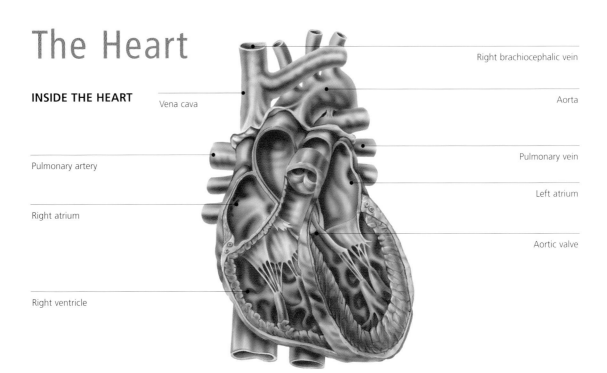

Vena cava

Pulmonary artery

Right atrium

Right ventricle

Right brachiocephalic vein

Aorta

Pulmonary vein

Left atrium

Aortic valve

HEART FRONT

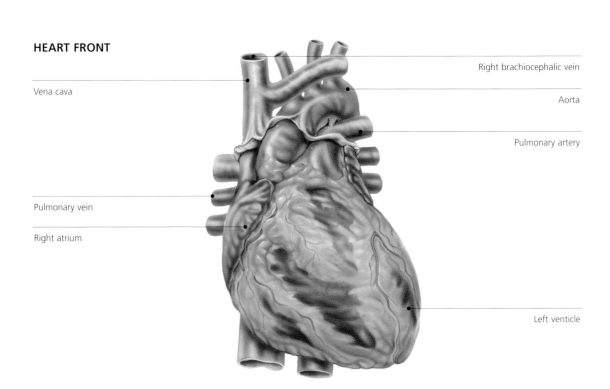

Vena cava

Pulmonary vein

Right atrium

Right brachiocephalic vein

Aorta

Pulmonary artery

Left venticle

HEART CYCLE

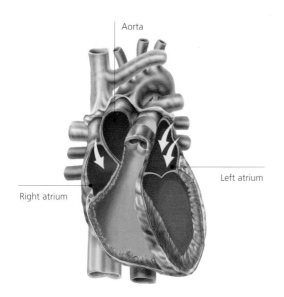

Aorta

Right atrium

Left atrium

Deoxygenated blood from the body pours into the right atrium. Oxygen-rich blood from the lungs fills the left atrium.

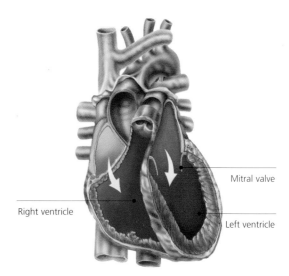

Right ventricle

Mitral valve

Left ventricle

The atria contract. Blood pushes open the valves leading to the heart's pumping chambers. The ventricles fill with blood.

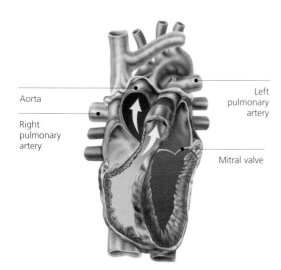

Aorta

Right pulmonary artery

Left pulmonary artery

Mitral valve

The ventricles contract, forcing open the valves to the aorta and pulmonary arteries. These fill with blood.

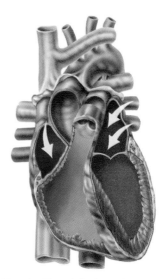

As the ventricles relax, the cycle begins again.

353

The Respiratory System

INSIDE THE LUNGS

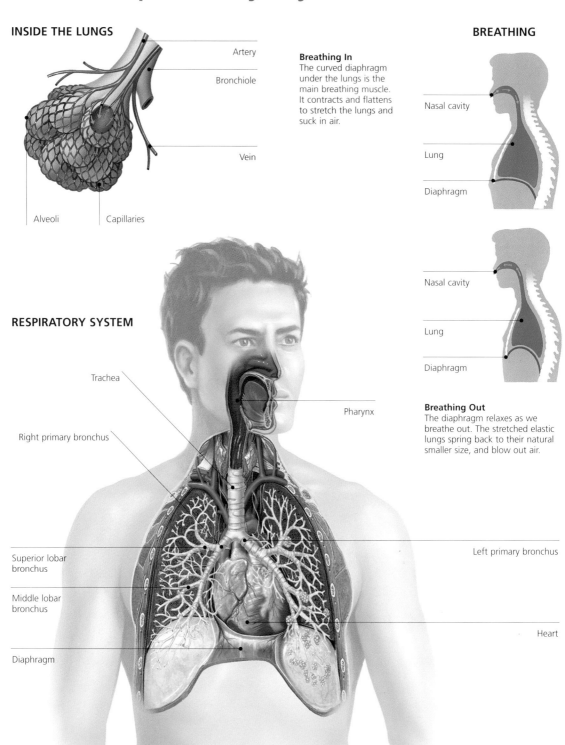

Artery

Bronchiole

Vein

Alveoli

Capillaries

BREATHING

Breathing In
The curved diaphragm under the lungs is the main breathing muscle. It contracts and flattens to stretch the lungs and suck in air.

Nasal cavity

Lung

Diaphragm

Nasal cavity

Lung

Diaphragm

Breathing Out
The diaphragm relaxes as we breathe out. The stretched elastic lungs spring back to their natural smaller size, and blow out air.

RESPIRATORY SYSTEM

Trachea

Pharynx

Right primary bronchus

Superior lobar bronchus

Left primary bronchus

Middle lobar bronchus

Heart

Diaphragm

BRONCHIAL TREE

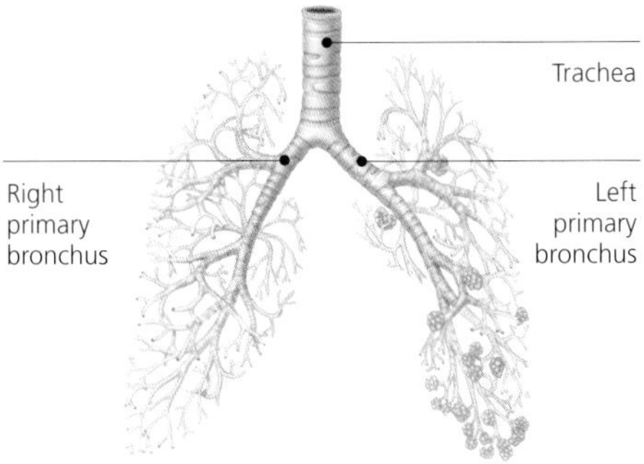

Trachea

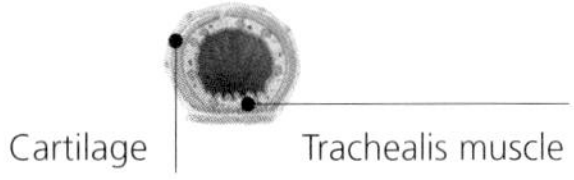

Right primary bronchus

Left primary bronchus

TRACHEA

Cartilage

Trachealis muscle

LUNGS

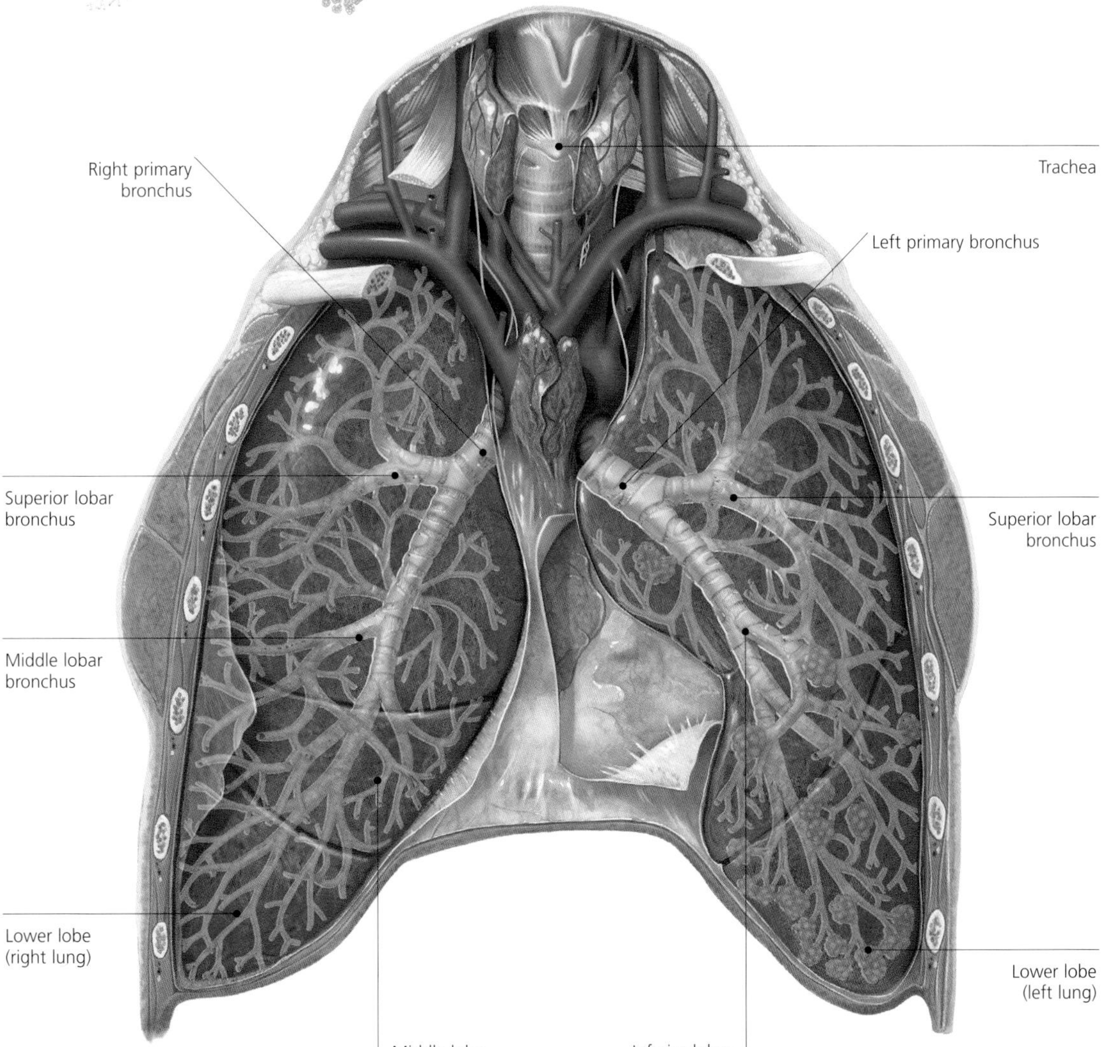

Right primary bronchus

Trachea

Left primary bronchus

Superior lobar bronchus

Superior lobar bronchus

Middle lobar bronchus

Lower lobe (right lung)

Lower lobe (left lung)

Middle lobe (right lung)

Inferior lobar bronchus

Digestion

STOMACH STRUCTURE

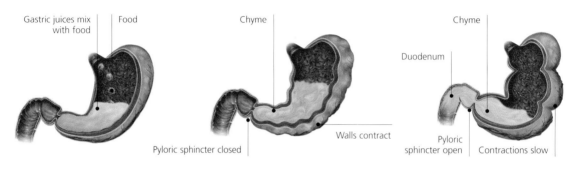

Duodenum

Gastroesophageal junction

Circular muscle layer

Mucosa and submucosa

Pyloric sphincter

Pylorus

STOMACH FUNCTION

Gastric juices mix with food

Food

Pyloric sphincter closed

Chyme

Walls contract

Chyme

Duodenum

Pyloric sphincter open

Contractions slow

DIGESTIVE ORGANS

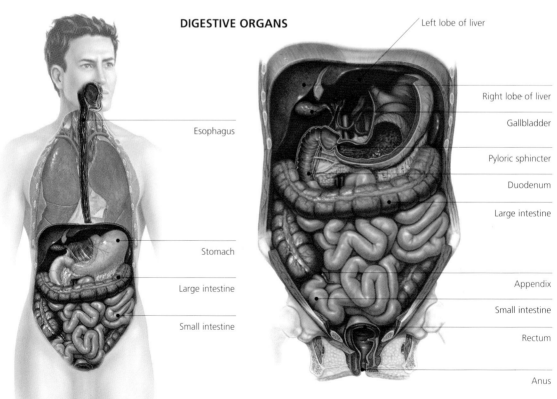

Left lobe of liver

Esophagus

Stomach

Large intestine

Small intestine

Right lobe of liver

Gallbladder

Pyloric sphincter

Duodenum

Large intestine

Appendix

Small intestine

Rectum

Anus

SALIVARY GLANDS

Salivary glands make watery spit, or saliva. Saliva makes food soft and easier to swallow. It also contains enzymes that start to digest food.

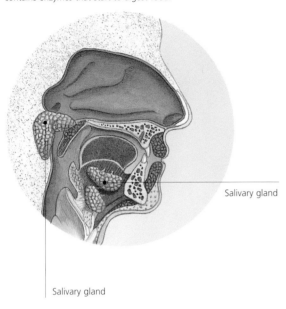

Salivary gland

Salivary gland

SMALL INTESTINE

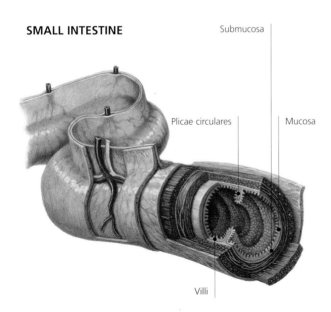

Submucosa

Plicae circulares

Mucosa

Villi

EATING

The tongue separates a small portion of the food in the mouth. It presses this against the mouth's roof, or hard palate, to shape it into a soft lump.

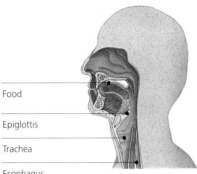

Food

Epiglottis

Trachea

Esophagus

The tongue pushes the food into the upper throat. The epiglottis closes over the trachea to stop food going down it.

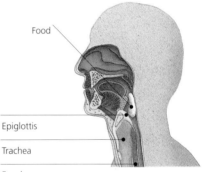

Food

Epiglottis

Trachea

Esophagus

Muscles in the walls of the lower throat and esophagus contract in waves. They force the food down the esophagus into the stomach.

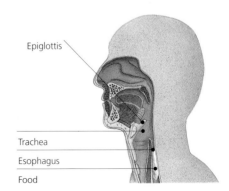

Epiglottis

Trachea

Esophagus

Food

Kidneys and Liver

KIDNEY CROSS-SECTION

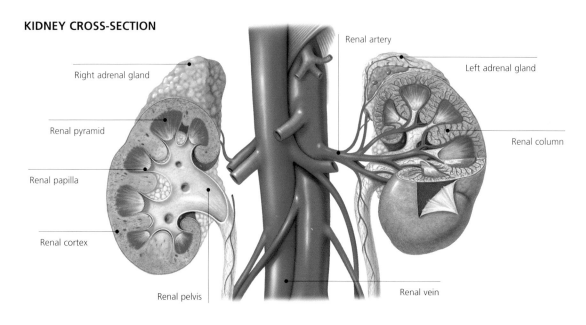

Right adrenal gland

Renal pyramid

Renal papilla

Renal cortex

Renal pelvis

Renal artery

Left adrenal gland

Renal column

Renal vein

URINARY SYSTEM

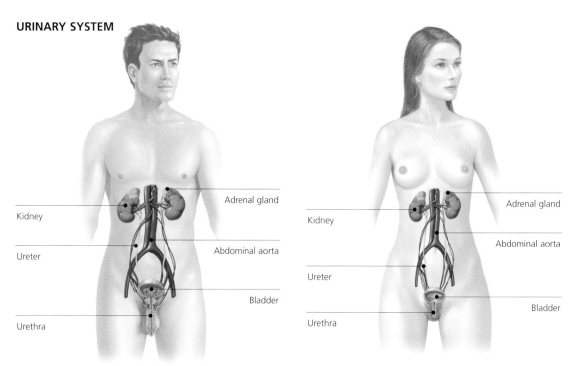

Kidney

Ureter

Urethra

Adrenal gland

Abdominal aorta

Bladder

Kidney

Ureter

Urethra

Adrenal gland

Abdominal aorta

Bladder

AROUND THE LIVER

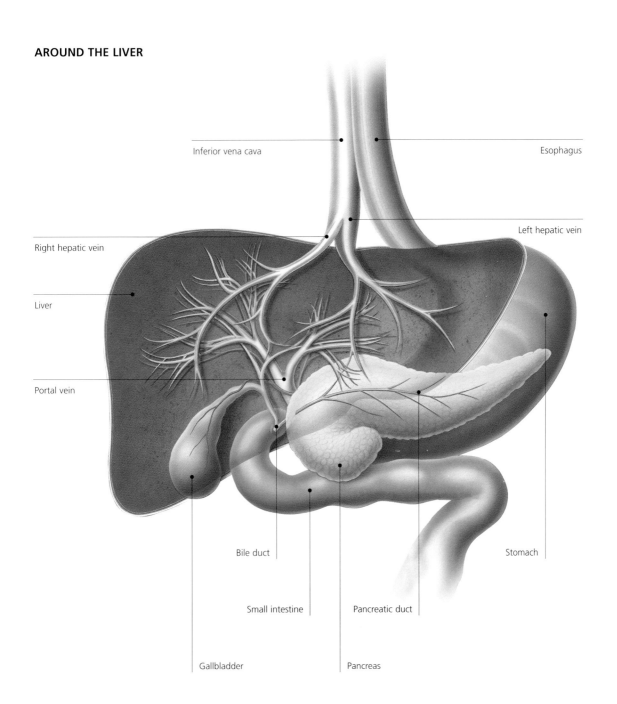

Inferior vena cava

Esophagus

Left hepatic vein

Right hepatic vein

Liver

Portal vein

Bile duct

Stomach

Small intestine

Pancreatic duct

Gallbladder

Pancreas

Reproductive Systems

BIRTH

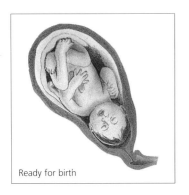

Ready for birth

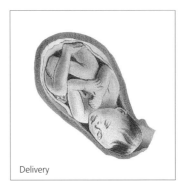

Delivery

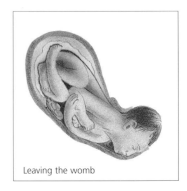

Leaving the womb

MALE REPRODUCTIVE ORGANS

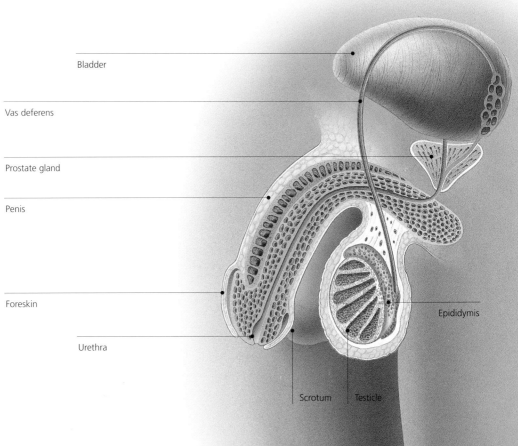

Bladder

Vas deferens

Prostate gland

Penis

Foreskin

Urethra

Epididymis

Scrotum

Testicle

BEGINNING LIFE

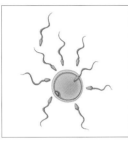

Fertilization
A sperm penetrates and fertilizes the egg. The egg is now called a zygote.

Implantation
The fertilized egg divides many times and attaches to the wall of the uterus.

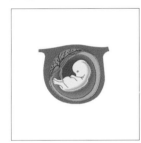

Embryo
At seven weeks the unborn child is called an embyro.

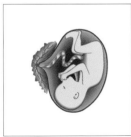

Fetus
At two months the embyro becomes a fetus. It is not much larger than a walnut.

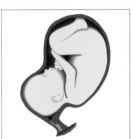

Birth
At nine months, strong uterine movements push the baby through the vagina into the world.

REPRODUCTIVE SYSTEM LOCATION

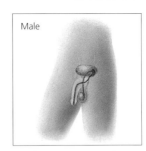

Male

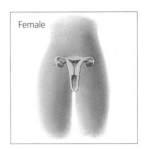

Female

FEMALE REPRODUCTIVE ORGANS

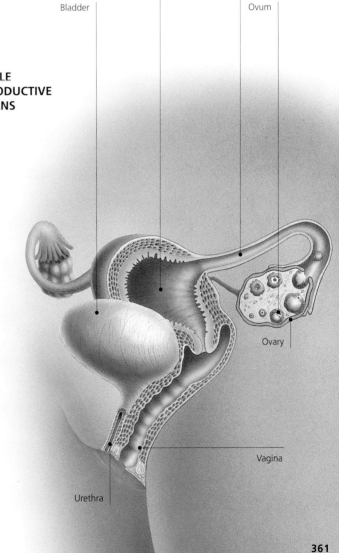

Bladder

Uterus

Fallopian tube

Ovum

Ovary

Vagina

Urethra

The Skeleton

FRONT VIEW

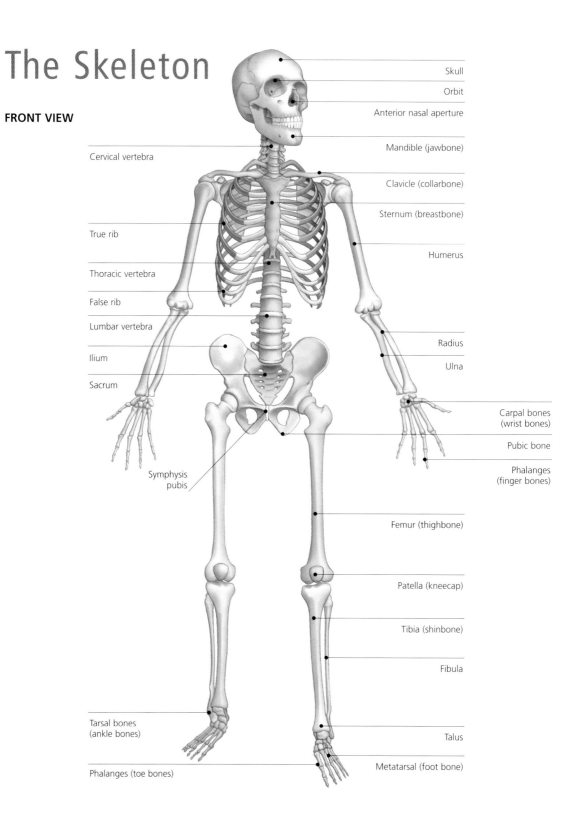

Skull

Orbit

Anterior nasal aperture

Mandible (jawbone)

Cervical vertebra

Clavicle (collarbone)

Sternum (breastbone)

True rib

Humerus

Thoracic vertebra

False rib

Lumbar vertebra

Radius

Ilium

Ulna

Sacrum

Carpal bones (wrist bones)

Pubic bone

Phalanges (finger bones)

Symphysis pubis

Femur (thighbone)

Patella (kneecap)

Tibia (shinbone)

Fibula

Tarsal bones (ankle bones)

Talus

Phalanges (toe bones)

Metatarsal (foot bone)

BACK VIEW

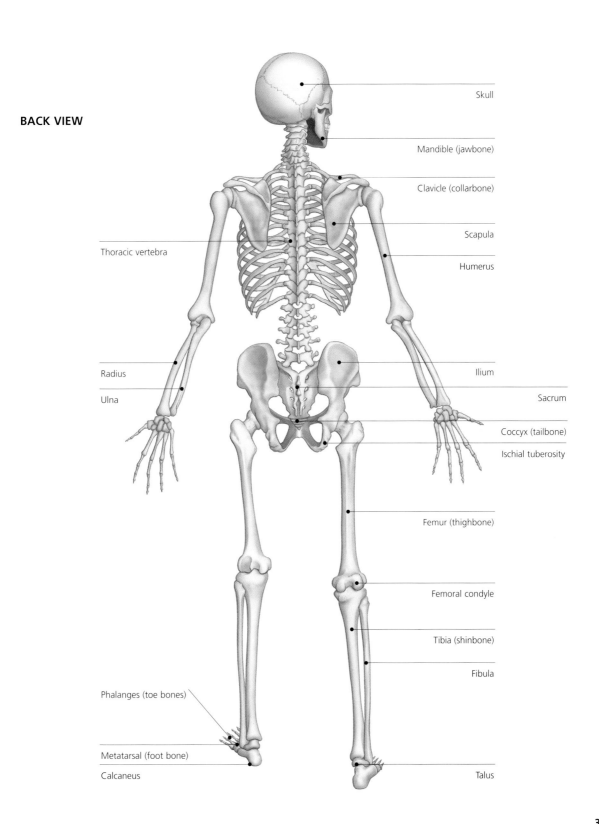

Skull

Mandible (jawbone)

Clavicle (collarbone)

Scapula

Thoracic vertebra

Humerus

Radius

Ilium

Ulna

Sacrum

Coccyx (tailbone)

Ischial tuberosity

Femur (thighbone)

Femoral condyle

Tibia (shinbone)

Fibula

Phalanges (toe bones)

Metatarsal (foot bone)

Calcaneus

Talus

The Skeleton

TEETH TYPES

Molar

Premolar

Canine

Incisor

SIDE VIEW

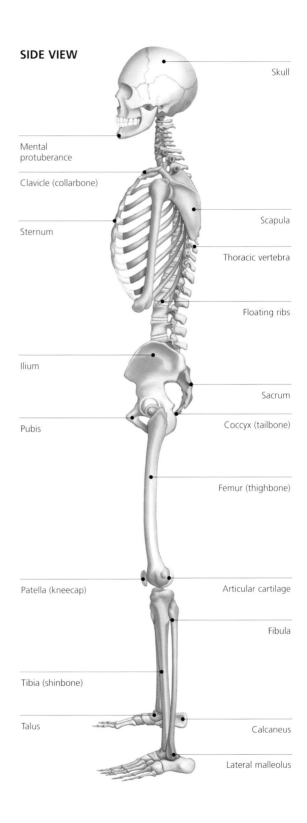

Skull

Mental protuberance

Clavicle (collarbone)

Scapula

Sternum

Thoracic vertebra

Floating ribs

Ilium

Sacrum

Pubis

Coccyx (tailbone)

Femur (thighbone)

Patella (kneecap)

Articular cartilage

Fibula

Tibia (shinbone)

Talus

Calcaneus

Lateral malleolus

SKULL SIDE VIEW

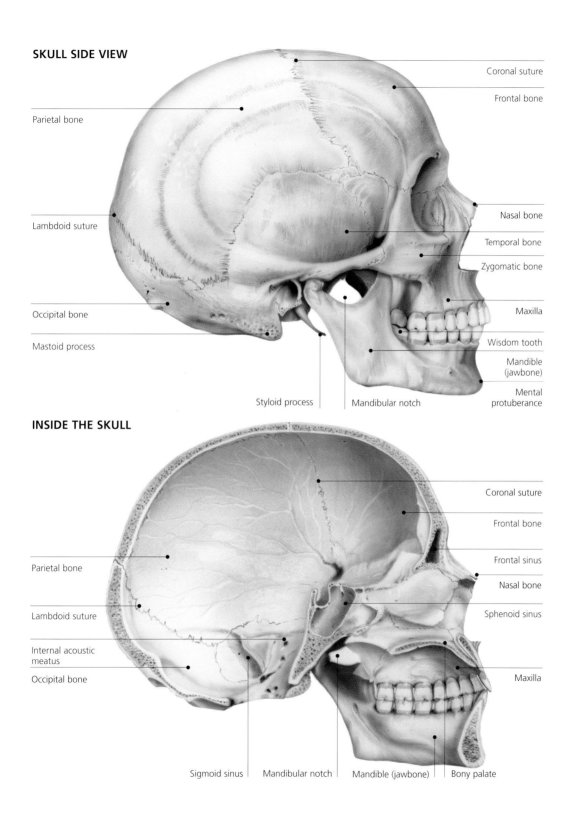

Coronal suture

Frontal bone

Parietal bone

Nasal bone

Lambdoid suture

Temporal bone

Zygomatic bone

Occipital bone

Maxilla

Mastoid process

Wisdom tooth

Mandible
(jawbone)

Mental
protuberance

Styloid process

Mandibular notch

INSIDE THE SKULL

Coronal suture

Frontal bone

Parietal bone

Frontal sinus

Nasal bone

Lambdoid suture

Sphenoid sinus

Internal acoustic
meatus

Occipital bone

Maxilla

Sigmoid sinus

Mandibular notch

Mandible (jawbone)

Bony palate

Bones and Joints

HEALING BROKEN BONES

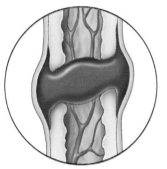

1. When a bone breaks, so do blood vessels. Blood flows into the fracture.

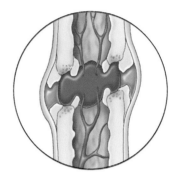

2. The blood grows sticky and thickens, forming a clot. The clot hardens. It will provide the platform on which the new bone will form.

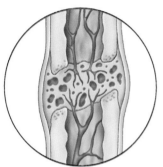

3. Cells from the broken ends rush to the clot. They quickly form a dense web of support tissue called a callus.

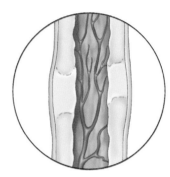

4. Over time the callus hardens into bone. At first, the bone bulges slightly but special cells reshape the bone, returning it to its original shape.

JOINTS

Joints are where two bones meet. Smooth cartilage coats the end of each bone. Synovial fluid moistens the joint. Ligaments lash the joint together and keep it from moving too much.

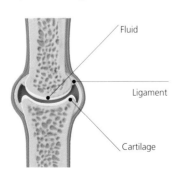

Fluid

Ligament

Cartilage

TYPES OF BROKEN BONE

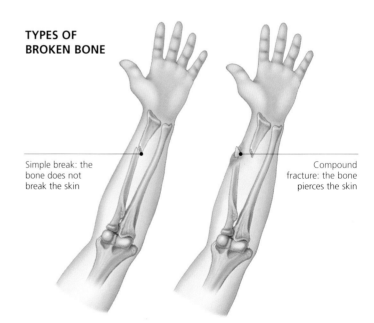

Simple break: the bone does not break the skin

Compound fracture: the bone pierces the skin

AT THE JOINT

Ball-and-socket joint

Hip joint

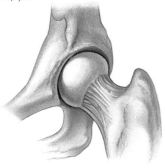

Hinge joint

Elbow joint

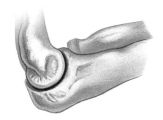

INSIDE A BONE

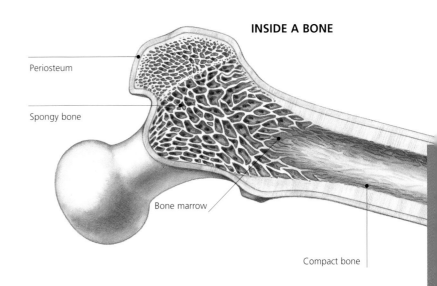

Periosteum

Spongy bone

Bone marrow

Compact bone

SPINE

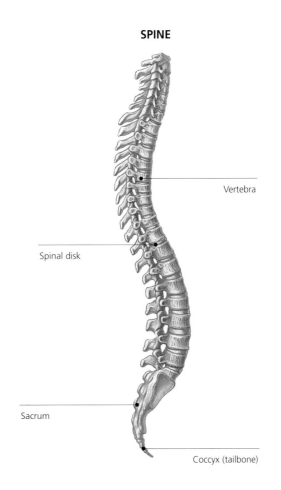

Vertebra

Spinal disk

Sacrum

Coccyx (tailbone)

Muscles

TYPES OF MUSCLES

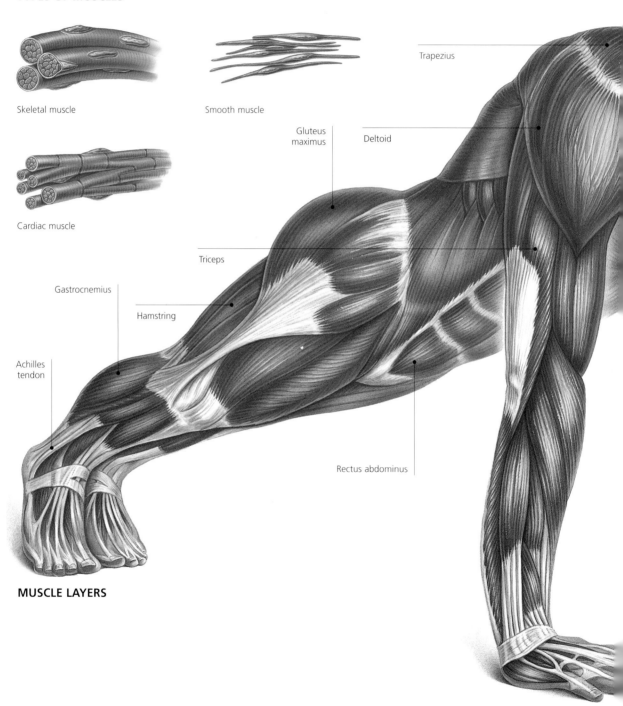

Skeletal muscle

Smooth muscle

Cardiac muscle

Trapezius

Gluteus
maximus

Deltoid

Triceps

Gastrocnemius

Hamstring

Achilles
tendon

Rectus abdominus

MUSCLE LAYERS

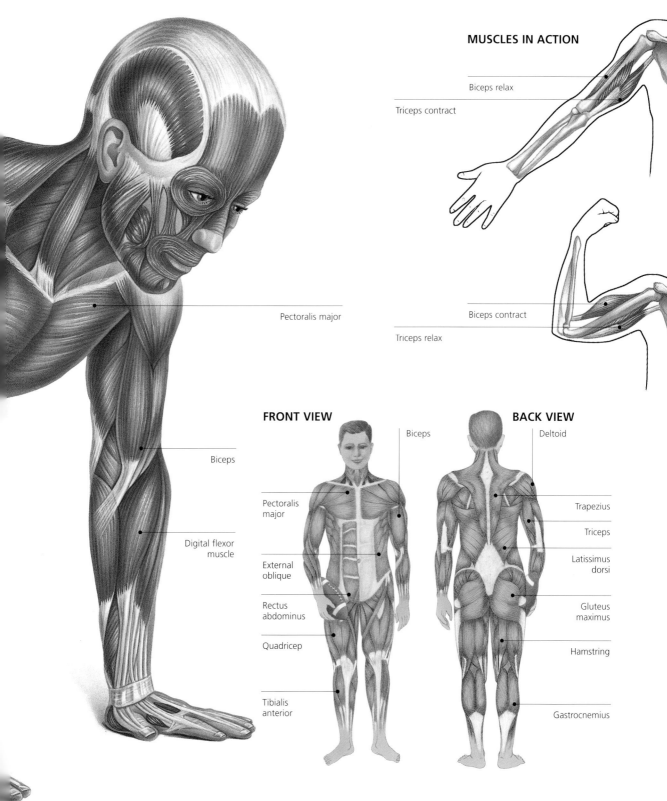

Pectoralis major

Biceps

Digital flexor
muscle

MUSCLES IN ACTION

Biceps relax

Triceps contract

Biceps contract

Triceps relax

FRONT VIEW

Biceps

Pectoralis
major

External
oblique

Rectus
abdominus

Quadricep

Tibialis
anterior

BACK VIEW

Deltoid

Trapezius

Triceps

Latissimus
dorsi

Gluteus
maximus

Hamstring

Gastrocnemius

Skin and Nails

SKIN COLOR

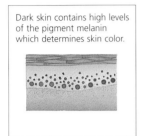

Dark skin contains high levels of the pigment melanin which determines skin color.

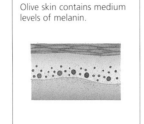

Olive skin contains medium levels of melanin.

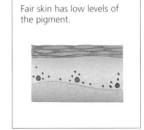

Fair skin has low levels of the pigment.

UNDER THE SKIN

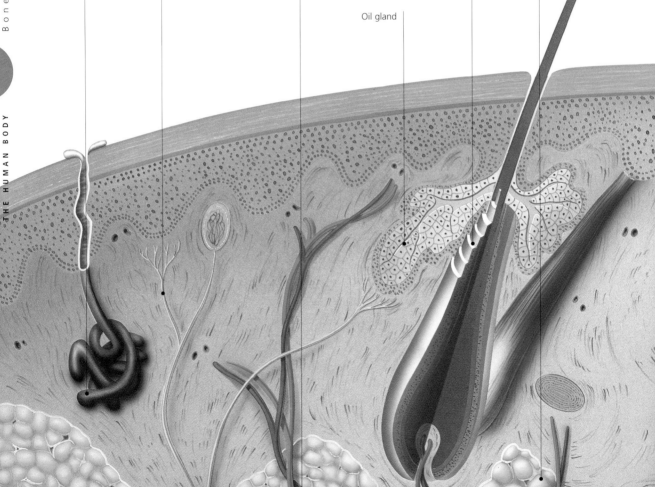

Sweat gland

Cold sensor

Blood vessel

Oil gland

Hair follicle

Fat under skin

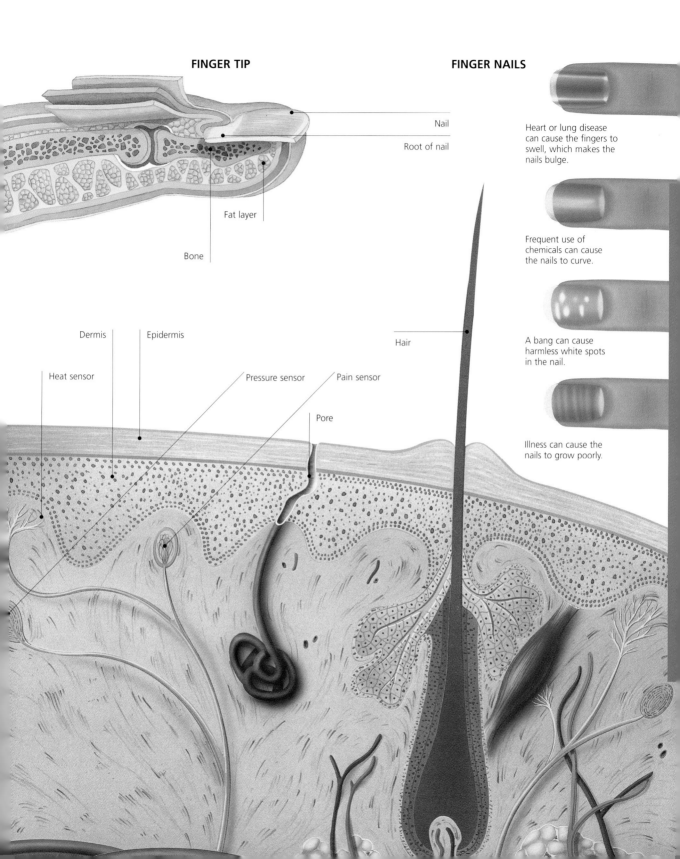

FINGER TIP

Nail

Root of nail

Fat layer

Bone

Dermis

Epidermis

Heat sensor

Pressure sensor

Pain sensor

Pore

FINGER NAILS

Heart or lung disease can cause the fingers to swell, which makes the nails bulge.

Frequent use of chemicals can cause the nails to curve.

A bang can cause harmless white spots in the nail.

Illness can cause the nails to grow poorly.

Hair

The Brain

BRAIN FUNCTIONS

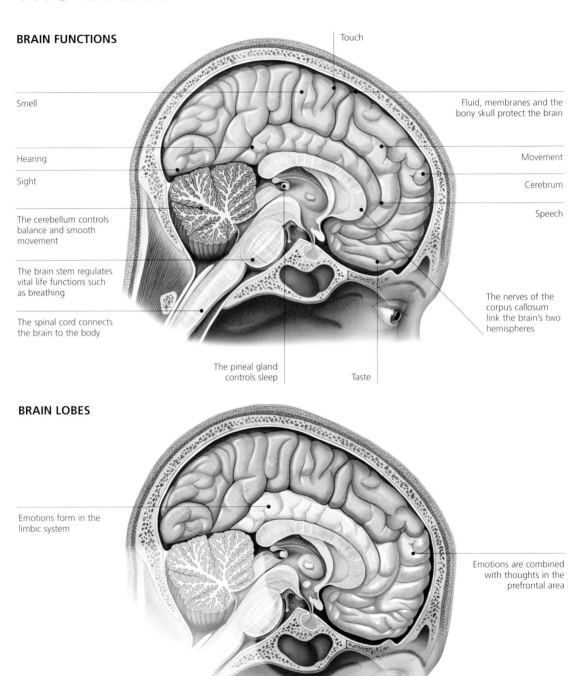

Touch

Smell

Fluid, membranes and the bony skull protect the brain

Hearing

Movement

Sight

Cerebrum

The cerebellum controls balance and smooth movement

Speech

The brain stem regulates vital life functions such as breathing

The nerves of the corpus callosum link the brain's two hemispheres

The spinal cord connects the brain to the body

The pineal gland controls sleep

Taste

BRAIN LOBES

Emotions form in the limbic system

Emotions are combined with thoughts in the prefrontal area

BRAIN CROSS SECTION

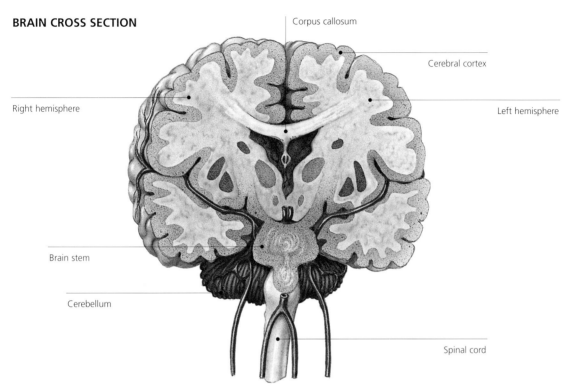

Corpus callosum

Cerebral cortex

Right hemisphere

Left hemisphere

Brain stem

Cerebellum

Spinal cord

BRAIN STEM
LATERAL VIEW

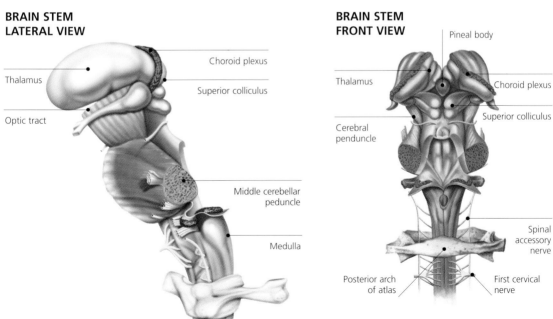

Thalamus

Choroid plexus

Superior colliculus

Optic tract

Middle cerebellar
peduncle

Medulla

BRAIN STEM
FRONT VIEW

Pineal body

Thalamus

Choroid plexus

Superior colliculus

Cerebral
penduncle

Spinal
accessory
nerve

Posterior arch
of atlas

First cervical
nerve

Sight

TEARS

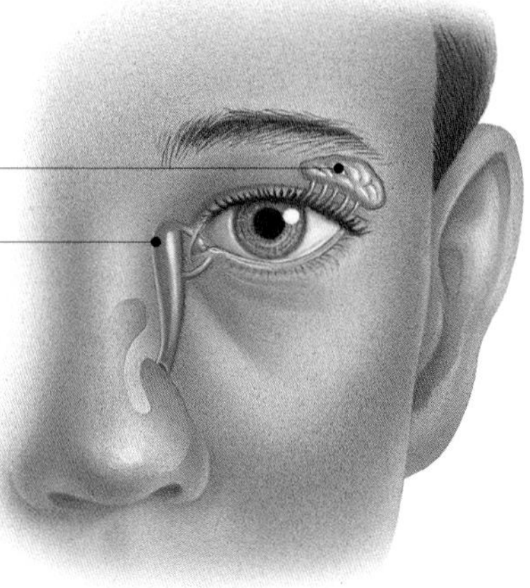

Tear gland

Tear duct

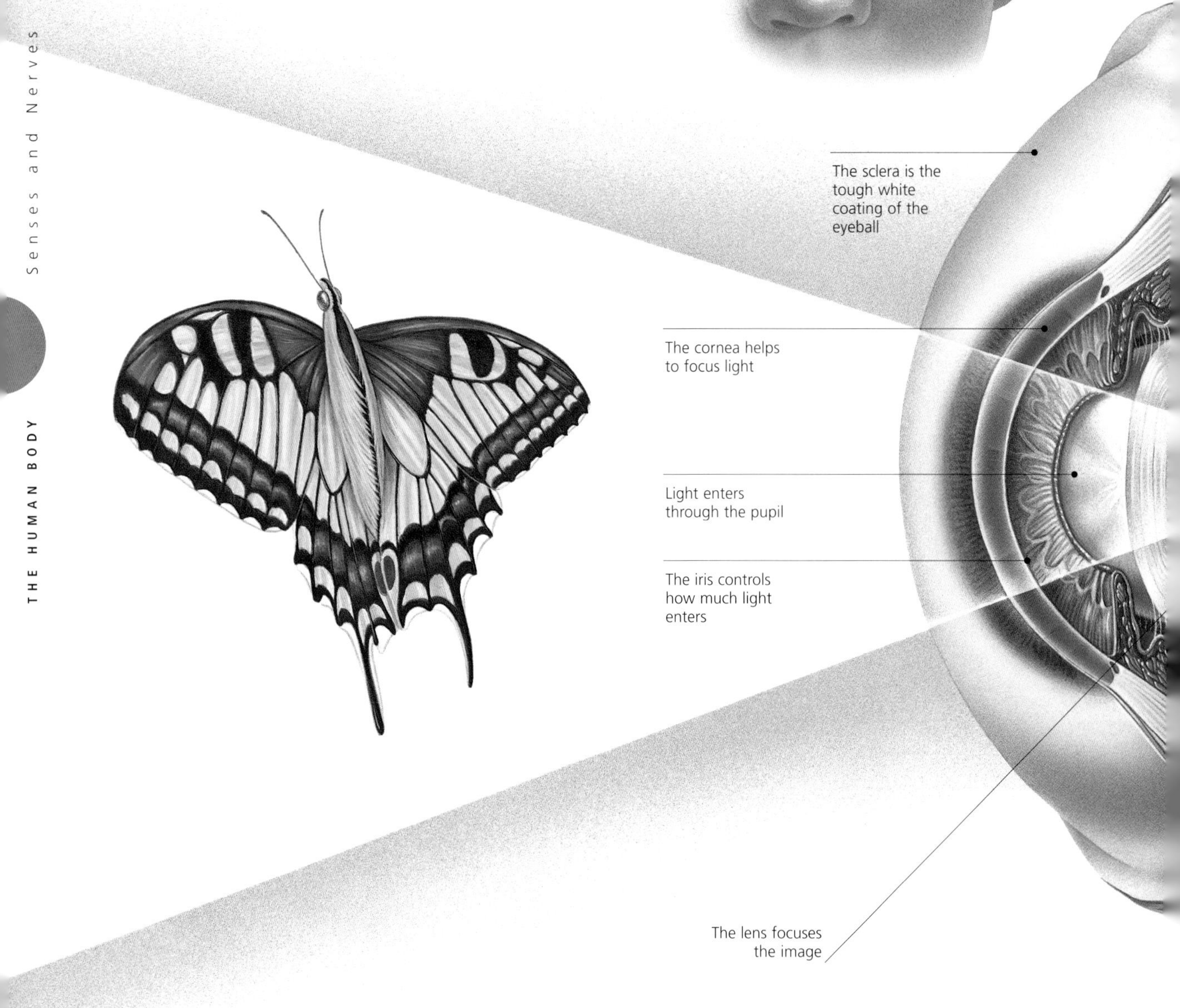

The sclera is the tough white coating of the eyeball

The cornea helps to focus light

Light enters through the pupil

The iris controls how much light enters

The lens focuses the image

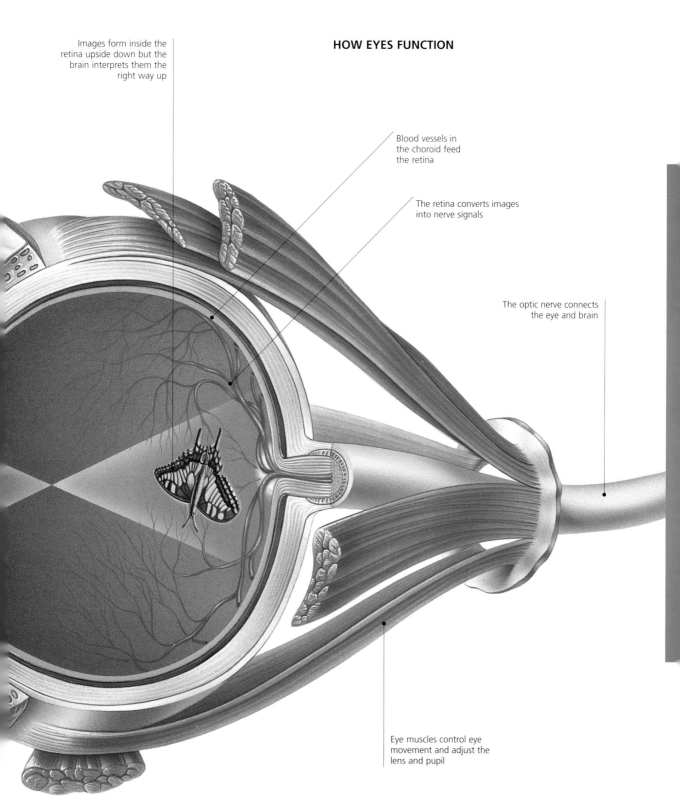

HOW EYES FUNCTION

Images form inside the retina upside down but the brain interprets them the right way up

Blood vessels in the choroid feed the retina

The retina converts images into nerve signals

The optic nerve connects the eye and brain

Eye muscles control eye movement and adjust the lens and pupil

Hearing and Speaking

EAR LOCATION

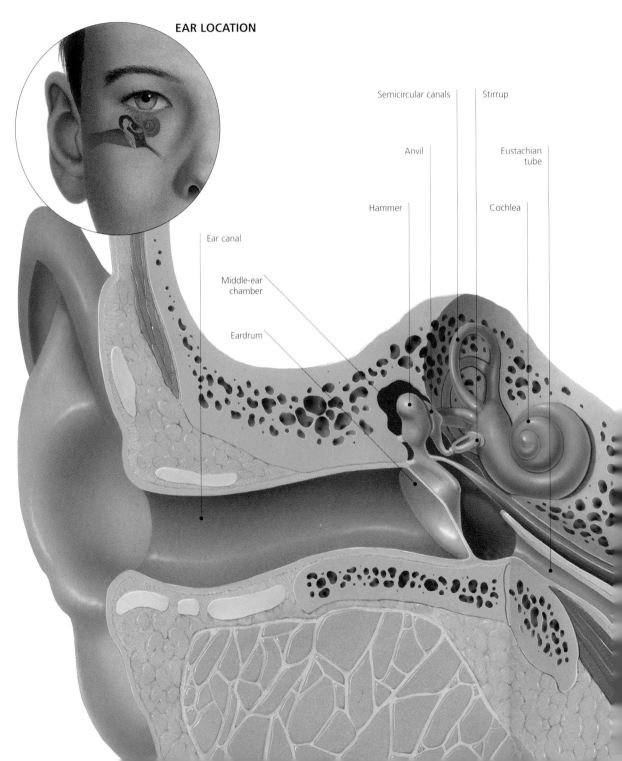

Semicircular canals

Stirrup

Anvil

Eustachian tube

Hammer

Cochlea

Ear canal

Middle-ear chamber

Eardrum

EAR PRESSURE

The middle-ear chamber is a tiny air pocket behind the eardrum. The Eustachian tube links it to the throat and so to the outside air.

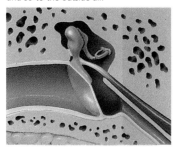

Outside pressure is less at altitude. Because the middle-ear pressure remains the same the ear drum bulges and hearing fades.

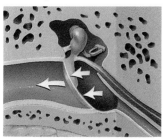

If you swallow hard the Eustachian tube opens. Air rushes out of the middle ear to relieve the pressure.

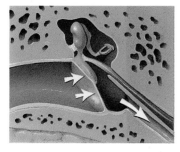

SPEECH

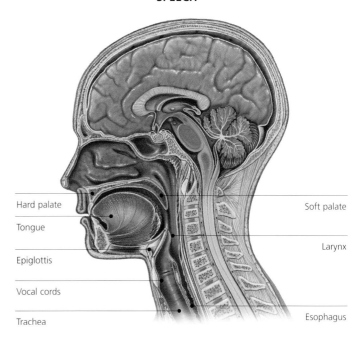

Hard palate

Tongue

Epiglottis

Vocal cords

Trachea

Soft palate

Larynx

Esophagus

VOICEBOX

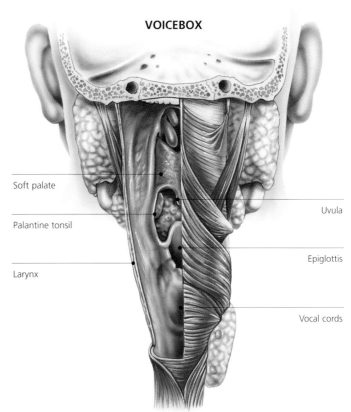

Soft palate

Palantine tonsil

Larynx

Uvula

Epiglottis

Vocal cords

Taste and Smell

SNEEZING

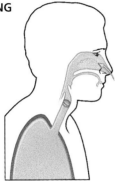

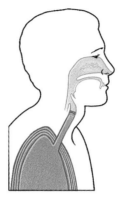

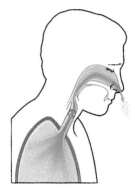

Dust, animal fur or pollen irritate the sensitive lining of the nose.

The throat and windpipe close. Muscles in the chest and abdomen press the lungs and squash the air inside.

When the windpipe and throat open again, high-pressure air blasts through the nose to blow away the irritants.

TASTE

Olfactory centers

Olfactory centers

Olfactory bulb

Olfactory nerves

Nerves from tongue and taste buds

Salivary gland

Salivary gland

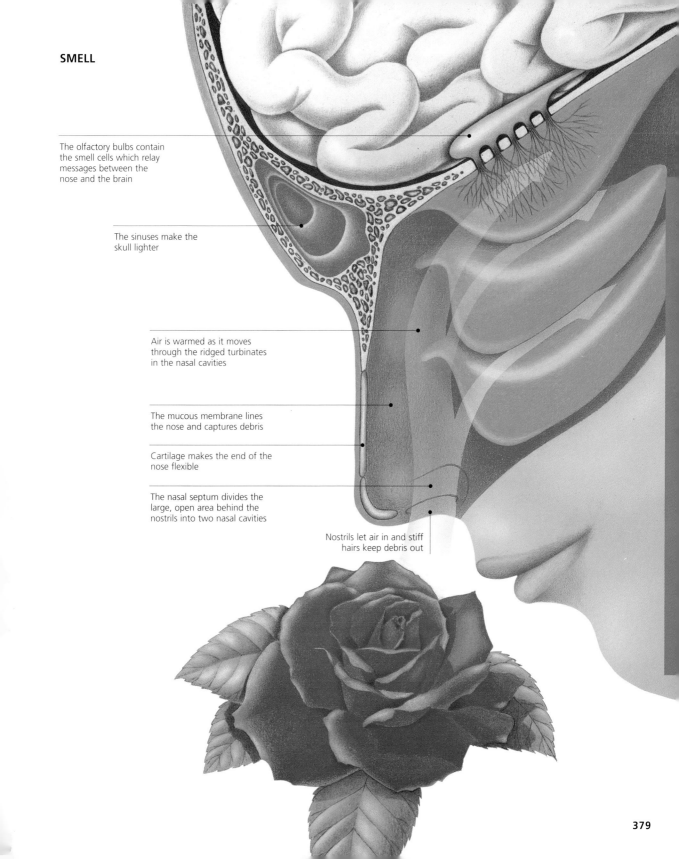

SMELL

The olfactory bulbs contain the smell cells which relay messages between the nose and the brain

The sinuses make the skull lighter

Air is warmed as it moves through the ridged turbinates in the nasal cavities

The mucous membrane lines the nose and captures debris

Cartilage makes the end of the nose flexible

The nasal septum divides the large, open area behind the nostrils into two nasal cavities

Nostrils let air in and stiff hairs keep debris out

Nerves and Hormones

NERVES

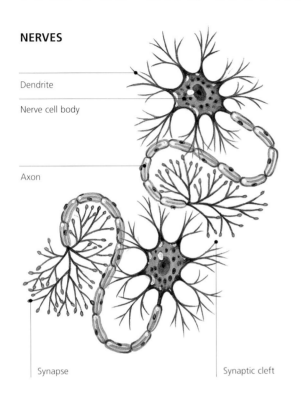

Dendrite

Nerve cell body

Axon

Synapse

Synaptic cleft

INSIDE THE SPINE

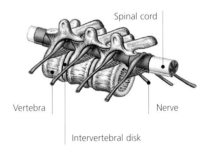

Spinal cord

Vertebra

Nerve

Intervertebral disk

SYNAPSE

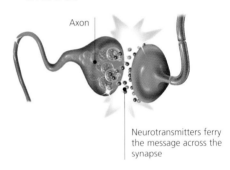

Axon

Neurotransmitters ferry the message across the synapse

HORMONE GLANDS

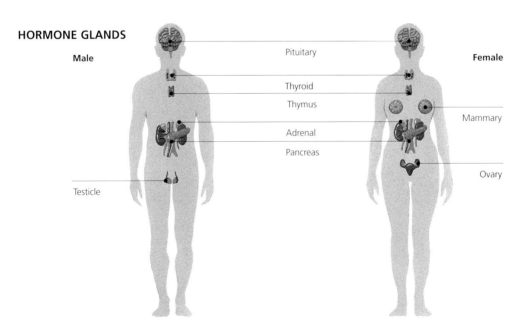

Male

Female

Pituitary

Thyroid

Thymus

Mammary

Adrenal

Pancreas

Ovary

Testicle

NERVOUS SYSTEM

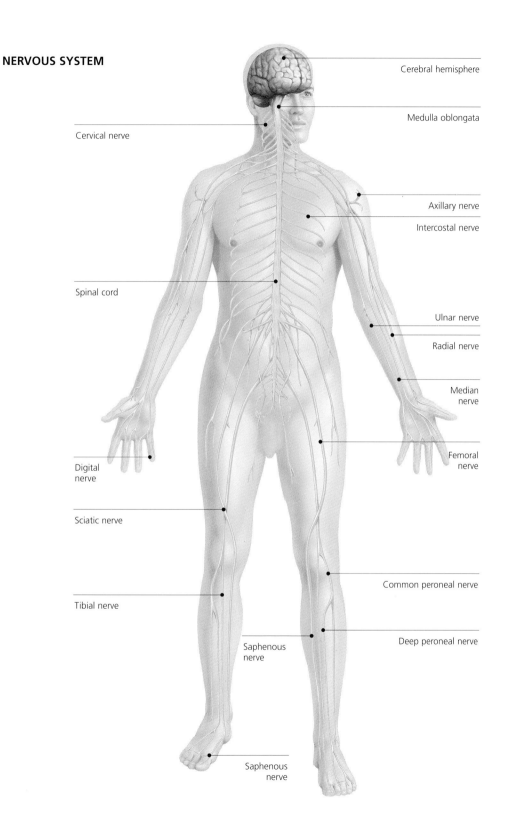

Cerebral hemisphere

Medulla oblongata

Cervical nerve

Axillary nerve

Intercostal nerve

Spinal cord

Ulnar nerve

Radial nerve

Median nerve

Digital nerve

Femoral nerve

Sciatic nerve

Common peroneal nerve

Tibial nerve

Deep peroneal nerve

Saphenous nerve

Saphenous nerve

The Egyptian Empire

CROWNS OF THE PHAROAH

White crown of
Upper Egypt

Red crown of
Lower Egypt

Double crown of
united Egypt

Blue crown

Atef crown
of Osiris

QUEEN HATSHEPSUT

When Queen Hatshepsut's husband died she took over the government and held power for about 20 years—statues show her wearing the false beard of kingship

LAND OF THE LOTUS

People in modern times likened ancient Egypt to a lotus plant, with its valley as the stem and its delta as the flower

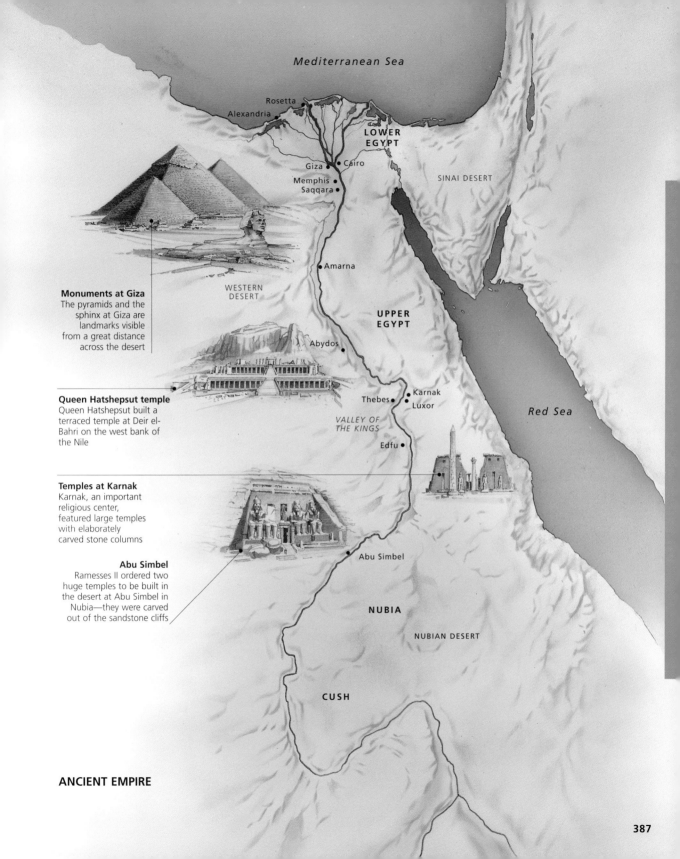

Monuments at Giza
The pyramids and the sphinx at Giza are landmarks visible from a great distance across the desert

Queen Hatshepsut temple
Queen Hatshepsut built a terraced temple at Deir el-Bahri on the west bank of the Nile

Temples at Karnak
Karnak, an important religious center, featured large temples with elaborately carved stone columns

Abu Simbel
Ramesses II ordered two huge temples to be built in the desert at Abu Simbel in Nubia—they were carved out of the sandstone cliffs

Mediterranean Sea

Rosetta
Alexandria

LOWER EGYPT

SINAI DESERT

Giza · Cairo
Memphis
Saqqara

Amarna

WESTERN DESERT

UPPER EGYPT

Abydos

Karnak
Thebes · Luxor

VALLEY OF THE KINGS

Edfu

Red Sea

Abu Simbel

NUBIA

NUBIAN DESERT

CUSH

ANCIENT EMPIRE

Worshiping the Gods

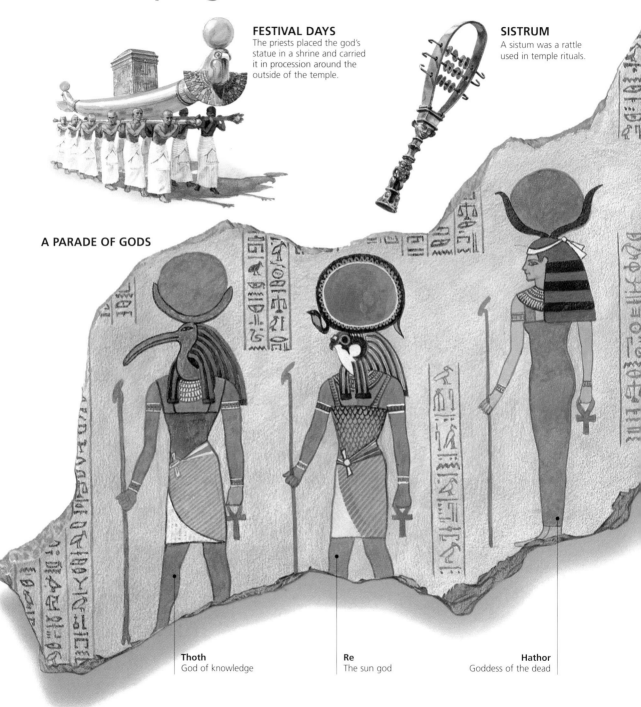

FESTIVAL DAYS
The priests placed the god's statue in a shrine and carried it in procession around the outside of the temple.

SISTRUM
A sistum was a rattle used in temple rituals.

A PARADE OF GODS

Thoth
God of knowledge

Re
The sun god

Hathor
Goddess of the dead

Anubis
God of the dead and embalming

Osiris
God of the underworld

Isis
Goddess of motherhood and healing

Horus
God of the sky

ENTERTAINING THE GODS

In temple courtyards, women sang, danced and put on acrobatic displays for the gods.

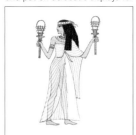   

Burial and the Afterlife

PREPARING THE MUMMY

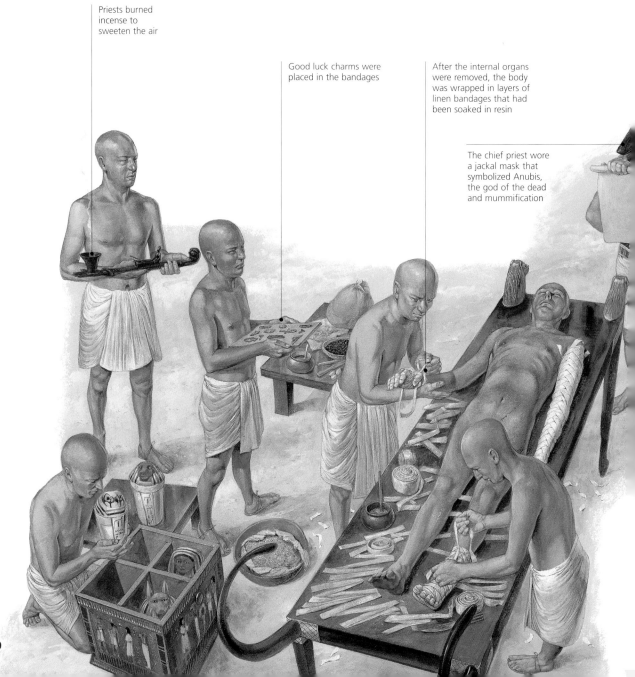

Priests burned incense to sweeten the air

Good luck charms were placed in the bandages

After the internal organs were removed, the body was wrapped in layers of linen bandages that had been soaked in resin

The chief priest wore a jackal mask that symbolized Anubis, the god of the dead and mummification

MUMMY CASES

Coffins were made of wood or cartonnage, which was a kind of papier-mâché

Lid of outer mummy case

Lid of inner mummy case

Linen wrappings

Wrapped mummy with mask

Two coffins for protection from animals and tomb robbers

Paintings of gods, spells, and hieroglyphs

Bottom of inner mummy case

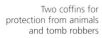

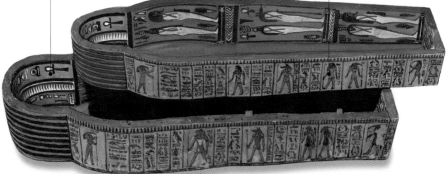

Bottom of outer mummy case

Writing and Art

HIEROGLYPHS

Owl

Water

Bread

Man

Arm

Reed

Mouth

Flax

Basket

WRITING KIT

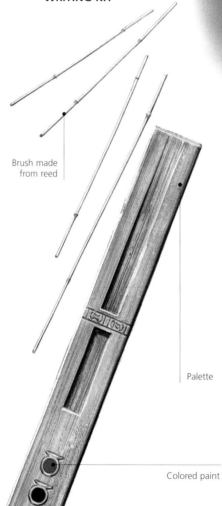

Brush made
from reed

Palette

Colored paint

A stonemason smoothed
the wall and covered it
with a layer of thin plaster

TRAVELING SYMBOLS

Traveling north

Traveling south

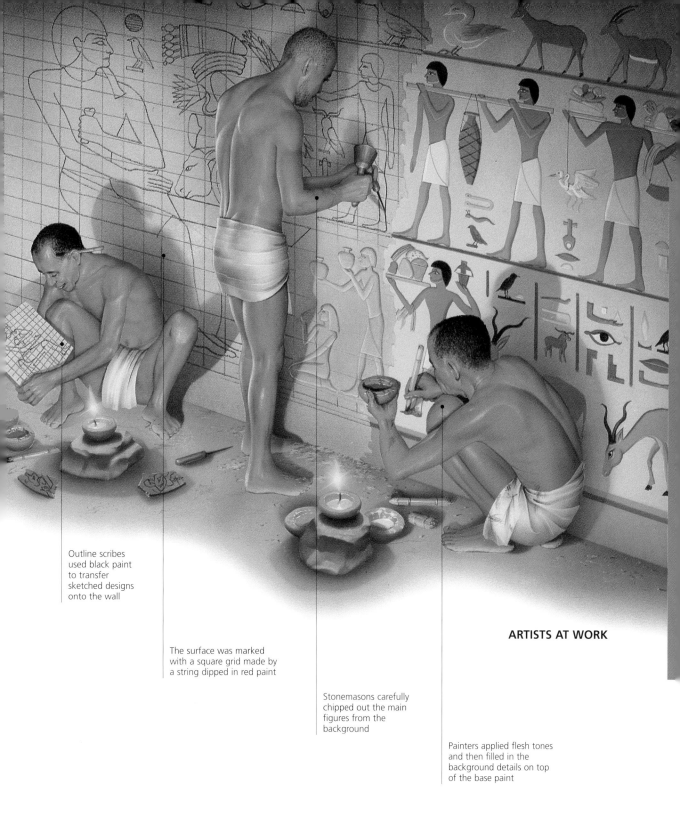

Outline scribes used black paint to transfer sketched designs onto the wall

The surface was marked with a square grid made by a string dipped in red paint

Stonemasons carefully chipped out the main figures from the background

ARTISTS AT WORK

Painters applied flesh tones and then filled in the background details on top of the base paint

Empire and Emperors

IMPERIAL PALACE

The Imperial Palace was called the Forbidden City because few people were allowed inside

The elaborate roof represented the heavens

The Hall of Supreme Harmony was built during the Ming dynasty (1368–1644) as part of the Imperial Palace

FIRST EMPEROR
Qin Shi Huangdi unified ancient China by making strict laws, taxing everyone in the country and introducing one script for writing.

DEFENDING THE EMPIRE

The Long Wall of ancient China snaked up and down mountains and across semi-desert plains. It was built to keep out invaders from the north.

The Emperor was called a Son of Heaven—the people believed he received heavenly approval to rule China

Society and Culture

SOCIAL ORDERS

Scholar

Peasant

Artisan

Merchant

CLOTHING

Woman

Short-sleeved
upper garment

Flowing silk skirt

Man

Loose robes

Wide sleeves

MAGISTRATE'S COURT

When the court believed the evidence was enough to prove a person's guilt, the accused was encouraged to confess

A district magistrate was a low-ranking official who enforced law and order; collected taxes; registered births, deaths and marriages; supervised building programs; and judged court cases

Science and Communication

ACUPUNCTURE

Ancient Chinese physicians believed that life-giving energy flowed along 12 lines in the body called meridians

Doctors were able to ease pain and treat certain illnesses by sticking acupuncture needles just below the skin at points along the meridians

MEDICINAL HERBS

Cilantro (coriander)

Garlic

Ginseng

Star anise

CHINESE CHARACTERS

Ruler or king

Moon

Mouth

Sun

CALLIGRAPHY

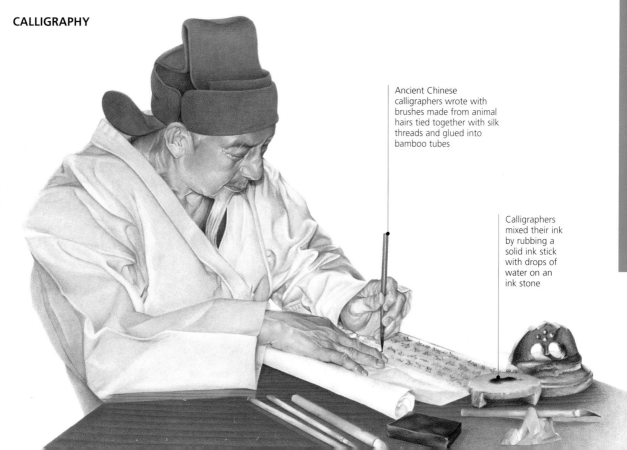

Ancient Chinese calligraphers wrote with brushes made from animal hairs tied together with silk threads and glued into bamboo tubes

Calligraphers mixed their ink by rubbing a solid ink stick with drops of water on an ink stone

Craft and Trade

BRONZE AGE CRAFT

Clay core

Artisans poured molten bronze into a carved ceramic mold

When the metal cooled, the bronzesmith broke the mold, removed the clay core and polished the metal surface

THE SILK ROAD

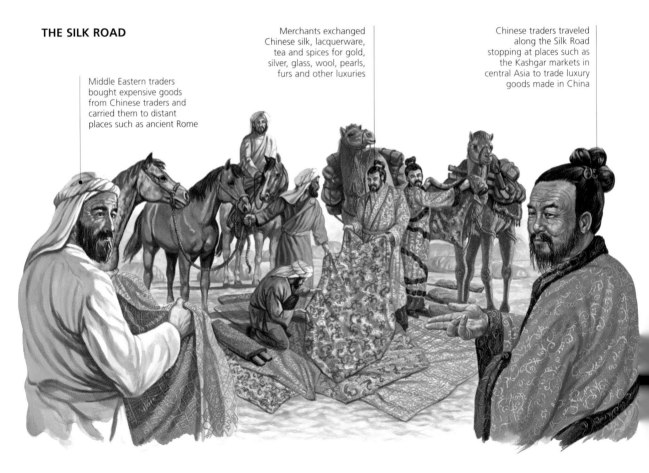

Merchants exchanged Chinese silk, lacquerware, tea and spices for gold, silver, glass, wool, pearls, furs and other luxuries

Chinese traders traveled along the Silk Road stopping at places such as the Kashgar markets in central Asia to trade luxury goods made in China

Middle Eastern traders bought expensive goods from Chinese traders and carried them to distant places such as ancient Rome

SILK PRODUCTION

Cocoon

Silkworm

The ancient Chinese gathered mulberry leaves to feed their silkworms

Women rinsed the silkworm cocoons in hot water to loosen the filaments

LACQUER ART
Sap from the lacquer tree is the oldest industrial plastic known to humans

The ancient Chinese used colored lacquer in the popular colors of red, black, brown, yellow, gold and green

The Greek World

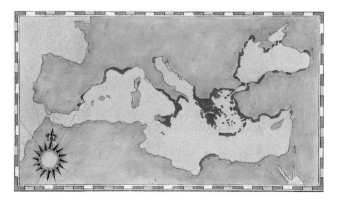

GREEK COLONIES
The red areas indicate where Greeks settled around the edges of the seas.

Ionian Sea

LIGHTHOUSE AT ALEXANDRIA
Alexander the Great set up many new cities called Alexandria. The first one was in Egypt.

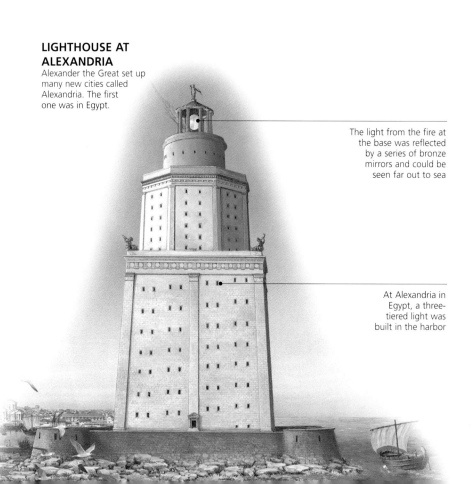

The light from the fire at the base was reflected by a series of bronze mirrors and could be seen far out to sea

At Alexandria in Egypt, a three-tiered light was built in the harbor

ANCIENT GREECE

MACEDONIA

Mount Olympus •

Thermopylae •

• Delphi

• Thebes

Marathon •

Corinth • • Athens

• Olympia

• Sparta

Aegean Sea

ASIA MINOR

• Ephesus

Cyclades

Rhodes

Mediterranean Sea

Knossos •

Crete

Society and Culture

GREEK ALPHABET

GREEK GODS

Athena
Goddess of
wisdom, art
and war

Zeus
God of the sky
and thunder

Aphrodite
Goddess of love
and beauty

Hestia
Goddess of
the family and
the hearth

Poseidon
God of earthquakes,
the sea, horses and bulls

Hermes
Messenger of
the gods and
protector of
travelers

Ares
God of war

THEATRICAL MASKS

Ancient Greek actors performed wearing masks.

The large mouths helped carry the actor's voice.

Masks were made from fabric stiffened with plaster.

Actors changed masks every time they changed character.

There was a range of theatrical masks.

Hera
Goddess of marriage and childbirth

Apollo
God of the sun, music and poetry

Artemis
Goddess of the moon, hunting and protector of girls

Demeter
Goddess of crops, especially grain

Hephaestus
God of fire and metalworkers

Daily Life

GREEK CLOTHING

Women wore a long tunic made of wool or linen, fastened on the shoulder with brooches or pins and tied at the waist and sometimes the hips

Men and boys wore thigh-length tunics; winter cloaks were often draped to leave one shoulder bare

Women's quarters
Women wove cloth in the loom room

INSIDE A GREEK HOUSE

Men's quarters
The head of the household entertained guests in a dining room furnished with couches

TUNIC STYLES

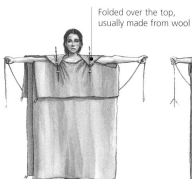

Folded over the top, usually made from wool

Fastened on the shoulders in several places, usually made from linen

Kitchen
Slaves baked bread in a pottery oven and cooked on an open fire—smoke escaped through a hole in the roof

Home furnishings
Couches, tables, stools, chairs, beds and storage chests were made from wood and bronze

Bathroom
Wealthy people had bathrooms in their homes and slaves filled the tubs with water

407

War and Warfare

HOPLITE

Greek foot soldiers, called hoplites, carried shields made of leather or bronze to protect them from neck to thigh

FIGHTING IN FORMATION

Phillip II of Macedon trained his hoplites to fight in a formation called a phalanx

BATTLE AT SEA

Soldiers wore bronze or leather breast and back plates joined on the shoulders and at the sides

Helmets protected soldiers' heads and faces

Athenian triremes were long, three-layered timber warships

Triremes were powered by 170 oarsmen

HOPLITE RACE

The hoplite race was part of the ancient Olympic games

Contestants were naked except for their leg-protectors and helmets, and they carried their shield as they raced

In 480 BC the Persians invaded Greece and destroyed Athens, after which the Greek fleet trapped the Persian fleet in the channel between the island of Salamis and the Greek mainland

At the Battle of Salamis Greek triremes rammed the larger Persian warships and forced them to retreat

The Roman World

ROMAN ARCHITECTURE

ROMAN EMPIRE

Hadrian's Arch

The Pantheon

The Colosseum

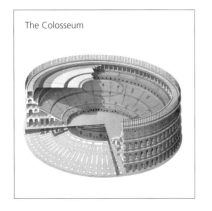

BRITANNIA

London

GAUL

Marseilles

HISPANIA

AFRICA

753 BC	753–510 BC	510–27 BC	27 BC	AD 395	AD 476	AD 1453
The legendary founding date of Rome.	Rome was ruled by a series of kings.	The Roman Republic.	The Roman Empire was established under Augustus.	The Empire was split into West and East.	The Western Empire collapsed.	The last city of the Eastern (Byzantine) Roman Empire was captured.

GERMANIA

DACIA

Black Sea

Ravenna

MACEDONIA

Constantinople

Corsica

Adriatic Sea

Rome

ASIA

Ostia

SYRIA

Pompeii

ACHAEA

CYPRUS

Sardinia

Damascus

Ionian Sea

Aegean Sea

Sicilia

CRETA

Jerusalem

Carthage

JUDAEA

Mediterranean Sea

Alexandria

AEGYPTUS

Engineering and Science

ROMAN NUMERALS

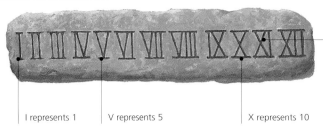

If "I" is before or after a letter it is subtracted from or added to the number—XI represents 11

I represents 1   V represents 5   X represents 10

BUILDER'S TOOLS

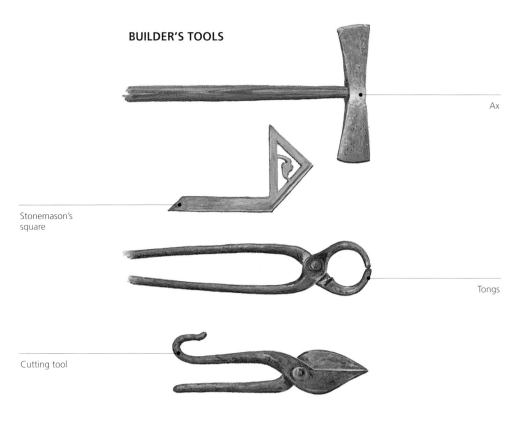

Ax

Stonemason's square

Tongs

Cutting tool

Scaled dividers

PANTHEON OF THE GODS
Rome's Pantheon honored all the state gods and still stands. Its domed roof, the largest of the time, represented the heavens; the circular opening stood for the sun.

Into Battle

GOING TO WAR

Legionaries marched with all their equipment and belongings—they carried food for three days, tools and weapons

Each century had its own standard-bearer

Each group of soldiers, called a century, was commanded by a centurion

ROMAN LEGIONS

 Legions were divided into nine cohorts of equal size which were led by a tenth, larger cohort

 A legion consisted of 5,000 foot soldiers

TORTOISE FORMATION

BATTERING RAM

ARMY CAMP

Armies on the march pitched a tent town each night. The camp was always arranged in the same way.

SIEGE WEAPONS

Catapult

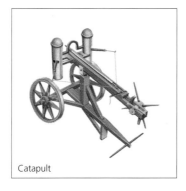

Catapult

Onager

Roman Baths

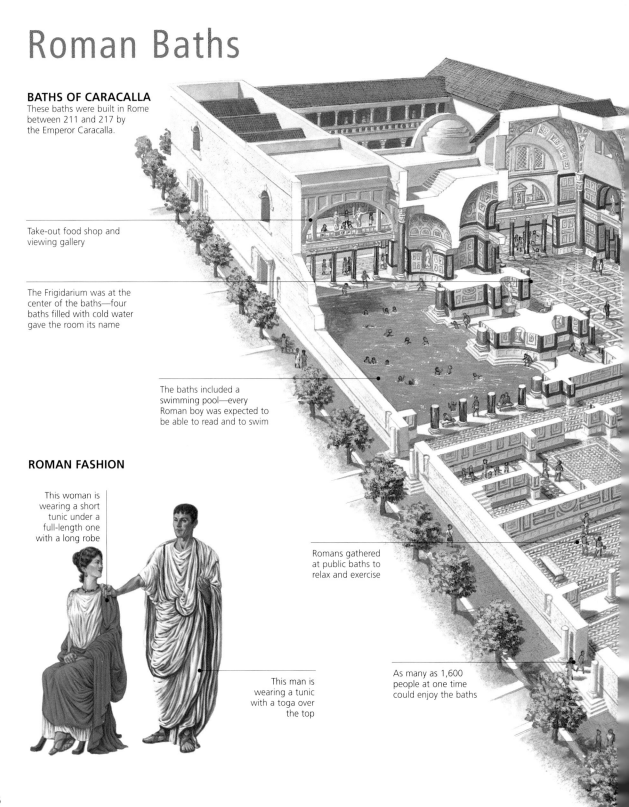

BATHS OF CARACALLA
These baths were built in Rome between 211 and 217 by the Emperor Caracalla.

Take-out food shop and viewing gallery

The Frigidarium was at the center of the baths—four baths filled with cold water gave the room its name

The baths included a swimming pool—every Roman boy was expected to be able to read and to swim

ROMAN FASHION

This woman is wearing a short tunic under a full-length one with a long robe

Romans gathered at public baths to relax and exercise

This man is wearing a tunic with a toga over the top

As many as 1,600 people at one time could enjoy the baths

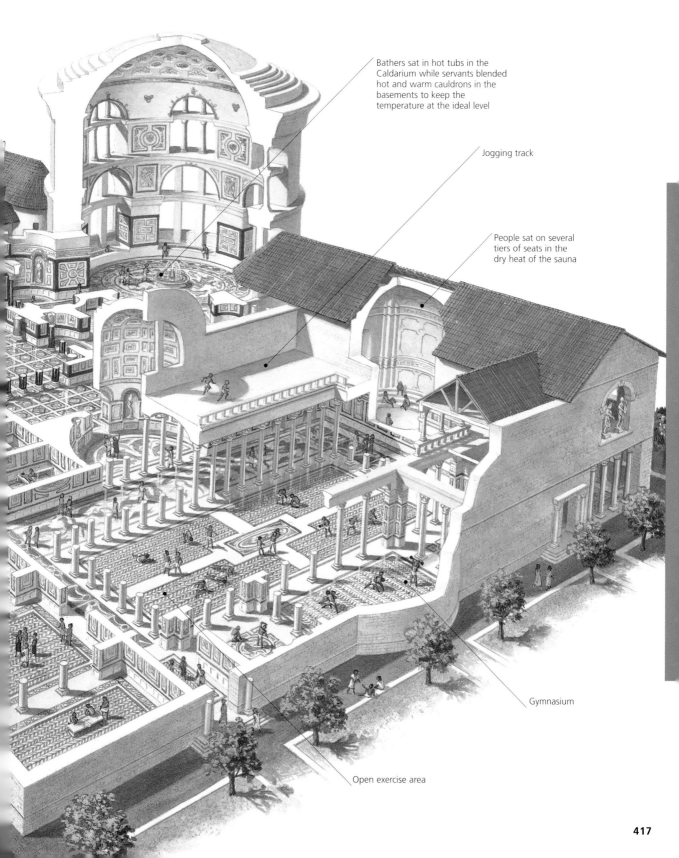

Bathers sat in hot tubs in the Caldarium while servants blended hot and warm cauldrons in the basements to keep the temperature at the ideal level

Jogging track

People sat on several tiers of seats in the dry heat of the sauna

Gymnasium

Open exercise area

Village Life

INSIDE A TEPEE

Smoke flaps could be opened from the inside with a pair of long poles

The tepee was laced from the bottom to the smoke flaps with pins carved from flexible willow wood

A decorated lining called a dew cloth was tied inside the tepee—it kept out moisture and helped insulate the tepee

The door was made from a flap of skin and was oval or V-shaped

Families kept everything they owned inside their tepee

Painted symbols protected the owners

The hem was pegged to the ground

418

SIGN LANGUAGE

Friend

Hello

Peace

Riding a horse

TARGET PRACTICE

TEPEE CAMP

PREPARING FOOD

Plains Indian women filled buffalo-hide containers with water and added hot stones to make the water boil

Women used stones to pound vegetables and grains for cooking

Travel and Hunting

A cedar log was split lengthwise. Shaping began with stone tools.

CEREMONIAL CANOE

MAKING A DUGOUT CANOE

The sides were chipped away to reach the required thickness.

Hollowing the inside to the correct thickness took skill and time.

Water heated with hot rocks softened the wood. Thwarts were fitted to broaden the interior.

The bow and stern pieces were attached and the hull was sanded and decorated.

DOG SLEDDING

Arctic tribes trained huskies to pull sleds

Sleds were made by laying a platform of driftwood or caribou antlers on wooden or whalebone runners

DOG TRAVOIS

Native Americans used buffalo hides for clothing and shelter, dung for fuel, fat for lamps, horns for spoons, bones for tools, stomachs for cooking pots, hooves for glue and meat for food

Plains Indians hunted buffalo from horseback

BUFFALO HUNT

Culture and Ceremonies

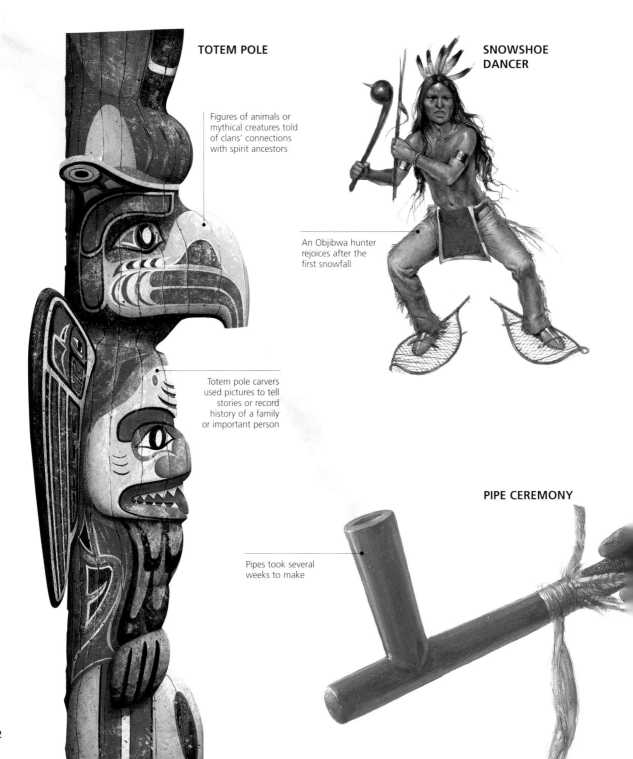

TOTEM POLE

Figures of animals or mythical creatures told of clans' connections with spirit ancestors

Totem pole carvers used pictures to tell stories or record history of a family or important person

SNOWSHOE DANCER

An Objibwa hunter rejoices after the first snowfall

PIPE CEREMONY

Pipes took several weeks to make

CEREMONIAL DANCE

Kwakiutl shamans wore bark costumes and painted wooden masks to represent birdlike friends of the fearsome Cannibal Spirit

Native Americans used solemn pipe-smoking rituals to ask for the spirits' help to make war, peace, rain, to hunt successfully, or to seal a good trade bargain

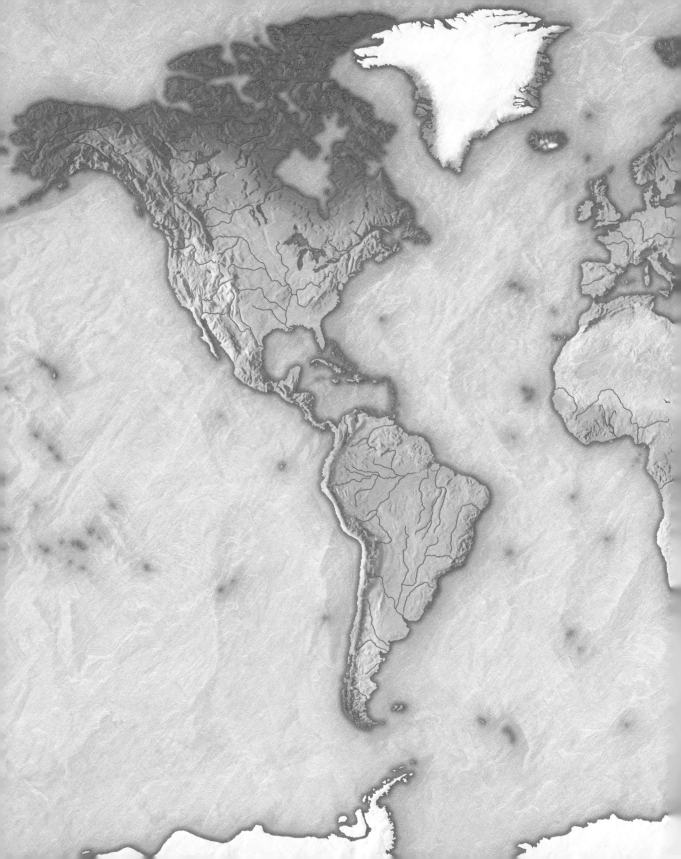

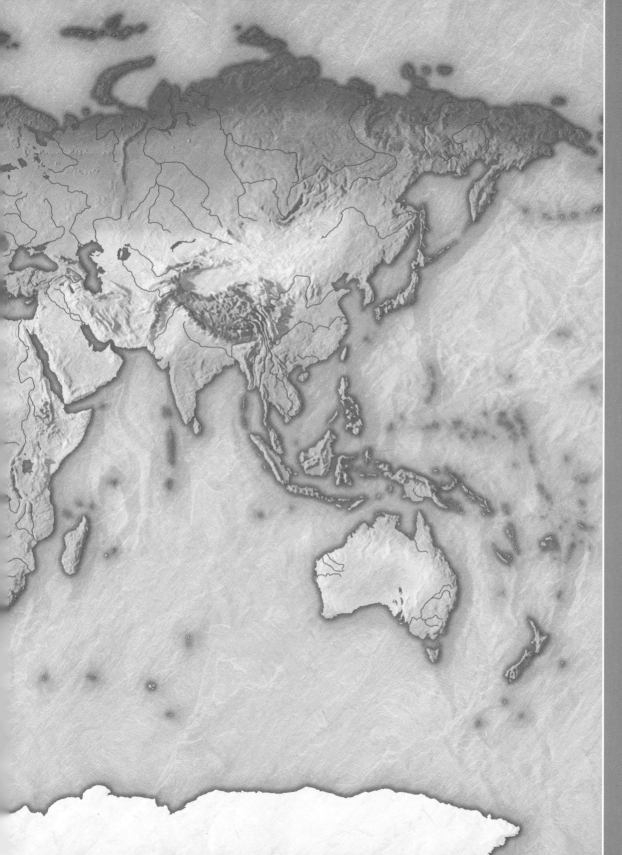

United Kingdom

BAGPIPE PLAYER

STONEHENGE
Wiltshire, England

BRIGHTON PAVILION
Brighton, England

COLDSTREAM GUARD

BLARNEY CASTLE
Blarney, Ireland

CRICKET PLAYER

HAMMER THROWER

SCOTLAND

Lerwick

Shetland Islands

Kirkwall   *Orkney Islands*

Thurso   John o'Groats

Lewis with Harris   Stornoway

North Uist

Skye   Inverness

South Uist   Ben Nevis
4,406 ft (1,343 m)   Aberdeen

H E B R I D E S

Mull   Oban   Dundee

Islay   Glasgow   **Edinburgh**

Arran

North Sea

GRAMPIAN MTS

Londonderry   Stranraer   Carlisle   Newcastle

NORTHERN IRELAND   Bangor   *PENNINES*   Middlesbrough

Sligo   **Belfast**

Dundalk   *Isle of Man*   York

IRELAND   *Irish Sea*   Blackpool   Leeds   Hull

Galway   Liverpool   Manchester   Sheffield

DUBLIN   *Anglesey*

Carlow   ▲ Mt. Snowdon
3,561 ft (1,085 m)   Nottingham   **ENGLAND**

Limerick   Leicester   Norwich

Tipperary   Aberystwyth   Birmingham   Coventry

Waterford   **WALES**   Cambridge   Ipswich

Carrantuohill
3,414 ft (1,041 m)   Milford Haven   Oxford   **LONDON**

Bantry   Cork   Swansea   **Cardiff**   Reading   *Thames*

St. George's Channel   Bristol   Bath

Southampton   Brighton

C e l t i c   S e a   Exeter   *Isle of Wight*

Plymouth

Land's End   *LOCATION*

Isles of Scilly

E n g l i s h   C h a n n e l

Channel Islands **(U.K.)**

Guernsey

Jersey   FRANCE

Liffey   *Shannon*   *Dee*   *Tay*   *Forth*   *Clyde*   *Tweed*   *Tyne*   *Trent*   *Severn*   *Wye*

Spain and Portugal

BULLFIGHTER

TORRE DE BELEM
Lisbon, Portugal

FLAMENCO DANCER

FISHERMAN

Azores
Madeira
Canary Islands

AZORES (PORTUGAL)

Corvo
Flores
Graciosa
Terceira
Faial
Pico
São Jorge
São Miguel
Santa Maria

MILES
0   50   100
0 50 100 150
KILOMETERS

MADEIRA (PORTUGAL)

Funchal

MILES
0   25   50
0   25 50 75
KILOMETERS

THE ALCAZAR
Segovia, Spain

CANARY ISLANDS (SPAIN)

La Palma
Tenerife
Gomera
Santa Cruz
de Tenerife
Lanzarote
Las Palmas
Fuerteventura
Hierro
Grand
Canary

MILES
0   25   50   75
0 50 100 150
KILOMETERS

Bay of Biscay

FRANCE

N
W E
S

La Coruña   Gijón   Santander
   Oviedo   Bilbao
Santiago   CANTABRIAN MOUNTAINS   Donostia–
        San Sebastián
        PYRENEES
      Pamplona   ANDORRA
Vigo   Ebro   Pico de Aneto   ANDORRA
       (11,168 ft (3,404 m))   LA VELLA
    Douro   Saragossa   COSTA BRAVA
Valladolid   Barcelona

Porto   Douro

ATLANTIC OCEAN

Salamanca   Segovia

PORTUGAL   SPAIN

    ☆ MADRID
Mondego   Coimbra

Alcántara   Toledo   MESETA   Valencia
Reservoir   Tagus

Tagus   Balearic Islands   Minorca
       Majorca
☆ LISBON   Badajoz   Guadiana   Palma
Setúbal   Evora   Ibiza
      Alicante   Ibiza

    SIERRA MORENA   Murcia
    Guadalquivir   Córdoba   Cartagena
ALGARVE   Seville
Guadiana   Granada
CAPE   Faro   Mulhacén 11,407 ft   Almería
ST. VINCENT   (3,477 m)
    Jerez   Málaga
Gulf of Cádiz   Cádiz   COSTA DEL SOL
    Algeciras   GIBRALTAR (U.K.)
     Ceuta (SPAIN)

Mediterranean Sea

ALGERIA

   Melilla (SPAIN)

MOROCCO

SCALE
MILES
0 25 50 75 100
0 50 100 150
KILOMETERS

LOCATION

431

France

TGV TRAIN

BOULES PLAYER

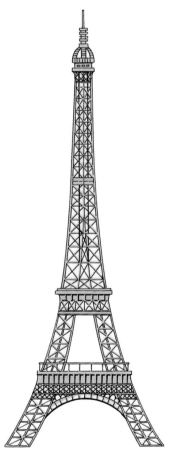

CAFE

FASHION MODEL

EIFFEL TOWER
Paris

CAMEMBERT CHEESE

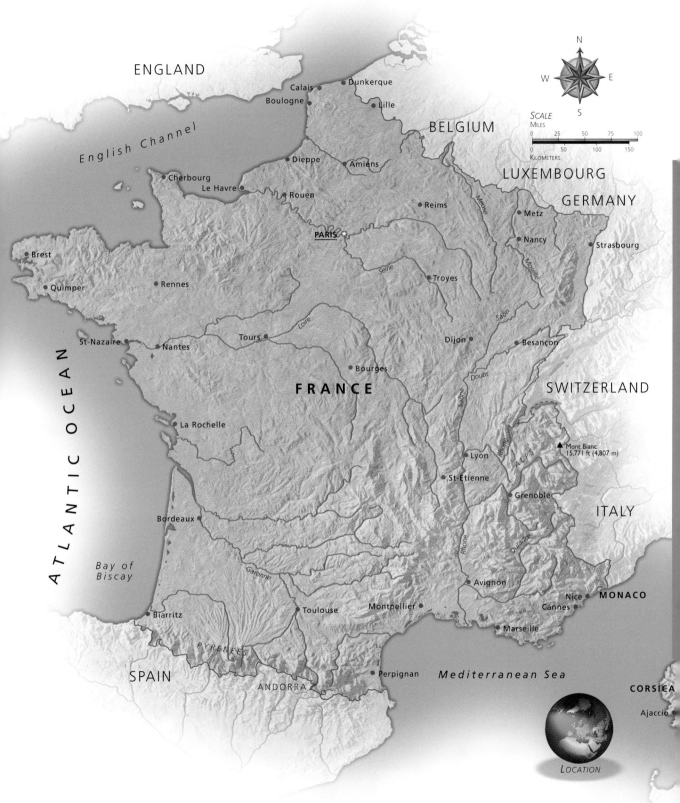

ENGLAND

English Channel

BELGIUM

LUXEMBOURG

GERMANY

Calais
Dunkerque
Boulogne
Lille
Dieppe
Amiens
Cherbourg
Le Havre
Rouen
Reims
Metz
Nancy
Strasbourg
PARIS
Brest
Seine
Troyes
Moselle
Quimper
Rennes
Meuse
ATLANTIC OCEAN
St-Nazaire
Nantes
Tours
Loire
Dijon
Saône
Besançon
FRANCE
Bourges
Doubs
SWITZERLAND
La Rochelle
Saône
Mont Blanc
15,771 ft (4,807 m)
Lyon
ALPS
St-Étienne
Grenoble
ITALY
Bordeaux
Rhône
Bay of
Biscay
Garonne
Durance
Avignon
Nice
MONACO
Biarritz
Toulouse
Montpellier
Cannes
Marseille
PYRENEES
Perpignan
Mediterranean Sea
CORSICA
SPAIN
ANDORRA
Ajaccio

N
W E
S

SCALE
MILES
0 25 50 75 100
0 50 100 150
KILOMETERS

LOCATION

The Low Countries

FOLK DANCERS
The Netherlands

WINDMILL

WOODEN CLOGS

ZUIDER ZEE FOLK COSTUME
The Netherlands

DAMME CANAL
Damme, Belgium

N
W   E
S

SCALE
MILES
0   10   20   30
0   10   20   30   40   50
KILOMETERS

Ameland

Terschelling

West Frisian Islands

Vlieland

Groningen

• Leeuwarden

Waddenzee

Texel

IJsselmeer

• Alkmaar

**THE
NETHERLANDS**

Haarlem •

✪ **AMSTERDAM**

Apeldoorn •

• Utrecht

Arnhem •

Lek

✪ **THE HAGUE**

• Rotterdam

Waal

Nijmegen •

Rhine

Dordrecht •

Maas

• Breda   • Tilburg

• Eindhoven

BAARLE-HERTOG
(BELGIUM)

North Sea

• Ostende   • Brugge

• Antwerp

GERMANY

Ghent •

FLANDERS

✪ **BRUSSELS**

BELGIUM   Liège •

Sambre

Meuse

FRANCE

LUXEMBOURG

✪ **LUXEMBOURG**

• Esch-sur-Alzette

LOCATION

435

Western Central Europe

ALPENHORN PLAYER
Swiss Alps, Switzerland

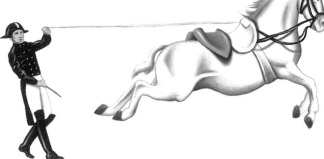

LIPIZZANER HORSE AND TRAINER
Vienna, Austria

FOLK COSTUME
Switzerland

HURDY-GURDY PLAYER
Germany

VIENNA PHILHARMONIC ORCHESTRA
Austria

NEUSCHWANSTEIN CASTLE
Bavaria, Germany

BAVARIAN BRASS BAND
Germany

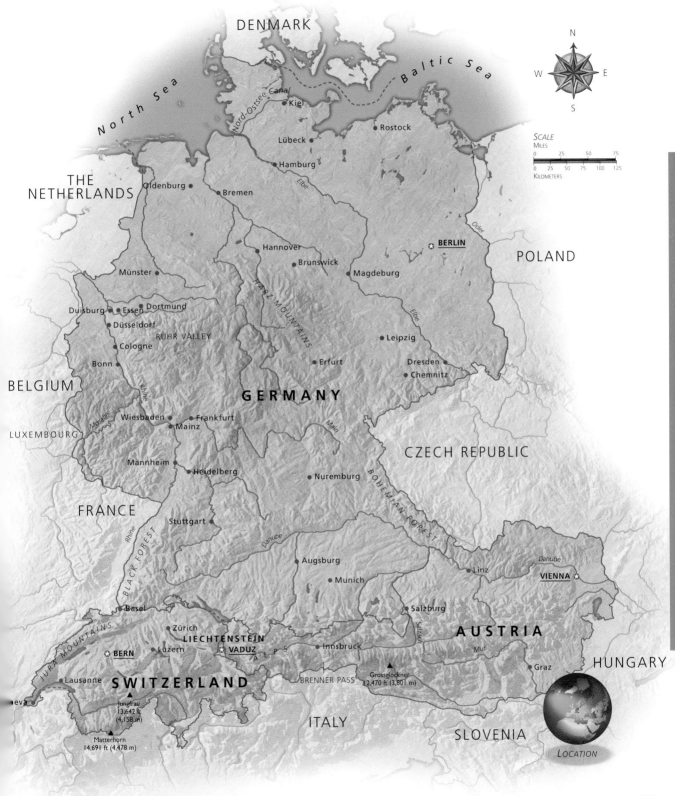

DENMARK

North Sea

Baltic Sea

Nord-Ostsee Canal

Kiel

Rostock

Lübeck

Hamburg

THE
NETHERLANDS

Oldenburg

Bremen

Elbe

Hannover

BERLIN

Brunswick

Magdeburg

POLAND

Oder

Münster

HARZ MOUNTAINS

Elbe

Duisburg Essen Dortmund

Düsseldorf

RUHR VALLEY

Leipzig

Cologne

Erfurt

Dresden

Bonn

Chemnitz

Rhine

GERMANY

BELGIUM

Mosselle

Wiesbaden Frankfurt

Mainz

Main

LUXEMBOURG

CZECH REPUBLIC

Mannheim

Heidelberg

Nuremburg

BOHEMIAN FOREST

FRANCE

Stuttgart

Danube

Augsburg

Linz

Danube

BLACK FOREST

Munich

VIENNA

Rhine

Salzburg

Basel

Salzach

AUSTRIA

Zürich

LIECHTENSTEIN

Innsbruck

HUNGARY

BERN

Luzern

VADUZ

A L P S

Mur

Graz

Lausanne

SWITZERLAND

BRENNER PASS

Grossglockner
12,470 ft (3,801 m)

JURA MOUNTAINS

Geneva

Jungfrau
13,642 ft
(4,158 m)

ITALY

SLOVENIA

Matterhorn
14,691 ft (4,478 m)

LOCATION

Italy

WINE MAKER

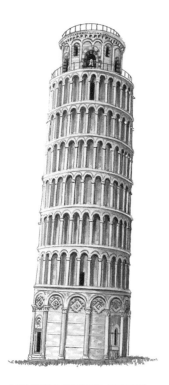

LEANING TOWER OF PISA

PIZZA MAKER

CHIANTI WINE

RIALTO BRIDGE
Venice

VATICAN GUARD

N
W   E
S

SCALE
MILES
0   25   50   75
0   50   100   150
KILOMETERS

FRANCE

SWITZERLAND

AUSTRIA

Mont Blanc
15,771 ft
(4,807 m)
Matterhorn
14,691 ft
(4,478 m)
Monte Rosa
15,203 ft
(4,634 m)

*Lake
Maggiore*

*Lake
Como*

DOLOMITES

Bolzano

ALPS

Turin

Milan
Brescia

*Lake
Garda*

Verona

Po

Padua

Venice

Trieste

SLOVENIA

Genoa

Parma

Ferrara

CROATIA

La Spezia

Modena

Bologna

Ravenna

*Gulf of
Venice*

*Ligurian
Sea*

Pisa

Arno

Florence

Rimini

☉ SAN MARINO
SAN MARINO

Livorno

Siena

Arezzo

APENNINES

Ancona

Elba

Perugia

*Corsica
(FRANCE)*

Giglio

Tiber

Pescara

*Adriatic
Sea*

VATICAN
CITY

☉ ROME

Sassari

ITALY

SARDINIA

Foggia

Ischia

Naples ▲

Bari

Capri

Salerno

Cagliari

Mt. Vesuvius
4,190 ft (1,277 m)

Taranto

Brindisi

*Tyrrhenian
Sea*

Gulf of Taranto

Strait of Otranto

Ustica

Cosenza

*Ionian
Sea*

Stromboli

*Lipari
Islands*

Palermo

Messina

Reggio di
Calabria

SICILY

Mt. Etna
10,902 ft
(3,323 m)

*Mediterranean
Sea*

Syracuse

MALTA

☆ VALLETTA

LOCATION

439

Southeastern Europe

FOLK COSTUME
Romania

SARAJEVO FOLK DANCER
Bosnia and Herzegovina

EVZONES GUARDS
Athens, Greece

CITY OF DUBROVNIK
Croatia

MOSTAR BRIDGE
Bosnia and Herzegovina

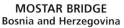

CASTLE OF VLAD TEPES
Transylvania, Romania

BOUZOUKI
Greece

KING AGAMEMNON'S DEATH MASK
Mycenae, Greece

AUSTRIA

SLOVENIA
LJUBLJANA

Rijeka

Pula

CROATIA

ZAGREB

Drava

Osijek

HUNGARY

VOJVODINA

Novi Sad

Arad

Oradea

Cluj-Napoca

ROMANIA

Timişoara

Mureş

Sibiu

Braşov

Galaţi

Ploieşti

UKRAINE

Iaşi

Prut

Siret

MOLDOVA

CARPATHIAN MTS.

TRANSYLVANIAN ALPS

Banja Luka

Bosna

Danube

BELGRADE

DALMATIA

BOSNIA AND
HERZEGOVINA

PINARIC ALPS

SARAJEVO

SERBIA

Craiova

BUCHAREST

Constanţa

Split

Mostar

YUGOSLAVIA

Niš

Danube

Morava

BULGARIA

Varna

N

MONTENEGRO

Priština

BALKAN MOUNTAINS

W   E

Dubrovnik

Podgorica

KOSOVO

Morava

SOFIA
Mt. Musala
9,596 ft (2,925 m)

Burgas

Black
Sea

S

Shkodër

Adriatic Sea

Vardar

SKOPJE

MACEDONIA

Struma

Plovdiv

RHODOPE MTS.

TURKEY

SCALE
MILES

0   25   50   75   100

Durrës

TIRANE

Bitola

Alexandroupolis

Thásos

0   50   100   150
KILOMETERS

ALBANIA

Vlorë

Korçë

Thessaloniki

Samothrace

Lemnos

Mt. Olympus
9,570 ft (2,917 m)

Aegean Sea

Lesbos

Corfu

GREECE

Volos

Northern
Sporades

Skyros

Chios

TURKEY

Levkás

Euboea

Ionian Islands

Khalkís

Sámos

Cephalonia

Patras

Piraeus

ATHENS

Ándros

Tinos

Mykonos

Zákinthos

PELOPONNESE

Tripolis

Cyclades

Náxos

Páros

DODECANESE

Kithira

Thira

Rhodes

Ionian Sea

Sea of Crete

Kárpathos

Canea

Crete   Iraklion

LOCATION

Mediterranean Sea

Eastern Europe

FOLK COSTUME
Poland

CITY OF RIGA
Latvia

FOLK DANCERS
Ukraine

STRAW FIGURES
Belarus

HORTOBAGY HORSEMAN
Hungary

Gulf of Finland

TALLINN

ESTONIA

Lake Peipus

Gulf of Riga

LATVIA

RIGA

Daugava

Baltic Sea

LITHUANIA

Vitsyebsk

RUSSIA

KALININGRAD
OBLAST
(RUSSIA)

Gdańsk

VILNIUS

Dnieper

Szczecin

Neman

MINSK

Mahilyow

Bydgoszcz

Poznań

BELARUS

POLAND

WARSAW

Pripyat

Homyel

Łódź

GERMANY

Odra

Wrocław

PRAGUE

Katowice

Vistula

KIEV

Kharkiv

Plzeň

Kraków

CZECH
REPUBLIC

Brno

L'viv

UKRAINE

Dnieper

Dnipropetrovs'k

BOHEMIAN FOREST

SUDETEN MTS

SLOVAKIA

Košice

Donets'k

AUSTRIA

BRATISLAVA

Bug

*Kakhovka
Reservoir*

CARPATHIAN MTS

BUDAPEST

Debrecen

Dniester

Prut

CHISINAU

SLOVENIA

HUNGARY

ROMANIA

MOLDOVA

Odessa

Sea of Azov

Danube

Pécs

CRIMEAN MTS

CROATIA

YUGOSLAVIA

Sevastapol'

Black Sea

N
W   E
S

SCALE
MILES
0   50   100   150
0   50   100   150   200   250
KILOMETERS

COSSACK DANCER
Belarus

LOCATION

443

Northern Europe

SAMI (LAPP) PEOPLE
Northern Scandinavia

BERGEN WHARF
Norway

ICE FISHING

KICK-SLEDDING

LITTLE MERMAID STATUE
Copenhagen, Denmark

ARCTIC CIRCLE PYRAMID
Norway

KALMAR CASTLE
Sweden

ICELAND

Akureyri

VATNAJÖKULL

⋆ **REYKJAVIK**

ATLANTIC OCEAN

MILES
0   50   100   150
0   100   200
KILOMETERS

NORTH
CAPE

Barents Sea

Hammerfest

Tromso

LAPLAND

*Lake
Inari*

*Lofoten
Islands*   Narvik

Kebnekaise
6,965 ft
(2,123 m)

Gällivare

Torne

Kemi

FINLAND

RUSSIA

Bodo

Norwegian Sea

Luleå

Skellefte

Oulu

Oulujärvi

SWEDEN

Ume

Umeå

Trondheim

Gulf of Bothnia

Vaasa

Kuopio

Joensuu

Jyväskylä

*Lake
Saimaa*

Nordfjord   Galdhøpiggen
8,100 ft (2,469 m)

Indal

Sundsvall

Pori

Tampere

Sognefjord

*JOTUNHEIM
MOUNTAINS*

Österdal

Lahti

Bergen

NORWAY

Turku

HELSINKI ⊛

⊛ **OSLO**

*Aland
Islands*

Gulf of Finland

Drammen

Uppsala

Stavanger

Karlstad

Orebro

⋆ **STOCKHOLM**

ESTONIA

Fredrikstad

Norrköping

Kristiansand

*Lake
Vänern*

Linköping

*Lake
Vättern*

Skagerrak

Goteborg

Borås

Jönköping

Gotland

SCALE
MILES
0   25   50   75   100   125
0   50   100   150   200
KILOMETERS

LATVIA

Alborg

DENMARK

Oland

*North
Sea*

Arhus

Hälsingborg

Baltic Sea

Esbjerg

⊛ **COPENHAGEN**

Odense   *Sjaelland*

Malmö

Fyn

Bornholm

Lolland

LOCATION

GERMANY   POLAND   445

Western Canada and Alaska

ALASKAN FERRY

IDITAROD MUSHER AND DOG TEAM
Alaska

Bering Strait

Nome

**ALASKA
(U.S.A.)**

ALASKA RANG

Anchorage

Aleutlian Islands

*Kodiak
Island*

Gulf of Ala

P A C I F I C   O C E A N

SNOWMOBILE RIDER

INUIT ICE-FISHERMAN
Canada

TRADITIONAL CHURCH
Northwest Territories, Canada

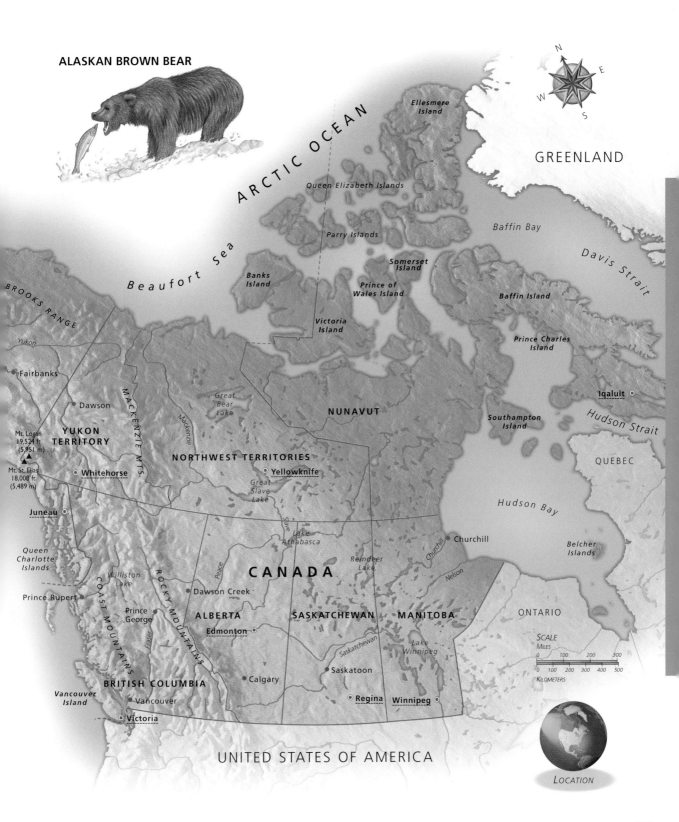

ALASKAN BROWN BEAR

ARCTIC OCEAN

GREENLAND

Ellesmere
Island

Queen Elizabeth Islands

Baffin Bay

Davis Strait

Beaufort Sea

Parry Islands

Banks
Island

Somerset
Island

Prince of
Wales Island

Baffin Island

BROOKS RANGE

Victoria
Island

Prince Charles
Island

Yukon

Fairbanks

Dawson

Great
Bear
Lake

NUNAVUT

Iqaluit

MACKENZIE MTS.

Mackenzie

Southampton
Island

Hudson Strait

Mt. Logan
19,524 ft
(5,951 m)

YUKON
TERRITORY

NORTHWEST TERRITORIES

Yellowknife

QUEBEC

Mt. St. Elias
18,008 ft
(5,489 m)

Whitehorse

Great
Slave
Lake

Juneau

Slave

Hudson Bay

Queen
Charlotte
Islands

Williston
Lake

Peace

Lake
Athabasca

Reindeer
Lake

Churchill

Churchill

Belcher
Islands

Prince Rupert

COAST MOUNTAINS

ROCKY MOUNTAINS

Dawson Creek

CANADA

Nelson

Prince
George

Fraser

ALBERTA

SASKATCHEWAN

MANITOBA

ONTARIO

Edmonton

Saskatchewan

Lake
Winnipeg

BRITISH COLUMBIA

Calgary

Saskatoon

SCALE
MILES
0   100   200   300
0 100 200 300 400 500
KILOMETERS

Vancouver
Island

Vancouver

Regina

Winnipeg

Victoria

UNITED STATES OF AMERICA

LOCATION

447

Eastern Canada

ICE HOCKEY PLAYERS

TRADITIONAL CHURCH
Newfoundland

CAP-DES-ROSIERS LIGHTHOUSE
Gaspé Peninsula, Québec

CN TOWER
Toronto

CHATEAU FRONTENAC
Québec City

ROYAL CANADIAN MOUNTED POLICE (MOUNTIES)

MANITOBA

ONTARIO

Lake
Nipig

Nipigon

Thunder Bay

Lake
Superior

UNITED STATES
OF AMERICA

Lak
Michi

N
W   E
S

SCALE
MILES
0   50   100   150   200
0   100   200   300   400
KILOMETERS

Ivujivik

Hudson Strait

PÉNINSULE D'UNGAVA
(UNGAVA PENINSULA)

Hudson Bay

*Ungava
Bay*

*Belcher
Islands*

Feuilles

Labrador Sea

Nain

A T L A N T I C   O C E A N

QUEBEC

*James
Bay*

*Réservoir de
la Grande
Deux*

LABRADOR

*Smallwood
Reservoir*

N E W F O U N D L A N D

Albany

Lac Sakami

Churchill

Happy
Valley —
Goose Bay

Moosonee

Hearst

*Lac
Mistassini*

Sault Ste. Marie

*Lac
Saint-Jean*

Saguenay

Sudbury

PENINSULE
DE LA GASPESIE
(GASPE PENINSULA)

*Ile d'Anticosti
(Anticosti Island)*

Gulf of St. Lawrence

Newfoundland

*Lake
Huron*

St. Lawrence

Québec

NEW
BRUNSWICK

*Prince
Edward
Island*

St. John's

OTTAWA

Montréal

Fredericton

Charlottetown

*St-Pierre and
Miquelon*
(FRANCE)

Toronto

London

Lake Ontario

Saint John

indsor

Lake Erie

NOVA
SCOTIA

Halifax

Bay of Fundy

UNITED STATES
OF AMERICA

LOCATION

Northeastern United States

AMISH PEOPLE
Pennsylvania

LIBERTY BELL
Philadelphia, Pennsylvania

STATUE OF LIBERTY
New York City

CHRYSLER BUILDING
New York City

KENTUCKY DERBY

CAPITOL BUILDING
Washington, D.C.

INDIANA

ILLINOIS

Louisville

Frankfort

Licking

KENTUCKY

TENNESSEE

BASKETBALL PLAYER

CANADA

MAINE

VERMONT

Fort Kent

Augusta

Montpelier

NEW
HAMPSHIRE

Portland

NEW YORK

Lake Ontario

Concord

Manchester

Lake Erie

Buffalo

Albany

Boston

MASSACHUSETTS

CONNECTICUT

Providence

Hartford

RHODE
ISLAND

PENNSYLVANIA

New York

Pittsburgh

Harrisburg

OHIO

Trenton

Philadelphia

NEW
JERSEY

Atlantic City

WEST VIRGINIA

Baltimore

Dover

Annapolis

WASHINGTON, D.C.

DELAWARE

Charleston

MARYLAND

ATLANTIC OCEAN

N

W   E

S

Richmond

Roanoke

VIRGINIA

Norfolk

SCALE
MILES
0   25   50   75   100   125

0   50   100   150   200
KILOMETERS

NORTH
CAROLINA

LOCATION

451

Central United States

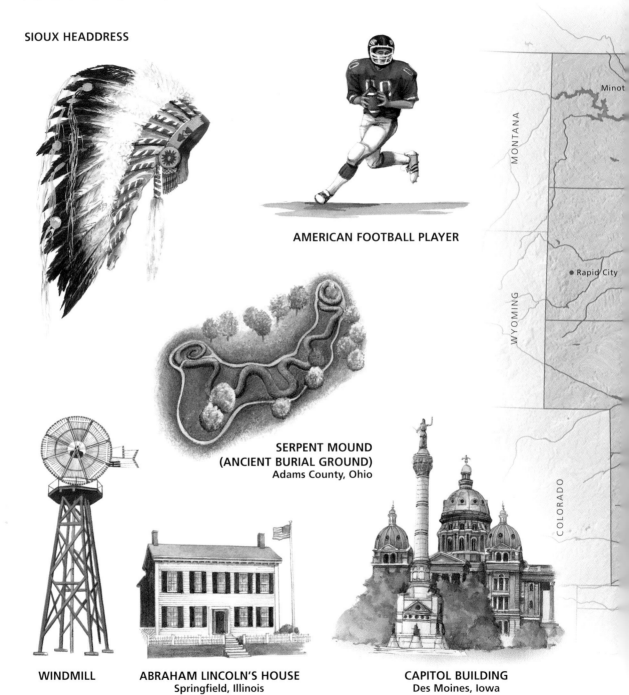

SIOUX HEADDRESS

AMERICAN FOOTBALL PLAYER

SERPENT MOUND
(ANCIENT BURIAL GROUND)
Adams County, Ohio

WINDMILL

ABRAHAM LINCOLN'S HOUSE
Springfield, Illinois

CAPITOL BUILDING
Des Moines, Iowa

MONTANA

Minot

WYOMING

Rapid City

COLORADO

North America

COUNTRIES OF THE WORLD

N

W · E

S

CANADA

CANADA

CANADA

Lake
Superior

Lake
Huron

Lake
Michigan

Lake Erie

MINNESOTA

Grand Forks

**NORTH
DAKOTA**

ismarck

Fargo   Moorhead

Duluth   Superior

Marquette

Sault Ste. Marie

Escanaba

Red

Lake of the
Woods

Mississippi

St. Croix

WISCONSIN

Green Bay
Appleton

MICHIGAN

Bay City

Saginaw

**SOUTH
DAKOTA**

Pierre

Minnesota

Minneapolis   St. Paul

Rochester

La Crosse

Madison

Milwaukee

Grand Rapids   Lansing

Detroit

James

Sioux Falls

Missouri

Mississippi

Dubuque

Chicago

Gary

Fort Wayne

Toledo   Cleveland

G R E A T   P L A I N S

Sioux City

IOWA

Davenport

Rock Island

Des Moines

NEBRASKA

Omaha   Council Bluffs

Peoria

OHIO

Columbus

rth Platte

Grand
Island   Lincoln

St. Joseph

Hannibal

Illinois

Springfield

Indianapolis

INDIANA

Cincinnati

Wabash

**WEST
VIRGINIA**

Kansas

Topeka

Kansas City

St. Louis   East St. Louis

ILLINOIS

Ohio

Salina

KANSAS

Dodge City   Wichita

Arkansas

Jefferson City

MISSOURI

Springfield

Mississippi

Cairo

O Z A R K   P L A T E A U

Evansville

KENTUCKY

Ohio

OKLAHOMA

ARKANSAS

LOCATION

453

Southern United States

COUNTRY MUSICIAN

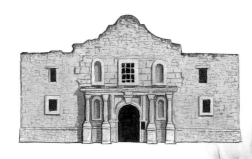

THE ALAMO
San Antonio, Texas

RODEO

New Mexico

Amarillo

Lubbock

El Paso

Pecos

TEXAS

Rio Grande

MEXICO

Laredo

MISSISSIPPI RIVER PADDLE STEAMER

JAZZ MUSICIAN

KANSAS

MISSOURI

KENTUCKY

VIRGINIA

OZARK PLATEAU

• Tulsa

◉ Oklahoma City

OKLAHOMA

Arkansas

Little Rock ◦

ARKANSAS

• Memphis

◉ Nashville

TENNESSEE

Tennessee

Birmingham •

MISSISSIPPI

ALABAMA

APPALACHIAN MTS.

▲ Mt. Mitchell
6,684 ft
(2,037 m)

◉ Raleigh

NORTH CAROLINA

• Charlotte

SOUTH
CAROLINA

Columbia ◉

• Wilmington

ATLANTIC COASTAL PLAIN

◉ Atlanta

Macon •
Columbus •

• Charleston

Savannah

• Savannah

ATLANTIC OCEAN

Red

Fort
Worth

• Dallas

Brazos

MISSISSIPPI

◉ Jackson

GEORGIA

• Albany

Chattahoochee

Alabama

◉ Austin

LOUISIANA

Mobile •

Tallahassee ◉

• Jacksonville

Houston •

San Antonio •

GULF COASTAL PLAIN

Lake •
Charles

◉ Baton Rouge

• New Orleans

Galveston

Orlando •

• Tampa

FLORIDA

N

W   E

S

The
Bahamas

Corpus
Christi •

Lake
Okeechobee

Gulf of Mexico

• Miami

Florida Keys

Brownsville •

Key West •

Straits of Florida

BASEBALL PLAYER

EPCOT CENTER
Orlando, Florida

SCALE
MILES
0   50   100   150   200
0   100   200   300
KILOMETERS

LOCATION

455

Western United States

IN-LINE SKATER

HULA DANCER
Hawaii

NAVAJO WEAVER
Arizona

GOLDEN GATE BRIDGE
San Francisco

PUEBLO POTTERY
New Mexico

DISNEYLAND
Anaheim, California

TAOS PUEBLO (NATIVE VILLAGE)
Taos, New Mexico

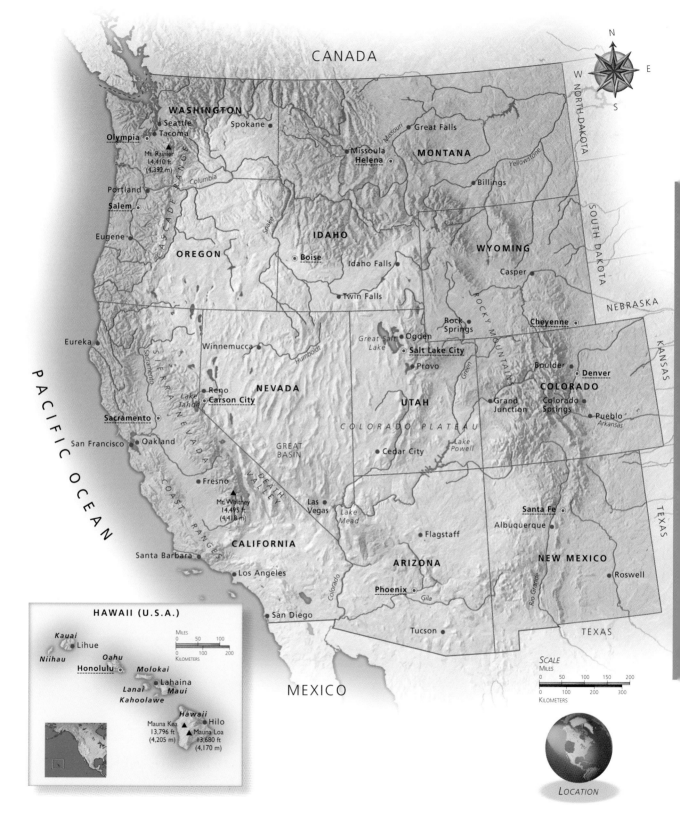

CANADA

N
W · E
S

WASHINGTON
Seattle
Tacoma
Olympia
Spokane
Mt. Rainier
14,410 ft
(4,392 m)
Columbia
Portland
Salem
Eugene
OREGON

Missoula
Helena
Great Falls
Missouri
MONTANA
Yellowstone
Billings

NORTH DAKOTA

CASCADE RANGE

Snake
IDAHO
Boise
Idaho Falls
Twin Falls

WYOMING
Casper

SOUTH DAKOTA

NEBRASKA

Eureka

Winnemucca

Sacramento
NEVADA

SIERRA NEVADA

Reno
Carson City
Lake
Tahoe

Sacramento

San Francisco
Oakland

COAST RANGES

Fresno

GREAT
BASIN

DEATH VALLEY

Mt. Whitney
14,495 ft
(4,418 m)

CALIFORNIA

Santa Barbara

Los Angeles

San Diego

Humboldt

Great Salt
Lake
Ogden
Salt Lake City
Provo

UTAH

COLORADO PLATEAU

Cedar City

Lake
Powell

Las
Vegas
Lake
Mead

Colorado

ARIZONA

Phoenix
Gila

Tucson

Rock
Springs

ROCKY MOUNTAINS

Green

Grand
Junction

Flagstaff

Cheyenne

Boulder
Denver
COLORADO
Colorado
Springs
Pueblo
Arkansas

KANSAS

Santa Fe
Albuquerque

NEW MEXICO

Roswell

Rio Grande

TEXAS

MEXICO

TEXAS

PACIFIC OCEAN

N
E

LOCATION

SCALE
MILES
0   50   100 150 200
0   100 200 300
KILOMETERS

HAWAII (U.S.A.)

Kauai
Lihue
Niihau
Oahu
Honolulu
Molokai
Lanai
Lahaina
Maui
Kahoolawe
Hawaii
Mauna Kea
13,796 ft
(4,205 m)
Mauna Loa
13,680 ft
(4,170 m)
Hilo

MILES
0   50   100
0   100   200
KILOMETERS

457

Central America and the Caribbean

FOLK DANCER
Mexico

METROPOLITAN CATHEDRAL
Mexico City, Mexico

OLMEC STONE CARVING
Mexico

STEEL BAND
The Caribbean

TRADITIONAL FARMER
Guatemala

THATCHED CORNCRIB
Mexico

UNITED STATES
OF AMERICA

Tijuana
Mexicali
Ciudad
Juárez
Hermosillo
Chihuahua
BAJA CALIFORNIA
Gulf of California
Rio Grande
SIERRA MADRE OCCIDENTAL
Culiacán
Monterrey
Torreón
Matamoros
La Paz
Tampico
MEXICO
Guadalajara
MEXICO CITY
Veracruz
Orizaba
18,700 ft
(5,700 m)
Acapulco

PACIFIC OCEAN

ATLANTIC OCEAN

Gulf of Mexico

NASSAU

THE BAHAMAS

Turks and
Caicos Islands
(U.K.)

HAVANA

CUBA

Virgin Islands
(U.S.A./U.K.)

Anguilla (U.K.)

Antigua and
Barbuda

San Juan

St. Kitts–
Nevis

Guadeloupe
(FRANCE)

Bay of
Campeche

YUCATAN
PENINSULA

Cayman Islands
(U.K.)

SANTO DOMINGO

PORT-AU-PRINCE

HAITI

DOMINICAN
REPUBLIC

Puerto Rico
(U.S.A.)

Montserrat
(U.K.)

Dominica

Martinique
(FRANCE)

Fort-de-France

JAMAICA

KINGSTON

St. Lucia

Barbados

St. Vincent and
the Grenadines

Caribbean Sea

Belize City

BELMOPAN

BELIZE

HONDURAS

Netherlands
Antilles
(NETHERLANDS)

Grenada

Aruba
(NETHERLANDS)

PORT-OF-SPAIN

TRINIDAD
AND TOBAGO

GUATEMALA

GUATEMALA

TEGUCIGALPA

VENEZUELA

SAN SALVADOR

EL SALVADOR

NICARAGUA

MANAGUA

COSTA RICA

SAN JOSE

PANAMA

PANAMA

COLOMBIA

N
W   E
S

SCALE
MILES
0   100   200   300

0   100 200 300 400 500
KILOMETERS

MARIACHI BAND
Mexico

LOCATION

459

Northern South America

QUECHUA MAN
Peru

CARNIVAL DANCER
Rio de Janeiro, Brazil

KAYAPO MAN
Brazil

TXUKAHAMAI HUNTERS WITH ANACONDA
Brazil

NOSSO SENHOR DO BOMFIM CHURCH
Salvador, Brazil

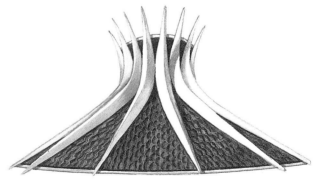

BRASILIA CATHEDRAL
Brasília, Brazil

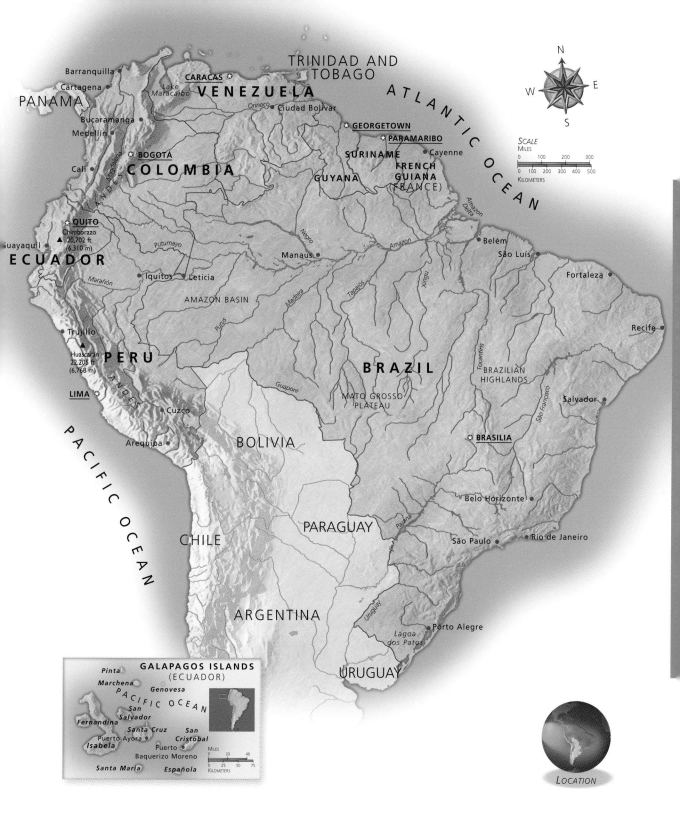

PANAMA

Barranquilla
Cartagena

CARACAS ✪

TRINIDAD AND
TOBAGO

VENEZUELA

Bucaramanga
Medellín

Lake
Maracaibo

Orinoco

Ciudad Bolívar

ATLANTIC

Cali

✪ **BOGOTÁ**

COLOMBIA

✪ **GEORGETOWN**

✪ **PARAMARIBO**

Cayenne

SURINAME

GUYANA

**FRENCH
GUIANA
(FRANCE)**

OCEAN

Amazon
Delta

✪ **QUITO**
Chimborazo
▲ 20,702 ft
(6,310 m)

Putumayo

Negro

Amazon

Belém

São Luís

ECUADOR

uayaquil

Marañón

Iquitos

Leticia

Manaus

Fortaleza

AMAZON BASIN

Purus

Madeira

Tapajós

Xingu

Trujillo

Huascarán
22,205 ft
(6,768 m)

PERU

Guaporé

BRAZIL

**BRAZILIAN
HIGHLANDS**

Recife

Tocantins

São Francisco

Salvador

LIMA

ANDES

Cuzco

**MATO GROSSO
PLATEAU**

Arequipa

BOLIVIA

✪ **BRASILIA**

PACIFIC

Belo Horizonte

PARAGUAY

Paraná

CHILE

São Paulo

Rio de Janeiro

OCEAN

ARGENTINA

Uruguay

Pôrto Alegre

Lagoa
dos Patos

URUGUAY

N
W   E
S

SCALE
MILES
0   100   200   300
0 100 200 300 400 500
KILOMETERS

Pinta

GALAPAGOS ISLANDS
(ECUADOR)

Marchena

Genovesa

PACIFIC OCEAN

San
Salvador

Fernandina

Santa Cruz

San
Cristóbal

Puerto Ayora

Isabela

Puerto
Baquerizo Moreno

MILES
0   20   40

Santa María

Española

0   25   50   75
KILOMETERS

LOCATION

461

Southern South America

VILLAGE MUSICIANS
Bolivia

FOLK COSTUME
Bolivia

TANGO DANCERS
Argentina

PRESIDENTIAL PALACE
Asunción, Paraguay

CONGRESO NACIONAL
Buenos Aires, Argentina

TRADITIONAL JESUIT CHURCH
Argentina

GIANT BROMELIAD
The Andes, Bolivia

GUANACOS
Argentina

PERU

BRAZIL

Guaporé

Trinidad

BOLIVIA

Lake Titicaca

LA PAZ ⚙ ▲
Mt. Illimani
21,201 ft
(6,462 m)

Cochabamba

Santa Cruz

Arica

Lake Poopó

⚙ **SUCRE**

Iquique

A T A C A M A   D E S E R T

PARAGUAY

Pilcomayo

G R A N   C H A C O

Antofagasta

Cerro Ojos
del Salado
22,664 ft (6,908 m)

Copiapó

Bonete
22,546 ft
(6,872 m)

San Miguel
de Tucumán

Paraguay

⚙ **ASUNCION**

Corrientes

Río Salado

BRAZIL

La Serena

Aconcagua
22,834 ft
(6,960 m)

San Juan

Mendoza

Córdoba

P A M P A S

Rosario

Paraná

Uruguay

URUGUAY

Valparaíso

⚙ **SANTIAGO**

BUENOS AIRES

La Plata

⚙ **MONTEVIDEO**

Concepción

A N D E S

ARGENTINA

Colorado

Mar del Plata

CHILE

Negro

Bahía Blanca

P A C I F I C   O C E A N

Puerto Montt

VALDES
PENINSULA

P A T A G O N I A

A T L A N T I C   O C E A N

Comodoro
Rivadavia

Puerto
Deseado

*Falkland Islands
(U.K.)*

Stanley

Río Gallegos

Strait of
Magellan

Punta
Arenas

Tierra del Fuego

Ushuaia

Cape Horn

N

W **E**

S

SCALE
MILES

	100	200	300
0
KILOMETERS
0 100 200 300 400 500

EASTER ISLAND
(CHILE)

Mataveri

P A C I F I C   O C E A N

MILES
0   5   10   15

0   10   20
KILOMETERS

LOCATION

Russia

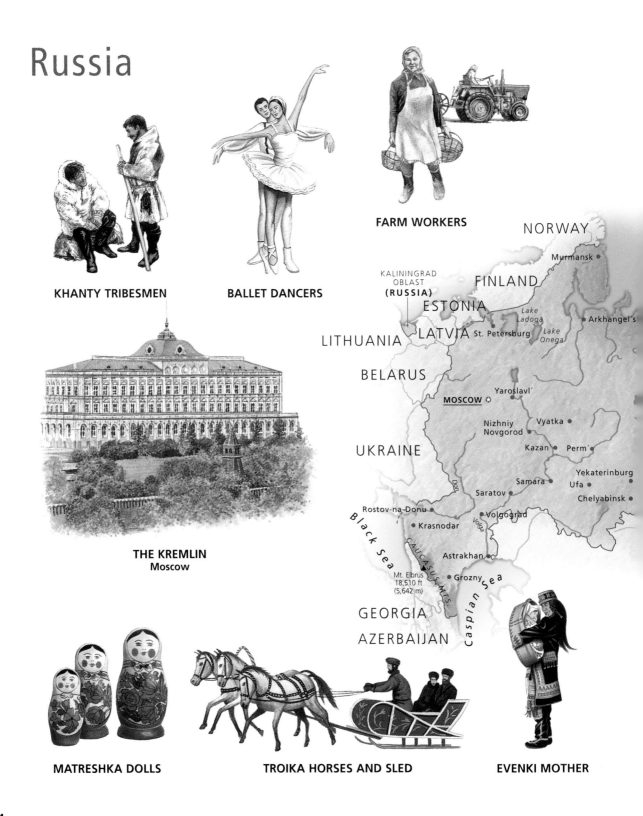

KHANTY TRIBESMEN

BALLET DANCERS

FARM WORKERS

THE KREMLIN
Moscow

KALININGRAD
OBLAST
(RUSSIA)

NORWAY

FINLAND

ESTONIA

LATVIA

LITHUANIA

BELARUS

UKRAINE

GEORGIA

AZERBAIJAN

Murmansk

Lake
Ladoga

Arkhangel's

Lake
Onega

St. Petersburg

Yaroslavl'

MOSCOW

Nizhniy
Novgorod

Vyatka

Kazan

Perm'

Yekaterinburg

Samara

Ufa

Saratov

Chelyabinsk

Rostov-na-Donu

Volgograd

Krasnodar

Volga

Don

Astrakhan

Black Sea

CAUCASUS MTS.

Grozny

Caspian Sea

Mt. Elbrus
18,510 ft
(5,642 m)

MATRESHKA DOLLS

TROIKA HORSES AND SLED

EVENKI MOTHER

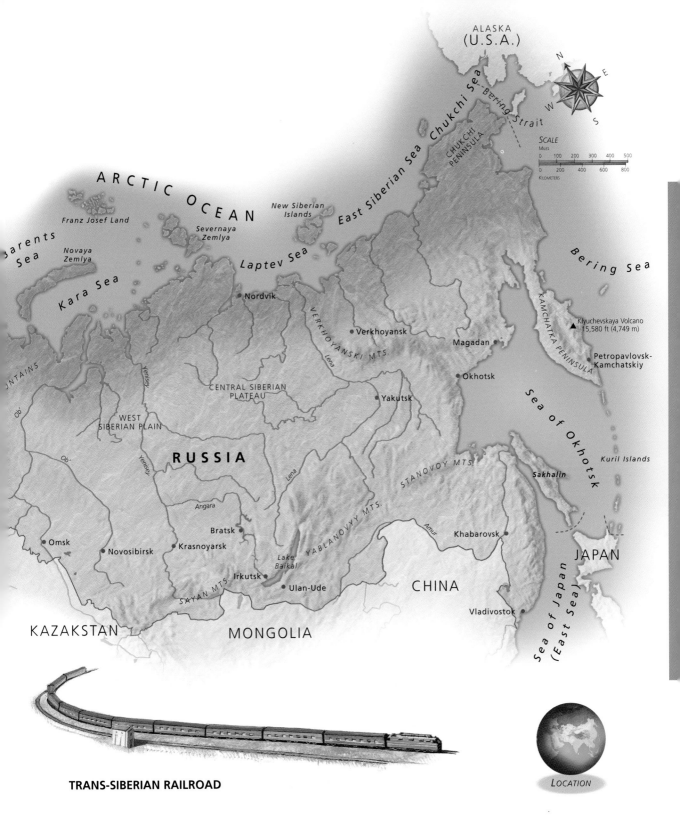

ALASKA
(U.S.A.)

ARCTIC OCEAN

Barents Sea

Franz Josef Land

Novaya Zemlya

Kara Sea

Severnaya Zemlya

New Siberian Islands

Laptev Sea

East Siberian Sea

Chukchi Sea

Bering Strait

CHUKCHI PENINSULA

Bering Sea

KAMCHATKA PENINSULA

Klyuchevskaya Volcano
15,580 ft (4,749 m)

Petropavlovsk-Kamchatskiy

Sea of Okhotsk

Kuril Islands

Sakhalin

Nordvik

Verkhoyansk

VERKHOYANSKI MTS.

Lena

Magadan

Okhotsk

Yakutsk

CENTRAL SIBERIAN PLATEAU

WEST SIBERIAN PLAIN

Yenisey

Ob

Ob

Yenisey

RUSSIA

Lena

STANOVOY MTS.

Amur

Khabarovsk

JAPAN

Sea of Japan (East Sea)

Angara

Bratsk

Krasnoyarsk

YABLANOVYY MTS.

Lake Baikal

Omsk

Novosibirsk

SAYAN MTS.

Irkutsk

Ulan-Ude

CHINA

Vladivostok

KAZAKSTAN

MONGOLIA

SCALE

MILES
0 100 200 300 400 500

KILOMETERS
0 200 400 600 800

N
E
W
S

TRANS-SIBERIAN RAILROAD

Location

Central Eurasia

STREET VENDOR
Kazakstan

FOLK COSTUME
Georgia

WHIRLING DERVISH
Turkey

GREECE

BULGARIA

EUROPE

Dardanelles

Istanbul

Izmir • Bursa *Bosporus*

B l a c

TURKEY

ANKARA ✪

Antalya •

Mediterranean Sea

• Adana

CYPRUS

NICOSIA ✿

Euphrates

TURKISH FEDERATED STATE OF CYPRUS

SYRIA

BLUE MOSQUE
Istanbul, Turkey

LONGHORN MUSICIAN
Tajikistan

SARSEMBEK HERDER
Kazakstan

EARLY VILLAGE OF CAPPADOCIA
Turkey

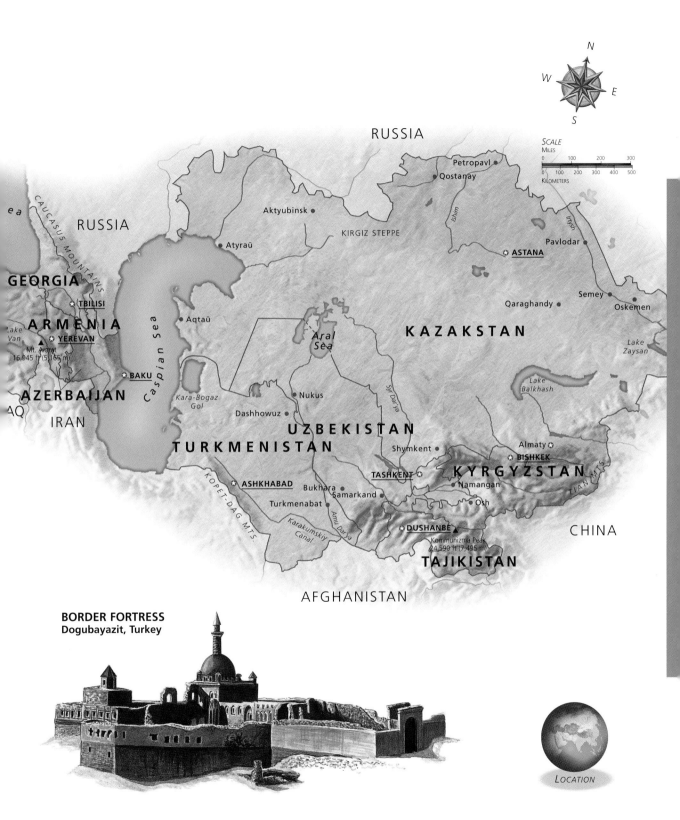

RUSSIA

N
W · E
S

SCALE
MILES
0   100   200   300

0 100 200 300 400 500
KILOMETERS

Petropavl
Qostanay

Aktyubinsk

e a

CAUCASUS MOUNTAINS

RUSSIA

Atyraū

KIRGIZ STEPPE

Ishim

Irtysh

Pavlodar

⊛ **ASTANA**

GEORGIA

☆ **TBILISI**

ARMENIA

Aqtaū

*Aral
Sea*

KAZAKSTAN

Semey

Oskemen

*Lake
Van*

▲ ☆ **YEREVAN**
Mt. Ararat
16,945 ft (5,165 m)

Qaraghandy

*Lake
Zaysan*

Caspian Sea

☆ **BAKU**

Nukus

Syr Dar'ya

*Lake
Balkhash*

AZERBAIJAN

*Kara-Bogaz
Gol*

Dashhowuz

UZBEKISTAN

Almaty ⊛

IRAN

AQ

TURKMENISTAN

Shymkent

⊛ **BISHKEK**

KYRGYZSTAN

TIAN MTS.

KOPET-DAG MTS.

☆ **ASHKHABAD**

Bukhara

TASHKENT ⊛

Namangan

Turkmenabat

Samarkand

Osh

*Karakumskiy
Canal*

Amu Dar'ya

☆ **DUSHANBE** ▲

CHINA

Kommunizma Peak
24,590 ft (7,495 m)

TAJIKISTAN

AFGHANISTAN

BORDER FORTRESS
Dogubayazit, Turkey

LOCATION

467

The Middle East

BEDOUINS

VEILED WOMAN

MEN WITH NARGHILE PIPE

WALLED CITY
Bam, Iran

ISRAELI MAN
Western Wall, Jerusaleum

CITY OF AL HAJRAH
Yemen

TRADITIONAL MUSICIAN
Iran

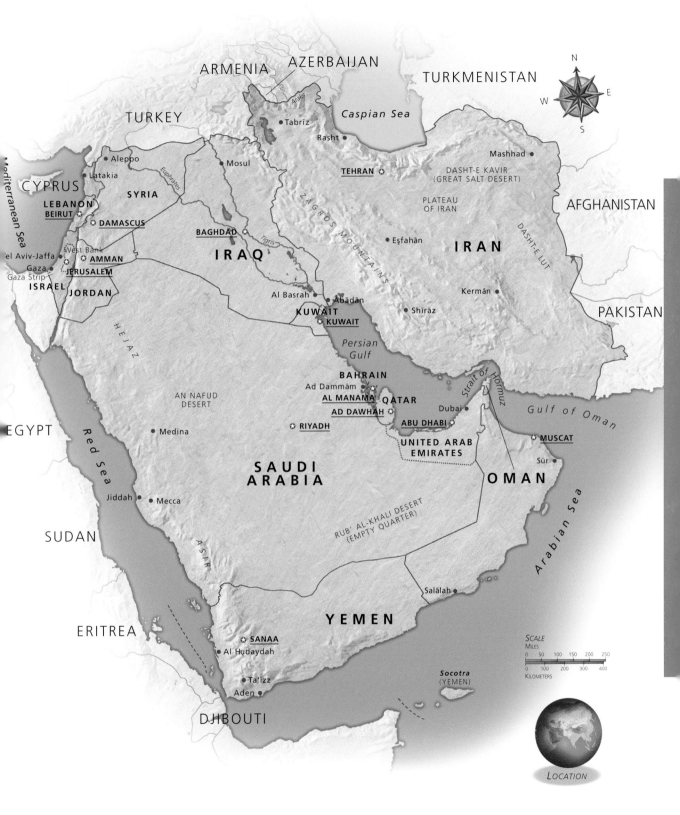

N

W · E

S

ARMENIA   AZERBAIJAN

TURKMENISTAN

TURKEY

Caspian Sea

Araks

• Tabrīz

Rasht •

Mashhad •

TEHRAN ⬡

DASHT-E KAVIR
(GREAT SALT DESERT)

AFGHANISTAN

• Aleppo

Latakia

CYPRUS

SYRIA

LEBANON
BEIRUT ⬡

Euphrates

• Mosul

PLATEAU
OF IRAN

BAGHDAD ⬡

Z A G R O S

⬡ **DAMASCUS**

Mediterranean Sea

el Aviv-Jaffa •

Gaza •

Gaza Strip

ISRAEL

West Bank

⬡ **AMMAN**

⬡ **JERUSALEM**

JORDAN

IRAQ

Tigris

I R A N

• Eşfahān

• Kermān

M O U N T A I N S

DASHT-E LUT

PAKISTAN

Al Basrah •

Ābādān •

KUWAIT

⬡ **KUWAIT**

• Shīrāz

*Persian
Gulf*

H E J A Z

AN NAFUD
DESERT

BAHRAIN

Ad Dammām •

AL MANAMA ⬡

QATAR

AD DAWHAH ⬡

Straat of Hormuz

Dubai •

Gulf of Oman

EGYPT

Red Sea

• Medina

⬡ **RIYADH**

ABU DHABI ⬡

**UNITED ARAB
EMIRATES**

⬡ **MUSCAT**

Sūr •

Jiddah •   • Mecca

**S A U D I
A R A B I A**

O M A N

SUDAN

A S I R

RUB' AL-KHALI DESERT
(EMPTY QUARTER)

Arabian Sea

Salālah •

ERITREA

Y E M E N

⬡ **SANAA**

Socotra
(YEMEN)

SCALE
MILES
0 50 100 150 200 250

0 100   200   300   400
KILOMETERS

• Al Ḩudaydah

• Ta'izz

Aden •

DJIBOUTI

LOCATION

469

Southern Asia

FOLK DANCER
Bhutan

HERATI WOMAN
Afghanistan

SIKH MEN

SNAKE CHARMER
India

SITAR
India

TAJ MAHAL
Agra, India

PAINTED PALACE ELEPHANT
Jaipur, India

MEENAKSHI TEMPLE
Madurai, India

LINE FISHERMEN
Sri Lanka

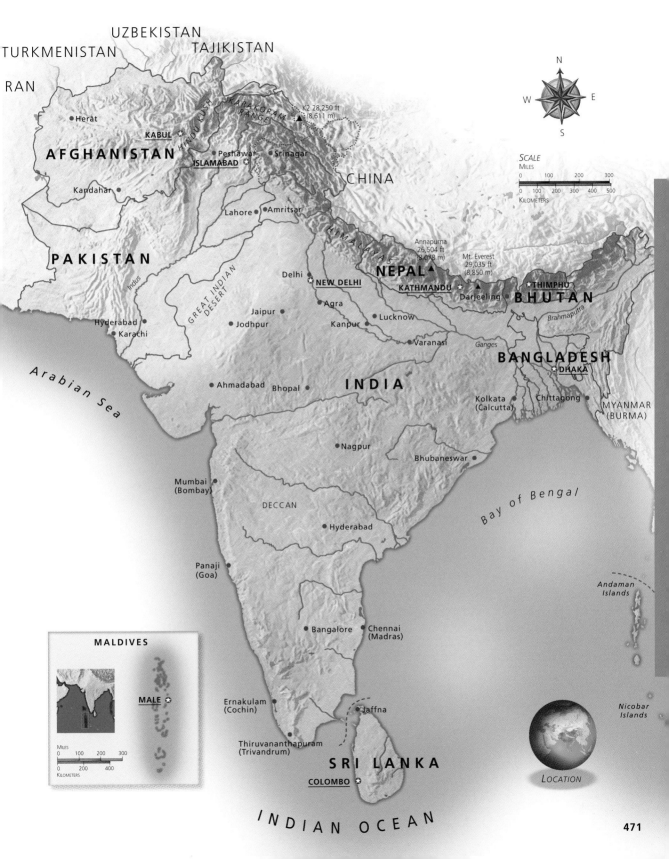

TURKMENISTAN

UZBEKISTAN

TAJIKISTAN

IRAN

HINDU KUSH

KARAKORAM RANGE

K2 28,250 ft
(8,611 m)

AFGHANISTAN

Herât

KABUL

Peshawar

Srinagar

CHINA

ISLAMABAD

Kandahar

Lahore

Amritsar

HIMALAYAS

Annapurna
26,504 ft
(8,078 m)

Mt. Everest
29,035 ft
(8,850 m)

PAKISTAN

Indus

GREAT INDIAN DESERT

Delhi

NEW DELHI

NEPAL

KATHMANDU

Darjeeling

THIMPHU

BHUTAN

Agra

Jaipur

Jodhpur

Kanpur

Lucknow

Brahmaputra

Hyderabad

Karachi

Varanasi

Ganges

BANGLADESH

DHAKA

Arabian Sea

Ahmadabad

Bhopal

INDIA

Kolkata
(Calcutta)

Chittagong

MYANMAR
(BURMA)

Nagpur

Bhubaneswar

Mumbai
(Bombay)

DECCAN

Hyderabad

Bay of Bengal

Panaji
(Goa)

Andaman
Islands

Bangalore

Chennai
(Madras)

MALDIVES

MALE

Ernakulam
(Cochin)

Jaffna

Nicobar
Islands

MILES
0   100   200   300

KILOMETERS
0   200   400

Thiruvananthapuram
(Trivandrum)

SRI LANKA

COLOMBO

LOCATION

INDIAN OCEAN

SCALE
MILES
0   100   200   300

0   100   200   300   400   500
KILOMETERS

N
W   E
S

471

Southeast Asia

FOLK COSTUME
Borneo

SINGKIL DANCER
The Philippines

BUDDHIST MONKS

INDIA

BANGLADES

**M Y A N M A R
(B U R M A)**

*Bay of
Bengal*

YANGON
(RANGOON

*Andan
Sea*

Strait

I N D I A

JEEPNEY BUS
The Philippines

TOWN HALL
Ho Chi Minh City (Saigon), Vietnam

SHADOW PUPPET
Indonesia

SINGAPORE

FLOATING MARKET
Bangkok, Thailand

472

N
W E
S

SCALE
MILES
0   100   200   300   400
0 150   300   450   600
KILOMETERS

CHINA

ndalay

Hong (Red)

HANOI   Haiphong

VIETNAM

LAOS

hiang
ai

VIENTIANE

Hue
Da Nang

THAILAND

BANGKOK

CAMBODIA

PHNOM PENH

Ho Chi Minh City
(Saigon)

Gulf
of Thailand

huket

Hat Yai

South China Sea

George
Town   Kuala
       Terengganu
Ipoh

MALAYSIA

an   KUALA LUMPUR

Johor Baharu

SINGAPORE

SINGAPORE

Padang

*Java
Sea*

Sumatra

Palembang

a

OCEAN

JAKARTA

Yogyakarta   *Java*   Surabaya

INDONESIA

Bali   *Sumbawa*   *Flores*

Lombok   *Sumba*

Luzon

Baguio

MANILA

Legazpi

PHILIPPINES

Mindoro

Panay   *Samar*

Palawan   Bacolod   Cebu

Negros

Mindanao
Davao

PACIFIC OCEAN

Mt. Kinabalu
13,455 ft (4,101 m)
Kota Kinabalu ▲   Sandakan

BANDAR SERI BEGAWAN   SABAH

BRUNEI

SARAWAK

Kuching

Borneo

Pontianak

KALIMANTAN

Balikpapan

Banjarmasin

Sulu Sea

Celebes Sea

Manado

Halmahera

Sulawesi

Buru   *Ceram*
       Ambon

Ujung
Pandang

Banda Sea

Kai

Aru

Jayapura

IRIAN
JAYA

Puncak Jaya
16,535 ft
(5,040 m)

NEW
GUINEA

Flores Sea

Tanimbar

Arafura Sea

DILI

EAST TIMOR

Kupang   *Timor Sea*

AUSTRALIA

LOCATION

473

Eastern Asia

TIBETAN MONKS

CYCLISTS

FOLK COSTUME
South Korea

TAJIKISTA

PAKISTA

INDI

JUNK
Hong Kong

TEMPLE OF HEAVEN
Beijing, China

GIANT PANDA

POTALA PALACE
Lhasa, Tibet

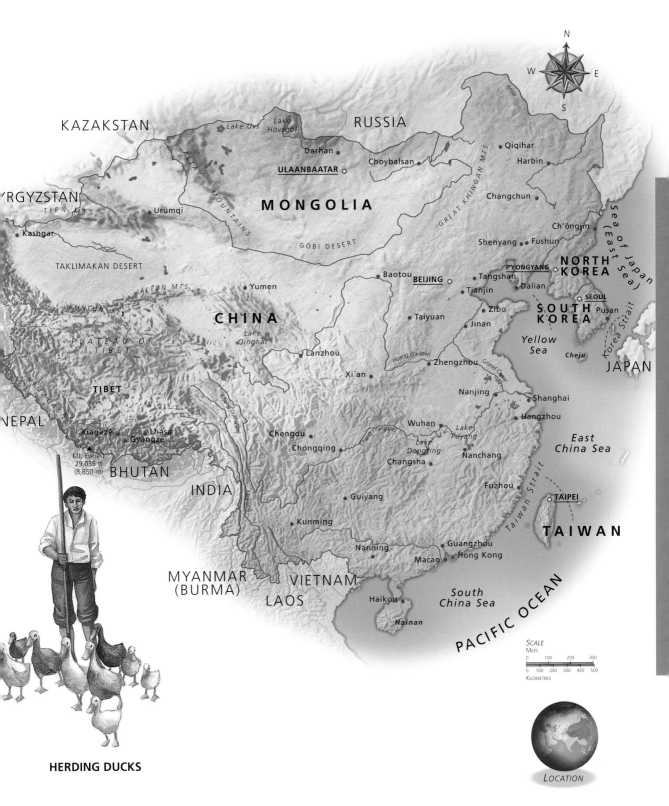

HERDING DUCKS

SCALE
MILES
0   100   200   300

0 100 200 300 400 500
KILOMETRES

LOCATION

475

Japan

Asia

COUNTRIES OF THE WORLD

GEISHA PREPARING TEA

SUMO WRESTLERS

NINJA

CARP STREAMERS

TEMPLE OF THE GOLDEN PAVILION
Kyoto

KOKECHI DOLL

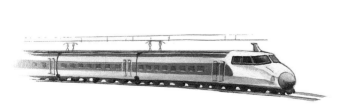

BULLET TRAIN

SHIOGAMA FESTIVAL BOAT

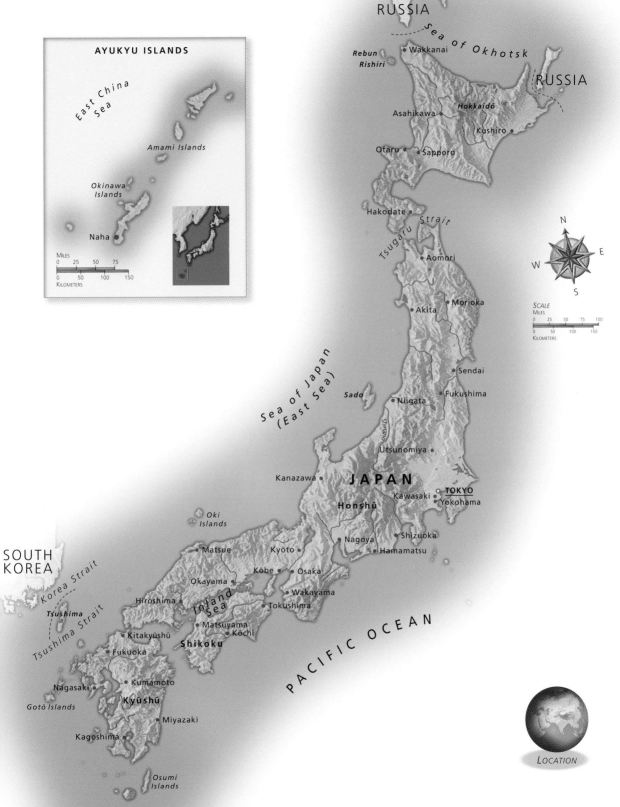

AYUKYU ISLANDS

East China Sea

Amami Islands

Okinawa Islands

Naha

MILES
0   25   50   75
0   50   100   150
KILOMETERS

RUSSIA

Sea of Okhotsk

Rebun
Rishiri

Wakkanai

RUSSIA

Asahikawa

Hokkaidō

Kushiro

Otaru   Sapporo

Hakodate

Tsugaru Strait

Aomori

N
W   E
S

SCALE
MILES
0   25   50   75   100
0   50   100   150
KILOMETERS

Akita   Morioka

Sea of Japan (East Sea)

Sado   Niigata   Sendai

Fukushima

Shinano

Utsunomiya

Kanazawa

JAPAN

Kawasaki   TOKYO
Yokohama

Honshū

SOUTH KOREA

Korea Strait

Tsushima

Tsushima Strait

Oki Islands

Matsue   Kyōto
Kōbe   Osaka
Okayama

Nagoya   Shizuoka
Hamamatsu

Hiroshima

Inland Sea

Wakayama
Tokushima

Matsuyama   Kōchi

Kitakyūshū

Shikoku

Fukuoka

Nagasaki

Kumamoto

Gotō Islands

Kyūshū

Miyazaki

Kagoshima

PACIFIC OCEAN

Osumi Islands

Tokara Islands

LOCATION

477

Northern Africa

ELEPHANT AND CALF

ALGERIAN NOMAD

BORORRO MAN
Niger

POUNDING MILLET
Senegal

CARRYING PALM WINE
Côte d'Ivoire

MADEIRA
(PORTUGAL)

Casab

CANARY
ISLANDS
(SPAIN)

Marrak
Mt. Toubkal
13,665 ft (4,165

El Aaiún

WESTERN
SAHARA
(MOROCCO)

MAURITANIA

NOUAKCHOTT

Senegal

DAKAR   SENEGAL
BANJUL
GAMBIA
GUINEA-   Ségou
BISSAU   BISSAU   BA
GUINEA

CONAKRY   CO
FREETOWN   D'IV
SIERRA LEONE   (IVORY

MONROVIA   YAMOU
LIBERIA   ABIDJ.

A T L A N T I C   O C E A N

GIRAFFES

KOUTTOUBIA MOSQUE
Morocco

GIZA PYRAMIDS
Egypt

SPAIN

Ceuta (SPAIN)
Tangier
Fès
Melilla (SPAIN)
Oran

BAT
TS.

MOROCCO

ALGIERS
TUNIS
Constantine

TUNISIA

ITALY

MALTA

GREECE

TURKEY

CYPRUS

SYRIA

LEBANON
ISRAEL

Mediterranean Sea

ALGERIA

TRIPOLI
Misrātah
Benghazi

Ghadāmis

LIBYA

Suez Canal

Alexandria
CAIRO

Port Said
Suez

EGYPT

Luxor

Aswān

Nile

SAUDI ARABIA

LIBYAN DESERT

Tamanrasset

SAHARA DESERT

AHAGGAR MTS.

TIBESTI MTS.

Lake
Nasser

*NUBIAN
DESERT*

Red Sea

MALI

Tombouctou
(Timbuktu)

SAHEL

NIGER

CHAD

SUDAN

Port Sudan

Nile

ERITREA
☆ **ASMARA**

YEMEN

*Gulf of
Aden*

Kassala

**URKINA
FASO**
ADOUGOU

Maradi
☆ **NIAMEY**
Zinder

Lake
Chad

KHARTOUM

El Obeid

White Nile

Blue Nile

Ras Dashen
15,158 ft (4,620 m)
▲

DJIBOUTI
DJIBOUTI

Berbera

SOMALIA

BENIN

Kano

☆ **N'DJAMENA**

*ETHIOPIAN
PLATEAU*

Dire Dawa

Lake
Volta
TOGO
ABUJA
☆

NIGERIA

Ibadan
Lagos

Chari

Sarh

ADDIS ABABA
☆

ETHIOPIA

ANA COTONOU
LOME
☆

PORTO-NOVO

RA

CAMEROON

**CENTRAL
AFRICAN REPUBLIC**

Juba

MALABO
Bioko
**EQUATORIAL
GUINEA**

☆ **YAOUNDE**

☆ **BANGUI**

**DEMOCRATIC
REPUBLIC OF
THE CONGO
(ZAIRE)**

UGANDA

KENYA

☆ **MOGADISHU**

Guinea

GABON

CONGO

Kismaayo

INDIAN OCEAN

MALI MAN WITH FISHING TRAPS

CAPE VERDE ISLANDS

*Santo
Antão*
*São
Vicente*
Mindelo
*São
Nicolau*

Sal

*Boa
Vista*

Fogo
Brava
*São
Tiago*

Maio
☆ **PRAIA**

MILES
0   10   15
0   10   20
KILOMETERS

LOCATION

SCALE
MILES
0   100   200   300
0   100 200 300 400 500
KILOMETERS

Southern Africa

WATA WOODCARVERS
Kenya

TRADITIONAL DANCERS
Zaire

NINGA DRUMMERS
Zaire

MASAI WARRIOR
Kenya

HERERO WOMAN
Namibia

ZULUS
South Africa

KHOISAN HUNTERS
Southern Africa

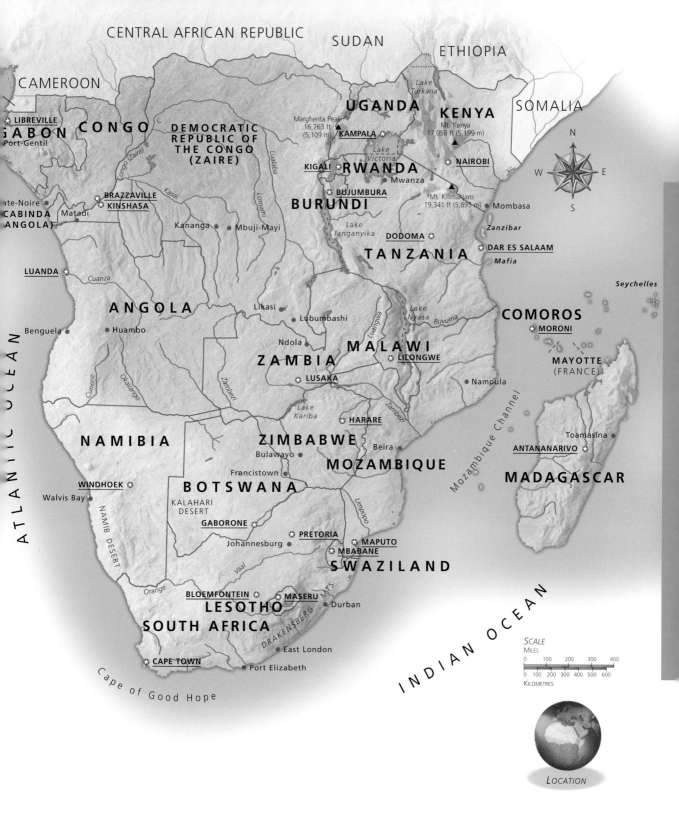

CENTRAL AFRICAN REPUBLIC

SUDAN

ETHIOPIA

CAMEROON

GABON CONGO

LIBREVILLE

Port-Gentil

DEMOCRATIC
REPUBLIC OF
THE CONGO
(ZAIRE)

Margherita Peak
16,763 ft
(5,109 m)

UGANDA

KAMPALA

Lake
Turkana

KENYA

Mt. Kenya
17,058 ft
(5,199 m)

SOMALIA

NAIROBI

KIGALI RWANDA

Lake
Victoria

Mwanza

te-Noire
CABINDA
NGOLA)

BRAZZAVILLE
KINSHASA

Congo (Zaire)

Matadi

Kasai

BUJUMBURA

BURUNDI

Lualaba

Lomami

Mt. Kilimanjaro
19,341 ft (5,895 m)

Mombasa

Zanzibar

LUANDA

Kananga

Mbuji-Mayi

Lake
Tanganyika

DODOMA

TANZANIA

DAR ES SALAAM

Mafia

Cuanza

Seychelles

ANGOLA

Likasi

Lubumbashi

Luangwa

Lake
Nyasa

Ruvuma

COMOROS

MORONI

Benguela

Huambo

Ndola

ZAMBIA

MALAWI

LILONGWE

MAYOTTE
(FRANCE)

Cunene

Okavango

Zambezi

LUSAKA

Nampula

Lake
Kariba

Zambezi

HARARE

ATLANTIC OCEAN

NAMIBIA

ZIMBABWE

Bulawayo

Beira

ANTANANARIVO

Toamasina

MADAGASCAR

NAMIB DESERT

WINDHOEK

Walvis Bay

BOTSWANA

KALAHARI
DESERT

Francistown

GABORONE

MOZAMBIQUE

Mozambique Channel

Limpopo

Johannesburg

PRETORIA

MAPUTO

MBABANE

SWAZILAND

Vaal

Orange

BLOEMFONTEIN

MASERU

DRAKENSBERG MTS.

LESOTHO

Durban

SOUTH AFRICA

DRAKENSBERG

East London

CAPE TOWN

Port Elizabeth

Cape of Good Hope

INDIAN OCEAN

N
W E
S

SCALE
MILES
0   100   200   300   400

0   100 200 300 400 500 600
KILOMETRES

LOCATION

481

Australia and Papua New Guinea

SURF LIFESAVERS
Australia

MUD-MASKED WARRIOR
Papua New Guinea

RED KANGAROO
Australia

ULURU (AYERS ROCK)
Central Australia

SPIRIT HOUSE
Papua New Guinea

ABORIGINAL DANCERS
Australia

OPERA HOUSE AND HARBOR BRIDGE
Sydney, Australia

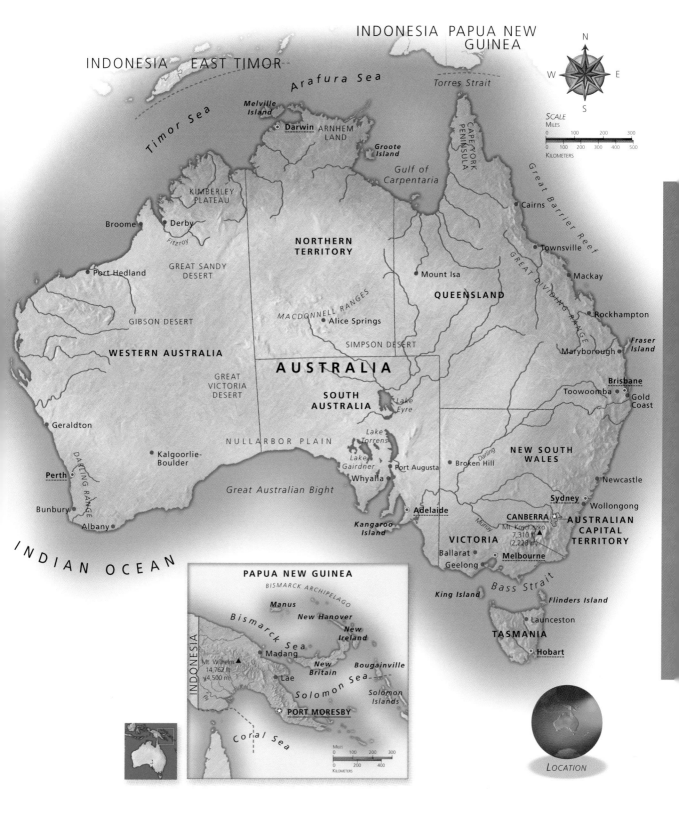

INDONESIA PAPUA NEW GUINEA

INDONESIA   EAST TIMOR

Arafura Sea

Timor Sea

Torres Strait

N
W   E
S

SCALE
MILES
0   100   200   300
0 100 200 300 500
KILOMETERS

Melville Island

Darwin   ARNHEM LAND

Groote Island

Gulf of Carpentaria

CAPE YORK PENINSULA

KIMBERLEY PLATEAU

Broome   Derby

Fitzroy

Port Hedland

GREAT SANDY DESERT

NORTHERN TERRITORY

Mount Isa

Cairns

Great Barrier Reef

Townsville

Mackay

QUEENSLAND

GREAT DIVIDING RANGE

Rockhampton

GIBSON DESERT

MACDONNELL RANGES

Alice Springs

SIMPSON DESERT

Maryborough

Fraser Island

WESTERN AUSTRALIA

AUSTRALIA

Geraldton

GREAT VICTORIA DESERT

SOUTH AUSTRALIA

Lake Eyre

Brisbane

Toowoomba

Gold Coast

NULLARBOR PLAIN

Lake Torrens

Lake Gairdner

Port Augusta

Broken Hill

Darling

NEW SOUTH WALES

Newcastle

Kalgoorlie-Boulder

Whyalla

Perth

DARLING RANGE

Great Australian Bight

Sydney

Wollongong

Bunbury

Adelaide

CANBERRA

AUSTRALIAN CAPITAL TERRITORY

Albany

Kangaroo Island

Murray

Mt. Kosciuzko 7,310 ft (2,228 m)

INDIAN OCEAN

VICTORIA

Ballarat

Geelong

Melbourne

King Island

Bass Strait

Flinders Island

Launceston

TASMANIA

Hobart

PAPUA NEW GUINEA

BISMARCK ARCHIPELAGO

Manus

New Hanover

INDONESIA

Bismarck Sea

Madang

New Ireland

New Britain

Bougainville

Solomon Sea

Mt. Wilhelm 14,762 ft (4,500 m)

Lae

Solomon Islands

PORT MORESBY

Coral Sea

MILES
0   100   200   300
0   200   400
KILOMETERS

LOCATION

483

New Zealand and the Southwestern Pacific

RUGBY PLAYER

TAHITIAN SURFER

TRADITIONAL MAORI
New Zealand

SCUBA DIVER

KIWI
New Zealand

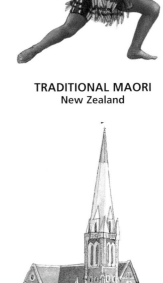

CHRISTCHURCH CATHEDRAL
Christchurch, New Zealand

WALKING ON HOT COALS
Fiji

PARLIAMENT HOUSE
Wellington, New Zealand

FIJI

Vanua Levu
Taveuni
Koro
Koro Sea
Viti Levu
Gau
SUVA
Lau Group
Lakeba
Moala
Kandavu

MILES
0 25 50 75
KILOMETERS
0 50 100 150

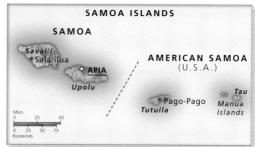

SAMOA ISLANDS

SAMOA

Savai'i
Sala'ilua
APIA
Upolu

AMERICAN SAMOA
(U.S.A.)

Tau
Pago-Pago
Manua
Tutuila
Islands

MILES
0 25 50
KILOMETERS
0 25 50 75

N
W   E
S

VANUATU AND NEW CALEDONIA

VANUATU

Banks
Islands
Espiritu
Santo
Maéwo
Luganville
Pentecost
Aoba
Ambrim
Malekula
Epi
Coral Sea
Efate
PORT VILA

NEW
CALEDONIA
(FRANCE)

Erromango

Tanna

Loyalty Islands

Pouembout

Nouméa

MILES
0 100 200
KILOMETERS
0 100 200 300

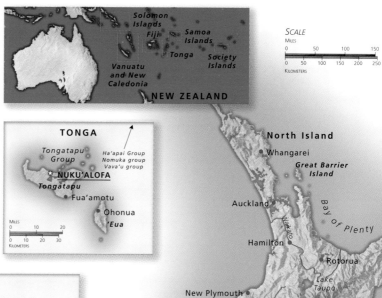

Solomon
Islands
Fiji
Samoa
Islands
Tonga
Society
Islands
Vanuatu
and New
Caledonia
NEW ZEALAND

SCALE
MILES
0 50 100 150
KILOMETERS
0 50 100 150 200 250

TONGA

Tongatapu
Group
Ha'apai Group
Nomuka group
Vava'u group
NUKU'ALOFA
Tongatapu
Fua'amotu
Ohonua
'Eua

MILES
0 10 20
KILOMETERS
0 10 20 30

SOCIETY ISLANDS

Tupai
Atoll
Maupiti
Bora-Bora
Tahaa
Huahine
Raiatea
Islands
Tetiaroa
Atoll
Leeward Islands
Windward Islands
Paopao
Moorea
Papeete
Maiao
Tahiti
Taravao

FRENCH POLYNESIA
(FRANCE)

MILES
0 25 50
KILOMETERS
0 25 50 75

SOLOMON ISLANDS

Choiseul
Santa
Isabel
New
Georgia Islands
Malaita
HONIARA
Guadalcanal
San Cristóbal
Rennell
Santa
Coral Sea
Cruz Islands

MILES
0 100 200
KILOMETERS
0 100 200 300

North Island
Whangarei
Great Barrier
Island
Auckland
Bay of Plenty
Waikato
Hamilton
Rotorua
Lake
Taupo
New Plymouth
Ruapehu
9,175 ft
Mt. Egmont (Taranaki)
(2,796 m)
8,260 ft (2,518 m)
Napier
Wanganui
Hastings
Palmerston North
Nelson
Cook Strait
Lower Hutt
WELLINGTON

Tasman Sea

**NEW
ZEALAND**

Greymouth

South Island
Christchurch

SOUTHERN ALPS
Mt. Cook
12,349 ft
(3,764 m)
Timaru
Waitaki
Lake
Wakatipu
Queenstown
Clutha
Dunedin

PACIFIC OCEAN

Foveaux Strait
Invercargill
Stewart
Island

LOCATION

485

PLACES OF WORSHIP

PUBLIC BUILDINGS

CASTLES, PALACES AND HOUSES

Classical Style

GREEK COLUMNS

Doric order

Ionic order

Corinthian order

THE PARTHENON
Athens, Greece

A narrow band of carving encircles the top of the temple wall

Walls and columns set close together hold up the timber frame for the tiled roof

The tall wooden statue of the goddess Athena wore clothing made of gold plates that weighed 2,500 pounds (1,134 kg)

THE PANTHEON
Rome, Italy

The dome is made of concrete that becomes lighter as it gets higher because each level is mixed with lighter stones such as volcanic pumice

Painted sculpture adorns the tympanum

Parthenon frieze depicts the procession of Athena

Athena's marble temple is surrounded by 46 Doric columns

491

Gothic Tradition

GOTHIC WINDOW TRACERIES

NOTRE DAME CATHEDRAL
Paris, France

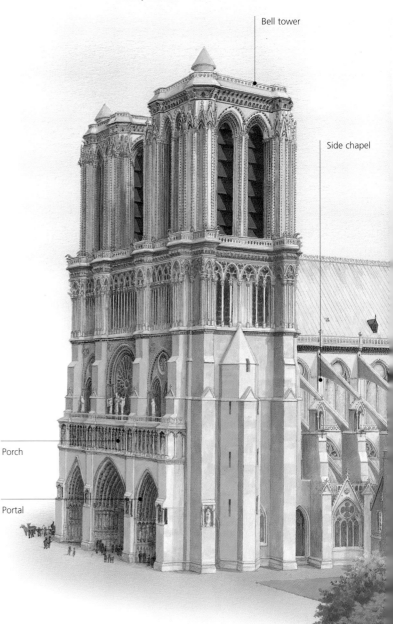

Bell tower

Side chapel

Porch

Portal

FLOOR PLAN

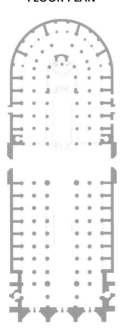

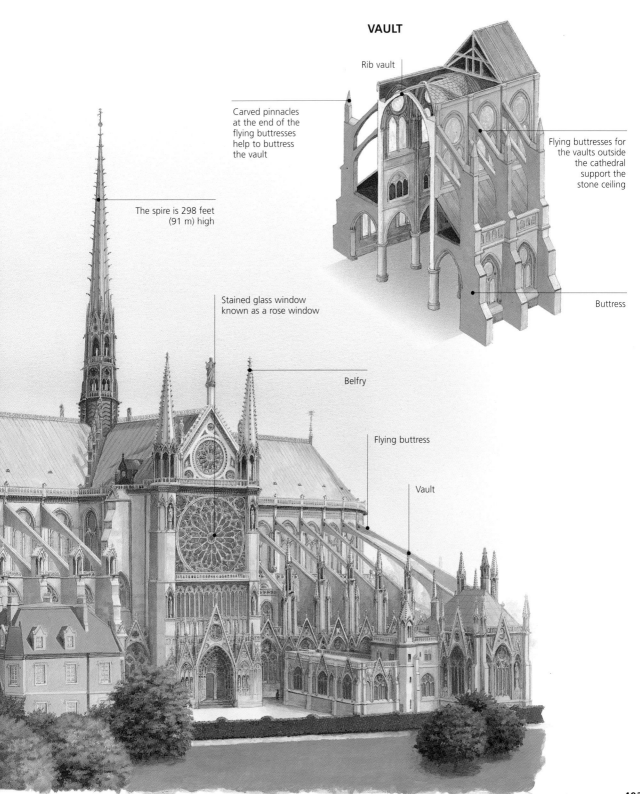

VAULT

Rib vault

Carved pinnacles
at the end of the
flying buttresses
help to buttress
the vault

Flying buttresses for
the vaults outside
the cathedral
support the
stone ceiling

The spire is 298 feet
(91 m) high

Buttress

Stained glass window
known as a rose window

Belfry

Flying buttress

Vault

St Peter's Basilica

ROME, ITALY

BRAMANTE'S FLOORPLAN

MICHELANGELO'S FLOORPLAN

The gold cross is
450 feet
(137 m) high

The interior is
decorated in the
Baroque style

Renaissance-style
dome seems to float,
as it does not have
supports directly
below it

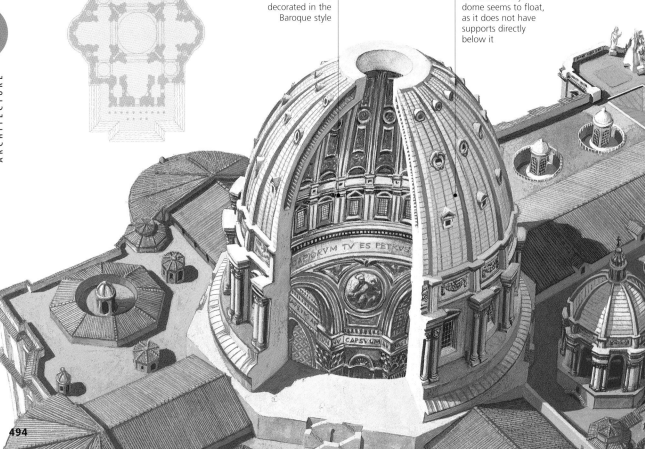

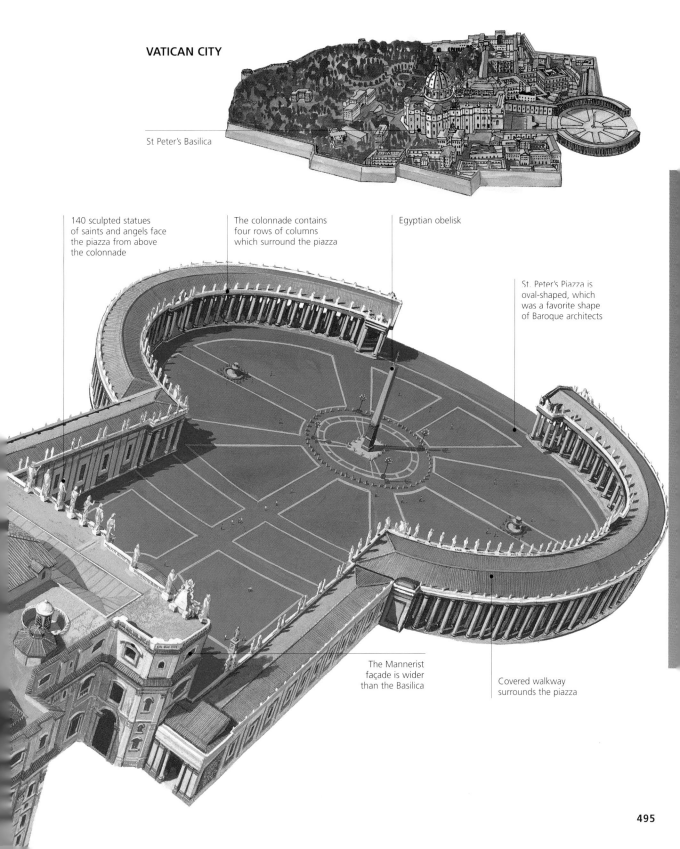

VATICAN CITY

St Peter's Basilica

140 sculpted statues
of saints and angels face
the piazza from above
the colonnade

The colonnade contains
four rows of columns
which surround the piazza

Egyptian obelisk

St. Peter's Piazza is
oval-shaped, which
was a favorite shape
of Baroque architects

The Mannerist
façade is wider
than the Basilica

Covered walkway
surrounds the piazza

495

Religious Buildings of Europe

CSEMPESZKOPACS CHURCH
Csempeszkopacs, Hungary

KECSKEMET CHURCH
Kecskemet, Hungary

LA SAGRADA FAMILIA
Barcelona, Spain

COLOGNE CATHEDRAL
Cologne, Germany

PARMA BAPTISTRY
Parma, Italy

MILAN CATHEDRAL
Milan, Italy

THIRA CHURCH
Santorini, Greece

SHIPKA MEMORIAL CHURCH
Shipka, Bulgaria

ST. SOPHIA'S CATHEDRAL
Kiev, Ukraine

CHARTRES CATHEDRAL
Chartres, France

DOM CATHEDRAL TOWER
Utrecht, The Netherlands

CHURCH OF SAN VITALE
Ravenna, Italy

BAVARIAN CHURCH
Bavaria, Germany

ALEXANDER NEVSKY CATHEDRAL
Sofia, Bulgaria

EASTERN ORTHODOX CHURCH
Lake Ohrid, Macedonia

497

Mosques of the World

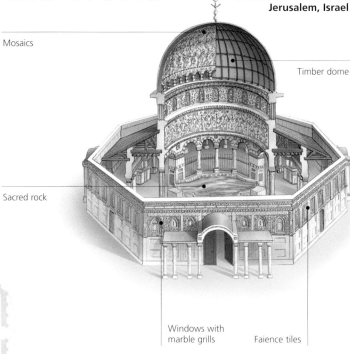

DOME OF THE ROCK
Jerusalem, Israel

Mosaics

Timber dome

Sacred rock

Windows with
marble grills

Faience tiles

FLOOR PLAN

MOSQUE FEATURES

Arch decoration

Minaret

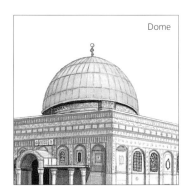

Dome

MASJID UBUDIAH
Kuala Kangsar, Malaysia

BLUE MOSQUE
Istanbul, Turkey

AL KHUWAIR MOSQUE
Al Khuwair, Oman

ROYAL MOSQUE
Eşfahān, Iran

GOL GUMBAZ MOSQUE
Bijapur, India

IMPERIAL MOSQUE
Lahore, Pakistan

Early American Buildings

GREAT PLAZA
Tikal, Guatemala

TAOS PUEBLO
New Mexico, USA

EL CASTILLO
Chichen Itza, Mexico

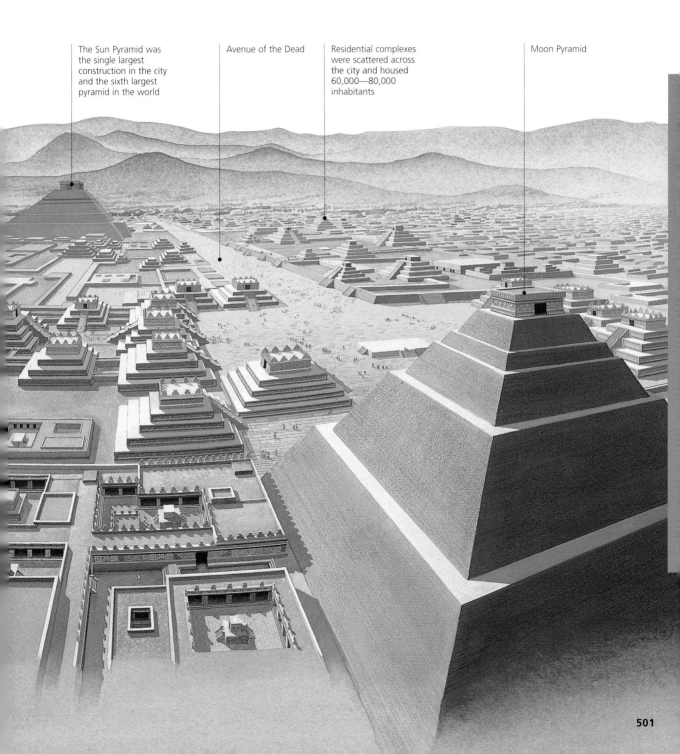

CITY OF TEOTIHUACAN
Mexico, AD 1— 200

The Sun Pyramid was the single largest construction in the city and the sixth largest pyramid in the world

Avenue of the Dead

Residential complexes were scattered across the city and housed 60,000—80,000 inhabitants

Moon Pyramid

Statues and Monuments

MOAI STATUES
Easter Island

TOLTEC STATUE
Mexico

STATUE OF THE LION
Ethiopia

MOUNT RUSHMORE
South Dakota, USA

TERRA-COTTA WARRIORS
Xi'an, China

GIZA SPHINX
Giza, Egypt

STATUE OF LIBERTY
New York, USA

From the base up to the tip of the flame, the statue measures 151 feet (46 m)

A single fingernail measures 13 by 10 inches (33 x 25 cm)

The seven rays in her crown represent the seven continents and seven seas

A 12-storey spiral staircase leads from the plinth to an observatory in the crown

This tablet is inscribed proclaiming the date of American Independence —July 4, 1776

The internal skeleton is iron

Copper surrounds the iron framework

Chains under the feet depict the breaking away from slavery

Viewing area

The pedestal is made of granite and measures 151 feet (46 m) high

Doric columns surround the pedestal on all sides

Tombs and Memorials

PREHISTORIC BURIAL GROUND
Newgrange, Ireland

ROCK TOMBS
Madain Salah, Saudi Arabia

BEEHIVE TOMB
Mycenae, Greece

ATOMIC DOME
Hiroshima, Japan

TOMB OF BIBI JAIWINDI
Uch Sharif, Pakistan

APAK HOJA TOMB
Kashgar, China

CROSS SECTION

GREAT PYRAMID
Giza, Egypt

1 King's chamber

2 Queen's chamber

3 Underground chamber

4 Grand gallery

5 Entrance

479 feet (146 m)

Over 2,500,000 blocks
of limestone were used
in its construction

Adventurous Shapes

CASA MILA
Barcelona, Spain

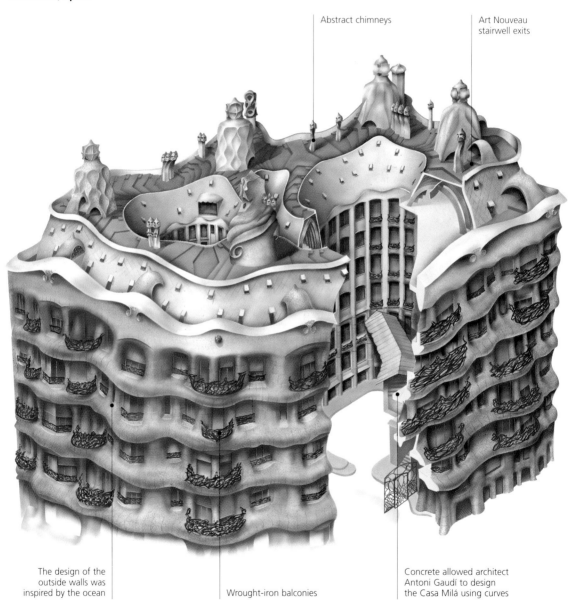

Abstract chimneys

Art Nouveau stairwell exits

The design of the outside walls was inspired by the ocean

Wrought-iron balconies

Concrete allowed architect Antoni Gaudí to design the Casa Milà using curves

NOTRE DAME DU HAUT
Ronchamp, France

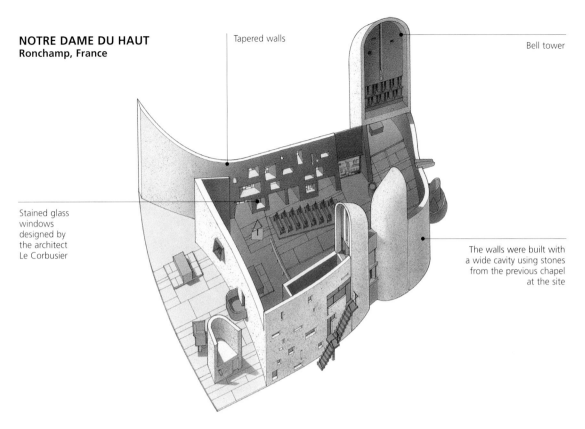

Tapered walls

Bell tower

Stained glass
windows
designed by
the architect
Le Corbusier

The walls were built with
a wide cavity using stones
from the previous chapel
at the site

GUGGENHEIM MUSEUM
New York, USA

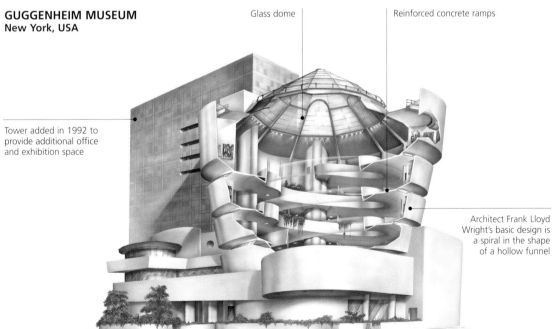

Glass dome

Reinforced concrete ramps

Tower added in 1992 to
provide additional office
and exhibition space

Architect Frank Lloyd
Wright's basic design is
a spiral in the shape
of a hollow funnel

Leisure Spaces

COLOSSEUM
Rome, Italy

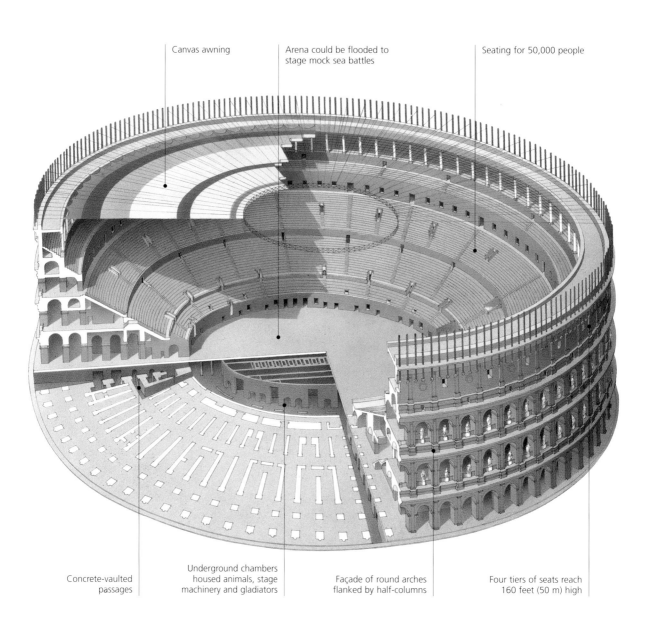

Canvas awning

Arena could be flooded to stage mock sea battles

Seating for 50,000 people

Concrete-vaulted passages

Underground chambers housed animals, stage machinery and gladiators

Façade of round arches flanked by half-columns

Four tiers of seats reach 160 feet (50 m) high

THE SKYDOME
Toronto, Canada

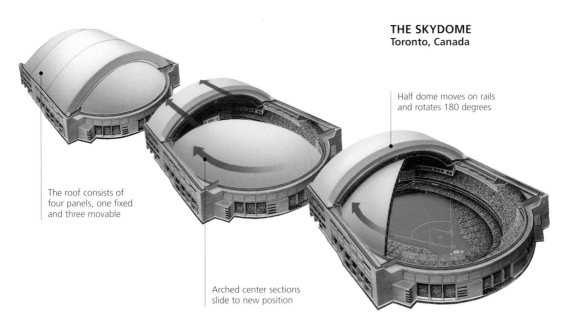

Half dome moves on rails and rotates 180 degrees

The roof consists of four panels, one fixed and three movable

Arched center sections slide to new position

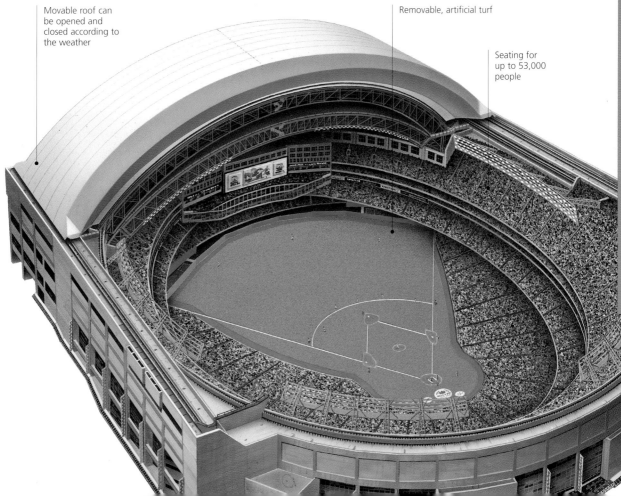

Movable roof can be opened and closed according to the weather

Removable, artificial turf

Seating for up to 53,000 people

Early Settlement

CITY OF CATAL HUYUK
Turkey, 6500—5400 BC

Sprawling mudbrick buildings were laid out like modern apartment complexes. Each family lived in an almost identical three-room unit—complete with a sleeping space, sitting nooks, a storage area and a kitchen

Houses were built directly against one another— sometimes with intervening courtyards. There were no streets or lanes through the city

Access to the buildings was from the roofs

The site covered 32 acres (13 ha) and housed 6,000 inhabitants —making it the most populated city on earth at the time

One out of every three rooms at Catal Hüyük was a shrine. Each of these worship rooms was different, but all had a similar bull motif

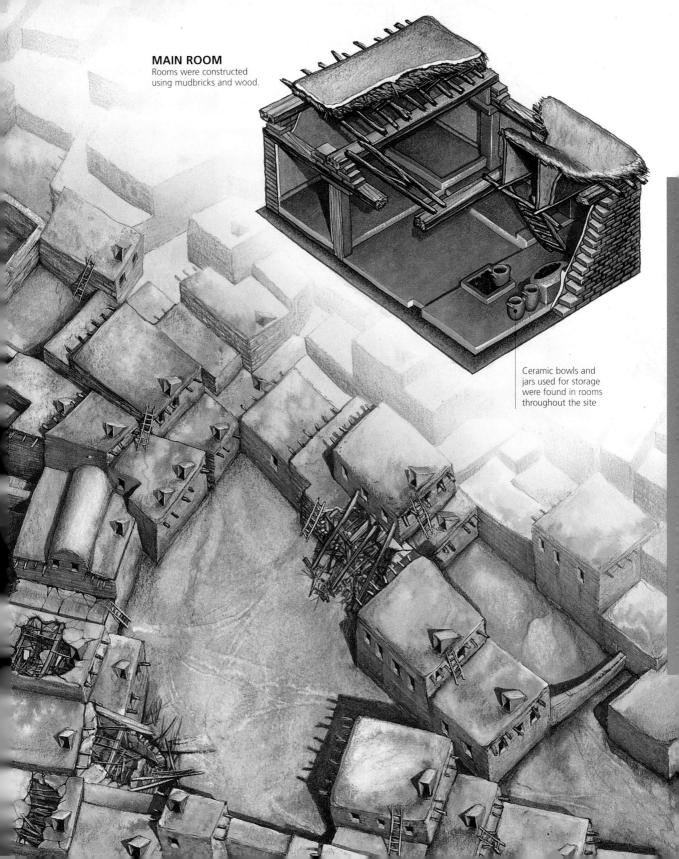

MAIN ROOM
Rooms were constructed using mudbricks and wood.

Ceramic bowls and jars used for storage were found in rooms throughout the site.

Traditional Houses

CHIAPAS HUT
Mexico

TRADITIONAL FARMHOUSE
China

TRADITIONAL HUT
Zimbabwe

NUNAVUT HOUSE
Canada

THATCHED COTTAGE
England

CROFTER'S COTTAGE
Ireland

LESOTHO HUT
South Africa

CHIPAYA SOD HUT
Peru

IGLOO
Canada

STILT HOUSE
Solomon Islands

WOVEN HUT
South Pacific

A waterproof roof is made from grass by thatching—bundles of swamp grass are tied to a wooden frame so that each bundle overlaps the ones next to it and below it

The walls are constructed by weaving mats from palm fronds or leaves—the weaving stiffens the fronds

513

Castles

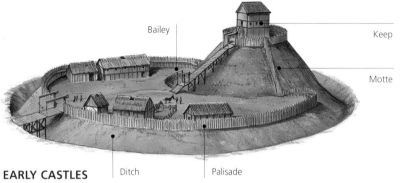

EARLY CASTLES

Bailey

Keep

Motte

Ditch

Palisade

CONWAY CASTLE
Conway, Wales

Lookout post

Rampart

Internal spiral
staircases

Royal bedchamber

Cellar where treasure
was often stored

ROYAL CASTLE
Warsaw, Poland

CHATEAU DE CHAMBORD
Chambord, France

Great Hall

Portcullis

Arrow loops

Stone walls
16 feet (5 m) thick

Drawbridge

Guards
on duty

A series of wheels
and pulleys was
used for lifting
heavy objects

515

Classical Influence

ATHENAEUM
Bucharest, Romania

CAPITOL BUILDING
Washington, USA

MONTICELLO HOUSE
Charlottesville, USA

OPERA HOUSE
Manaus, Brazil

CONGRESO NACIONAL
Buenos Aires, Argentina

PRESIDENTIAL PALACE
Asunción, Paraguay

LEGISLATIVE BUILDING
Regina, Canada

VILLA CAPRA
Vincenza, Italy

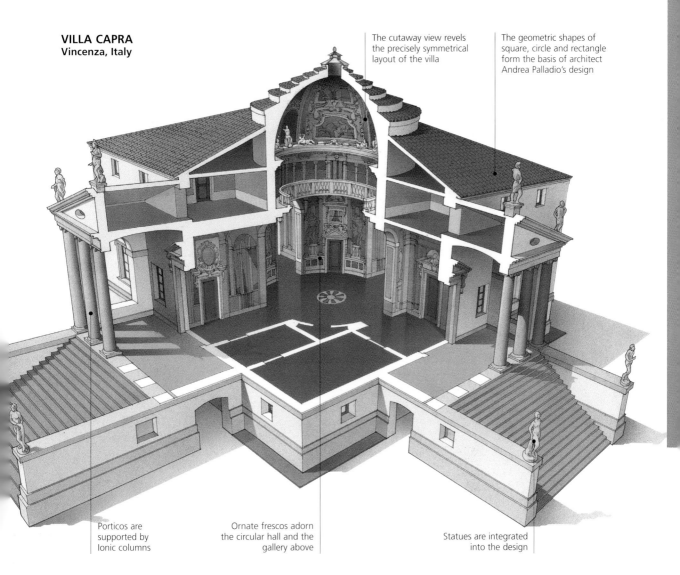

The cutaway view revels the precisely symmetrical layout of the villa

The geometric shapes of square, circle and rectangle form the basis of architect Andrea Palladio's design

Porticos are supported by Ionic columns

Ornate frescos adorn the circular hall and the gallery above

Statues are integrated into the design

TRANSPORT

EVERYDAY TECHNOLOGY

COMMUNICATIONS AND INDUSTRY

Land Transport

AUTOMOBILE

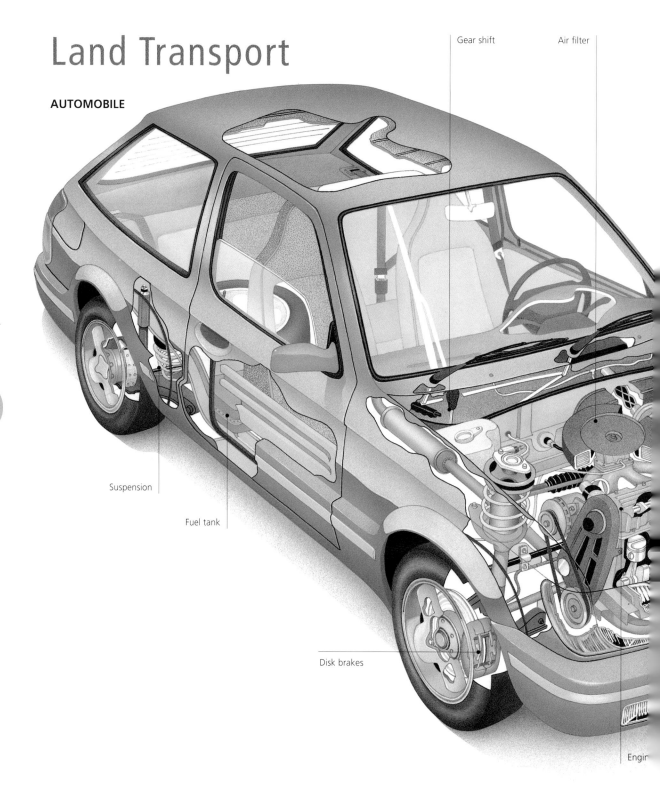

Gear shift

Air filter

Suspension

Fuel tank

Disk brakes

Engin

A HISTORY OF BICYCLES

Dandy horse
1790

Penny-farthing
1870

Safety bike
1879

Aerodynamic bike
Early 1980s

Distributor

Alternator

Battery

Radiator

Fan

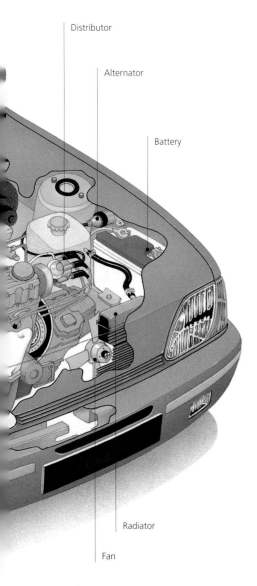

SEMITRAILER TRUCK

LONG DISTANCE PASSENGER COACH

Steam Trains

MALLARD STEAM TRAIN

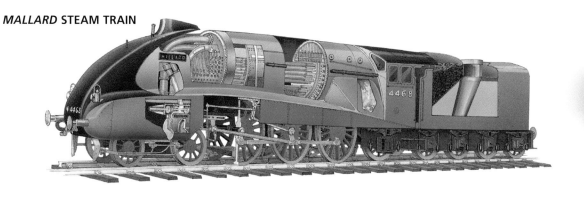

HOW STEAM ENGINES WORK

Fuel burnt in the firebox is the source of power

The engineer uses the throttle (regulator) valve to control the supply of steam to the cylinders

Air passes through the firegate to aid combustion

These tubes are surrounded by water which is heated until it boils, so creating steam

The backward and forward thrusts of the pistons are transmitted to the driving wheels by a coupling rod and crank

HOW PISTONS TURN WHEELS

Inlet valve admits steam under pressure in front of piston.

Rear inlet valve opens. Steam enters at rear of piston.

Valve closes. Steam in cyclinder expands.

Exhaust valve lets expanded steam out.

Steam almost spent. Piston nears one extreme.

Two cycles complete one revolution of driving wheels.

Steam is exhausted through the blastpipe and chimney

Steam exhausting from the blastpipe and out of the chimney draws the heat of the fire through fire tubes in the boiler

Steam enters the cylinders and forces the pistons backward and forward

Water Transport

CHINESE JUNK
Mid-15th century

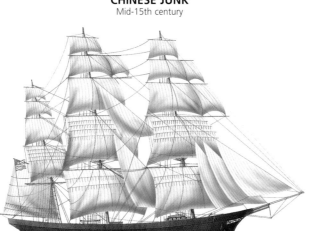

CLIPPER
1845 to 1890s

STEAMSHIP
1800 to 1900s

**A HISTORY OF
SAILING VESSELS**

Egyptian trading vessel
3000 BC to 500 BC

Phoenician trading vessel
1000 BC to 300 BC

Viking knorr
AD 800 to AD 1070

Polynesian canoe
Early AD onward

Hanseatic cog
1350–1450

Caravel
1430–1520

CATAMARAN
Twin hulls

YACHT
Single hull

TRIMARAN
Three hulls

CANOE
Open boat with
single-bladed paddle

KAYAK
Enclosed craft with
double-bladed paddle

ESKIMO ROLL
This maneuver allows a paddler to
roll the kayak over if it capsizes.

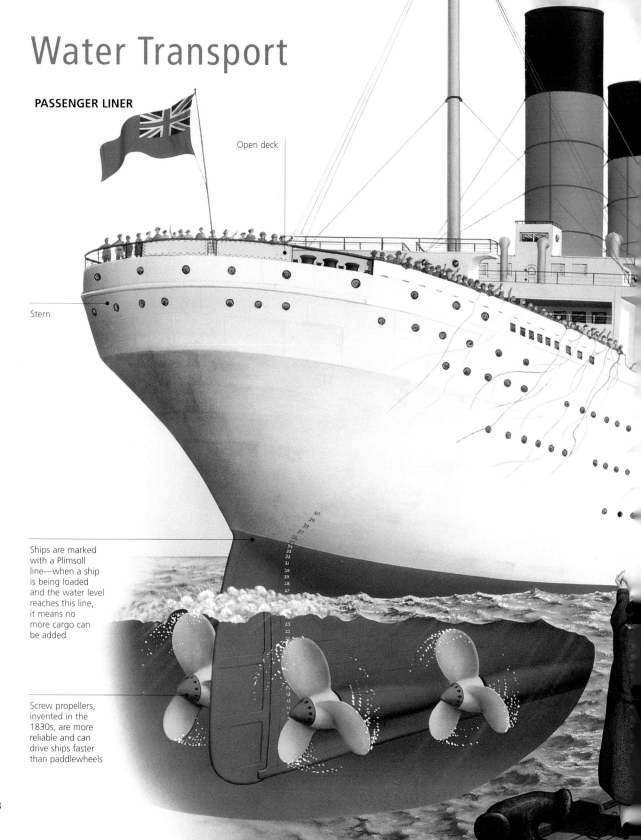

Water Transport

PASSENGER LINER

Open deck

Stern

Ships are marked with a Plimsoll line—when a ship is being loaded and the water level reaches this line, it means no more cargo can be added

Screw propellers, invented in the 1830s, are more reliable and can drive ships faster than paddlewheels

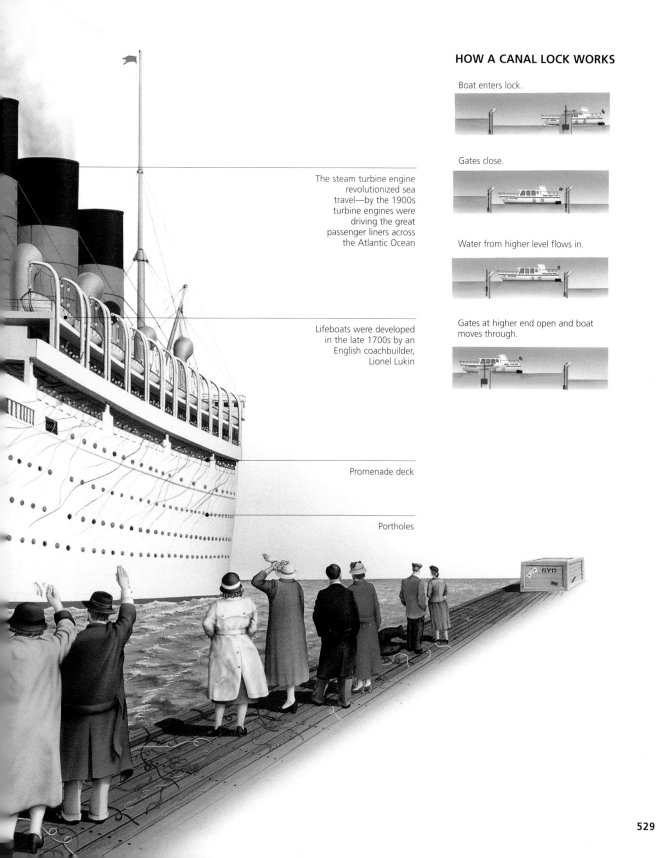

The steam turbine engine revolutionized sea travel—by the 1900s turbine engines were driving the great passenger liners across the Atlantic Ocean

Lifeboats were developed in the late 1700s by an English coachbuilder, Lionel Lukin

Promenade deck

Portholes

HOW A CANAL LOCK WORKS

Boat enters lock.

Gates close.

Water from higher level flows in.

Gates at higher end open and boat moves through.

Flight

PROPELLER PLANE IN FLIGHT

Banking

Left aileron down

Right aileron up

Pitching

Elevators up

Turning

Rudder right

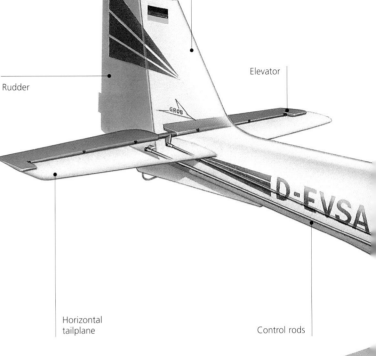

Vertical tailplane (tailfin)

Rudder

Elevator

Horizontal tailplane

Control rods

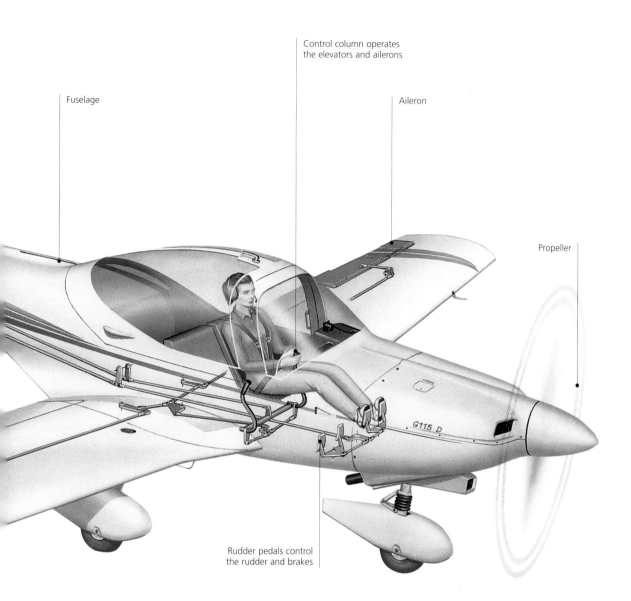

Fuselage

Control column operates the elevators and ailerons

Aileron

Propeller

Rudder pedals control the rudder and brakes

G115 D

HELICOPTER FLIGHT

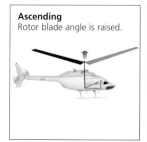

Ascending
Rotor blade angle is raised.

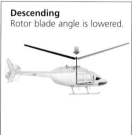

Descending
Rotor blade angle is lowered.

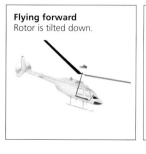

Flying forward
Rotor is tilted down.

Flying sideways
Rotor is tilted sideways.

Passenger Aircraft

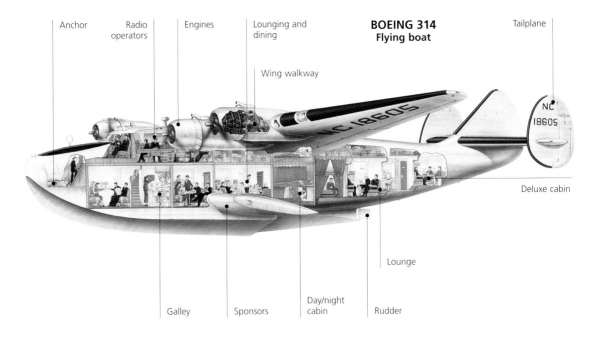

Anchor

Radio operators

Engines

Lounging and dining

BOEING 314
Flying boat

Tailplane

Wing walkway

Deluxe cabin

Lounge

Galley

Sponsors

Day/night cabin

Rudder

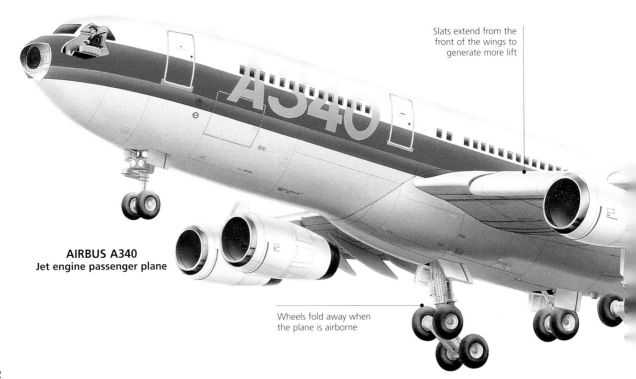

Slats extend from the front of the wings to generate more lift

AIRBUS A340
Jet engine passenger plane

Wheels fold away when the plane is airborne

AIRSHIPS

USS *Macon*
This US Navy airship was built in 1933 as a patrol carrier.

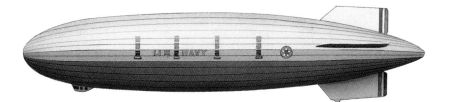

Graf Zeppelin
This airship made its first flight in 1928 and could carry 20 passengers.

R-34
In 1919, this became the first airship to cross the North Atlantic.

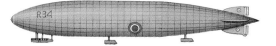

Norge
Explorers Nobile and Amundsen traveled to the North Pole in this airship in 1926.

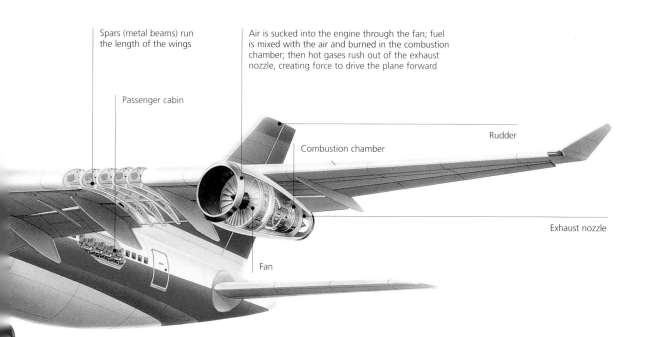

Spars (metal beams) run the length of the wings

Air is sucked into the engine through the fan; fuel is mixed with the air and burned in the combustion chamber; then hot gases rush out of the exhaust nozzle, creating force to drive the plane forward

Passenger cabin

Rudder

Combustion chamber

Exhaust nozzle

Fan

Military Aircraft

JUMP JET
McDonnell Douglas AV-8B

Called a V/STOL (Vertical/
Short Take Off and
Landing) plane because it
can hover, land and take
off like a helicopter

Jet nozzles direct the
exhaust downward for
landing and take off

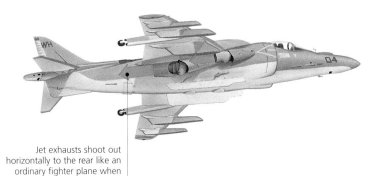

Jet exhausts shoot out
horizontally to the rear like an
ordinary fighter plane when
jump jet is flying normally

A HISTORY OF
MILITARY AIRCRAFT

**1915 German Fokker
E.1 Eindecker**
This fighter plane flew at
79 miles (128 km) per hour.

1917 French Spad X11
This biplane fighter flew
at 129 miles (208 km)
per hour.

**1917 English Handley
Page 0/400**
This bomber could carry
2,002 pounds (906 kg).

**1938 English Supermarine
Spitfire**
This fighter plane flew at
357 miles (576 km) per hour.

AIRWING OF AIRCRAFT CARRIER USS *AMERICA*

Intruder

Hawkeye

Prowler

Viking

Tomcat

Sea King

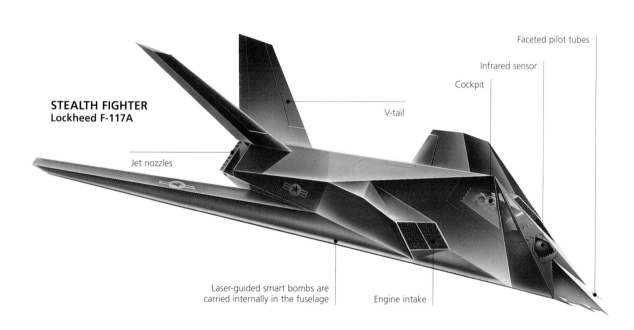

STEALTH FIGHTER
Lockheed F-117A

Faceted pilot tubes

Infrared sensor

Cockpit

V-tail

Jet nozzles

Laser-guided smart bombs are carried internally in the fuselage

Engine intake

1943 English Gloster Meteor
The first British jet fighter flew at 600 miles (969 km) per hour.

1952 US Boeing B-52 Stratofortress
This bomber flew at 595 miles (960 km) per hour.

1974 German, English and Italian Panavia Tornado
This strike aircraft flies at 1,446 miles (2,333 km) per hour.

1978 US McDonnell Douglas F/A 18C Hornet
This fighter flies at 1,317 miles (2,124 km) per hour.

Supersonic Flight

SUPERSONIC WING SHAPES

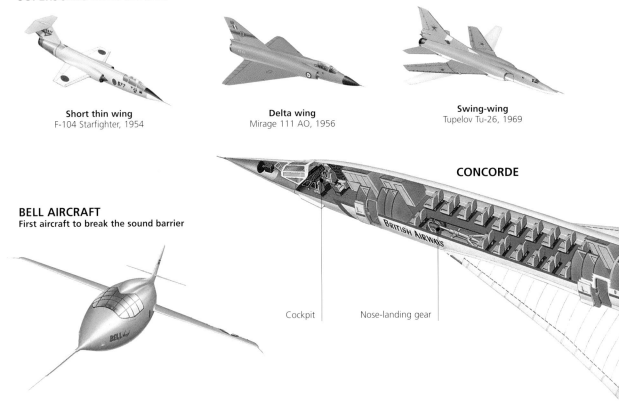

Short thin wing
F-104 Starfighter, 1954

Delta wing
Mirage 111 AO, 1956

Swing-wing
Tupelov Tu-26, 1969

CONCORDE

BELL AIRCRAFT
First aircraft to break the sound barrier

Cockpit

Nose-landing gear

THE SOUND BARRIER

Subsonic Flight: Below Mach 1
Pressure waves radiate in front of and behind the aircraft.

Transonic Flight: At Mach 1
The aircraft catches up with its own pressure waves.

Supersonic Flight: Above Mach 1
Shock waves form a cone. This causes a sonic boom when it hits the ground.

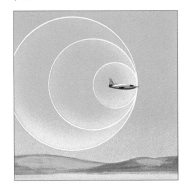

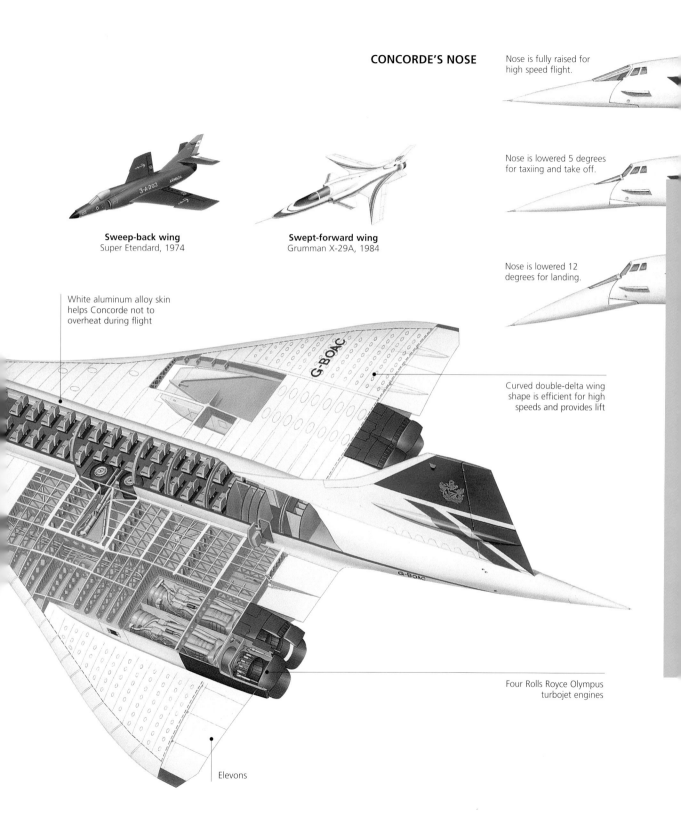

CONCORDE'S NOSE

Nose is fully raised for high speed flight.

Nose is lowered 5 degrees for taxiing and take off.

Nose is lowered 12 degrees for landing.

Sweep-back wing
Super Etendard, 1974

Swept-forward wing
Grumman X-29A, 1984

White aluminum alloy skin helps Concorde not to overheat during flight

Curved double-delta wing shape is efficient for high speeds and provides lift

Four Rolls Royce Olympus turbojet engines

Elevons

Forces at Work

PERMANENT MAGNET

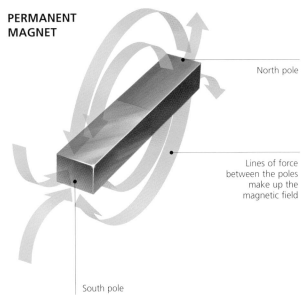

North pole

Lines of force between the poles make up the magnetic field

South pole

MAGNETISM AND ELECTRICITY

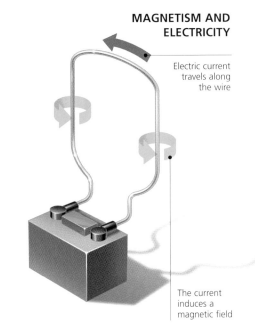

Electric current travels along the wire

The current induces a magnetic field

FINDING THE WAY

A compass needle always faces north because it is attracted to Earth's magnetic pole near the geographic north pole

ATTRACTION

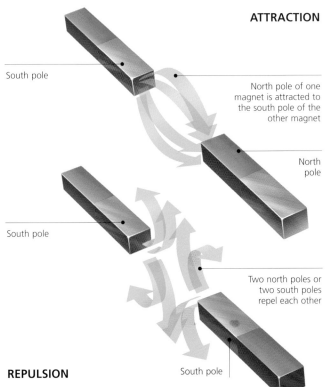

South pole

North pole of one magnet is attracted to the south pole of the other magnet

North pole

South pole

Two north poles or two south poles repel each other

South pole

REPULSION

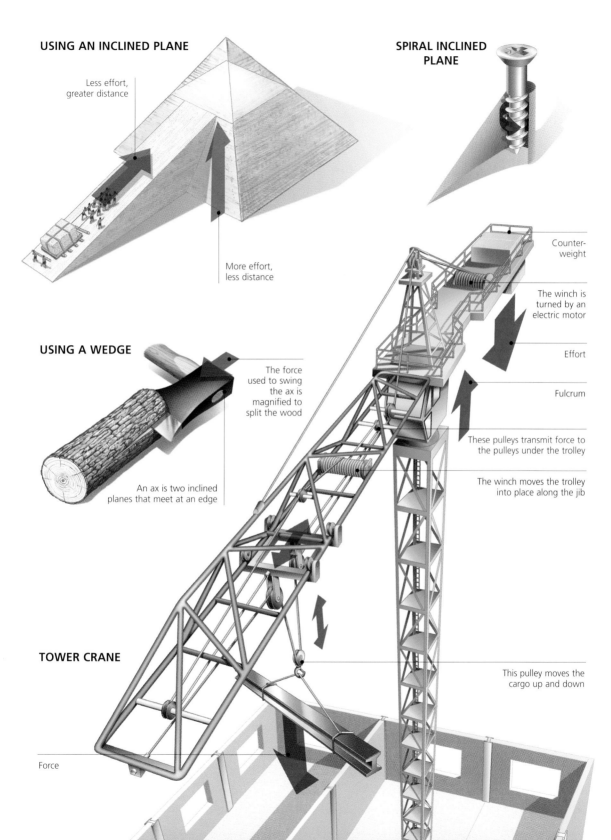

USING AN INCLINED PLANE

Less effort, greater distance

More effort, less distance

SPIRAL INCLINED PLANE

USING A WEDGE

The force used to swing the ax is magnified to split the wood

An ax is two inclined planes that meet at an edge

TOWER CRANE

Counter-weight

The winch is turned by an electric motor

Effort

Fulcrum

These pulleys transmit force to the pulleys under the trolley

The winch moves the trolley into place along the jib

This pulley moves the cargo up and down

Force

Home Appliances

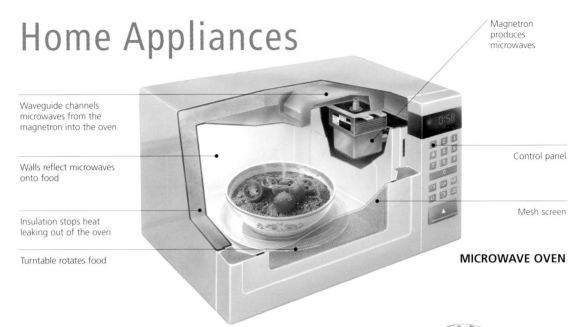

Magnetron produces microwaves

Waveguide channels microwaves from the magnetron into the oven

Walls reflect microwaves onto food

Insulation stops heat leaking out of the oven

Turntable rotates food

Control panel

Mesh screen

MICROWAVE OVEN

TELEVISION

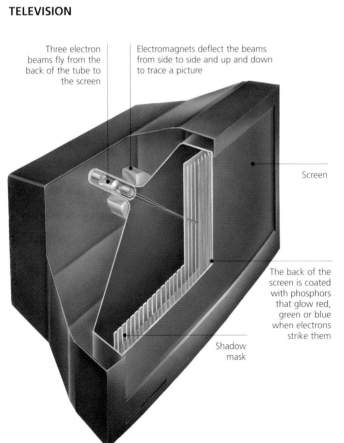

Three electron beams fly from the back of the tube to the screen

Electromagnets deflect the beams from side to side and up and down to trace a picture

Screen

The back of the screen is coated with phosphors that glow red, green or blue when electrons strike them

Shadow mask

FOOD PROCESSOR

Pusher

Feed tube

Lid

Slicing disk

Blade

Handle

Bowl

Spindle

Speed selector

Motor unit

WASHING MACHINE

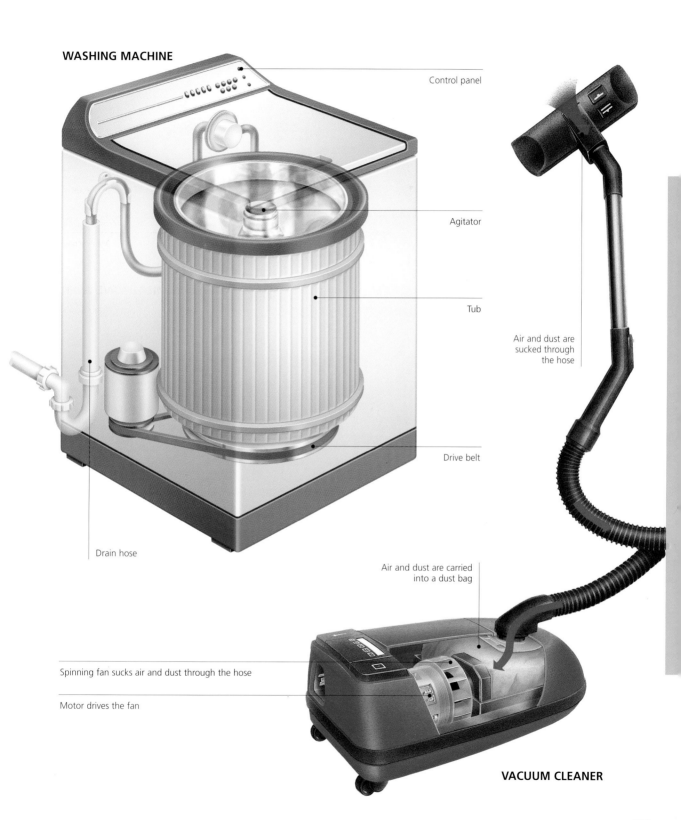

Control panel

Agitator

Tub

Air and dust are sucked through the hose

Drive belt

Drain hose

Air and dust are carried into a dust bag

Spinning fan sucks air and dust through the hose

Motor drives the fan

VACUUM CLEANER

Computers

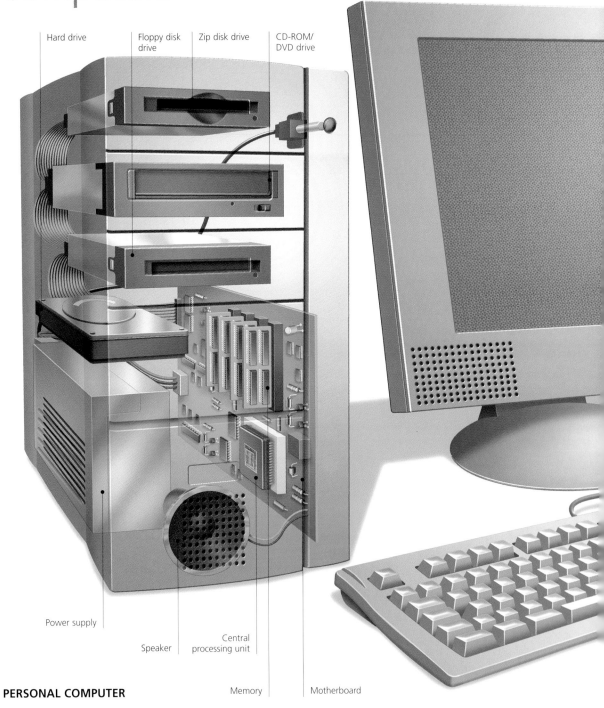

Hard drive

Floppy disk drive

Zip disk drive

CD-ROM/ DVD drive

Power supply

Speaker

Central processing unit

Memory

Motherboard

PERSONAL COMPUTER

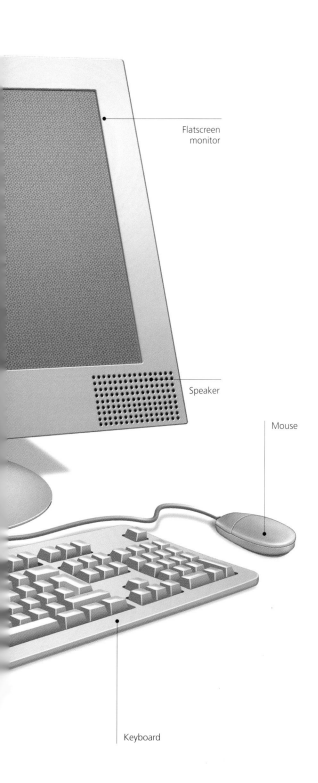

Flatscreen
monitor

Speaker

Mouse

Keyboard

FLATBED SCANNER

LASER PRINTER

PERSONAL ORGANIZER

Medical Technology

X-RAY MACHINE

X-ray gun takes an image of a hand.

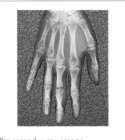

Processed x-ray image

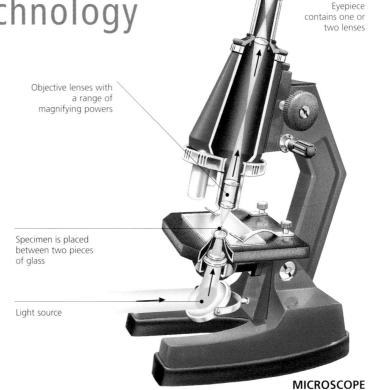

Eyepiece contains one or two lenses

Objective lenses with a range of magnifying powers

Specimen is placed between two pieces of glass

Light source

MICROSCOPE

ULTRASOUND MACHINE

Hand-held probe sends bursts of ultrasound into the body and receives reflections bouncing back

Image created from the reflected ultrasound

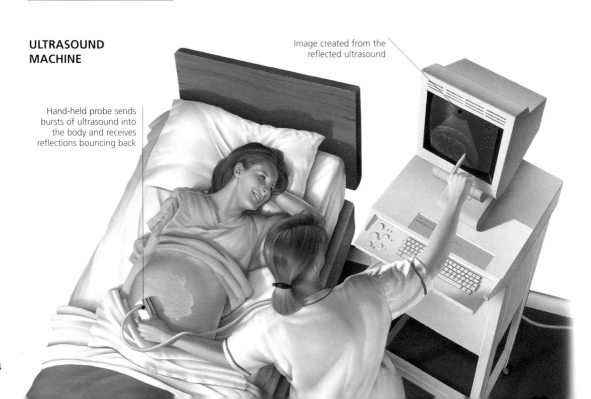

STETHOSCOPE

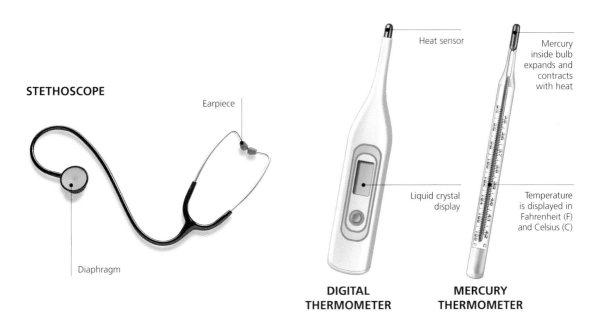

Earpiece

Diaphragm

Heat sensor

Mercury inside bulb expands and contracts with heat

Liquid crystal display

Temperature is displayed in Fahrenheit (F) and Celsius (C)

DIGITAL THERMOMETER

MERCURY THERMOMETER

COCHLEAR IMPLANT

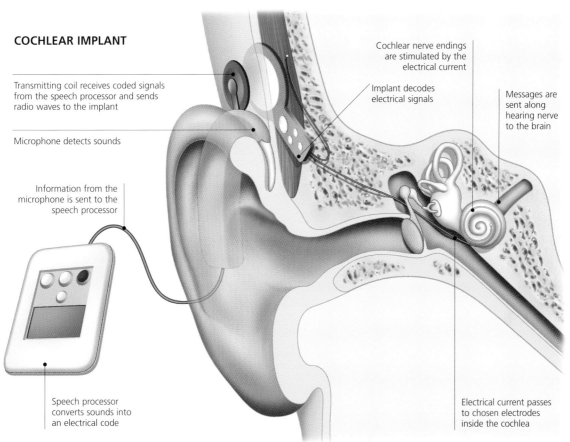

Transmitting coil receives coded signals from the speech processor and sends radio waves to the implant

Microphone detects sounds

Information from the microphone is sent to the speech processor

Cochlear nerve endings are stimulated by the electrical current

Implant decodes electrical signals

Messages are sent along hearing nerve to the brain

Speech processor converts sounds into an electrical code

Electrical current passes to chosen electrodes inside the cochlea

545

Communications

TELEPHONE

An electric signal received by the earpiece passes through a coil and creates a magnetic field around it; a magnet makes the coil vibrate then the diaphragm vibrates to create sound

The mouthpiece works in the opposite way to the earpiece—the caller's voice makes the diaphragm vibrate

VIDEO CONFERENCE

Web-enabled camera

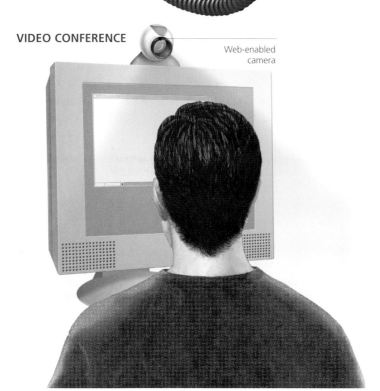

COMMUNICATION SATELLITES

Solar panels change sunlight into electricity to supply power for the satellite's radio equipment

A low-flying
satellite orbits Earth
at a height of
155–186 miles
(250–300 km)

Optics

BINOCULARS

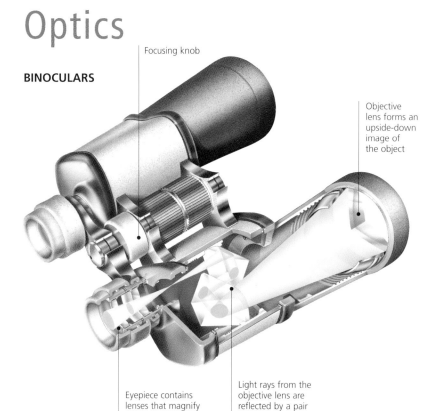

Focusing knob

Objective lens forms an upside-down image of the object

Eyepiece contains lenses that magnify the image

Light rays from the objective lens are reflected by a pair of prisms

Film winder moves a new piece of film behind the shutter

LENSES

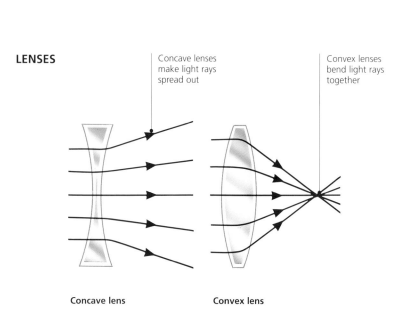

Concave lenses make light rays spread out

Convex lenses bend light rays together

Concave lens

Convex lens

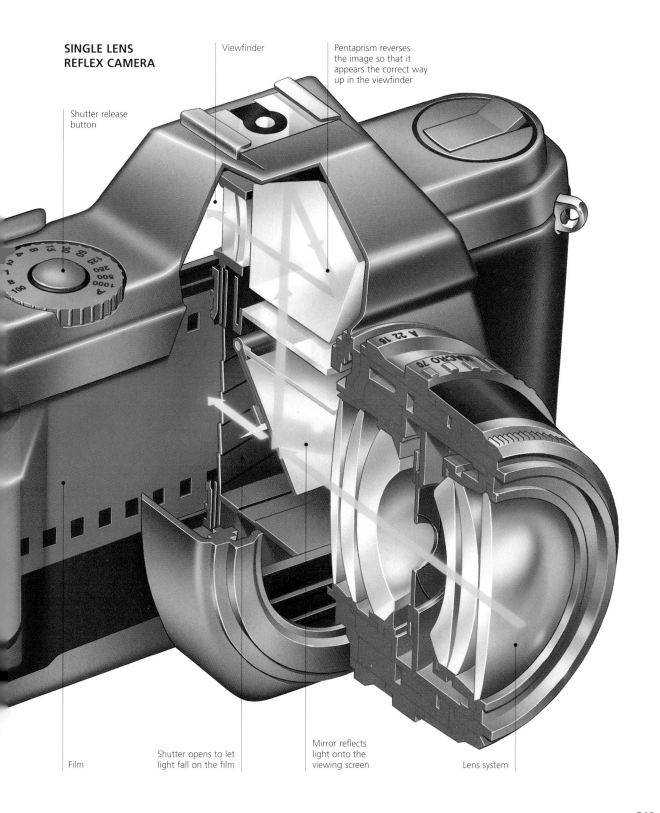

SINGLE LENS REFLEX CAMERA

Viewfinder

Pentaprism reverses the image so that it appears the correct way up in the viewfinder

Shutter release button

Shutter opens to let light fall on the film

Film

Mirror reflects light onto the viewing screen

Lens system

Sound

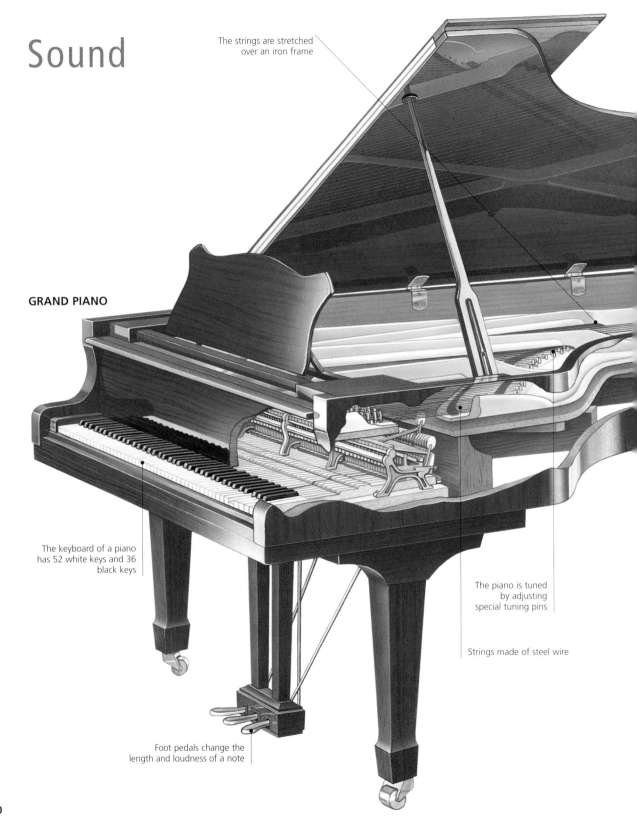

The strings are stretched over an iron frame

GRAND PIANO

The keyboard of a piano has 52 white keys and 36 black keys

The piano is tuned by adjusting special tuning pins

Strings made of steel wire

Foot pedals change the length and loudness of a note

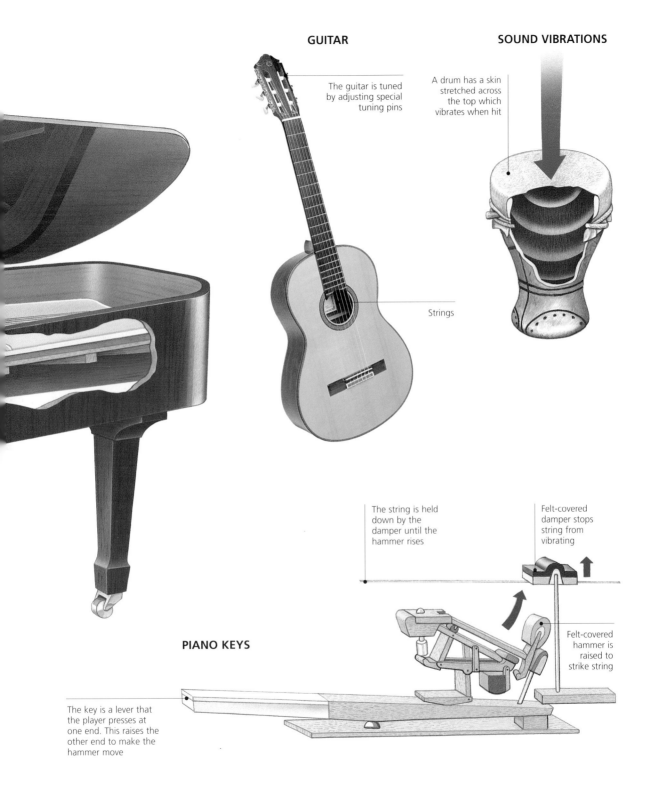

GUITAR

The guitar is tuned by adjusting special tuning pins

Strings

SOUND VIBRATIONS

A drum has a skin stretched across the top which vibrates when hit

The string is held down by the damper until the hammer rises

Felt-covered damper stops string from vibrating

Felt-covered hammer is raised to strike string

PIANO KEYS

The key is a lever that the player presses at one end. This raises the other end to make the hammer move

Power and Energy

TURBOGENERATOR

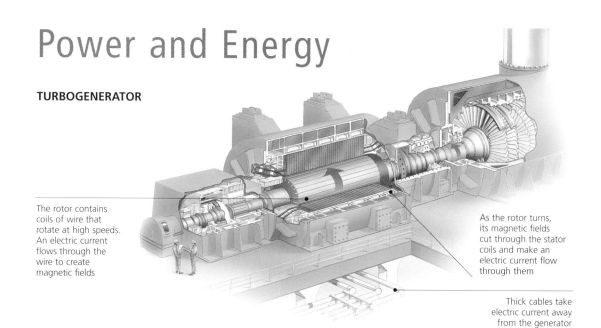

The rotor contains coils of wire that rotate at high speeds. An electric current flows through the wire to create magnetic fields

As the rotor turns, its magnetic fields cut through the stator coils and make an electric current flow through them

Thick cables take electric current away from the generator

STEAM POWER

Steam-powered merry-go-round

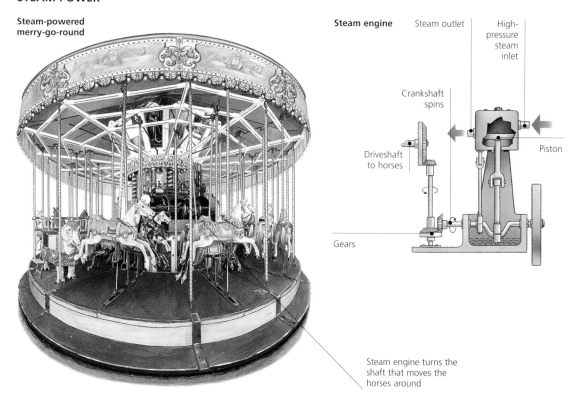

Steam engine

Steam outlet

High-pressure steam inlet

Crankshaft spins

Driveshaft to horses

Piston

Gears

Steam engine turns the shaft that moves the horses around

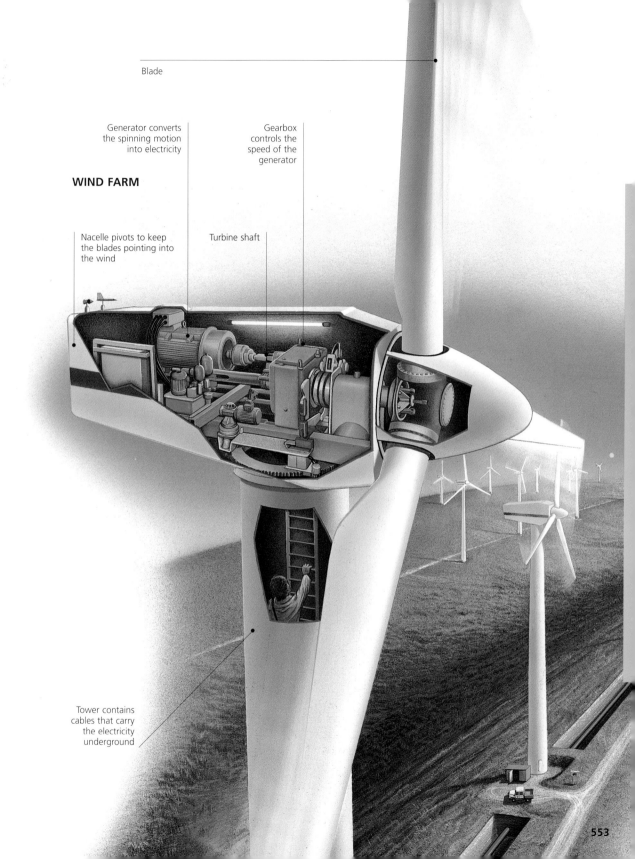

Blade

Generator converts
the spinning motion
into electricity

Gearbox
controls the
speed of the
generator

WIND FARM

Nacelle pivots to keep
the blades pointing into
the wind

Turbine shaft

Tower contains
cables that carry
the electricity
underground

World Map

COUNTRY FORMATION

Early on, people lived in small family groups and their ways of life, or cultures, were shaped by the physical demands of the regions they lived in. Eventually, as the family groups grew larger, relations between the groups helped form the regions into countries. Today, there are 193 independent countries and a small number of territories or dependencies of those countries.

KEY TO NUMBERED COUNTRIES

1	The Netherlands
2	Belgium
•3	Luxembourg
4	Czech Republic
5	Slovakia
6	Switzerland
•7	Liechtenstein
8	Slovenia
9	Croatia
•10	Andorra
•11	Monaco
•12	San Marino
•13	Vatican City
14	Bosnia-Herzegovina
15	Moldova
16	Yugoslavia
17	Albania
18	Macedonia
•19	Gibraltar (U.K.)
20	Armenia
21	Azerbaijan
22	United Arab Emirates
23	Rwanda
24	Burundi

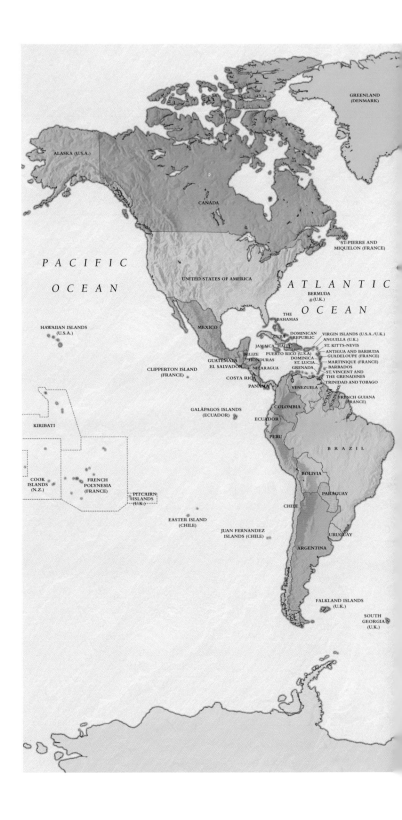

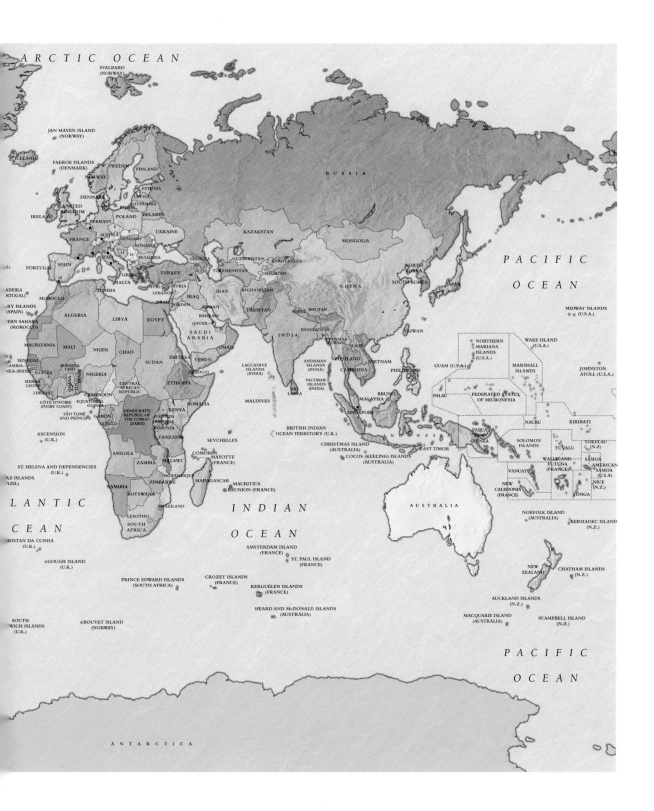

ARCTIC OCEAN

SVALBARD
(NORWAY)

JAN MAYEN ISLAND
(NORWAY)

ICELAND

FAEROE ISLANDS
(DENMARK)

RY ISLANDS
(SPAIN)

ERN SAHARA
(MOROCCO)

SWEDEN

NORWAY

FINLAND

DENMARK

UNITED
KINGDOM

IRELAND

GERMANY

AUSTRIA

FRANCE

ESTONIA

LATVIA

LITHUANIA

RUSSIA

POLAND

BELARUS

UKRAINE

HUNGARY

ROMANIA

ITALY

BULGARIA

RUSSIA

KAZAKSTAN

MONGOLIA

NORTH
KOREA

SOUTH KOREA

JAPAN

PACIFIC

OCEAN

PORTUGAL

SPAIN

GREECE

MALTA

TURKEY

CYPRUS

LEBANON

SYRIA

GEORGIA

UZBEKISTAN

KYRGYZSTAN

TURKMENISTAN

TAJIKISTAN

CHINA

TAIWAN

MIDWAY ISLANDS
(U.S.A.)

ADEIRA
RTUGAL)

MOROCCO

TUNISIA

ISRAEL

JORDAN

IRAQ

KUWAIT

IRAN

AFGHANISTAN

NEPAL

BHUTAN

ALGERIA

LIBYA

EGYPT

BAHRAIN

QATAR

SAUDI
ARABIA

OMAN

PAKISTAN

BANGLADESH

INDIA

MYANMAR
(BURMA)

LAOS

THAILAND

VIETNAM

PHILIPPINES

GUAM (U.S.A.)

NORTHERN
MARIANA
ISLANDS
(U.S.A.)

WAKE ISLAND
(U.S.A.)

MARSHALL
ISLANDS

JOHNSTON
ATOLL (U.S.A.)

MAURITANIA

MALI

NIGER

CHAD

SUDAN

ERITREA

YEMEN

DJIBOUTI

LACCADIVE
ISLANDS
(INDIA)

ANDAMAN
ISLANDS
(INDIA)

CAMBODIA

PALAU

FEDERATED STATES
OF MICRONESIA

SENEGAL
GAMBIA
NEA-BISSAU

GUINEA

SIERRA
LEONE

LIBERIA

BURKINA
FASO

NIGERIA

GHANA

BENIN

TOGO

CENTRAL
AFRICAN
REPUBLIC

ETHIOPIA

NICOBAR
ISLANDS
(INDIA)

SRI
LANKA

MALAYSIA

BRUNEI

NAURU

KIRIBATI

CÔTE D'IVOIRE
(IVORY COAST)

CAMEROON

EQUATORIAL
GUINEA

SÃO TOMÉ
AND PRÍNCIPE

GABON

CONGO

DEMOCRATIC
REPUBLIC OF
THE CONGO
(ZAIRE)

KENYA

SOMALIA

UGANDA

RWANDA

BURUNDI

MALDIVES

SINGAPORE

I N D O N E S I A

PAPUA
NEW
GUINEA

SOLOMON
ISLANDS

TUVALU

TOKELAU
(N.Z.)

ASCENSION
(U.K.)

TANZANIA

BRITISH INDIAN
OCEAN TERRITORY (U.K.)

EAST TIMOR

WALLIS AND
FUTUNA
(FRANCE)

SAMOA

AMERICAN
SAMOA
(U.S.A)

ST. HELENA AND DEPENDENCIES
(U.K.)

ANGOLA

ZAMBIA

MALAWI

SEYCHELLES

COMOROS

MAYOTTE
(FRANCE)

CHRISTMAS ISLAND
(AUSTRALIA)

COCOS (KEELING) ISLANDS
(AUSTRALIA)

VANUATU

NEW
CALEDONIA
(FRANCE)

Fiji

TONGA

NIUE
(N.Z.)

AZ ISLANDS
AZIL)

NAMIBIA

ZIMBABWE

MOZAMBIQUE

BOTSWANA

MADAGASCAR

MAURITIUS

RÉUNION (FRANCE)

LANTIC

CEAN

RISTAN DA CUNHA
(U.K.)

GOUGH ISLAND
(U.K.)

SWAZILAND

LESOTHO

SOUTH
AFRICA

INDIAN

OCEAN

AMSTERDAM ISLAND
(FRANCE)

ST. PAUL ISLAND
(FRANCE)

AUSTRALIA

NORFOLK ISLAND
(AUSTRALIA)

KERMADEC ISLAND
(N.Z.)

PRINCE EDWARD ISLANDS
(SOUTH AFRICA)

CROZET ISLANDS
(FRANCE)

KERGUÉLEN ISLANDS
(FRANCE)

HEARD AND McDONALD ISLANDS
(AUSTRALIA)

NEW
ZEALAND

CHATHAM ISLANDS
(N.Z.)

AUCKLAND ISLANDS
(N.Z.)

MACQUARIE ISLAND
(AUSTRALIA)

CAMPBELL ISLAND
(N.Z.)

SOUTH
WICH ISLANDS
(U.K.)

BOUVET ISLAND
(NORWAY)

PACIFIC

OCEAN

ANTARCTICA

NORTH AMERICA

CANADA

Pronunciation: KA-nuh-duh
Area: 3,851,809 sq. miles (9,976,185 sq. km)
Population: 31,902,268
Capital: Ottawa
Currency: 100 cents = 1 Canadian dollar (CAD)
Official Languages: English, French
Main Religion: Christianity 82%
Exports: Newsprint, wood pulp, timber, crude petroleum, machinery, natural gas, aluminum, motor vehicles and parts, telecommunications equipment, electricity

UNITED STATES OF AMERICA

Pronunciation: yoo-NEYE-tuhd STAYTS of uh-MEHR-uh-kuh
Area: 3,717,800 sq. miles (9,629,091 sq. km)
Population: 280,562,489
Capital: Washington, D.C.
Currency: 100 cents = 1 United States dollar (USD)
Official Language: English
Other Language: Spanish
Main Religions: Christianity 84%, Judaism 2%
Exports: Motor vehicles, raw materials, consumer goods, agricultural products, industrial supplies

Territories and Dependencies

American Samoa: South Pacific Ocean; 76 sq. miles (197 sq. km); population 68,688
Guam: Western Pacific Ocean; 209 sq. miles (541 sq. km); population 160,796
Midway: Central Pacific Ocean; 2 sq. miles (5 sq. km); no permanent population
Northern Mariana Islands: North Pacific Ocean; 184 sq. miles (477 sq. km); population 77,311
Puerto Rico: Caribbean Sea; 3,515 sq. miles (9,104 sq. km); population 3,888,000
Virgin Islands of the United States: Caribbean Sea; 133 sq. miles (345 sq. km); population 123,498
Wake Island: North Pacific Ocean; 3 sq. miles (7.7 sq. km); population 124

MEXICO

Pronunciation: MEK-si-koh
Area: 761,600 sq. miles (1,972,544 sq. km)
Population: 103,400,165
Capital: Mexico City
Currency: 100 centavos = 1 Mexican peso (MXN)
Official Language: Spanish
Other Languages: Regional languages
Main Religion: Christianity 95%
Exports: Crude oil, oil products, coffee, silver, engines, motor vehicles, cotton, electronic goods

GUATEMALA

Pronunciation: gwah-tuh-MAH-luh
Area: 42,042 sq. miles (108,889 sq. km)
Population: 13,314,079
Capital: Guatemala
Currency: 100 centavos = 1 Guatemalan quetzal (GTQ)
Official Language: Spanish

Other Languages: Quiche, Cakchiquel, Kekchi, other regional languages
Main Religions: Christianity 99%, traditional Mayan religions
Exports: Coffee, bananas, cotton, sugar, minerals, textiles, petroleum

BELIZE

Pronunciation: buh-LEEZ
Area: 8,867 sq. miles (22,966 sq. km)
Population: 262,999
Capital: Belmopan
Currency: 100 cents = 1 Belizean dollar (BZD)
Official Language: English
Other Languages: Spanish, Maya, Garifuna, Creole
Main Religion: Christianity 92%
Exports: Sugar, molasses, citrus fruit, bananas, clothing, fish products, timber

HONDURAS

Pronunciation: hahn-DER-uhs
Area: 43,277 sq. miles (112,087 sq. km)
Population: 6,560,608
Capital: Tegucigalpa
Currency: 100 centavos = 1 lempira (HNL)
Official Language: Spanish
Other Languages: Regional languages
Main Religion: Christianity 97%
Exports: Sugar, coffee, textiles, clothing, timber and timber products

EL SALVADOR

Pronunciation: el SAL-vuh-dor
Area: 8,260 sq. miles (21,393 sq. km)
Population: 6,353,681
Capital: San Salvador

Currency: 100 centavos = 1 Salvadoran colón (SVC)
Official Language: Spanish
Other Language: Nahua
Main Religion: Christianity 92%
Exports: Coffee, sugarcane, shrimp, raw materials

NICARAGUA

Pronunciation: ni-kuh-RAH-gwuh
Area: 49,998 sq. miles (129,494 sq. km)
Population: 5,023,818
Capital: Managua
Currency: 100 centavos = 1 gold cordoba (NIO)
Official Language: Spanish
Other Languages: English, regional languages
Main Religion: Christianity 100%
Exports: Coffee, cotton, sugar, bananas, seafood, gold, beef, tobacco

COSTA RICA

Pronunciation: kaws-tuh REE-kuh
Area: 19,652 sq. miles (50,899 sq. km)
Population: 3,834,934
Capital: San José
Currency: 100 centimos = 1 Costa Rican colón (CRC)
Official Language: Spanish
Other Language: English
Main Religion: Christianity 92%
Exports: Coffee, bananas, sugar, textiles, pineapples

PANAMA

Pronunciation: PA-nuh-mah
Area: 33,659 sq. miles (87,177 sq. km)
Population: 2,882,329
Capital: Panama
Currency: 100 centesimos = 1 balboa (PAB)
Official Language: Spanish
Other Languages: English, regional languages
Main Religion: Christianity 100%
Exports: Bananas, shrimp, sugar, coffee, clothing

THE BAHAMAS

Pronunciation: the buh-HAH-muhz
Area: 5,386 sq. miles (13,950 sq. km)
Population: 300,529
Capital: Nassau
Currency: 100 cents = 1 Bahamian dollar (BSD)
Official Language: English
Other Language: Bahamian creole
Main Religion: Christianity 95%
Exports: Pharmaceuticals, cement, rum, crayfish, refined petroleum products

CUBA

Pronunciation: KYOO-buh
Area: 42,804 sq. miles (110,862 sq. km)
Population: 11,224,321
Capital: Havana
Currency: 100 centavos = 1 Cuban peso (CUP)
Official Language: Spanish
Main Religion: Christianity 85%
Exports: Sugar, fish and shellfish, citrus fruit, coffee, tobacco, nickel, medical products

JAMAICA

Pronunciation: juh-MAY-kuh
Area: 4,243 sq. miles (10,990 sq. km)
Population: 2,680,029
Capital: Kingston
Currency: 100 cents = 1 Jamaican dollar (JMD)
Official Language: English
Other Language: Jamaican creole
Main Religion: Christianity 65%
Exports: Bauxite, sugar, bananas, rum, alumina

HAITI

Pronunciation: HAY-tee
Area: 10,714 sq. miles (27,749 sq. km)
Population: 7,063,722
Capital: Port-au-Prince
Currency: 100 centimes = 1 gourde (HTG)
Official Languages: French, Haitian creole
Main Religion: Christianity 96%
Exports: Clothing, coffee, sugar, manufactured goods, oils, mangoes

DOMINICAN REPUBLIC

Pronunciation: duh-MI-ni-kuhn ri-PUH-blik
Area: 18,657 sq. miles (48,322 sq. km)
Population: 8,721,594
Capital: Santo Domingo
Currency: 100 centavos = 1 Dominican peso (DOP)
Official Language: Spanish
Main Religion: Christianity 95%
Exports: Minerals, coffee, cocoa, gold, tobacco

ANTIGUA AND BARBUDA

Pronunciation: an-TEE-guh and bar-BOO-duh
Area: 171 sq. miles (443 sq. km)
Population: 67,448
Capital: St. John's
Currency: 100 cents = 1 East Caribbean dollar (XCD)
Official Language: English
Other Languages: Regional languages
Main Religions: Christianity 97%, indigenous religions 3%
Exports: Petroleum products, manufactured goods, machinery and transportation equipment, food and livestock

ST. KITTS–NEVIS

Pronunciation: saynt KITS NEE-vuhs
Area: 104 sq. miles (269 sq. km)
Population: 38,736
Capital: Basseterre
Currency: 100 cents = 1 East Caribbean dollar (XCD)
Official Language: English
Main Religion: Christianity 86%
Exports: Machinery, food, beverages, electronics, tobacco

DOMINICA

Pronunciation: dah-muh-NEE-kuh
Area: 289 sq. miles (749 sq. km)
Population: 70,158
Capital: Roseau
Currency: 100 cents = 1 East Caribbean dollar (XCD)
Official Language: English

Other Language: French patois
Main Religion: Christianity 92%
Exports: Bananas, grapefruit, oranges, vegetables, soap, bay oil

ST. LUCIA

Pronunciation: saynt LOO-shuh
Area: 238 sq. miles (616 sq. km)
Population: 160,145
Capital: Castries
Currency: 100 cents = 1 East Caribbean dollar (XCD)
Official Language: English
Other Language: French patois
Main Religion: Christianity 100%
Exports: Bananas, clothing, cocoa, coconut oil, fruit and vegetables

BARBADOS

Pronunciation: bar-BAY-dohs
Area: 166 sq. miles (430 sq. km)
Population: 276,607
Capital: Bridgetown
Currency: 100 cents = 1 Barbadian dollar (BBS)
Official Language: English
Other Language: Barbadian creole
Main Religion: Christianity 71%
Exports: Sugar and molasses, rum, chemicals, foods and beverages, electrical components, clothing

ST. VINCENT AND THE GRENADINES

Pronunciation: saynt VIN-suhnt and the gren-uh-DEENZ
Area: 150 sq. miles (389 sq. km)
Population: 116,394

Capital: Kingstown
Currency: 100 cents = 1 East Caribbean dollar (XCD)
Official Language: English
Other Language: French patois
Main Religion: Christianity 75%
Exports: Bananas, taro, tennis rackets, arrowroot

GRENADA

Pronunciation: gruh-NAY-duh
Area: 133 sq. miles (344 sq. km)
Population: 89,211
Capital: St. George's
Currency: 100 cents = 1 East Caribbean dollar (XCD)
Official Language: English
Other Language: French patois
Main Religion: Christianity 100%
Exports: Bananas, fruit and vegetables, cocoa, nutmeg, clothing, mace

TRINIDAD AND TOBAGO

Pronunciation: TRI-nuh-dad and tuh-BAY-goh
Area: 1,980 sq. miles (5,128 sq. km)
Population: 1,163,724
Capital: Port-of-Spain
Currency: 100 cents = 1 Trinidad and Tobago dollar (TTD)
Official Language: English
Other Languages: Hindi, French, Spanish, Chinese
Main Religions: Christianity 44%, Hinduism 24%, Islam 6%
Exports: Petroleum and petroleum products, chemicals, steel products, fertilizer, sugar, cocoa, coffee, citrus fruit, flowers

SOUTH AMERICA

COLOMBIA

Pronunciation: kuh-LUHM-bee-uh
Area: 439,735 sq. miles (1,138,914 sq. km)
Population: 41,008,227
Capital: Bogota
Currency: 100 centavos = 1 Colombian peso (COP)
Official Language: Spanish
Main Religion: Christianity 90%
Exports: Petroleum, coffee, coal, bananas, flowers

VENEZUELA

Pronunciation: ve-nuh-ZWAY-luh
Area: 352,143 sq. miles (912,050 sq. km)
Population: 24,287,670
Capital: Caracas
Currency: 100 centimos = 1 bolivar (VEB)
Official Language: Spanish
Other Languages: Regional languages
Main Religion: Christianity 98%
Exports: Petroleum, bauxite and aluminum, steel, chemicals, agricultural products, basic manufactured goods

GUYANA

Pronunciation: geye-AH-nuh
Area: 83,000 sq. miles (214,970 sq. km)
Population: 698,209
Capital: Georgetown
Currency: 100 cents = 1 Guyanese dollar (GYD)
Official Language: English
Other Languages: Local languages, Hindi, Urdu
Main Religions: Christianity 50%, Hinduism 33%, Islam 9%
Exports: Sugar, molasses, bauxite, rice, shrimp

SURINAME

Pronunciation: SUR-uh-nah-muh
Area: 63,039 sq. miles (163,270 sq. km)
Population: 436,494
Capital: Paramaribo
Currency: 100 cents = 1 Surinamese guilder or florin (SRG)
Official Language: Dutch
Other Languages: English, Sranang Tongo, Hindustani, Javanese
Main Religions: Christianity 48%, Hinduism 27%, Islam 20%, indigenous religions 5%
Exports: Aluminum, fish, shrimp, timber, rice, bananas, crude oil

ECUADOR

Pronunciation: E-kwuh-dor
Area: 109,483 sq. miles (283,561 sq. km)
Population: 13,447,494

Capital: Quito
Currency: 100 cents = 1 United States dollar (USD)
Official Language: Spanish
Other Languages: Quechua, other regional languages
Main Religion: Christianity 95%
Exports: Petroleum, bananas, shrimp, cocoa, coffee, flowers, fish

PERU

Pronunciation: puh-ROO
Area: 496,222 sq. miles (1,285,215 sq. km)
Population: 27,949,639
Capital: Lima
Currency: 100 centimos = 1 nuevo sol (PEN)
Official Languages: Spanish, Quechua
Other Language: Aymara
Main Religion: Christianity 90%
Exports: Copper, zinc, petroleum products, lead, coffee, cotton, fish and fish products, sugar

BRAZIL

Pronunciation: bruh-ZIL
Area: 3,284,426 sq. miles (8,506,663 sq. km)
Population: 176,029,560
Capital: Brasília
Currency: 100 centavos = 1 real (BRL)
Official Language: Portuguese
Other Languages: Spanish, English, French
Main Religion: Christianity 80%
Exports: Iron ore, soybean bran, coffee, sugar, footwear, manufactured goods

BOLIVIA

Pronunciation: buh-LI-vee-uh
Area: 424,162 sq. miles (1,098,579 sq. km)
Population: 8,445,134
Capitals: La Paz (seat of government),
Sucre (legal and judicial)
Currency: 100 centavos = 1 boliviano (BOB)
Official Languages: Spanish, Quechua,
Aymara
Main Religion: Christianity 100%
Exports: Natural gas, soybeans, zinc, gold
jewelry, timber

CHILE

Pronunciation: CHI-lee
Area: 292,257 sq. miles (756,946 sq. km)
Population: 15,498,930
Capital: Santiago
Currency: 100 centavos = 1 Chilean peso
(CLP)
Official Language: Spanish
Other Languages: Regional languages
Main Religion: Christianity 99%
Exports: Copper, metals and minerals, timber
products, fish, fruit, chemicals

PARAGUAY

Pronunciation: PAR-uh-gweye
Area: 157,043 sq. miles
(406,741 sq. km)
Population: 5,884,491
Capital: Asunción
Currency: 100 centimos = 1 guarani (PYG)

Official Languages: Spanish, Guarani
Main Religion: Christianity 97%
Exports: Cotton, soybeans, timber, vegetable
oils, meat products, coffee, electricity, feed
for livestock

ARGENTINA

Pronunciation: ar-juhn-TEE-nuh
Area: 1,068,296 sq. miles (2,766,884 sq. km)
Population: 37,812,817
Capital: Buenos Aires
Currency: 100 centavos = 1 Argentine
peso (ARS)
Official Language: Spanish
Other Languages: English, Italian,
German, French
Main Religions: Christianity 92%,
Judaism 2%
Exports: Manufactured goods, meat, wheat,
corn, vegetable oil, fuel and energy

URUGUAY

Pronunciation: OOR-uh-gweye
Area: 68,039 sq. miles (176,221 sq. km)
Population: 3,386,575
Capital: Montevideo
Currency: 100 centesimos = 1 Uruguayan
peso (UYU)
Official Language: Spanish
Other Language: Brazilero
Main Religions: Christianity 68%,
Judaism 1%
Exports: Wool, textiles, beef and other animal
products, leather, rice

DISPUTED TERRITORIES WORLDWIDE

GAZA STRIP (PALESTINE)
Location: Middle East
Disputed By: Israel and Palestine,
Palestinian interim self-government
Size: 139 sq. miles (360 sq. km)
Population: 1,225,911

KASHMIR
Location: Southern Asia
Disputed By: India and Pakistan
Size: 85,085 sq. miles
(222,236 sq. km)
Population: 7,718,700

**TURKISH FEDERATED STATE
OF CYPRUS**
Location: Mediterranean Sea
Disputed By: Turkey and Cyprus
Size: 1,295 sq. miles (3,355 sq. km)
Population: 177,120

WEST BANK (PALESTINE)
Location: Middle East
Disputed By: Israel and Palestine,
Palestinian interim self-government
Size: 2,263 sq. miles (5,860 sq. km)
Population: 1,612,000

WESTERN SAHARA
Location: Northwestern Africa
Disputed By: Morocco and separatist
movement
Size: 102,703 sq. miles
(266,001 sq. km);
Population: 256,177

EUROPE

UNITED KINGDOM

Pronunciation: yoo-NEYE-tuhd KING-duhm
Area: 94,525 sq. miles (244,820 sq. km)
Population: 58,836,700
Capital: London
Currency: 100 pence = 1 British pound (GBP)
Official Language: English
Other Languages: Welsh, Scottish Gaelic, Irish Gaelic
Main Religions: Christianity 90%, Islam 3%, Sikh 1%, Hinduism 1%, Judaism 1%
Exports: Manufactured goods, machinery, fuels, chemicals, food and beverages, tobacco

Territories and Dependencies

Anguilla: Caribbean Sea; 35 sq. miles (91 sq. km); population 12,446
Bermuda: North Atlantic Ocean; 20 sq. miles (52 sq. km); population 63,960
British Indian Ocean Territory: Indian Ocean; 23 sq. miles (60 sq. km); no permanent population
British Virgin Islands: Caribbean Sea; 59 sq. miles (153 sq. km); population 21,272
Cayman Islands: Caribbean Sea; 118 sq. miles (306 sq. km); population 36,273

Falkland Islands and Dependencies (South Georgia and South Sandwich Islands): South Atlantic Ocean; 4,700 sq. miles (12,173 sq. km); population 2,967
Gibraltar: Southern Spain; 2.25 sq. miles (6 sq. km); population 27,714
Guernsey: English Channel; 30 sq. miles (78 sq. km); population 64,587
Isle of Man: Irish Sea; 221 sq. miles (572 sq. km); population 73,873
Jersey: English Channel; 45 sq. miles (116 sq. km); population 89,775
Montserrat: Caribbean Sea; 40 sq. miles (104 sq. km); population 8,437
Pitcairn Islands: South Pacific Ocean; 18 sq. miles (47 sq. km); population 47
St. Helena and Dependencies (Ascension Island and Tristan da Cunha): South Atlantic Ocean; 158 sq. miles (410 sq. km); population 7,317
Turks and Caicos Islands: Caribbean Sea; 166 sq. miles (430 sq. km); population 18,738

IRELAND

Pronunciation: EYER-luhnd
Area: 26,600 sq. miles (68,894 sq. km)
Population: 3,883,159
Capital: Dublin
Currency: 100 cents = 1 euro (EUR)
Official Languages: English, Irish Gaelic
Main Religion: Christianity 94%
Exports: Chemicals, data processing equipment, industrial machinery, livestock, animal products, pharmacueticals

PORTUGAL

Pronunciation: POR-chi-guhl
Area: 35,383 sq. miles (91,642 sq. km)
Population: 10,084,245
Capital: Lisbon
Currency: 100 cents = 1 euro (EUR)
Official Language: Portuguese
Main Religion: Christianity 98%
Exports: Clothing, footwear, machinery, cork, paper products, animal hides, chemicals

SPAIN

Pronunciation: spayn
Area: 194,881 sq. miles (504,742 sq. km)
Population: 40,077,100
Capital: Madrid
Currency: 100 cents = 1 euro (EUR)
Official Language: Castilian Spanish
Other Languages: Catalan, Galician, Basque
Main Religion: Christianity 99%
Exports: Motor vehicles, manufactured goods, food, machinery, consumer goods

ANDORRA

Pronunciation: an-DOR-uh
Area: 180 sq. miles (482 sq. km)
Population: 68,403
Capital: Andorra la Vella
Currencies: 100 cents = 1 euro (EUR)
Official Language: Catalan
Other Languages: French, Castilian Spanish
Main Religion: Christianity 95%
Exports: Electricity, tobacco products, timber, furniture

FRANCE

Pronunciation: frans
Area: 211,209 sq. miles (547,030 sq. km)
Population: 59,765,983
Capital: Paris
Currency: 100 cents = 1 euro (EUR)
Official Language: French
Other Languages: Occitan, Breton, Catalan, Basque, Arabic, Corsican, Flemish, Alsatian
Main Religions: Christianity 92%, Judaism 1%, Islam 3%

Exports: Machinery and transportation equipment, chemicals, food, agricultural products, iron and steel, textiles, clothing, pharmacueticals

Territories and Dependencies

French Guiana: Northern South America; 35,126 sq. miles (90,976 sq. km); population 182,333
French Polynesia: South Pacific Ocean; 1,609 sq. miles (4,167 sq. km); population 257,847
Guadeloupe: Caribbean Sea; 852 sq. miles (1,507 sq. km); population 435,739
Martinique: Caribbean Sea; 425 sq. miles (1,101 sq. km); population 422,277
Mayotte: Mozambique Channel, Africa; 144 sq. miles (373 sq. km); population 170,879
New Caledonia: South Pacific Ocean; 7,367 sq. miles (19,081 sq. km); population 207,858
Réunion: Indian Ocean; 969 sq. miles (2,510 sq. km); population 743,981
St-Pierre and Miquelon: North Atlantic Ocean; 93 sq. miles (241 sq. km); population 6,954
Wallis and Futuna Islands: South Pacific Ocean; 106 sq. miles (275 sq. km); population 15,585

MONACO

Pronunciation: MAH-nuh-koh
Area: 0.58 sq. miles (1.5 sq. km)
Population: 31,987
Capital: Monaco
Currency: 100 cents = 1 euro (EUR)
Official Language: French
Other Languages: English, Italian, Monégasque
Main Religion: Christianity 95%
Exports: Pharmaceuticals, perfumes, clothing

THE NETHERLANDS

Pronunciation: the NE-ther-luhndz
Area: 16,033 sq. miles (41,525 sq. km)
Population: 16,067,754
Capitals: Amsterdam (official); The Hague (seat of government)
Currency: 100 cents = 1 euro (EUR)
Official Language: Dutch
Main Religions: Christianity 52%, Islam 4%
Exports: Metal products, chemicals, processed food, tobacco, agricultural products, machinery and equipment

Territories and Dependencies

Aruba: Caribbean Sea; 69 sq. miles (179 sq. km); population 70,441
Netherlands Antilles: Caribbean Sea; 371 sq. miles (961 sq. km); population 214,258

BELGIUM

Pronunciation: BEL-juhm
Area: 11,781 sq. miles (30,513 sq. km)
Population: 10,274,595
Capital: Brussels
Currency: 100 cents = 1 euro (EUR)
Official Languages: Dutch (Flemish), French
Other Language: German
Main Religion: Christianity 100%
Exports: Iron and steel, machinery and equipment, chemicals, diamonds, petroleum products

LUXEMBOURG

Pronunciation: LUK-suhm-berg
Area: 999 sq. miles (2,587 sq. km)
Population: 429,100
Capital: Luxembourg
Currency: 100 cents = 1 euro (EUR)
Official Languages: Luxembourgish (Letzeburgesh), German, French
Other Language: English
Main Religions: Christianity 99%, Judaism 1%
Exports: Steel products, chemicals, rubber products, glass, aluminum, machinery and equipment

GERMANY

Pronunciation: JER-muh-nee
Area: 137,735 sq. miles (356,734 sq. km)
Population: 83,251,851
Capital: Berlin

Currency: 100 cents = 1 euro (EUR)
Official Language: German
Main Religions: Christianity 72%, Islam 2%
Exports: Machines and machine tools, motor vehicles, chemicals, iron and steel products, textiles, agricultural products, raw materials

AUSTRIA

Pronunciation: AWS-tree-uh
Area: 32,375 sq. miles (83,851 sq. km)
Population: 8,169,929
Capital: Vienna
Currency: 100 cents = 1 euro (EUR)
Official Language: German
Main Religion: Christianity 82%
Exports: Machinery, electrical equipment, iron and steel, lumber, textiles, paper and paper products, chemicals, foodstuffs, metal goods

VATICAN CITY

Pronunciation: VA-ti-kuhn city
Area: 0.17 sq. miles (0.44 sq. km)
Population: 900
Capital: Vatican City
Currency: 100 cents = 1 euro (EUR)
Official Languages: Italian, Latin, French
Main Religion: Christianity 100%
Exports: None

SWITZERLAND

Pronunciation: SWIT-suhr-luhnd
Area: 15,941 sq. miles (41,287 sq. km)
Population: 7,301,994
Capital: Bern
Currency: 100 centimes = 1 Swiss franc (CHF)
Official Languages: German, French, Italian
Other Language: Romansch
Main Religion: Christianity 86%
Exports: Machinery, precision instruments, metal products, food, textiles, chemicals

ITALY

Pronunciation: IT-uh-lee
Area: 116,313 sq. miles (301,251 sq. km)
Population: 57,715,625
Capital: Rome
Currency: 100 cents = 1 euro (EUR)
Official Language: Italian
Other Languages: German, French, Slovene
Main Religion: Christianity 98%
Exports: Textiles, clothing, machinery, motor vehicles, transportation equipment, chemicals, food products, minerals

MALTA

Pronunciation: MAWL-tuh
Area: 122 sq. miles (316 sq. km)
Population: 397,499
Capital: Valletta
Currency: 100 cents = 1 Maltese lira (MTL)
Official Languages: Maltese, English
Main Religion: Christianity 98%
Exports: Machinery and transportation equipment, clothing, footwear

LIECHTENSTEIN

Pronunciation: LIK-tuhn-shteyen
Area: 62 sq. miles (161 sq. km)
Population: 32,842
Capital: Vaduz
Currency: 100 centimes = 1 Swiss franc (CHF)
Official Language: German
Main Religion: Christianity 87%
Exports: Machinery, dental products, stamps, hardware, pottery

SAN MARINO

Pronunciation: san muh-REE-noh
Area: 24 sq. miles (62 sq. km)
Population: 27,730
Capital: San Marino
Currency: 100 cents = 1 euro (EUR)
Official Language: Italian
Main Religion: Christianity 95%
Exports: Building stone, lime, timber, chestnuts, wheat, wine, baked goods, animal skins, ceramics

SLOVENIA

Pronunciation: sloh-VEE-nee-uh
Area: 7,819 sq. miles (20,251 sq. km)
Population: 1,932,917
Capital: Ljubljana
Currency: 100 stotins = 1 tolar (SIT)
Official Language: Slovenian
Other Language: Serbo-Croatian
Main Religions: Christianity 72%, Islam 1%
Exports: Motor vehicles, furniture, machinery, manufactured goods, chemicals, textiles, food, raw materials

CROATIA

Pronunciation: kroh-AY-shuh
Area: 21,829 sq. miles (56,537 sq. km)
Population: 4,390,751
Capital: Zagreb
Currency: 100 lipas = 1 Croatian kuna (HRK)
Official Language: Serbo-Croatian
Main Religions: Christianity 88%, Islam 1%
Exports: Machinery and transportation equipment, other manufactured goods, chemicals, food, livestock, raw materials, fuels, textiles

BOSNIA AND HERZEGOVINA

Pronunciation: BAHZ-nee-uh and hert-suh-goh-VEE-nuh
Area: 19,740 sq. miles (51,129 sq. km)
Population: 3,964,388
Capital: Sarajevo
Currency: 100 pfenniga = 1 marka (BAM)
Official Languages: Serbo-Croatian, Bosnian
Main Religions: Christianity 50%, Islam 40%
Exports: Timber, furniture

YUGOSLAVIA

Pronunciation: yoo-goh-SLAH-vee-uh
Area: 39,449 sq. miles (102,173 sq. km)
Population: 10,656,929
Capital: Belgrade
Currency: 100 paras = 1 Yugoslav new dinar (YUM)

Official Language: Serbo-Croatian
Other Language: Albanian
Main Religions: Christianity 70%, Islam 19%
Exports: Manufactured goods, raw materials, food

ROMANIA

Pronunciation: roh-MAY-nee-uh
Area: 91,699 sq. miles (237,500 sq. km)
Population: 22,317,730
Capital: Bucharest
Currency: 100 bani = 1 leu (ROL)
Official Language: Romanian
Other Languages: Hungarian, German
Main Religion: Christianity 82%
Exports: Metals and metal products, minerals and fuels, textiles and footwear, electrical goods, machinery and equipment

BULGARIA

Pronunciation: buhl-GAIR-ee-uh
Area: 42,823 sq. miles (110,912 sq. km)
Population: 7,621,337
Capital: Sofia
Currency: 100 stotinki = 1 lev (BGL)
Official Language: Bulgarian
Main Religions: Christianity 86%, Islam 13%, Judaism 1%
Exports: Machinery and equipment, fuels, minerals and raw materials, metals, clothing, footwear

ALBANIA

Pronunciation: al-BAY-nee-uh
Area: 11,100 sq. miles (28,749 sq. km)
Population: 3,544,841
Capital: Tiranë

Currency: 100 qintars = 1 lek (ALL)
Official Language: Albanian (Tosk dialect)
Other Language: Greek
Main Religions: Islam 70%, Christianity 30%
Exports: Asphalt, metals and metallic ores, electricity, crude oil, fruit and vegetables, tobacco

MACEDONIA

Pronunciation: ma-suh-DOH-nee-uh
Area: 9,928 sq. miles (25,714 sq. km)
Population: 2,054,800
Capital: Skopje
Currency: 100 deni = 1 Macedonian denar (MKD)
Official Language: Macedonian
Other Languages: Albanian, Turkish, Serbo-Croatian
Main Religions: Christianity 67%, Islam 30%
Exports: Manufactured goods, machinery and transportation equipment, food, beverages, tobacco, iron and steel

GREECE

Pronunciation: grees
Area: 50,944 sq. miles (131,945 sq. km)
Population: 10,645,343
Capital: Athens
Currency: 100 cents = 1 euro (EUR)
Official Language: Greek
Other Languages: English, French
Main Religions: Christianity 98%, Islam 1%
Exports: Manufactured goods, food, petroleum

ESTONIA

Pronunciation: e-STOH-nee-uh
Area: 17,413 sq. miles (45,100 sq. km)
Population: 1,415,681
Capital: Tallinn
Currency: 100 cents = 1 Estonian kroon (EEK)
Official Language: Estonian
Other Languages: Russian, Ukrainian, English
Main Religion: Christianity 99%
Exports: Textiles, food, machinery, timber

LATVIA

Pronunciation: LAT-vee-uh
Area: 24,938 sq. miles (64,589 sq. km)
Population: 2,366,515
Capital: Riga
Currency: 100 santims = 1 Latvian lat (LVL)
Official Language: Latvian (Lettish)
Other Languages: Lithuanian, Russian
Main Religion: Christianity 100%
Exports: Timber, metals, dairy products, furniture, textiles, machinery and equipment

LITHUANIA

Pronunciation: li-thuh-WAY-nee-uh
Area: 25,174 sq. miles (65,201 sq. km)
Population: 3,601,138
Capital: Vilnius
Currency: 100 centas = 1 Lithuan litas (LTL)
Official Language: Lithuanian
Other Languages: Polish, Russian
Main Religion: Christianity 98%
Exports: Machinery, minerals, chemicals, textiles and clothing, food

BELARUS

Pronunciation: be-luh-ROOS
Area: 80,154 sq. miles (207,599 sq. km)
Population: 10,335,382
Capital: Minsk
Currency: Belarusian rubel (BYR)
Official Language: Belarusian
Other Language: Russian
Main Religion: Christianity 80%
Exports: Machinery and equipment, chemicals, food, metals, textiles

POLAND

Pronunciation: POH-luhnd
Area: 120,756 sq. miles (312,758 sq. km)
Population: 38,625,478
Capital: Warsaw
Currency: 100 groszy = 1 zloty (PLN)
Official Language: Polish
Main Religion: Christianity 95%
Exports: Machinery and transportation equipment, manufactured goods, food and livestock, fuels

CZECH REPUBLIC

Pronunciation: chek ri-PUH-blik
Area: 30,450 sq. miles (78,866 sq. km)
Population: 10,256,760
Capital: Prague

Currency: 100 haleru = 1 Czech koruna (CZK)
Official Language: Czech
Main Religion: Christianity 47%
Exports: Manufactured goods, raw materials and fuels, machinery and transportation equipment, chemicals, agricultural products

SLOVAKIA

Pronunciation: sloh-VAH-kee-uh
Area: 18,923 sq. miles (49,011 sq. km)
Population: 5,422,366
Capital: Bratislava
Currency: 100 halierov = 1 Slovak koruna (SKK)
Official Language: Slovak
Other Language: Hungarian
Main Religion: Christianity 73%
Exports: Machinery and transportation equipment, chemicals, minerals and metals, manufactured goods, agricultural products

UKRAINE

Pronunciation: yoo-KRAYN
Area: 233,089 sq. miles (603,701 sq. km)
Population: 48,396,470
Capital: Kiev
Currency: 100 kopiykas = 1 hryvnia (UAH)
Official Language: Ukrainian
Other Languages: Russian, Romanian, Polish, Hungarian
Main Religions: Christianity 90%, Judaism 2%
Exports: Metals, chemicals, machinery and transportation equipment, grain, meat, fuel and petroleum products

HUNGARY

Pronunciation: HUHNG-uh-ree
Area: 35,919 sq. miles (93,030 sq. km)
Population: 10,075,034
Capital: Budapest
Currency: 100 filler = 1 forint (HUF)
Official Language: Hungarian
Main Religion: Christianity 93%
Exports: Raw materials, machinery and transportation equipment, manufactured goods, food products, agriculture, fuels, energy

MOLDOVA

Pronunciation: mawl-DOH-vuh
Area: 13,012 sq. miles (33,701 sq. km)
Population: 4,434,547
Capital: Chişinău
Currency: Moldovan Leu (MDL)
Official Language: Moldovan
Other Languages: Russian, Gagauz
Main Religions: Christianity 98%, Judaism 2%
Exports: Food, wine, tobacco, textiles, footwear, machinery, chemicals

ICELAND

Pronunciation: EYES-luhnd
Area: 39,702 sq. miles (102,828 sq. km)
Population: 279,384

Capital: Reykjavík
Currency: 100 aurar = 1 Icelandic krona (ISK)
Official Language: Icelandic
Main Religion: Christianity 99%
Exports: Fish and fish products, animal products, minerals

NORWAY

Pronunciation: NOR-way
Area: 125,181 sq. miles (324,220 sq. km)
Population: 4,525,116
Capital: Oslo
Currency: 100 oere = 1 Norwegian krone (NOK)
Official Language: Norwegian
Other Languages: Finnish, Sami
Main Religion: Christianity 89%
Exports: Petroleum and petroleum products, metals, fish and fish products, chemicals, ships, machinery and equipment, natural gas

Territories and dependencies
Bouvet Island: South Atlantic Ocean; 22.6 sq. miles (58.5 sq. km); no permanent population
Jan Mayen Island: North Atlantic Ocean; 144 sq. miles (373 sq. km); no permanent population
Svalbard: Arctic Ocean; 23,958 sq. miles (62,052 sq. km); population 2,868

SWEDEN

Pronunciation: SWEE-duhn
Area: 173,665 sq. miles (449,792 sq. km)
Population: 8,912,000
Capital: Stockholm
Currency: 100 oere = 1 Swedish krona (SEK)
Official Language: Swedish

Other Languages: Finnish, Sami
Main Religion: Christianity 96%
Exports: Machinery, motor vehicles, paper products, pulp and wood, iron and steel products, chemicals, petroleum products

FINLAND

Pronunciation: FIN-luhnd
Area: 130,128 sq. miles (337,032 sq. km)
Population: 5,183,545
Capital: Helsinki
Currency: 100 cents = 1 euro (EUR)
Official Languages: Finnish, Swedish
Other Languages: Sami, Russian
Main Religion: Christianity 90%
Exports: Paper and pulp, machinery and equipment, chemicals, metals, timber

DENMARK

Pronunciation: DEN-mark
Area: 16,629 sq. miles (43,069 sq. km)
Population: 5,368,854
Capital: Copenhagen
Currency: 100 ore = 1 Danish krone (DKK)
Official Language: Danish
Other Languages: Faroese, Greenlandic, German
Main Religion: Christianity 98%
Exports: Meat and meat products, dairy products, ships, fish, chemicals, machinery and instruments, furniture, windmills

Territories and dependencies
Faroe Islands: North Atlantic Ocean; 540 sq. miles (1,399 sq. km); population 46,011
Greenland: North Atlantic Ocean; 836,326 sq. miles (2,166,086 sq. km); population 59,900

ASIA

RUSSIA

Pronunciation: RUH-shuh
Area: 6,592,812 sq. miles
(17,075,383 sq. km)
Population: 144,978,573
Capital: Moscow
Currency: 100 kopecks = 1 Russian ruble (RUR)
Official Language: Russian
Main Religions: Christianity 75%, Islam, Buddhism
Exports: Petroleum and petroleum products, natural gas, timber and timber products, metals, chemicals, manufactured goods

TURKEY

Pronunciation: TER-kee
Area: 301,380 sq. miles (780,574 sq. km)
Population: 67,308,928
Capital: Ankara
Currency: 100 kurus = 1 Turkish lira (TRL)
Official Language: Turkish
Other Languages: Kurdish, Arabic, Armenian
Main Religion: Islam 99%
Exports: Manufactured goods, food, textiles and clothing, transport equipment

CYPRUS

Pronunciation: SEYE-pruhs
Area: 3,572 sq. miles (9,251 sq. km)
Population: 767,314
Capital: Nicosia
Currency: 100 cents = 1 Cypriot pound (CYP);
100 kurus = 1 Turkish lira (TRL)
Official Languages: Greek, Turkish
Other Language: English
Main Religions: Christianity 78%, Islam 18%
Exports: Citrus fruit, potatoes, grapes, wine, cement, textiles and clothing, shoes

GEORGIA

Pronunciation: JOR-juh
Area: 26,911 sq. miles (69,699 sq. km)
Population: 4,960,951
Capital: T'bilisi
Currency: 100 tetri = 1 lari (GEL)
Official Language: Georgian
Other Languages: Russian, Armenian, Azeri
Main Religions: Christianity 83%, Islam 11%
Exports: Citrus fruit, tea, wine, machinery, metals, textiles, chemicals, fuel re-exports

ARMENIA

Pronunciation: ar-MEE-nee-uh
Area: 11,506 sq. miles (29,800 sq. km)
Population: 3,330,099
Capital: Yerevan
Currency: 100 luma = 1 dram (AMD)
Official Language: Armenian
Other Languages: Russian, Azeri
Main Religion: Christianity 94%
Exports: Diamonds, scrap metal, machinery and equipment, brandy, copper ore

AZERBAIJAN

Pronunciation: a-zuhr-beye-ZHAHN
Area: 33,436 sq. miles (86,599 sq. km)
Population: 7,798,497
Capital: Baku
Currency: 100 gopiks = 1 Azerbaijani manat (AZM)
Official Language: Azerbaijani
Other Languages: Russian, Armenian
Main Religions: Islam 94%, Christianity 5%
Exports: Oil, gas, chemicals, oil field equipment, textiles, cotton, foodstuffs

KAZAKSTAN

Pronunciation: kuh-zahk-STAHN
Area: 1,049,150 sq. miles (2,717,300 sq. km)
Population: 16,741,519
Capital: Astana
Currency: 100 tiyn = 1 tenge (KZT)
Official Languages: Kazak, Russian
Main Religions: Islam 47%, Christianity 46%
Exports: Oil, metals, chemicals, grain, wool, cotton, machinery, ferrous and non-ferrous metals, meat and livestock, coal

UZBEKISTAN

Pronunciation: uz-be-ki-STAN
Area: 172,741 sq. miles (447,400 sq. km)
Population: 25,563,441
Capital: Tashkent
Currency: Uzbekistani Sum (UZS)
Official Language: Uzbek
Other Languages: Russian, Tajik
Main Religions: Islam 88%, Christianity 9%
Exports: Cotton, gold, natural gas, mineral fertilizer, metals, textiles, food, automobiles

TURKMENISTAN

Pronunciation: terk-me-nuh-STAN
Area: 188,455 sq. miles (488,098 sq. km)
Population: 4,688,963
Capital: Ashkhabad
Currency: 100 tenesi = 1 Turkmen manat (TMM)
Official Language: Turkmen
Other Languages: Russian, Uzbek
Main Religions: Islam 89%, Christianity 9%
Exports: Natural gas, cotton, petroleum products, textiles, carpets

KYRGYZSTAN

Pronunciation: kihr-gi-STAN
Area: 76,641 sq. miles (198,500 sq. km)
Population: 4,822,166
Capital: Bishkek
Currency: 100 tyiyn = 1 Kyrgyzstani som (KGS)
Official Languages: Kyrgyz (Kirghiz), Russian
Main Religions: Islam 75%, Christianity 20%
Exports: Wool, chemicals, cotton, metals, shoes, machinery, tobacco, potatoes, fruits, vegetables, sheep, goats, cattle

TAJIKISTAN

Pronunciation: tah-ji-ki-STAN
Area: 55,251 sq. miles (143,100 sq. km)
Population: 6,719,567
Capital: Dushanbe

Currency: 100 diram = 1 somoni (TJS)
Official Language: Tajik
Other Language: Russian
Main Religion: Islam 85%
Exports: Cotton, aluminum, fruits, vegetable oil, textiles, electricity

SYRIA

Pronunciation: SIHR-ee-uh
Area: 71,498 sq. miles (185,180 sq. km)
Population: 17,155,814
Capital: Damascus
Currency: 100 piastres = 1 Syrian pound (SYP)
Official Language: Arabic
Other Languages: Kurdish, Armenian, Aramaic, Circassian, French, English
Main Religions: Islam 90%, Christianity 10%
Exports: Petroleum, textiles, raw cotton, fruit and vegetables, live sheep, phosphates

IRAQ

Pronunciation: i-RAHK
Area: 168,927 sq. miles (437,521 sq. km)
Population: 24,001,816
Capital: Baghdad
Currency: 1,000 fils = 1 Iraqi dinar (IQD)
Official Languages: Arabic, Kurdish (in Kurdish regions)
Other Languages: Assyrian, Armenian
Main Religions: Islam 97%, Christianity 3%
Exports: Crude oil and refined products, fertilizer, sulfur

IRAN

Pronunciation: i-RAHN
Area: 635,932 sq. miles (1,647,064 sq. km)
Population: 66,622,704
Capital: Tehran

Currency: 100 dinars = 1 Iranian rial (IRR)
Official Language: Farsi (Persian)
Other Languages: Turkic, Kurdish, Luri
Main Religion: Islam 99%
Exports: Petroleum, carpets, fruit, nuts, iron and steel, chemicals

LEBANON

Pronunciation: LE-buh-nuhn
Area: 3,949 sq. miles (10,228 sq. km)
Population: 3,677,780
Capital: Beirut
Currency: 100 piastres = 1 Lebanese pound (LBP)
Official Language: Arabic
Other Languages: Armenian, English, French
Main Religions: Islam 70%, Christianity 30%
Exports: Agricultural products, chemicals, paper, textiles, metals, jewelry, electrical products

ISRAEL

Pronunciation: IZ-ray-uhl
Area: 7,992 sq. miles (20,699 sq. km)
Population: 6,029,529
Capital: Jerusalem
Currency: 100 new agorot = 1 new Israeli shekel (ILS)
Official Languages: Hebrew, Arabic
Other Language: English
Main Religions: Judaism 80%, Islam 15%, Christianity 2%
Exports: Machinery, cut diamonds, chemicals, textiles, agricultural products, metals, software

JORDAN

Pronunciation: JOR-duhn
Area: 35,637 sq. miles (92,300 sq. km)
Population: 5,307,470
Capital: Amman
Currency: 1,000 fils = 1 Jordanian dinar (JOD)
Official Language: Arabic
Other Language: English
Main Religions: Islam 92%, Christianity 6%
Exports: Phosphates, fertilizer, agricultural products, potash, manufactured goods

SAUDI ARABIA

Pronunciation: SOW-dee uh-RAY-bee-uh
Area: 756,981 sq. miles (1,960,582 sq. km)
Population: 23,513,330
Capital: Riyadh
Currency: 100 halalas = 1 Saudi riyal (SAR)
Official Language: Arabic
Main Religion: Islam 100%
Exports: Petroleum and petroleum products

KUWAIT

Pronunciation: koo-WAYT
Area: 6,880 sq. miles (17,819 sq. km)
Population: 2,111,561
Capital: Kuwait
Currency: 1,000 fils = 1 Kuwaiti dinar (KD)
Official Language: Arabic
Other Language: English
Main Religions: Islam 85%, Christianity 8%, Hinduism and Zoroastrianism 2%
Exports: Oil and refined products, fertilizers

BAHRAIN

Pronunciation: bah-RAYN
Area: 255 sq. miles (661 sq. km)
Population: 656,397
Capital: Manama
Currency: 1,000 fils = 1 Bahraini dinar (BHD)
Official Language: Arabic
Other Languages: English, Farsi, Urdu
Main Religion: Islam 100%
Exports: Petroleum and petroleum products, aluminum

QATAR

Pronunciation: KAH-tuhr
Area: 4,400 sq. miles (11,395 sq. km)
Population: 793,341
Capital: Doha
Currency: 100 dirhams = 1 Qatari rial (QAR)
Official Language: Arabic
Other Language: English
Main Religion: Islam 95%
Exports: Petroleum products, steel, fertilizer

UNITED ARAB EMIRATES

Pronunciation: yoo-NEYE-tuhd a-ruhb EM-uh-ruhts
Area: 32,000 sq. miles (82,880 sq. km)
Population: 2,445,989
Capital: Abu Dhabi
Currency: 100 fils = 1 Emirati dirham (AED)
Official Language: Arabic
Other Languages: Persian, English, Hindi, Urdu
Main Religion: Islam 96%
Exports: Crude oil, natural gas, dried fish, dates

OMAN

Pronunciation: oh-MAHN
Area: 82,000 sq. miles (212,380 sq. km)
Population: 2,713,462
Capital: Muscat
Currency: 1,000 baiza = 1 Omani rial (OMR)
Official Language: Arabic
Other Languages: English, Baluchi, Urdu, Indian languages
Main Religions: Islam 86%, Hinduism 13%
Exports: Petroleum, fish, metals, textiles

YEMEN

Pronunciation: YE-muhn
Area: 203,849 sq. miles (527,969 sq. km)
Population: 18,701,257
Capital: Sanaa
Currency: 100 fils = 1 Yemeni rial (YER)
Official Language: Arabic
Main Religion: Islam 99%
Exports: Crude oil, cotton, coffee, animal skins, vegetables, dried and salted fish

AFGHANISTAN

Pronunciation: af-GA-nuh-stan
Area: 250,775 sq. miles (649,507 sq. km)
Population: 27,755,775
Capital: Kabul
Currency: 100 puls = 1 afghani (AFA)
Official Languages: Afghan, Persian (Dari), Pashtu
Other Languages: Uzbek, Turkmen, Balochi
Main Religions: Islam 99%, Hinduism and Judaism 1%
Exports: Opium, fruit, nuts, handwoven carpets, wool, cotton, animal skins, precious and semiprecious gemstones

PAKISTAN

Pronunciation: pa-ki-STAN
Area: 310,403 sq. miles (803,944 sq. km)
Population: 147,663,429
Capital: Islamabad
Currency: 100 paisa = 1 Pakistani
rupee (PKR)
Official Languages: Urdu, English
Other Languages: Punjabi, Sindhi, Siraiki
Pashtu, Balochi, Hindko
Main Religion: Islam 97%
Exports: Cotton, textiles, clothing, rice, yarn,
leather, carpets, agricultural products

INDIA

Pronunciation: IN-dee-uh
Area: 1,269,338 sq. miles (3,287,590 sq. km)
Population: 1,045,845,226
Capital: New Delhi
Currency: 100 paise = 1 Indian rupee (INR)
Official Languages: Hindi, English, Bengali,
Telugu, Marathi, Tamil, Urdu, Gujarati,
Malayalam, Kannada, Oriya, Punjabi,
Assamese, Kashmiri, Sindhi, Sanskrit
Other Languages: Hindustani, Rajasthani
Main Religions: Hinduism 81%, Islam 12%,
Christianity 2%, Sikh 2%
Exports: Clothing and textiles, engineering
equipment, gemstones and jewelry, chemicals,
leather goods, cotton yarn, fabric

NEPAL

Pronunciation: nuh-PAHL
Area: 54,362 sq. miles (140,798 sq. km)
Population: 25,873,917
Capital: Kathmandu
Currency: 100 paisa = 1 Nepalese rupee (NPR)
Official Language: Nepali

Main Religions: Hinduism 86%,
Buddhism 8%, Islam 4%
Exports: Carpets, clothing, leather goods,
jute goods, grain

BHUTAN

Pronunciation: boo-TAHN
Area: 18,147 sq. miles (47,000 sq. km)
Population: 2,094,176
Capital: Thimphu
Currency: 100 chetrums = 1 ngultrum (BTN);
100 paise = 1 Indian rupee (INR)
Official Language: Dzongkha
Other Languages: Tibetan and Nepali
Main Religions: Buddhism 75%,
Hinduism 25%
Exports: Timber,
handicrafts, cement,
fruit, electricity, gemstones,
spices, gypsum

BANGLADESH

Pronunciation: bahng-gluh-DESH
Area: 55,598 sq. miles (144,000 sq. km)
Population: 133,376,684
Capital: Dhaka
Currency: 100 paisa = 1 taka (BDT)
Official Language: Bengali (Bangla)
Other Language: English
Main Religions: Islam 83%, Hinduism 16%
Exports: Clothing and textiles, jute and jute
goods, leather, frozen fish and seafood,
agricultural products

MALDIVES

Pronunciation: MAWL-deevz
Area: 115 sq. miles (298 sq. km)
Population: 320,165

Capital: Male
Currency: 100 laari = 1 rufiyaa (MVR)
Official Language: Maldivian Dhivehi
Other Language: English
Main Religion: Islam 100%
Exports: Fish, clothing

SRI LANKA

Pronunciation: sree LAHNG-kuh
Area: 25,332 sq. miles (65,610 sq. km)
Population: 19,576,783
Capital: Colombo
Currency: 100 cents = 1 Sri Lankan
rupee (LKR)
Official Languages: Sinhala, Tamil
Other Language: English
Main Religions: Buddhism 70%,
Hinduism 15%, Christianity 8%, Islam 7%
Exports: Textiles, tea, diamonds and other
precious gemstones, petroleum products,
rubber products, agricultural products,
marine products

MYANMAR (BURMA)

Pronunciation: MYAHN-mar (BER-muh)
Area: 261,789 sq. miles (678,034 sq. km)
Population: 42,238,224
Capital: Yangon (Rangoon)
Currency: 100 pyas = 1 kyat (MMK)
Official Language: Burmese
Other Languages: regional languages
Main Religions: Buddhism 89%,
Christianity 4%, Islam 4%,
animism 1%
Exports: Clothing, foodstuffs,
rice, precious stones, timber

LAOS

Pronunciation: lows
Area: 91,428 sq. miles (236,799 sq. km)
Population: 5,777,180
Capital: Vientiane
Currency: 100 at = 1 kip (LAK)
Official Language: Lao
Other Languages: French, English, regional languages
Main Religions: Buddhism 60%, animism 34%, Christianity 2%
Exports: Electricity, timber products, coffee, tin, textiles and clothing

VIETNAM

Pronunciation: vee-et-NAHM
Area: 127,243 sq. miles (329,560 sq. km)
Population: 81,098,416
Capital: Hanoi
Currency: 100 xu = 1 new dong (VND)
Official Language: Vietnamese
Other Languages: French, Chinese languages, English, Khmer, tribal languages
Main Religions: Buddhism 55%, Christianity 7%, Daoism (Taoism), indigenous religions, Islam
Exports: Crude oil, rice, clothing and footwear, rubber, tea, coffee marine products

THAILAND

Pronunciation: TEYE-land
Area: 198,455 sq. miles (513,998 sq. km)
Population: 62,354,402
Capital: Bangkok
Currency: 100 satang = 1 baht (THB)
Official Language: Thai

Other Languages: English, Chinese languages, Malay, regional languages
Main Religions: Buddhism 95%, Islam 4%
Exports: Computers and parts, textiles, integrated circuits, rice

CAMBODIA

Pronunciation: kam-BOH-dee-uh
Area: 69,898 sq. miles (181,036 sq. km)
Population: 12,775,324
Capital: Phnom Penh
Currency: 100 sen = 1 new riel (KHR)
Official Language: Khmer
Other Languages: French, English
Main Religions: Buddhism 95%, Islam 2%
Exports: Timber, rubber, clothing, rice, fish

MALAYSIA

Pronunciation: muh-LAY-zhuh
Area: 127,316 sq. miles (329,750 sq. km)
Population: 22,662,365
Capital: Kuala Lumpur
Currency: 100 sen = 1 ringgit (MYR)
Official Language: Malay (Bahasa Melayu)
Other Languages: English, Chinese languages, Tamil, Telugu, regional languages
Main Religions: Islam 53%, Buddhism 17%, Confucianism 12%, Christianity 9%, Hinduism 7%
Exports: Electronic equipment, petroleum, liquified natural gas, palm oil, timber and timber products, rubber, textiles

PHILIPPINES

Pronunciation: FI-luh-peenz
Area: 115,651 sq. miles (299,536 sq. km)
Population: 84,525,639
Capital: Manila

Currency: 100 centavos = 1 Philippine peso (PHP)
Official Languages: Filipino, English
Other Languages: Regional languages
Main Religions: Christianity 92%, Islam 5%, Buddhism 3%
Exports: Electronics, machinery and transport equipment, textiles, coconut products, copper, fish

SINGAPORE

Pronunciation: SING-uh-por
Area: 200 sq. miles (648 sq. km)
Population: 4,452,732
Capital: Singapore
Currency: 100 cents = 1 Singapore dollar (SGD)
Official Languages: Chinese, Malay, Tamil, English
Main Religions: Buddhism 28%, Islam 15%, Christianity 13%, Taoism 13%, Hinduism 5%
Exports: Computer equipment, chemicals, mineral fuels, telecommunications equipment

BRUNEI

Pronunciation: broo-NEYE
Area: 2,226 sq. miles (5,765 sq. km)
Population: 350,898
Capital: Bandar Seri Begawan
Currency: 100 cents = 1 Bruneian dollar (BND)
Official Language: Malay
Other Languages: English, Chinese languages
Main Religions: Islam 67%, Buddhist 13%, Christianity 10%, indigenous religions
Exports: Crude oil, liquefied natural gas, petroleum products

INDONESIA

Pronunciation: in-duh-NEE-zhuh
Area: 741,096 sq. miles (1,919,440 sq. km)
Population: 216,109,000
Capital: Jakarta
Currency: 100 sen = 1 Indonesian rupiah (IDR)
Official Language: Bahasa Indonesian
Other Languages: English, Dutch, Javanese, regional languages
Main Religions: Islam 88%, Christianity 8%, Hinduism 2%, Buddhism 1%
Exports: Manufactured goods, oil and gas, textiles, rubber, plywood

EAST TIMOR

Pronunciation: EEST TEE-mor
Area: 7,000 sq. miles (19,000 sq.km)
Population: 952,618
Capital: Dili
Currency: 100 cents = 1 United States dollar (USD)
Official Language: Tetum, Portuguese
Other Languages: Bahasa Indonesian, English
Main Religion: Christianity 93%, Islam 4%
Exports: Coffee, sandalwood, marble

CHINA

Pronunciation: CHEYE-nuh
Area: 3,705,386 sq. miles (9,596,960 sq. km)
Population: 1,284,303,705
Capital: Beijing
Currency: 10 jiao = 1 yuan (CNY)
Official Language: Mandarin
Other Languages: Cantonese, Shanghaiese, Fuzhou, Hokkien-Taiwanese, regional languages
Main Religions: Daoism (Taoism) 20%,

Buddhism 6%, Islam 3%, Christianity 1%
Exports: Textiles and clothing, shoes, toys, machinery and equipment, mineral fuels

MONGOLIA

Pronunciation: mahn-GOHL-yuh
Area: 604,247 sq. miles (1,565,000 sq. km)
Population: 2,694,432
Capital: Ulaanbaatar
Currency: 100 mongos = 1 togrog/tugrik (MNT)
Official Language: Khalkha Mongol
Other Languages: Turkic, Russian, Chinese
Main Religions: Buddhism 95%, Islam 4%
Exports: Copper, livestock, animal products, cashmere, wool, animal skins, non-ferrous metals

NORTH KOREA

Pronunciation: north kuh-REE-uh
Area: 46,609 sq. miles (120,717 sq. km)
Population: 22,224,195
Capital: P'yŏngyang
Currency: 100 chon = 1 North Korean won (KPW)
Official Language: Korean
Main Religions: Chondogyo 14%, Buddhism 2%, Christianity 1%
Exports: Minerals, metal products, agricultural and fishery products, manufactured goods

SOUTH KOREA

Pronunciation: sowth kuh-REE-uh
Area: 38,022 sq. miles (98,477 sq. km)
Population: 48,324,000
Capital: Seoul
Currency: 100 chon = 1 South Korean won (KRW)

Official Language: Korean
Other Language: English
Main Religions: Christianity 49%, Buddhism 47%, Confucianism 3%
Exports: Electronic and electrical equipment, machinery, steel, motor vehicles, ships, textiles, clothing, shoes, fish

TAIWAN

Pronunciation: TEYE-wahn
Area: 13,887 sq. miles (35,967 sq. km)
Population: 22,548,009
Capital: Taipei
Currency: 100 cents = 1 New Taiwan dollar (NTD)
Official Language: Mandarin
Other Languages: Taiwanese, Hakka dialects
Main Religions: Buddhism 43%, Daoism (Taoism) 21%, Christianity 5%, Confucianism
Exports: Electrical machinery, electronic goods, textiles, metals, plastics, chemicals

JAPAN

Pronunciation: juh-PAN
Area: 145,882 sq. miles (377,835 sq. km)
Population: 126,974,628
Capital: Tokyo
Currency: 100 sen = 1 yen (JPY)
Official Language: Japanese
Main Religions: Shinto and Buddhism 84%, Christianity 1%
Exports: Machinery, motor vehicles, consumer electronics, chemicals, semiconductors

AFRICA

MOROCCO

Pronunciation: muh-RAH-koh
Area: 172,413 sq. miles (446,550 sq. km)
Population: 31,167,783
Capital: Rabat
Currency: 100 centimes = 1 Moroccan dirham (MAD)
Official Language: Arabic
Other Languages: French, Berber dialects
Main Religions: Islam 99%, Christianity 1%
Exports: Food, beverages, consumer goods, phosphates and fertilizers, minerals

ALGERIA

Pronunciation: al-JIHR-ee-uh
Area: 919,590 sq. miles (2,381,740 sq. km)
Population: 32,277,942
Capital: Algiers
Currency: 100 centimes = 1 Algerian dinar (DZD)
Official Language: Arabic
Other Languages: French, Berber dialects
Main Religions: Islam 99%, Christianity and Judaism 1%
Exports: Petroleum products, natural gas

TUNISIA

Pronunciation: too-NEE-zhuh
Area: 63,378 sq. miles (164,149 sq. km)
Population: 9,815,644
Capital: Tunis
Currency: 1,000 millimes = 1 Tunisian dinar (TND)
Official Language: Arabic
Other Language: French
Main Religions: Islam 98%, Christianity 1%, Judaism 1%
Exports: Agricultural products, chemicals, textiles, mechanical goods, phosphates

LIBYA

Pronunciation: LI-bee-uh
Area: 679,360 sq. miles (1,759,540 sq. km)
Population: 5,368,585
Capital: Tripoli
Currency: 1,000 dirhams = 1 Libyan dinar (LYD)
Official Language: Arabic
Other Languages: Italian, English
Main Religion: Islam 97%
Exports: Crude oil, refined petroleum products

CAPE VERDE ISLANDS

Pronunciation: kayp VAIRD islands
Area: 1,557 sq. miles (4,033 sq. km)
Population: 408,760

Capital: Praia
Currency: 100 centavos = 1 Cape Verdean escudo (CVE)
Official Language: Portuguese
Other Language: Cape Verde creole (Crioulo)
Main Religion: Christianity 97%
Exports: Fish, bananas, animal skins, clothing, fuel

EGYPT

Pronunciation: EE-juhpt
Area: 386,660 sq. miles (1,001,450 sq. km)
Population: 70,712,345
Capital: Cairo
Currency: 100 piasters = 1 Egyptian pound (EGP)
Official Language: Arabic
Other Languages: English, French
Main Religions: Islam 94%, Christianity 6%
Exports: Crude oil and petroleum products, cotton, textiles, metal products, chemicals

MAURITANIA

Pronunciation: maw-ruh-TAY-nee-uh
Area: 397,955 sq. miles (1,030,807 sq. km)
Population: 2,828,858
Capital: Nouakchott
Currency: 5 khoums = 1 ouguiya (MRO)
Official Languages: Hasaniya Arabic, Wolof
Other Languages: French, Pular, Soninke
Main Religion: Islam 100%
Exports: Iron ore, fish and fish products, gold

MALI

Pronunciation: MAH-lee
Area: 478,652 sq. miles (1,239,709 sq. km)
Population: 11,340,480
Capital: Bamako
Currency: 100 centimes = 1 CFA franc (XOF)
Official Language: French
Other Languages: Bambara, regional languages
Main Religions: Islam 90%, indigenous religions 9%, Christianity 1%
Exports: Cotton, livestock, gold

BURKINA FASO

Pronunciation: ber-KEE-nuh FAH-soh
Area: 105,869 sq. miles (274,201 sq. km)
Population: 12,603,185
Capital: Ouagadougou
Currency: 100 centimes = 1 CFA franc (XOF)
Official Language: French
Other Languages: Tribal languages
Main Religions: Islam 50%, indigenous religions 40%, Christianity 10%
Exports: Cotton, gold, animal products

NIGER

Pronunciation: NEYE-juhr
Area: 459,073 sq. miles (1,188,999 sq. km)
Population: 10,639,744

Capital: Niamey
Currency: 100 centimes = 1 CFA franc (XOF)
Official Language: French
Other Languages: Hausa, Djerma
Main Religions: Islam 80%, indigenous religions 14%, Christianity 1%
Exports: Uranium ore, livestock, cowpeas, onions

CHAD

Pronunciation: chad
Area: 495,752 sq. miles (1,283,998 sq. km)
Population: 8,997,237
Capital: N'Djamena
Currency: 100 centimes = 1 CFA franc (XOF)
Official Languages: French, Arabic
Other Languages: Sara, Sango, tribal languages
Main Religions: Islam 50%, Christianity 25%, indigenous religions and animism 25%
Exports: Cotton, cattle, textiles

SUDAN

Pronunciation: soo-DAN
Area: 967,500 sq. miles (2,505,825 sq. km)
Population: 37,090,298
Capital: Khartoum
Currency: 100 girsh = 1 Sudanese dinar (SDD)

Official Language: Arabic
Other Languages: Nubian, Ta Bedawie, Nilotic, Nilo-Hamitic, regional languages, English
Main Religions: Islam 70%, indigenous religions 25%, Christianity 5%
Exports: Oil, livestock, cotton, sesame, peanuts

ERITREA

Pronunciation: ehr-uh-TREE-uh
Area: 46,842 sq. miles (121,320 sq. km)
Population: 4,465,651
Capital: Asmara
Currency: 100 cents = 1 nafka (ERN)
Official Languages: Arabic, Tigrinya, Tigre
Other Languages: Regional languages
Main Religions: Islam 50%, Christianity 50%
Exports: Livestock, sorghum, textiles, food

ETHIOPIA

Pronunciation: ee-thee-OH-pee-uh
Area: 435,184 sq. miles (1,127,127 sq. km)
Population: 67,673,031
Capital: Addis Ababa
Currency: 100 cents = 1 birr (ETB)
Official Languages: Amharic, Tigrinya, Oromigna, Guiragigna, Somali
Other Languages: Arabic, English
Main Religions: Islam 45%, Christianity 35%, animism 12%
Exports: Coffee, leather products, gold, oilseeds, qat

DJIBOUTI

Pronunciation: ji-BOO-tee
Area: 8,494 sq. miles (22,000 sq. km)
Population: 472,810
Capital: Djibouti
Currency: 100 centimes = 1 Djiboutian franc (DJF)
Official Languages: French, Arabic
Other Languages: Somali, Afar
Main Religions: Islam 94%, Christianity 6%
Exports: Animal skins, coffee

SOMALIA

Pronunciation: soh-MAH-lee-uh
Area: 246,154 sq. miles (637,539 sq. km)
Population: 7,753,310
Capital: Mogadishu
Currency: 100 cents = 1 Somali shilling (SOS)
Official Language: Somali
Other Languages: Arabic, Italian, English
Main Religion: Islam 99%
Exports: Bananas, livestock, fish, animal skins

SENEGAL

Pronunciation: sen-i-GAWL
Area: 75,749 sq. miles (196,190 sq. km)
Population: 10,589,571
Capital: Dakar
Currency: 100 centimes = 1 CFA franc (XOF)
Official Language: French
Other Languages: Wolof, Pulaar, Jola, Mandinka

Main Religions: Islam 92%, indigenous religions 6%, Christianity 2%
Exports: Fish, peanuts, petroleum products, phosphates, cotton

GAMBIA

Pronunciation: GAM-bee-uh
Area: 4,363 sq. miles (11,300 sq. km)
Population: 1,455,842
Capital: Banjul
Currency: 100 bututs = 1 dalasi (GMD)
Official Language: English
Other Languages: Mandinka, Wolof, Fula
Main Religions: Islam 90%, Christianity 9%, indigenous religions 1%
Exports: Peanuts, fish, palm kernels, cotton lint

GUINEA-BISSAU

Pronunciation: gi-nee-bi-SOW
Area: 13,948 sq. miles (36,125 sq. km)
Population: 1,345,479
Capital: Bissau
Currency: 100 centimes = 1 CFA franc (XOF)
Official Language: Portuguese
Other Languages: Crioulo, tribal languages
Main Religions: Indigenous religions 50%, Islam 45%, Christianity 5%
Exports: Cashews, shrimp, palm kernels, peanuts, timber

GUINEA

Pronunciation: GI-nee
Area: 94,925 sq. miles (245,856 sq. km)
Population: 7,775,065

Capital: Conakry
Currency: 100 centimes = 1 Guinean franc (GNF)
Official Language: French
Other Languages: Tribal languages
Main Religions: Islam 85%, Christianity 8%, indigenous religions 7%
Exports: Bauxite, alumina, diamonds, gold, coffee, fish, agricultural products

SIERRA LEONE

Pronunciation: see-EHR-uh lee-OHN
Area: 27,699 sq. miles (71,740 sq. km)
Population: 5,614,743
Capital: Freetown
Currency: 100 cents = 1 leone (SLL)
Official Language: English
Other Languages: Mende, Temne, Krio
Main Religions: Islam 60%, indigenous religions 30%, Christianity 10%
Exports: Diamonds and other minerals, coffee, cocoa, fish

LIBERIA

Pronunciation: leye-BIHR-ee-uh
Area: 43,000 sq. miles (111,370 sq. km)
Population: 3,288,198
Capital: Monrovia
Currency: 100 cents = 1 Liberian dollar (LRD)
Official Language: English
Other Languages: Tribal languages
Main Religions: Indigenous religions 40%, Christianity 40%, Islam 20%
Exports: Iron ore, rubber, timber, coffee, diamonds

COTE D'IVOIRE (IVORY COAST)

Pronunciation: koht dee-VWAR
Area: 124,503 sq. miles (322,463 sq. km)
Population: 16,804,784
Capitals: Abidjan (seat of government), Yamoussoukro (official)
Currency: 100 centimes = 1 CFA franc (XOF)
Official Language: French
Other Languages: Regional languages
Main Religions: Christianity 34%, Islam 27%, animism 15%
Exports: Cocoa, coffee, timber, petroleum, cotton, bananas, pineapples, palm oil, fish

GHANA

Pronunciation: GAH-nuh
Area: 92,100 sq. miles (238,539 sq. km)
Population: 20,244,154
Capital: Accra
Currency: 100 pesewas = 1 new cedi (GHC)
Official Language: English
Other Languages: Regional languages
Main Religions: Indigenous religions 38%, Islam 30%, Christianity 24%
Exports: Cocoa, gold, timber, tuna, bauxite, aluminum, manganese ore, diamonds

TOGO

Pronunciation: TOH-goh
Area: 21,853 sq. miles (56,599 sq. km)
Population: 5,285,501

Capital: Lomé
Currency: 100 centimes = 1 CFA franc (XOF)
Official Language: French
Other Languages: Regional languages
Main Religions: Indigenous religions 59%, Christianity 29%, Islam 12%
Exports: Phosphates, cotton, cocoa, coffee

BENIN

Pronunciation: buh-NEEN
Area: 43,483 sq. miles (112,621 sq. km)
Population: 6,787,625
Capitals: Cotonou (seat of government), Porto-Novo (official)
Currency: 100 centimes = 1 CFA franc (XOF)
Official Language: French
Other Languages: Fon, Yoruba, tribal languages
Main Religions: Indigenous religions 50%, Islam 20%, Christianity 30%
Exports: Cotton, crude oil, palm products, cocoa

NIGERIA

Pronunciation: neye-JIHR-ee-uh
Area: 356,669 sq. miles (923,773 sq. km)
Population: 129,934,911
Capital: Abuja
Currency: 100 kobo = 1 naira (NGN)
Official Language: English
Other Languages: Regional languages
Main Religions: Islam 50%, Christianity 40%, indigenous religions 10%
Exports: Oil and petroluem products, cocoa, rubber

CAMEROON

Pronunciation: ka-muh-ROON
Area: 183,591 sq. miles (475,501 sq. km)
Population: 16,184,748
Capital: Yaoundé
Currency: 100 centimes = 1 CFA franc (XOF)
Official Languages: English, French
Other Languages: Regional languages
Main Religions: Indigenous religions 40%, Christianity 40%, Islam 20%
Exports: Crude oil, petroleum products, timber, cocoa beans, aluminum, coffee, cotton

EQUATORIAL GUINEA

Pronunciation: e-kwuh-TOR-ee-uhl GI-nee
Area: 10,825 sq. miles (28,037 sq. km)
Population: 498,144
Capital: Malabo
Currency: 100 centimes = 1 CFA franc (XOF)
Official Languages: Spanish, French
Other Languages: Pidgin English, Fang, Bubi, Ibo, other regional languages
Main Religion: Christianity 85%
Exports: Timber, cocoa, petroleum

CENTRAL AFRICAN REPUBLIC

Pronunciation: SEN-truhl AF-ri-kuhn
ri-PUH-blik
Area: 240,534 sq. miles (622,984 sq. km)
Population: 3,642,739
Capital: Bangui
Currency: 100 centimes = 1 CFA franc (XOF)
Official Language: French
Other Languages: Sangho, Arabic, Hunsa,
Swahili
Main Religions: Christianity 50%,
indigenous religions 24%, Islam 15%
Exports: Diamonds, timber, cotton,
coffee, tobacco

SAO TOME AND PRINCIPE

Pronunciation: SOW tuh-MAY and
PRIN-suh-pee
Area: 372 sq. miles (963 sq. km)
Population: 170,372
Capital: São Tomé
Currency: 100 centimos = 1 dobra (STD)
Official Language: Portuguese
Main Religion: Christianity 80%
Exports: Cocoa, copra, coffee, palm oil

GABON

Pronunciation: ga-BOHN
Area: 103,346 sq. miles (267,667 sq. km)
Population: 1,233,353
Capital: Libreville
Currency: 100 centimes = 1 CFA franc (XOF)
Official Language: French
Other Languages: Regional languages
Main Religions: Christianity 60%,
animism 40%, Islam 1%
Exports: Crude oil, timber, manganese,
uranium

CONGO

Pronunciation: KAHN-goh
Area: 132,047 sq. miles (342,002 sq. km)
Population: 2,958,448
Capital: Brazzaville
Currency: 100 centimes = 1 CFA franc (XOF)
Official Language: French
Other Languages: Lingala, Monokutuba
Main Religions: Christianity 50%,
animism 48%, Islam 2%
Exports: Petroleum, timber, sugar, cocoa,
coffee, diamonds

DEMOCRATIC REPUBLIC OF
THE CONGO (ZAIRE)

Pronunciation: de-muh-KRA-tik ri-PUH-blik
of the KAHN-goh
Area: 905,356 sq. miles (2,344,872 sq. km)
Population: 55,225,478
Capital: Kinshasa
Currency: Congolese franc (CDF)
Official Language: French
Other Languages: Lingala, Kingwana,
Kikongo, Tshiluba
Main Religions: Christianity 70%,
Islam 10%, Kimbanguism 10%,
indigenous beliefs 10%
Exports: Copper, coffee,
diamonds, crude oil

UGANDA

Pronunciation: yoo-GAN-duh
Area: 91,134 sq. miles (236,037 sq. km)
Population: 24,699,073
Capital: Kampala
Currency: 100 cents = 1 Ugandan
shilling (UGX)

Official Language: English
Other Languages: Ganda or Luganda,
Swahili, other regional languages
Main Religions: Christianity 66%, indigenous
religions 18%, Islam 16%
Exports: Coffee, cotton, tea,
fish, iron and steel

KENYA

Pronunciation: KEN-yuh
Area: 224,960 sq. miles
(582,646 sq. km)
Population: 31,138,735
Capital: Nairobi
Currency: 100 cents = 1 Kenyan shilling
(KES)
Official Languages: English, Kiswahili
Other Languages: Regional languages
Main Religions: Christianity 66%, indigenous
religions 26%, Islam 7%
Exports: Tea, coffee, petroleum products, fish

RWANDA

Pronunciation: ruh-WAHN-duh
Area: 10,169 sq. miles (26,338 sq. km)
Population: 7,398,074
Capital: Kigali
Currency: 100 centimes = 1 Rwandan
franc (RWF)
Official Languages: Kinyarwanda, French,
English
Other Language: Kiswahili
Main Religions: Christianity 87%, indigenous
religions 7%, Islam 2%
Exports: Coffee, tea, animal skins, tin ore

BURUNDI

Pronunciation: boo-RUN-dee
Area: 10,759 sq. miles (27,866 sq. km)
Population: 6,373,002
Capital: Bujumbura
Currency: 100 centimes = 1 Burundi franc (BIF)
Official Languages: Kirundi, French
Other Language: Swahili
Main Religions: Christianity 67%, indigenous religions 23%, Islam 10%
Exports: Coffee, tea, cotton, animal skins, sugar

TANZANIA

Pronunciation: tan-zuh-NEE-uh
Area: 364,900 sq. miles (945,091 sq. km)
Population: 37,187,939
Capitals: Dar es Salaam (seat of government), Dodoma (official)
Currency: 100 cents = 1 Tanzanian shilling (TZS)
Official Languages: Swahili, English
Other Languages: Arabic, regional languages
Main Religions: Christianity 45%, Islam 35%, indigenous religions 20%
Exports: Coffee, cotton, tobacco, cashews, minerals

ANGOLA

Pronunciation: ang-GOH-luh
Area: 481,351 sq. miles (1,246,699 sq. km)
Population: 10,593,171
Capital: Luanda

Currency: 100 lwei = 1 kwanza (AOA)
Official Language: Portuguese
Other Languages: Bantu, other regional languages
Main Religions: Christianity 53%, indigenous religions 47%
Exports: Crude oil, diamonds, gas, refined petroleum products, coffee, sisal (fiber), fish and fish products, timber, cotton

ZAMBIA

Pronunciation: ZAM-bee-uh
Area: 290,585 sq. miles(752,615 sq. km)
Population: 9,959.037
Capital: Lusaka
Currency: 100 ngwee = 1 Zambian kwacha (ZMK)
Official Language: English
Other Languages: Regional languages
Main Religions: Christianity 62%, Islam and Hinduism 36%, indigenous religions 1%
Exports: Copper, cobalt, electricity, tobacco

ZIMBABWE

Pronunciation: zim-BAH-bway
Area: 150,820 sq. miles (390,624 sq. km)
Population: 11,376,676
Capital: Harare
Currency: 100 cents = 1 Zimbabwean dollar (ZWD)
Official Language: English
Other Languages: Shona, regional languages
Main Religions: Syncretic (part Christianity, part indigenous religions) 50%, Christianity 25%, indigenous religions 24%, Islam 1%
Exports: Tobacco, manufactured goods, metals, cotton, gold

MALAWI

Pronunciation: muh-LAH-wee
Area: 45,747 sq. miles (118,485 sq. km)
Population: 10,701,824
Capital: Lilongwe
Currency: 100 tambala = 1 Malawian kwacha (MWK)
Official Languages: English, Chichewa
Other Languages: Regional languages
Main Religions: Christianity 75%, Islam 20%, indigenous religions 5%
Exports: Tobacco, tea, sugar, cotton, coffee, peanuts, timber products

MOZAMBIQUE

Pronunciation: moh-zahm-BEEK
Area: 309,494 sq. miles (801,590 sq. km)
Population: 19,607,519
Capital: Maputo
Currency: 100 centavos = 1 metical (MZM)
Official Language: Portuguese
Other Languages: Regional languages
Main Religions: Indigenous religions 50%, Christianity 30%, Islam 20%
Exports: Shrimp, cashews, cotton, sugar, citrus fruit, timber, bulk electricity

NAMIBIA

Pronunciation: nuh-MI-bee-uh
Area: 318,694 sq. miles (825,418 sq. km)
Population: 1,820,916
Capital: Windhoek
Currency: 100 cents = 1 Namibian dollar (NAD); 100 cents = 1 rand (ZAR)
Official Language: English
Other Languages: Afrikaans, German, Herero, Oshivambo, Nama

Main Religions: Christianity 85%, indigenous religions 15%
Exports: Diamonds, metals, cattle, processed fish

BOTSWANA

Pronunciation: bawt-SWAH-nuh
Area: 231,803 sq. miles (600,370 sq. km)
Population: 1,591,232
Capital: Gaborone
Currency: 100 thebe = 1 pula (BWP)
Official Language: English
Other Language: Setswana
Main Religions: Indigenous religions 50%, Christianity 50%
Exports: Diamonds, copper and nickel, meat

SOUTH AFRICA

Pronunciation: sowth AF-ri-kuh
Area: 471,008 sq. miles (1,219,912 sq. km)
Population: 43,427,000
Capitals: Pretoria (administrative), Bloemfontein (judicial), Cape Town (legislative)
Currency: 100 cents = 1 rand (ZAR)
Official Languages: Afrikaans, English, Ndebele, Pedi, Sotho, Swazi, Tsonga, Tswana, Venda, Xhosa, Zulu
Main Religions: Christianity 68%, animism 29%, Islam 2%, Hinduism 1%
Exports: Gold, diamonds and other minerals and metals, machinery and equipment

SWAZILAND

Pronunciation: SWAH-zee-land
Area: 6,705 sq. miles (17,366 sq. km)
Population: 1,123,605
Capital: Lobamba (royal and legislative), Mbabane (official)

Currency: 100 cents = 1 lilangeni (SZL)
Official Languages: English, Swazi
Main Religions: Christianity 60%, indigenous religions 30%, Islam 10%
Exports: Sugar, wood pulp, cotton, refridgerators

LESOTHO

Pronunciation: luh-SOH-toh
Area: 11,716 sq. miles (30,344 sq. km)
Population: 2,207,954
Capital: Maseru
Currency: 100 licente = 1 loti (LSL)
Official Languages: English, Sesotho
Other Languages: Zulu, Xhosa
Main Religions: Christianity 80%, indigenous religions 20%
Exports: Wool, mohair, food and livestock, clothing, footwear, road vehicles

COMOROS

Pronunciation: KAH-muh-rohz
Area: 719 sq. miles (1,862 sq. km)
Population: 614,382
Capital: Moroni
Currency: 100 centimes = 1 Comoran franc (KMF)
Official Languages: Arabic, French
Other Language: Comoran
Main Religions: Islam 98%, Christianity 2%
Exports: Vanilla, cloves, perfume oil, copra

MADAGASCAR

Pronunciation: ma-duh-GAS-kuhr
Area: 226,657 sq. miles (587,042 sq. km)
Population: 16,473,477
Capital: Antananarivo

Currency: 100 centimes = 1 Malagasy franc (MGF)
Official Languages: French, Malagasy
Main Religions: Indigenous religions 52%, Christianity 41%, Islam 7%
Exports: Coffee, vanilla, shellfish, chromite, sugar, petroleum products, cotton cloth

SEYCHELLES

Pronunciation: say-SHELZ
Area: 176 sq. miles (455 sq. km)
Population: 80,098
Capital: Victoria
Currency: 100 cents = 1 Seychelles rupee (SCR)
Official Languages: English, French
Other Language: Seychelles creole
Main Religion: Christianity 98%
Exports: Fish, cinnamon bark, copra, petroleum products

MAURITIUS

Pronunciation: maw-RI-shuhs
Area: 720 sq. miles (1,865 sq. km)
Population: 1,200,206
Capital: Port Louis
Currency: 100 cents = 1 Mauritian rupee (MUR)
Official Language: English
Other Languages: Mauritian creole, French, Hindi, Urdu, Hakka, Bojpoori
Main Religions: Hinduism 52%, Christianity 28%, Islam 17%
Exports: Textiles and clothing, sugar, cut flowers, molasses

AUSTRALIA
AND OCEANIA

World

FACT FILE

AUSTRALIA

Pronunciation: aw-STRAYL-yuh
Area: 2,967,909 sq. miles (7,686,884 sq. km)
Population: 19,546,792
Capital: Canberra
Currency: 100 cents = 1 Australian dollar (AUD)
Official Language: English
Other Languages: Aboriginal languages
Main Religion: Christianity 76%
Exports: Coal, gold, meat, wool, wheat, alumina, iron ore, machinery and transportation equipment

Territories and dependencies
Christmas Island: Indian Ocean; 52 sq. miles (135 sq. km); population 474
Cocos (Keeling) Islands: Indian Ocean; 9 sq. miles (23 sq. km); population 632
Heard and McDonald Islands: Indian Ocean; 159 sq. miles (412 sq. km); no permanent population
Norfolk Island: South Pacific Ocean; 13 sq. miles (34 sq. km); population 1,866

PAPUA NEW GUINEA

Pronunciation: PA-pyoo-uh noo GI-nee
Area: 178,703 sq. miles (462,840 sq. km)
Population: 5,172,033
Capital: Port Moresby
Currency: 100 toea = 1 kina (PGK)
Official Languages: English, pidgin English, Motu
Other Languages: Regional languages
Main Religions: Christianity 66%, indigenous religions 34%
Exports: Gold, copper ore, oil, lumber, palm oil, coffee, cocoa, lobster, crayfish

NEW ZEALAND

Pronunciation: noo ZEE-luhnd
Area: 103,736 sq. miles (268,676 sq. km)
Population: 3,908,037
Capital: Wellington
Currency: 100 cents = 1 New Zealand dollar (NZD)
Official Languages: English, Maori
Main Religion: Christianity 67%
Exports: Wool, lamb, mutton, beef, fish, cheese, chemicals, forestry products, fruit and vegetables, manufactured goods

Territories and dependencies
Cook Islands: South Pacific Ocean; 92 sq. miles (238 sq. km); population 20,811
Niue: South Pacific Ocean; 100 sq. miles (259 sq. km); population 2,134
Tokelau: South Pacific Ocean; 4 sq. miles (10 sq. km); population 1,431

SOLOMON ISLANDS

Pronunciation: SAH-luh-muhn islands
Area: 10,985 sq. miles (28,450 sq. km)
Population: 494,786
Capital: Honiara
Currency: 100 cents = 1 Solomon Islands dollar (SBD)
Official Language: Melanesian pidgin
Other Languages: English, regional languages
Main Religions: Christianity 96%, indigenous religions 4%
Exports: Fish, timber, palm oil, cocoa, copra

SAMOA

Pronunciation: suh-MOH-uh
Area: 1,100 sq. miles (2,850 sq. km)
Population: 178,631
Capital: Apia
Currency: 100 sene = 1 tala (WST)
Official Languages: Samoan (Polynesian), English
Main Religion: Christianity 99%
Exports: Coconut oil and cream, taro, fish, beer, copra

VANUATU

Pronunciation: van-wah-TOO
Area: 4,710 sq. miles (12,200 sq. km)
Population: 196,178
Capital: Port-Vila
Currency: 100 centimes = 1 vatu (VUV)
Official Languages: English, French

Other Language: Bislama (pidgin)
Main Religions: Christianity 77%,
indigenous religions 8%
Exports: Copra, kava, beef,
cocoa, timber, coffee

KIRIBATI

Pronunciation: kihr-uh-BAH-tee
Area: 277 sq. miles (717 sq. km)
Population: 96,335
Capital: Tarawa
Currency: 100 cents = 1 Australian
dollar (AUD)
Official Language: English
Other Language: I-Kiribati
Main Religion: Christianity 94%
Exports: Copra, coconuts, seaweed, fish

NAURU

Pronunciation: nah-OO-roo
Area: 8.5 sq. miles (22 sq. km)
Population: 12,329
Capital: None. Government offices in Yaren
district
Currency: 100 cents = 1 Australian
dollar (AUD)
Official Language: Nauruan
Other Language: English
Main Religion: Christianity 100%
Export: Phosphates

FIJI

Pronunciation: FEE-jee
Area: 7,055 sq. miles (18,272 sq. km)
Population: 856,346
Capital: Suva
Currency: 100 cents = 1 Fijian dollar (FJD)
Official Language: English
Other Languages: Fijian, Hindustani
Main Religions: Christianity 52%,
Hinduism 38%, Islam 8%
Exports: Sugar, clothing, gold, processed fish,
timber

MARSHALL ISLANDS

Pronunciation: MAR-shuhl islands
Area: 70 sq. miles (181 sq. km)
Population: 73,630
Capital: Majuro
Currency: 100 cents = 1 United States
dollar (USD)
Official Language: English
Other Languages: Marshallese, Japanese
Main Religion: Christianity 98%
Exports: Coconut oil, fish, trochus shells

PALAU

Pronunciation: puh-LOW
Area: 191 sq. miles (495 sq. km)
Population: 19,409
Capital: Koror
Currency: 100 cents = 1 United States
dollar (USD)
Official Language: English
Other Languages: Palauan, Sonsorolese,
Angaur, Japanese, Tobi
Main Religions: Christianity 67%, Modekngei
religion 33%
Exports: Shellfish, tuna, trochus shells, copra

TONGA

Pronunciation: TAHNG-guh
Area: 270 sq. miles (699 sq. km)
Population: 106,137
Capital: Nuku'alofa
Currency: 100 seniti = 1 pa'anga (TOP)
Official Languages: Tongan, English
Main Religion: Christianity 70%
Exports: Squash, vanilla, fish, root crops,
coconut oil

FEDERATED STATES
OF MICRONESIA

Pronunciation: FE-der-ayt-ed STAYTS
of meye-kruh-NEE-zhuh
Area: 266 sq. miles (689 sq. km)
Population: 135,869
Capital: Palikir
Currency: 100 cents = 1 United States
dollar (USD)
Official Language: English
Other Languages: Regional languages
Main Religion: Christianity 97%
Exports: Fish, clothing, bananas, black pepper

TUVALU

Pronunciation: too-VAH-loo
Area: 9 sq. miles (23 sq. km)
Population: 11,146
Capital: Funafuti
Currency: 100 cents = 1 Tuvaluan dollar
(TVD); 100 cents = 1 Australian dollar (AUD)
Official Languages: Tuvaluan, English
Main Religions: Christianity 98%, Baha'i 1%
Exports: Copra

Astronomy Timeline

30,000 BC Lunar phases scratched on bone —the oldest astronomical record?

4000 BC Sumerians of Mesopotamia make the first records of Leo, Taurus, and Scorpius, the oldest constellations still used today.

600 BC Greek philosopher Thales probably knows the cause of solar and lunar eclipses.

525 BC Greek philosopher Pythagoras recognizes that Earth is round.

350 BC Greek philosopher Aristotle provides a scientific explanation of why Earth is round.

325 BC Greek mathematician Eudoxus explains celestial motions in terms of several crystal spheres with Earth at their center.

300 BC Greek astronomer Aristarchus proposes a Sun-centered model for the universe. But his ideas are ignored until Copernicus's time, almost 2,000 years later.

200 BC Greek astronomer Eratosthenes measures the circumference of Earth, getting a result close to the modern one.

150 BC Greek astronomer Hipparchus creates system of magnitudes to measure star brightness, discovers a slow wobble in Earth's axis (precession), and compiles the first star catalog.

AD 150 Greek astronomer Claudius Ptolemy publishes the *Almagest,* a detailed summing-up of all the ancient world's astronomical knowledge. It dominates the subject for more than 1,000 years.

AD 165 Chinese astronomers make the first accurately dated observations, recording sunspots on the face of the Sun.

AD 635 A Chinese scholar records the rule that a comet's tail always points away from the Sun.

1543 Nicolaus Copernicus publishes his book *On the Revolutions of the Celestial Spheres,* proposing a Sun-centered solar system.

1572 Tycho Brahe sees a supernova in Cassiopeia and determines that it lies beyond the Moon. This discovery conflicts with ancient ideas of the heavens being unchangeable, and it encourages Tycho to make a whole new set of accurate observations.

1576 Tycho builds his Uraniborg observatory on an island in the Baltic Sea and begins compiling the world's most accurate observations of the motions of stars and planets.

1600 Tycho Brahe hires Johannes Kepler as his mathematical assistant to work on the observations.

1608 Hans Lippershey in the Netherlands invents the telescope.

1609 Using Tycho Brahe's observations, Kepler determines that Mars's orbit is elliptical, a key advance over ancient astronomy, which had insisted on circular orbits. Galileo Galilei hears of the telescope and, following the reported description, builds his own. He is the first person to use the telescope for astronomy.

1610 Galileo publishes his telescope discoveries of moons orbiting Jupiter, craters on the Moon, and stars in the Milky Way. He starts promoting a Copernican model of the solar system.

1616 The Roman Catholic Church bans Copernican ideas as "false and absurd."

1619 Kepler discovers a simple mathematical relationship between the length of a planet's year and its distance from the Sun.

1633 Galileo is put under house arrest by the Church for promoting Copernican ideas.

1665 Isaac Newton starts developing mathematical physics.

1687 Newton publishes his book *The Mathematical Principles of Natural Philosophy*, which links astronomy with physics and puts both on firm mathematical ground.

1727 James Bradley discovers the aberration of starlight, an apparent shift in the positon of a star caused by the motion of Earth. It is the first physical proof that Earth moves around the Sun.

1758 Comet Halley returns as forecast by Edmond Halley, the first predicted return of a comet.

1781 William Herschel discovers seventh planet, Uranus. This is the first planet to be discovered since prehistoric times.

1833 A spectacular Leonid meteor shower shows astronomers that meteors come from space and do not originate in the atmosphere.

1835 The Roman Catholic Church removes books by Copernicus and Galileo from its list of banned works.

1838 Friedrich Bessel measures the parallax of 61 Cygni, the first direct measurement of a star's distance.

1846 Johann Galle and Heinrich d'Arrest find the eighth planet, Neptune, following predictions made by Urbain Leverrier (and, independently, by John C. Adams).

1860s The spectroscope begins to show astronomers what stars and nebulas are made of.

1880s Photography becomes an important tool for astronomy because it can detect things in the sky that people cannot see and it provides a permanent record.

1905 Albert Einstein's special theory of relativity is published.

1908 Ejnar Hertzsprung divides the population of stars into two groups, giants and dwarfs. It is the first step in learning how stars change as they age.

1910 The return of comet Halley creates the world's first media event.

1912 Henrietta Leavitt discovers that Cepheid variable stars with long periods of variation are systematically brighter than those with shorter periods.
Vesto Slipher discovers that most "spiral nebulas" are flying away from Earth, the first detection of an expanding universe.

1916 Einstein publishes his general theory of relativity, which predicts that the universe is expanding.

1917 100-inch (2.5-m) Hooker reflector telescope completed at Mount Wilson, California, USA.

1919 Einstein's general theory of relativity is confirmed by observations of a total solar eclipse seen from Brazil and West Africa.

1923 Edwin Hubble uses Cepheid variables to show that "spiral nebulas" are galaxies lying outside the Milky Way.

1929 Hubble presents observational evidence for an expanding universe and provides the first estimates of its age and rate of expansion.

1930 Clyde Tombaugh discovers the ninth planet, Pluto.

1931 Karl Jansky builds a rotating aerial and discovers radio waves coming from space. These radio waves had been predicted in the 1880s but were not found because astronomers had no way to detect them.

1937 Grote Reber discovers radio waves coming from the center of the Milky Way, using a radio telescope built in his own backyard.

1938 Hans Bethe publishes a theory explaining how the Sun and other stars shine because of nuclear reactions.

1942 John Hey and colleagues discover radio noise coming from the Sun.

1946 Hey and colleagues identify the most powerful radio source in the sky, the radio galaxy Cygnus A.

1948 George Gamow, Ralph Alpher, and Robert Herman describe how chemical elements were formed in the Big Bang.

1948 200-inch (5-m) Hale Telescope is completed at Palomar Mountain, California, USA. Jan Oort proposes that comets come from a vast cloud orbiting far beyond Pluto.

1952 Walter Baade announces that galaxies are twice as far away as astronomers had previously assumed.

1957 Launch of Sputnik 1 satellite by the Soviet Union (now Russia) starts the Space Age.

1959 First photographs of the Moon's farside returned by Soviet probe, Luna 3.

1961 Yuri Gagarin from the Soviet Union is the first person to fly in space.

1962 Mariner 2 spacecraft flies past Venus, first probe to visit another planet, discovers dense atmosphere and verifies hot surface.
Orbiting Solar Observatory, the first astronomical satellite, is launched.

1963 Maarten Schmidt discovers that quasars are objects with big redshifts and must lie very far away.

1965 Arno Penzias and Robert Wilson discover the cosmic background radiation—the faded glow of the Big Bang explosion in which the universe began. Mariner 4 spacecraft is the first to fly past Mars. It discovers lots of craters.

1967 Jocelyn Bell-Burnell discovers pulsars, which are soon identified as neutron stars, one of the objects that massive stars can finish as.

1969 Apollo 11 astronauts Neil Armstrong and Edwin Aldrin make the first manned landing on the Moon.

1971 Mariner 9 is the first spacecraft to orbit another planet, Mars. Finds evidence of past water.

1973 Pioneer 10 makes first flyby of Jupiter and detects powerful radiation belts.

1974 Mariner 10 makes first two of three flybys of Mercury (third in 1975). Finds evidence of massive iron core and giant impacts.

1975 Venera 9 takes the first photos from the surface of Venus.

1976 Viking 1 and 2 land on Mars. They find no signs of life.

1977 Charles Kowal finds comet Chiron, the first in the outer solar system.

1977 Uranus's rings are discovered by astronomers aboard the Kuiper Airborne Observatory.

1978 James Christy discovers Charon, Pluto's moon.

1979 Voyager 1 and 2 spacecraft fly past Jupiter. Make detailed survey of planet and moons and find its rings. Pioneer 11 makes first flyby of Saturn.

1980 Alan Guth proposes a period of extremely fast expansion in the early history of the universe, which he calls cosmic inflation.
Voyager 1 spacecraft makes first detailed study of Saturn system.
Very Large Array radio telescope starts working in New Mexico, USA.

1983 Infrared Astronomical Satellite (IRAS) completes the first full survey of the infrared sky.

1985/6 Comet Halley's return is met by a fleet of space probes.

1986 Voyager 2 makes first flyby of Uranus.

1987 Supernova 1987A appears in the Large Magellanic Cloud.

1989 Voyager 2 spacecraft makes first flyby of Neptune. Captures details of the planet and its moons—and its rings, suspected to exist since 1981.
Margaret Geller and John Huchra announce evidence for walls and voids in the distribution of galaxies in the universe.

1990 Hubble Space Telescope is launched.

1991 Galileo spacecraft on the way to Jupiter makes first asteroid flyby, passing 951 Gaspra.
Compton Gamma-Ray Observatory begins survey of universe at high-energy wavelengths, seeking cause of mysterious bursts of high energy.

1992 COBE satellite observatory confirms predictions of Big Bang theory.

1993 First 394-inch (10-m) Keck telescope begins operation on Mauna Kea, Hawaii.
Hubble Space Telescope repaired and upgraded in orbit.

1994 Comet Shoemaker-Levy 9 crashes into Jupiter.

1995 Discovery of first planet to orbit ordinary star other than the Sun, orbiting 51 Pegasi.
Galileo spacecraft sends probe into Jupiter's atmosphere, begins tour of Jupiter's moons.

1996 Black hole confirmed at center of Milky Way galaxy.

1997 Burst of gamma rays tracked to source far from Milky Way, perhaps caused by colliding neutron stars.
Mars Pathfinder lands on Mars with Sojourner Rover.

1999 Chandra X-Ray Observatory is launched to look for X-rays from distant objects.

Universe Fact File

SUN

Apparent magnitude: −26.8
Absolute (actual) magnitude: 4.8
Rotation time: 25 Earth days at equator, 34 Earth days near poles
Diameter: 865,000 miles (1,392,000 km)
Mass: 332,946 x Earth's
Density: 1.4 x water's density
Surface gravity: 27.9 x Earth's
Composition: 92.1% hydrogen, 7.8% helium, 1% other elements
Surface temperature: 9,900°F (5,500°C)
Core temperature: 27,900,000°F (15,500,000°C)
Magnetic field strength: up to 10,000 x Earth's

MERCURY

When discovered: prehistoric
Who discovered it: unknown
How we can see it: naked eye
Apparent magnitude: −2 to +3
Distance from Sun: 0.4 AU, or 36 million miles (58 million km)
Length of year: 88 Earth days
Average speed: 30 miles per second (48 km/s)
Inclination of orbit: 7.0°
Eccentricity of orbit: 0.21
Tilt of axis: 0.5°
Rotation time: 59 Earth days
Solar day: 176 Earth days
Diameter: 3,029 miles (4,875 km)
Mass: 55% x Earth's
Density: 5.4 x water's density
Surface gravity: 0.38 x Earth's

Composition: iron and rock
Atmosphere: essentially none
Average temperature: −280°F to 800°F (−173°C to 427°C)
Magnetic field strength: 0.5% x Earth's
Number of moons: none
Number of rings: none
Number of probe visits: 1

VENUS

When discovered: prehistoric
Who discovered it: unknown
How we can see it: naked eye
Apparent magnitude: −4.0 to −4.6
Distance from Sun: 0.7 AU, or 67 million miles (108 million km)
Length of year: 225 Earth days
Average speed: 22 miles per second (35 km/s)
Inclination of orbit: 3.4°
Eccentricity of orbit: 0.01
Tilt of axis: 177.4°
Rotation time: 243 Earth days
Solar day: 117 Earth days
Diameter: 7,521 miles (12,104 km)
Mass: 82% x Earth's
Density: 5.2 x water's density
Surface gravity: 0.90 x Earth's
Composition: mostly rock
Atmosphere: 97% carbon dioxide, 3% nitrogen
Pressure of atmosphere: 96 x Earth's
Average temperature: 880°F (470°C)
Magnetic field strength: less than 0.05% x Earth's
Number of moons: none
Number of rings: none
Number of probe visits: 31

EARTH

When discovered: prehistoric
Who discovered it: unknown
Distance from Sun: 1.0 AU, or 93 million miles (150 million km)
Length of year: 365.25 days
Average speed: 18.5 miles per second (30 km/s)
Inclination of orbit: 0°
Eccentricity of orbit: 0.02
Tilt of axis: 23.5°
Rotation time: 23 hours 56 minutes
Solar day: 24 hours
Diameter: 7,926 miles (12,756 km)
Mass: 6×10^{24} tons (5.5×10^{24} tonnes)
Density: 5.5 x water's density
Composition: mostly rock
Atmosphere: 78% nitrogen, 21% oxygen, plus water, argon, carbon dioxide
Average temperature: 63°F (17°C)
Number of moons: 1
Number of rings: none

MARS

When discovered: prehistoric
Who discovered it: unknown
How we can see it: naked eye
Apparent magnitude: −2.6 to +1.8
Distance from Sun: 1.5 AU, or 142 million miles (228 million km)
Length of year: 687 Earth days
Average speed: 15 miles per second (24 km/s)
Inclination of orbit: 1.9°
Eccentricity of orbit: 0.09
Tilt of axis: 25.2°

Rotation time: 24 hours 37 minutes
Solar day: 24 hours 40 minutes
Diameter: 4,213 miles (6,780 km)
Mass: 64% x Earth's
Density: 3.9 x water's density
Surface gravity: 0.38 x Earth's
Composition: mostly rock
Atmosphere: 95% carbon dioxide, 2.7% nitrogen, 1.6% argon, plus others
Pressure of atmosphere: 0.6% x Earth's
Average temperature: −74°F (−59°C)
Magnetic field strength: less than 0.1% x Earth's
Number of moons: 2
Number of rings: none
Number of probe visits: 23

JUPITER

When discovered: prehistoric
Who discovered it: unknown
How we can see it: naked eye
Apparent magnitude: −2.5 to −1.2
Distance from Sun: 5.2 AU, or 483 million miles (778 million km)
Length of year: 11.9 Earth years
Average speed: 8 miles per second (13 km/s)
Inclination of orbit: 1.3°
Eccentricity of orbit: 0.05
Tilt of axis: 3.1°
Rotation time: 9 hours 55 minutes
Solar day: same as rotation time
Diameter: 88,846 miles (142,984 km)
Mass: 317.8 x Earth's
Density: 1.3 x water's density
Gravity at cloudtops: 2.6 x Earth's surface gravity
Composition: mostly gaseous
Atmosphere: 86% hydrogen, 13.6% helium, plus methane, ammonia, water
Average temperature at cloudtops: −162°F (−108°C)
Magnetic field strength: 7.1 x Earth's
Number of moons: 39
Number of rings: 3
Number of probe visits: 5

SATURN

When discovered: prehistoric
Who discovered it: unknown
How we can see it: naked eye
Apparent magnitude: 0.6 to 1.5
Distance from Sun: 9.6 AU, or 890 million miles (1,432 million km)
Length of year: 29.4 Earth years
Average speed: 6 miles per second (10 km/s)
Inclination of orbit: 2.5°
Eccentricity of orbit: 0.05
Tilt of axis: 26.7°
Rotation time: 10 hours 39 minutes
Solar day: same as rotation time
Diameter: 74,896 miles (120,533 km)
Mass: 95.2 x Earth's
Density: 0.7 x water's density
Gravity at cloudtops: 1.1 x Earth's surface gravity
Composition: mostly gaseous
Atmosphere: 96% hydrogen, 3.3% helium, plus methane, ammonia, and others
Average temperature at cloudtops: −218°F (−139°C)
Magnetic field strength: 0.34 x Earth's
Number of moons: at least 30
Number of rings: 7
Number of probe visits: 4

URANUS

When discovered: March 1781
Who discovered it: William Herschel
How we can see it: barely visible to the naked eye, but easy to see with a telescope
Apparent magnitude: 5.5 to 5.9
Distance from Sun: 19.2 AU, or 1,784 million miles (2,871 million km)
Length of year: 84.1 Earth years
Average speed: 4 miles per second (7 km/s)
Inclination of orbit: 0.8°
Eccentricity of orbit: 0.04
Tilt of axis: 97.9°
Rotation time: 17 hours 14 minutes
Solar day: same as rotation time
Diameter: 31,763 miles (51,118 km)
Mass: 14.5 x Earth's
Density: 1.3 x water's density
Gravity at cloudtops: 0.90 x Earth's surface gravity
Composition: mostly gaseous
Atmosphere: 83% hydrogen, 15% helium, 2% methane
Average temperature at cloudtops: −323°F (−197°C)
Magnetic field strength: 0.38 x Earth's
Number of moons: 21
Number of rings: 11
Number of probe visits: 1

NOTES ON PLANET FACTS

Apparent magnitude: How bright an object looks in the sky. Brighter objects have smaller numbers than dimmer ones.

Distance from Sun: The planet's average distance from the Sun.

Inclination of orbit: The angle of the planet's orbit relative to the plane of Earth's orbit.

Accentricity of orbit: How elliptical the planet's orbit is. The larger the number, the more elliptical the orbit is.

1 AU (astronomical unit): The average distance between Earth and the Sun, about 93 million miles (150 million km).

NEPTUNE

When discovered: September 1846
Who discovered it: Urbain Leverrier, John Couch Adams, Johann Galle, and Heinrich d'Arrest
How we can see it: telescope
Apparent magnitude: 7.9
Distance from Sun: 30.1 AU, or 2,795 million miles (4,498 million km)
Length of year: 164.9 Earth years
Average speed: 3.5 miles per second (5.5 km/s)
Inclination of orbit: 1.8°
Eccentricity of orbit: 0.01
Tilt of axis: 29.6°
Rotation time: 16 hours 7 minutes
Solar day: same as rotation time
Diameter: 30,775 miles (49,528 km)

Mass: 17.2 x Earth's
Density: 1.6 x water's density
Gravity at cloudtops: 1.1 x Earth's surface gravity
Composition: mostly gaseous
Atmosphere: 80% hydrogen, 19% helium, 1% methane
Average temperature at cloudtops: −330°F (−201°C)
Magnetic field strength: 22% x Earth's
Number of moons: 8
Number of rings: 6
Number of probe visits: 1

PLUTO

When discovered: February 1930
Who discovered it: Clyde Tombaugh
How we can see it: telescope

Apparent magnitude: 13.7
Distance from Sun: 39.5 AU, or 3,675 million miles (5,914 million km)
Length of year: 248 Earth years
Average speed: 3 miles per second (5 km/s)
Inclination of orbit: 17.1°
Eccentricity of orbit: 0.25
Tilt of axis: 122.5°
Rotation time: 6.4 Earth days
Solar day: same as rotation time
Diameter: 1,432 miles (2,304 km)
Mass: 0.2% x Earth's
Density: 2.1 x water's density
Surface gravity: 0.065 x Earth's
Composition: rock and ice
Atmosphere: methane, nitrogen
Pressure of atmosphere: about 3 millionths x Earth's
Average temperature: −387°F (−233°C)
Magnetic field strength: unknown
Number of moons: 1
Number of rings: none
Number of probe visits: none

COMET FACTS

NAME	FIRST RECORDED	FARTHEST FROM SUN	CLOSEST TO SUN	TYPE	ORBIT TIME	ORBIT INCLIN.	ORBIT ECCENT.
Encke	1786	4.1 AU	0.3 AU	short period	3.3 yrs	11.9°	0.85
Wirtanen	1954	5.1 AU	1.1 AU	short period	5.5 yrs	11.7°	0.65
Wild 2	1978	5.3 AU	1.6 AU	short period	6.4 yrs	3.2°	0.54
d'Arrest	1851	5.6 AU	1.4 AU	short period	6.5 yrs	19.5°	0.61
Tempel-Tuttle	1866	19.5 AU	1.0 AU	short period	32.9 yrs	163°	0.90
Halley	239 bc	35.0 AU	0.6 AU	short period	76.0 yrs	162°	0.97
Swift-Tuttle	1862	52.3 AU	1.0 AU	short period	137.3 yrs	113°	0.96
Bennett	1970	281.8 AU	0.5 AU	long period	1,678 yrs	90.0°	0.99
Donati	1858	311.6 AU	0.6 AU	long period	1,950 yrs	117°	0.99
Hale-Bopp	1995	370.6 AU	0.9 AU	long period	2,529 yrs	89.4°	0.99
Hyakutake	1996	2,006 AU	0.2 AU	long period	31,781 yrs	125°	0.99
Ikeya-Seki	1965	4,000 AU	0.01 AU	long period	89,443 yrs	129°	0.99

Name: Comets are named for their discoverers.
Orbit Time: All years listed are Earth years.
Orbit Inclin.: The inclination of the comet's orbit, relative to the plane of Earth's orbit.
Orbit Eccent.: The eccentricity of the comet's orbit. The larger the number, the more elliptical the orbit.

LUNAR ECLIPSES

DATE	TYPE	BEST SEEN FROM
May 16, 2003	total	North & South America
Nov 9, 2003	total	Europe, west Africa, North & South America
May 4, 2004	total	west Asia, Africa, Europe
Oct 28, 2004	total	North & South America
Oct 17, 2005	partial	central Pacific Ocean
Sept 7, 2006	partial	Indian Ocean, Asia, east Africa
Mar 3, 2007	total	Africa, Europe
Aug 28, 2007	total	central Pacific, west North & South America
Feb 21, 2008	total	North & South America, west Europe
Aug 16, 2008	partial	west Asia, Europe, Africa
Dec 21, 2009	partial	Asia, Indian Ocean, Africa, Europe
June 26, 2010	partial	central Pacific Ocean, west North & South America
Dec 21, 2010	total	North America, west South America
June 15, 2011	total	southwest Asia, Africa, Indian Ocean
Dec 10, 2011	total	west Pacific Ocean, east Asia, Alaska, Yukon
June 4, 2012	partial	central Pacific Ocean, west North & South America
Apr 15, 2014	total	North America, west South America, Pacific Ocean
Oct 8, 2014	total	Pacific Ocean, west North & South America
Apr 4, 2015	total	Pacific Ocean, west North & South America
Sept 28, 2015	total	west Europe & Africa, North & South America

MANNED MISSIONS TO THE MOON

NAME	CREW	LAUNCH DATE	ARRIVAL DATE	LANDING SITE	SAMPLES RETURNED
Apollo 8	Frank Borman, James Lovell, William Anders	Dec 21, 1968	Dec 24, 1968	no landing	no samples
Apollo 10	Thomas Stafford, John Young, Eugene Cernan	May 18, 1969	May 22, 1969	no landing	no samples
Apollo 11	*Neil Armstrong, Edwin Aldrin,* Michael Collins	July 16, 1969	July 20, 1969	Mare Tranquillitatis	49 pounds (22 kg)
Apollo 12	*Charles Conrad, Alan Bean,* Richard Gordon	Nov 14, 1969	Nov 19, 1969	Oceanus Procellarum	76 pounds (34 kg)
Apollo 13	James Lovell, John Swigert, Fred Haise	Apr 11, 1970	Apr 14, 1970	no landing	no samples
Apollo 14	*Alan Shepard, Edgar Mitchell,* Stuart Roosa	Jan 31, 1971	Feb 5, 1971	Fra Mauro highlands	93 pounds (42 kg)
Apollo 15	*David Scott, James Irwin,* Alfred Worden	July 26, 1971	July 30, 1971	Hadley Rille	171 pounds (77 kg)
Apollo 16	*John Young, Charles Duke,* Thomas Mattingly	Apr 16, 1972	Apr 21, 1972	Descartes highlands	213 pounds (96 kg)
Apollo 17	*Eugene Cernan, Harrison Schmitt,* Ronald Evans	Dec 7, 1972	Dec 11, 1972	Taurus-Littrow valley	247 pounds (111 kg)

* The names of the astronauts who landed on the Moon are in *italics*.

Universal Records

Hottest Planet Surface in our Solar System

The surface of Venus, 880°F (470°C). At its hottest, Mercury comes pretty close: 800°F (427°C). Venus's thick atmosphere traps the Sun's heat, so midnight temperatures are as hot as those at noontime. (And the rocks are hot enough to glow dull red.)

Coldest Planet Surface in our Solar System

Pluto when farthest from the Sun. The actual temperature at that point has not yet been measured because Pluto has not made a full orbit since it was discovered in 1930. Pluto will reach the farthest point in its orbit in February 2114. At present, Pluto's surface temperature is −387°F (−233°C)—and it is slowly falling!

Biggest Crater in our Solar System

South Pole-Aitken Basin on the Moon, roughly 1,600 miles (2,500 km) in diameter. This ancient impact scar is so heavily marked with smaller craters that it was not discovered until the Clementine probe visited the Moon in 1994. Scientists used data from Clementine to carefully map the Moon's surface. This mapping revealed the basin, a broad depression in the lunar farside that is more than 7 miles (12 km) deep.

Tallest Mountain in our Solar System

Olympus Mons on Mars, rising 15 miles (24 km) above its base. The second tallest is Maxwell Montes on Venus, which rises 7 miles (11 km) above the planet's average surface. Earth's officially tallest peak is Mount Everest, 5.5 miles (8.8 km) above sea level.

However, Hawaii's Mauna Kea can also claim to be the tallest on Earth, since it rises about 5.6 miles (9 km) above the ocean floor it stands on.

Biggest Canyon in our Solar System

Valles Marineris on Mars, roughly 2,500 miles (4,000 km) long, with a maximum width of about 370 miles (600 km) and a maximum depth of 5 miles (8 km). If it were in the United States, this canyon could extend from San Francisco on the west coast to the Appalachian Mountains in Virginia near the east coast. In Europe, it would stretch from Paris, France, to Russia's Ural Mountains.

Biggest Moon in our Solar System

Jupiter's Ganymede, 3,273 miles (5,268 km) in diameter. If Ganymede orbited the Sun instead of Jupiter, it would easily qualify as a planet. It is larger than either Mercury or Pluto.

Biggest Planet in our Solar System

Jupiter, with 317.8 times the mass of Earth, and about 11 times its diameter. Jupiter contains more mass than all the rest of the planets, moons, comets, and asteroids put together.

Biggest Known Planet

An unnamed planet orbiting the star HD 114762. This planet appears to have 11 times the mass of Jupiter, but some astronomers think it may actually be a brown dwarf, an object that is like a small, dim, cool star. If it is a brown dwarf, then the most massive planet would be one with 6.6 times Jupiter's mass

that orbits the star 70 Virginis. (This Universal Record is very likely to change as research continues.)

Greatest Meteor Shower

The Leonids on November 13, 1833, with up to 200,000 meteors per hour. Onlookers said that the meteors "fell like snowflakes," and many uneducated people thought the world was about to come to an end. The remarkable display helped astronomers realize that meteors were entering Earth's atmosphere from outer space, and were not just an Earth-based event like rain.

Biggest Meteorite

Hoba meteorite in Namibia, weighing 65 tons (60 tonnes)—about as heavy as nine elephants! Discovered in 1920, this iron meteorite almost 10 feet (3 m) long still lies in the ground where it landed. It was originally even larger—the discolored soil surrounding it shows that part of the meteorite has weathered away.

Biggest Asteroid

1 Ceres, 567 miles (913 km) in diameter. This largest of all asteroids was also the first one to be found—and its discovery came on the first day of the 19th century: January 1, 1801. The discoverer of Ceres was Giuseppe Piazzi (1746–1826) and the place was the Palermo Observatory in Sicily.

Closest Comet to Earth

Comet Lexell in 1770, at a distance of 1.4 million miles (2.2 million km) from Earth—less than six times the distance to the Moon. Despite coming so close, this comet never developed much of a tail and its head looked no bigger than five times the size of the Moon in our night sky.

Longest Comet Tail

Great Comet of March 1843, 190 million miles (300 million km) long. This tail was long enough to reach from the Sun to well past the orbit of Mars. When it passed closest to the Sun, the comet was only about 80,000 miles (130,000 km) above the Sun's surface. Planetary scientists call such comets "sungrazers."

Brightest Star in our Night Sky

Sirius, −1.46 magnitude. Sirius is actually a double star, and its dim companion was the first white dwarf star to be discovered.

Broadest Star

Betelgeuse in Orion, about 800 times the Sun's diameter. If it replaced the Sun in our solar system, this bloated red supergiant star would reach past the orbit of Jupiter.

Most Massive Star

Eta Carinae, about 150 times as massive as the Sun. Astronomers are not certain if Eta Carinae is really one star or two.

Least Massive Star

Gliese 105C, about 10 percent as massive as the Sun. This is about as small as a star can be and still be a true star (an object that fuses hydrogen into helium).

Nearest Star

Proxima Centauri, third member of the Alpha Centauri system. This cool red dwarf star lies about 4.2 light-years away, about 0.1 light-year closer to us than the other two stars in the system.

Globular Star Cluster with the Most Stars

Omega Centauri, with 1.1 million stars. This globular cluster measures about 180 light-years in diameter.

Most Massive Galaxy

Giant elliptical M87 in the constellation of Virgo, with at least 800 billion Suns worth of mass. M87 is a member of the Virgo cluster of galaxies.

Least Massive Galaxy

The Pegasus II dwarf elliptical, about 10 million solar masses. Smaller galaxies may exist, but because they are not very luminous, astronomers cannot detect them unless they also lie close to us.

Nearest Galaxy

Sagittarius dwarf elliptical, 80,000 light-years away. This galaxy is the current record holder, but surveys find new dwarf elliptical galaxies every year or so, and an even closer galaxy may yet be found.

Most Distant Object Visible to the Naked Eye

Andromeda galaxy (M31), 2.5 million light-years away. When you look at this galaxy, you are seeing light that left the galaxy when the most recent great Ice Ages were beginning on Earth.

Most Distant Object Detected

An unnamed galaxy in Ursa Major, 12.6 billion light-years away. This galaxy may not hold the record for very long. Astronomers working with giant telescopes on Earth and the Hubble Space Telescope find a new and more distant record-holder once or twice a year.

ASTEROID FACTS

NAME	DISCOVERY	DISTANCE FROM SUN	ORBIT TIME	ROTATION TIME	DIAMETER
1 Ceres	Piazzi, 1801	2.76 AU	4.6 yrs	9h 5m	567 miles (913 km)
2 Pallas	Olbers, 1802	2.77 AU	4.6 yrs	7h 49m	325 miles (523 km)
4 Vesta	Olbers, 1807	2.36 AU	3.6 yrs	5h 21m	323 miles (520 km)
10 Hygeia	De Gasparis, 1849	3.14 AU	5.6 yrs	27h 40m	267 miles (429 km)
511 Davida	Dugan, 1903	3.18 AU	5.7 yrs	5h 8m	209 miles (337 km)
704 Interamnia	Cerulli, 1910	3.06 AU	5.4 yrs	8h 44m	207 miles (333 km)
253 Mathilde	Palisa, 1885	2.65 AU	4.3 yrs	17h 24m	41 miles (66 km)
243 Ida	Palisa, 1884	2.86 AU	4.9 yrs	4h 38m	37 miles (60 km)
433 Eros	Witt & Charlois, 1898	1.46 AU	1.8 yrs	5h 18m	21 miles (33 km)
951 Gaspra	Neujmin, 1916	2.21 AU	3.3 yrs	7h 3m	11 miles (18 km)

Distance from Sun: The asteroid's average distance from the Sun.
Orbit Time: All years listed are Earth years.

Robot Missions

IMPORTANT MISSIONS TO THE PLANETS

MISSION	COUNTRY	TYPE*	LAUNCH	ARRIVAL	ACHIEVEMENTS
Mercury					
Mariner 10	USA	F	Nov 3, 1973	Mar 29, 1974	first close-up images show cratered surface
Venus					
Mariner 2	USA	F	Aug 27, 1962	Dec 14, 1962	first flyby finds heavy atmosphere, hot surface
Venera 4	Soviet Union	L	June 12, 1967	Oct 18, 1967	measures atmosphere, fails on descent
Mariner 5	USA	F	June 14, 1967	Oct 19, 1967	improves atmospheric measurements
Venera 5	Soviet Union	L	Jan 5, 1969	May 16, 1969	studies atmosphere
Venera 6	Soviet Union	L	Jan 10, 1969	May 17, 1969	studies atmosphere
Venera 8	Soviet Union	L	Mar 27, 1972	July 22, 1972	sends back first data from surface
Mariner 10	USA	F	Nov 4, 1973	Feb 5, 1974	flies past on way to Mercury, photographs clouds
Venera 9	Soviet Union	OL	June 8, 1975	Oct 22, 1975	first images of surface show volcanic rocks
Venera 10	Soviet Union	OL	June 14, 1975	Oct 25, 1975	photographs surface rocks and dirt
Pioneer Venus Orbiter	USA	O	May 20, 1978	Dec 4, 1978	first global radar map of landscape, studies clouds
Pioneer Venus Probes	USA	EP	Aug 8, 1978	Dec 9, 1978	five probes sample atmosphere
Venera 11	Soviet Union	OL	Sept 9, 1978	Dec 25, 1978	photographs surface, analyzes atmosphere
Venera 12	Soviet Union	OL	Sept 14, 1978	Dec 21, 1978	photographs surface, analyzes atmosphere
Venera 13	Soviet Union	OL	Oct 30, 1981	Mar 1, 1982	photographs surface, analyzes atmosphere
Venera 14	Soviet Union	OL	Nov 4, 1981	Mar 5, 1982	photographs surface, analyzes atmosphere
Venera 15	Soviet Union	O	June 2, 1983	Oct 10, 1983	radar mapping of northern hemisphere
Venera 16	Soviet Union	O	June 7, 1983	Oct 14, 1983	radar mapping of northern hemisphere
Vega 1	Soviet Union	LB	Dec 15, 1984	June 11, 1985	surveys atmosphere and winds with balloon
Vega 2	Soviet Union	LB	Dec 21, 1984	June 16, 1985	surveys atmosphere and winds with balloon
Magellan	USA	O	May 4, 1989	Aug 10, 1990	surveys geology over Venus using radar
Galileo	USA	F	Oct 18, 1989	Feb 10, 1990	flies past on way to Jupiter, studies clouds
Cassini	USA	F	Oct 15, 1997	Apr 26, 1998	flies past on way to Saturn, studies clouds
Cassini	USA	F	Oct 15, 1997	June 24, 1999	second Venus flyby, studies clouds
Mars					
Mariner 4	USA	F	Nov 28, 1965	July 14, 1965	first close-up images show craters, thin atmosphere
Mariner 6	USA	F	Feb 24, 1969	July 31, 1969	returns 75 photos, increases geological knowledge
Mariner 7	USA	F	Mar 27, 1969	Aug 5, 1969	returns 126 photos, increases geological knowledge
Mars 3	Soviet Union	OL	May 28, 1971	Dec 3, 1971	some data and few photos
Mariner 9	USA	O	May 30, 1971	Nov 12, 1971	first survey of surface, finds water channels, volcanoes
Mars 5	Soviet Union	O	July 25, 1973	Feb 12, 1974	lasts a few days
Mars 6	Soviet Union	OL	Aug 5, 1973	Mar 12, 1974	little data return
Mars 7	Soviet Union	OL	Aug 9, 1973	Mar 9, 1974	little data return
Viking 1	USA	OL	Aug 20, 1975	June 19, 1976	Survey from orbit, unsuccessful search for life
Viking 2	USA	OL	Sept 9, 1975	Aug 7, 1976	Survey from orbit, unsuccessful search for life
Mars Global Surveyor	USA	O	Nov 7, 1996	Sept 12, 1997	maps entire planet at high resolution
Mars Pathfinder	USA	LR	Dec 2, 1996	July 4, 1997	explores geology of a once-flooded landscape
Nozomi (Planet-B)	Japan	O	July 4, 1998	Dec 2003	studies upper atmosphere, magnetosphere, solar wind

MISSION	COUNTRY	TYPE*	LAUNCH	ARRIVAL	ACHIEVEMENTS
Mars					
Mars Climate Orbiter	USA	O	Dec 11, 1998	Sept 23, 1999	crashes on arrival, no data returned
Mars Polar Lander	USA	L	Jan 3, 1999	Dec 3, 1999	fails upon arrival, no data returned
Deep Space 2	USA	I	Jan 3, 1999	Dec 3, 1999	travels with Polar Lander, searches for subsurface ice
Jupiter					
Pioneer 10	USA	F	Mar 3, 1972	Dec 3, 1973	first detailed study of a gas-giant planet
Pioneer 11	USA	F	Apr 6, 1973	Dec 3, 1974	studies polar regions of Jupiter, magnetic environment
Voyager 1	USA	F	Sept 5, 1977	Mar 5, 1979	first detailed images of planet & moons, discovers rings
Voyager 2	USA	F	Aug 20, 1977	July 9, 1979	follow-up on Voyager 1's discoveries
Galileo	USA	OEP	Oct 18, 1989	Dec 7, 1995	first atmosphere probe, orbital tour of planet & moons
Saturn					
Pioneer 11	USA	F	Apr 6, 1973	Sept 1, 1979	first spacecraft visit, discovers new rings
Voyager 1	USA	F	Sept 5, 1977	Nov 12, 1980	detailed portraits of clouds, rings, and moons
Voyager 2	USA	F	Aug 20, 1977	Aug 25, 1981	follow-up on Voyager 1's discoveries
Cassini	USA	F	Oct 15, 1997	July 2004	orbital tour of planet and moons, lander for Titan
Uranus					
Voyager 2	USA	F	Aug 20, 1977	Jan 24, 1986	first visit, studies rings and moons, finds new moons
Neptune					
Voyager 2	USA	F	Aug 20, 1977	Aug 25, 1989	first visit, studies storms, finds geysers on Triton

Pluto

no mission yet flown

*Key to type F: flyby; L: lander; O: orbiter; B: balloon; I: impactor; R: rover; EP: entry probe

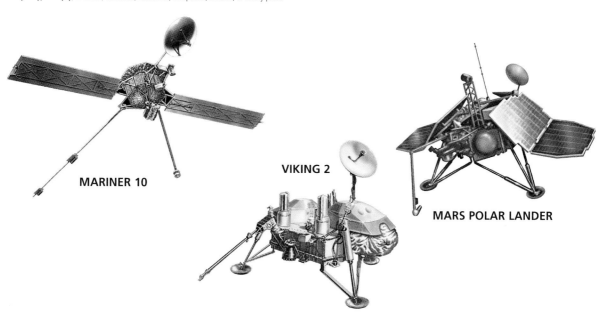

MARINER 10

VIKING 2

MARS POLAR LANDER

Index

INDEX

Acknowledgments

Weldon Owen would like to thank the following people for their assistance in the production of this book: Philippa Findlay and Sarah Plant at Puddingburn Publishing Services, Jacqueline Richards at Pinchme Design, Lithoteam, Greg Browne, Jessica Cox

The following illustrations are reproduced from *Anatomica: The Complete Reference Guide to the Human Body and How It Works*, Global Book Publishing, Australia: 351tl, 352t, 352b, 353tr, 353bl, 353br, 353tl, 354b, 355tl, 355tr, 355b, 356tr, 356cl, 356c, 356cr, 356bl, 356br, 357bl, 358t, 358bl, 358br, 362c, 362c, 364r, 365t, 365b, 373bl, 373br, 377tr, 377br, 381c (t=top, b=bottom, c=center, r=right, l=left)

Illustrators: Susanna Addario, Mike Atkinson/illustrationweb.com, Paul Bachem, Kenn Backhaus, Cy Baker/Wildlife Art Ltd., Alistair Barnard, Julian Baum, Andrew Beckett, Richard Bonson/Wildlife Art Ltd., Stuart Bowey, Anne Bowman, John Bull, Peter Bull Art Studio, Danny Burke, Martin Camm, Dan Cole/Wildlife Art Ltd., Leslye Cole/Wildlife Art Ltd., Sam and Amy Collins, Tom Connell, Marcus Cremonese, Marjorie Crosby-Fairall, Barry Croucher/Wildlife Art Ltd., Claire Davies/Wildlife Art Ltd., Fiammatte Dogi, Sandra Doyle/Wildlife Art Ltd., Levent Efe, Simone End, Christer Eriksson, Alan Ewart, Nick Farmer/Brihton Illustration, Rod Ferring, Cecilia Fitzsimons/Wildlife Art Ltd., Giuliano Fornari, Chris Forsey, Lloyd Foye, John Francis/Bernard Thornton Artists UK, Luigi Gallante/Wildlife Art Ltd., Lee Gibbons/Wildlife Art Ltd., Tony Gibbons/Bernard Thornton Artists UK, Jon Gittoes, Mike Gorman, Ray Grinaway, Terry Hadler, Langdon G. Halls, Gino Halser, Lorraine Hannay, David A Hardy/Wildlife Art Ltd., Tim Hayward, Phil Hood/Wildlife Art Ltd., Adam Hook/Bernard Thornton Artists UK, Christa Hook/Bernard Thornton Artists UK, Richard Hook/Bernard Thornton Artists UK, Robert Hynes, Mark Iley/Wildlife Art Ltd., Inklink, Ian Jackson/Wildlife Art Ltd., Gillian Jenkins, Janet Jones, Steve Kirk/Wildlife Art Ltd., David Kirshner, Frank Knight, Mike Lamble, Alex Lavroff, Connell Lee, John Mac/Folio, David Mackay, Iain McKellar, James McKinnon, Martin Macrae/Folio, Stuart McVicar/Geocart, Robert Mancini, David Mathews, Peter Mennim, Siri Mills, David Moore/Linden Artists, Colin Newman/Bernard Thornton Artists UK, Kevin O'Donnell, Nicola Oram, Matthew Ottley, Darren Pattenden/illustrationweb.com, Jane Pickering/Linden Artists, Sandra Pond/Wildlife Art Ltd., Marilyn Pride, Tony Pyrzakowski, Oliver Rennert, Luis Rey/Wildlife Art Ltd., John Richards, Edwinna Riddell, Steve Roberts/Wildlife Art Ltd., Trevor Ruth, Claudia Saraceni, Michael Saunders, Peter Schouten, Peter Scott/Wildlife Art Ltd., Stephen Seymour/Bernard Thornton Artists UK, Christine Shafner/K.E. Sweeny Illustration, Nick Shewring/illustrationweb.com, Chris Shields/Wildlife Art Ltd., Ray Sim, Marco Sparaciari, R. Spencer Phippen, Kevin Stead, Roger Stewart/Brihton Illustration, Irene Still, Roger Swainston, Kate Sweeney/K.E. Sweeny Illustration, Sharif Tarabay/illustrationweb.com, Steve Trevaskis, Thomas Trojer, Chris Turnbull/Wildlife Art Ltd., Glen Vause, Jane Walkins/Wildlife Art Ltd., Genevieve Wallace, Ross Watton/illustrationweb.com, Trevor Weekes, Rod Westblade, Steve Weston/Linden Artists, Laurie Whiddon, Simon Williams/illustrationweb.com, Ann Winterbotham, David Wood, David Wun

Countries of the World Maps: Digital Wisdom Publishing Ltd
Star Maps: Wil Tirion
Flags: Flag Society of Australia